IRREPRESSIBLE

IRREPRESSIBLE

THE LIFE AND TIMES OF JESSICA MITFORD

Leslie Brody

COUNTERPOINT
BERKELEY

PERMISSIONS

The author is grateful to the following for kindly granting permission for copyright material to be printed in this book: Constancia Romilly and Benjamin Treuhaft for the use of all unpublished and published material by permission of the estate of Jessica Mitford; *Decca* copyright © 2006 by Constancia Romilly and Benjamin Treuhaft, editing, commentary, and introduction copyright © by Peter Y. Sussman; Rare Books Room and Manuscript Library of the Ohio State University Libraries: The Jessica Mitford Collection; The Dowager Duchess of Devonshire for quotations from *The Mitfords: Letters Between Six Sisters* and *Love from Nancy: The Letters of Nancy Mitford*, both edited by Charlotte Mosley, and passages from Nancy Mitford's novels: *Noblesse Oblige* and *Don't Tell Alfred*; Virginia Foster Durr II, executor of the Durr estate for letters and for the use of content and quotes from *Outside the Magic Circle: The Autobiography of Virginia Foster Durr*, edited by Hollinger F. Barnard, and *Freedom Writer* by Patricia Sullivan; authorized quotations from filmed interviews included in the Jessica Mitford archive; Anthea Fursland for quotations from *Jessica Mitford: A Levinsonian Study of Mid-Life*, Berkeley, California: Wright Institute, 1990; "I am bound, and fast bound so / That from thee I cannot go / If I co'd, I wo'd not so," Robert Herrick, "The Bracelet to Julia" from *The Poems of Robert Herrick*, edited, with a biographical introduction, by John Masefield, London: E. Grant Richards, 1906; "No es sueño la vida," Federico Garcia Lorca, "Ciudad sin sueño," in *Poet in New York*, translated from the Spanish by Pablo Medina and Mark Statman, New York: Grove Press, 2008; "Murmur a little sadly how love fled / And paced upon the mountains overhead / And hid his face amid a crowd of stars," William Butler Yeats, "When You Are Old" from *The Collected Poems of W.B. Yeats*, Ware, Hertfordshire, England: Wordsworth Editions Limited, 1994.

Photographs from the Mitford/Treuhaft family photo archive used with permission. Otherwise credits have been listed on the photo insert.

Library of Congress Cataloging-in-Publication Data

Brody, Leslie.
  Irrepressible : the life and times of Jessica Mitford / by Leslie Brody.
    p. cm.

ISBN978-1-58243-767-5

1. Mitford, Jessica, 1917-1996. 2. Women communists—United States—Biography. 3. Women journalists—United States—Biography. 4. Women radicals—United States—Biography. 5. Women civil rights workers—United States—Biography. 6. British Americans—Biography. 7. Mitford, Jessica, 1917–1996—Family. I. Title. II. Title: Life and times of Jessica Mitford.

HX84.M55B76 2010
335.43092—dc22
[B]

2010017800

Jacket design by Ann Weinstock
Interior design by Megan Jones Design
Printed in the United States of America

COUNTERPOINT
2560 Ninth Street, Suite 318
Berkeley, CA 94710
www.counterpointpress.com

For Gary

Oh! Gossip is charming! History is merely gossip. But scandal is gossip made tedious by morality.

—OSCAR WILDE

CONTENTS

IRREPRESSIBLE

PART ONE

Two miles up the hill from the village is Swinbrook house, built by my father in 1926 to satisfy the needs as then seen, of a family of seven children plus two indoor servants, governess and nanny. We can look from the outside—but don't let's try to go on in. A nice place to visit but you wouldn't want to live there.

—JESSICA MITFORD,
SAN FRANCISCO CHRONICLE, MARCH 24, 1985

CHAPTER 1

SOON AFTER JESSICA Mitford moved with her family to Swinbrook House in Oxfordshire, she began to plot her escape from it. She was twelve years old, already an autodidact well aware of world events and with a practical sense concerning certain economic currents. That year—it was 1929—she wrote a letter to her family's London bank, requesting that a new kind of account be opened on her behalf, and she provided specifications. In reply, she received the following, written in handsome script by an unknown clerk:

> Dear Madam, We are pleased to acknowledge receipt of your ten shillings to open your Running Away Account. Passbook no. 437561 enclosed. We beg to remain, dear Madam, your obedient servants, Drummonds.

Later in life, she would recite those phrases as evidence of another world. Few things must have seemed less Californian than that letter. She delighted in the contrast between the ways things were done and said during her youth among the British aristocracy, including their "obedient servants," and her more than fifty years in the American West. "Bank of America's not your obedient servant," she once cracked on camera in her best Lady Bracknell-at-the-Kremlin-on-hashish tone of voice. "Rather marvelous, isn't it?"

"I was never at all attracted to the life my mother imagined for us," she said in the same interview. Her running-away fund began as a direct response to her mother's refusal to let her attend the local grammar school. She kept that Drummonds account active for seven years, applying to it any gifts, small wages, and "spare shillings." Then at the age of nineteen, with fifty pounds saved, she set off to the Spanish Civil War to fight fascism.

SHE WAS CHRISTENED Jessica Lucy Freeman Mitford in 1917, the sixth of seven children born to Lord and Lady Redesdale. Her mother Sydney, or "Muv," called her "Brave Little D." In childhood, she and her siblings invented languages and exchanged nicknames meant to be funny and mystifying to outsiders. Those that stuck for Jessica included "Boud," "Hen," and "Susan," though friends and family mainly called her "Decca." Most everyone who saw her in her youth remarked on her beauty, and by all accounts, she was always a fighter. The inscription on the Mitford family coat of arms was "God Careth for Us"—but embarrass the powerful, mock the hypocrite, and shift the complacent were always mottos more to Decca's taste.

What was Little D. running away from? The usual: parental rules and regulations, hothouse sibling rivalries, boredom; the more arcane: country estates, nannies, governesses, secret cupboards, and secret languages; conservatism and elitism in her relations; and fascism, in the body politic. Where was she running to? At first, she longed to go to school and, later, to the East End of London to live in a bedsit and be a Communist. To readers of the British press, the Mitfords were the subject of gossip and scrutiny for the fashions they wore and the odd things they did. Anyone not related to her seemed infinitely more fascinating to Decca.

Her father David built Swinbrook House on family land near the village of Burford. The eighteen-bedroom house gave a beautiful view from the top of a hill over the bucolic Cotswolds, but passersby noted the building's "uncompromising air." Decca, raised there from the age of nine, thought Swinbrook distinctly institutional in appearance, like an English "lunatic asylum." Its interior was drafty and damp. Seeking a warm hideaway, Decca and her younger sister, Deborah (nicknamed "Debo"), forged a secret Amazon club they called the Society of Hons, in a linen closet heated by hot water pipes. They invented and practiced a language called "Honnish," influenced both by the prefix *Hon*, short for Honorable, to which they were entitled as daughters of an English baron, and by their abiding interest in the chickens their mother raised. Decca and Debo called each other "Hen" all their lives. (Debo was reputed to give a good imitation of a chicken laying an egg.)

Among so many siblings, strategic teasing was a weapon for defense and destruction. Plotting to usurp the grown-ups, they played flesh-pinching and skin-scratching games, little teasing tortures designed to toughen up the players—making a younger sister cry was a foundation technique. The family custom of mockery made Decca unafraid of words and gave her confidence. Eldest sister Nancy was a supreme tease, with all the honors this conferred. She was also the younger girls' vile nemesis. Why so vile? "The others bored me and I made them feel it," Nancy admitted in her memoir, *The Water Beetle*.

The Mitford children had fields to roam, horses to ride; there was no terrible school food, dormitory discomfort, or group sports to dread. They had an extensive library to browse and could order all the magazines and books they liked. It was a good childhood for some; for instance, Debo loved country life, but Decca felt trapped. Muv considered school "unnecessary" and "expensive," the uniforms hideous, and the strange children overstimulating. She educated her daughters herself with nannies and a string of governesses, finishing the Mitford girls with a season abroad.

In 1937, when Decca was nineteen and fed up with the frills and ruffles of privilege, she met eighteen-year-old Esmond Romilly at the home of a mutual relation. She didn't yet know the means of her escape, but it would start that night with Romilly and an aperitif.

Romilly was Winston Churchill's nephew and Decca's second cousin. He had dropped out of one school, been expelled from another, spent time in a reformatory, lived in a Bloomsbury bookstore from which he'd published an underground newspaper called *Out of Bounds*, and was already a veteran of the Spanish Civil War. Decca passionately admired his book, which was also called *Out of Bounds* (a manifesto opposed to the conformism, drumbeating, and sadism of English boys schools) and had been published the year before. He was, she imagined, the only man on earth who might begin to understand her. "Are you planning to go back to Spain?"

she whispered to him over dinner. "I was wondering if you could possibly take me with you."

>«

EVEN AMONG so many siblings, in her youth Decca felt lonely and mis-understood, an intellectual forced to live in the body of a useless debu-tante. She read *Lady Chatterley's Lover*, "having smuggled a copy in from Paris," and appropriated the gramophone to listen to the études of Claude Debussy. Her elder sisters laughed at her pretensions when they weren't ignoring her, which was just as infuriating. She had so many sisters. Their parties filled society columns. They set styles in language and fashion. They inspired envy, lust, rage, and headlines. Deborah, the youngest, later became the Duchess of Devonshire. Nancy, the eldest, was a brilliant and jealous girl, a wit. She went on to become a celebrated writer of novels of manners and social satire, and of biographies of Parisian notables: Louis XIV, Voltaire, Frederick the Great, and Madame de Pompadour. Nancy adored France and was passionately America-phobic. She was also the per-son, more than any other, against whom Decca would measure her own accomplishments.

As a child, second sister Pam wanted to be a horse. She liked to cook and garden. The other sisters dubbed her "Woman" for her domesticity. To the younger girls, feeling thwarted as they did in the schoolroom, Pam's nickname was no compliment. She didn't possess the "restless, unformu-lated longing for change that, in one form or other, gripped the rest of us," Decca would write. What she and Pam did share was a work ethic and resourcefulness.

Diana was the sister Decca worshipped in childhood but later loathed. The fourth Mitford child, Diana was famously bored, restless, and fascist. To connoisseurs, she was the most beauteous of those prewar blondes, slim as a cigarette, and with swoony, blue eyes twice as large as other people's. A wandering shadow looking for somewhere to stick, she first married into the Irish Guinness beer fortune, and then into the British Union of Fascists (in 1940, she would go to prison alongside its leader, her second husband, Oswald Mosley). Seven years her senior, Diana would roar when little Decca played court jester to her languid empress. To roar was a requirement in Swinbrook House, amid the din of clanging personalities. Uproarious laughter, often dark, filled the time. Their father, the rampant Lord Redesdale known as "Farve," roared to laugh and to admonish. His mockery wasn't particularly witty, but his mean teasing could mortify. Decca loved their game playing and adored her father.

Sister Unity ("Bobo") was three years older than Decca and cultivated outrage. Decca and she called each other "Boud" in the language they invented called "Boudledidge." Unity liked the limelight. To command attention when surrounded by so many pretty and interesting sisters, Unity recited Blake and Coleridge from memory and, inspired by the artists Hieronymus Bosch and Henri Rousseau, made collages, the same one over and over: *Hannibal Crossing the Alps*. Defiant and adventurous, she cursed, clambered over rooftops, and ate all the ripe strawberries before a garden party. Rather enormous (her mother's description) at nearly six feet tall, she sulked, glowered, and shocked to get her way. At debutante dances, she was the one with the white rat on her shoulder. By age sixteen, Unity was reading *Jew Süss*, a malevolent novel that fueled German anti-Semitism and inspired many eruptions of hate and violence. Unity passionately cast herself into the dark side to become an outspoken hater and letter-to-the-editor writer. When she was twenty years old, she wrote to the German paper *Der Stürmer*: "We think with joy of the day when we shall be able to say with might and authority: England for the English! Out with the Jews! . . . PS: If you find room in your newspaper for this letter, please publish my name in full . . . I want everyone to know I'm a Jew hater."

Decca and Unity shared a room at the top of Swinbrook House, where they conspired and plotted their various plans to escape. By 1932, when she was fifteen, Decca's own interests had begun to coalesce against the "beastly fascists." In clarifying her opposition to Unity, Decca threw in with the crowd she thought would end suffering, injustice, poverty, and cruelty. She wouldn't join the Communist Party for ten more years, but it seemed to her the most powerful counterbalance.

Meanwhile, thanks to sister Diana's affair with Mosley, the leader of the British Union of Fascists, Unity enrolled, subscribed, and submerged herself in their cause. She would have found some way in, but such lubricated access suited her especially. She loved what groupies love, the reflected power and distinction of the limelight. When she sneaked away from Swinbrook to attend rallies or sell copies of the party organ, *Blackshirt*, she always wore her special fascist badge, awarded by Mosley himself. It had all seemed grand enough at first, but eventually, she had to move on to Berlin.

Unity met Hitler many times. He gave her other badges, autographs, possibly a gun. She dined with him and invited her visiting family to experience *der Führer*'s teatime sociability. (Decca and Nancy both declined.) Muv said Hitler had very nice manners. Later, Decca considered how easy it would have been to visit Unity and Hitler with a gun in her handbag. She was sorry she missed her chance to assassinate the Nazi leader. "Unfortunately, my will to live was too strong for me actually to carry out this scheme, which would have been fully practical and might have changed the course of history. I often bitterly regretted my lack of courage."

Back in England, Decca and Unity were star-crossed. Decca "still loved Boud for her huge, glittering personality, for her rare brand of eccentricity, for a kind of loyalty." The loyalty, forged in their early, more cheerful enmity, and a routine sense of gamesmanship was enough to sustain them. But Decca sensed that a "freezing shadow was approaching." (For the Mitfords' Oxfordshire neighbor J. R. R. Tolkien, then working on *The Hobbit*, the shadow grew along the lines of Mordor. Saruman the White was like Unity, caught on the verge of betraying Gandalf and all the creatures of Middle-Earth.)

》《

THERE IS A photo of Decca, aged four, arms crossed, mouth pursed, hat clamped down, ready to wait it out. A rebellious, pent-up spirit, burdened by the world's troubles, but always funny. Young Decca made fierce attachments. In nursery days, she loved their Nanny Blor. And in Diana's opinion, Blor loved Decca best. Blor, whose real name was Laura Dicks, was probably Decca's earliest progressive influence. Labour Party members were virtually unknown in the heavily conservative Swinbrook milieu, but Nanny Blor came from a liberal and nonconformist family and voted Labour herself. It was Blor who never stopped trying to move Decca along. She invented a prayer for the three youngest children: "God bless Muv, God Bless Farve . . . and make Decca a good girl, Amen."

In adolescence, Decca flailed at the injustice of it all. Why had Muv let Unity attend school and later Debo, but not Decca? Unity had been expelled, and there perhaps was the answer: Who would wish to repeat such an experiment in a hurry? Muv was reacting to the heat of Decca's passion, wishing to damp down what appeared excessive, unseemly, insincere. How could Decca *really* want to leave so *very* much? Muv refused to be stormed, chided, or charmed on this point, dressing her own stubbornness in drifty procrastinations and vague rebukes. Perhaps Muv just knew *this* daughter would not fail and would probably never look back.

Tom was the third Mitford child, a sweet, easy, indulged only son, who seemed to like everyone and whom everyone adored. Brother Tom introduced Decca to Milton, Balzac, and Boswell's *Life of Johnson* and helped guide his sister through Huxley, Lawrence, and Gide. From that jumping-off place, Decca tore through books about the brutality and horror of World War I and "about great movements in England and other countries to divest the rich of their wealth." She eavesdropped on the "irreverent outpourings of Nancy's liberal leaning friends" and sharpened her political claws battling with Unity. Using a diamond ring, Decca and Unity etched symbols of their political affiliations into the window of the room they shared at the top of the house—Unity drew a swastika; Decca a hammer and sickle.

Finally, at the age of eighteen, Decca was considered old enough to emerge formally from childhood. It was her debutante season, and despite its traditional purpose of parading new merchandise for breeding, coming out also implied various new degrees of freedom. Decca wore ostrich feathers in her hair and was presented at court, where she took the opportunity to steal some royal chocolates from the palace (having learned the finer points of shoplifting or "a little jiggery-pokery" from one of her governesses). Otherwise, she went through the motions.

For all the patronizing, condescending, and infantilizing Decca felt in her home, there was kindness. For all the benign neglect, there was tenderness. For all the sarcasm and teasing and hostile sibling parrying, there was usually some kind of comfort. She knew it was positively time to find more like-minded friends, but to do so, she needed a plan. She longed to escape but feared that she wouldn't get it right, that she'd make "an abortive attempt at running away, only to be ignominiously discovered and hauled back home to face greater strictness than ever."

CHAPTER 2

Y THE TIME she met Esmond Romilly, Decca was already a little in love with him. From childhood, the reports Decca heard on the Romilly cousins had typically teetered on scandal. *Had he really held Cousin Mary Churchill's head in a bucket of water until she'd said there was no god? Brilliant!* Later, along with the rest of England, Decca could follow Esmond's exploits in the tabloid press, each headline preceded by "Winston Churchill's Nephew." He was the "Public School Runaway," the "Red Menace," the "Precocious Author," and the "Gallant Young Soldier in the Spanish Civil War."

Both Esmond and his brother Giles attended Wellington College, a public school known for its particularly militaristic tone. Wellington's rigorous Officers' Training Corps emphasized conformity, obedience, discipline, and an unassailable hierarchy. The OTC, field games, and other physical competitions were held to be the essential medium for assessing future generals, leaders of industry, and cabinet ministers. While a boy learned the importance of being earnest, loyal, true, and brave, he might also be wrung dry of sweetness and sympathy. This brutal, rigidly formal world was dangerous territory for freethinkers and romantics. A boy needed to have either a tough skin like Esmond's or the lovers and intellectual allies whom Giles accumulated.

By the mid-1930s, radical politics was everywhere in the atmosphere. London was plastered with posters announcing protests and demonstrations for or against Mosley's British Union of Fascists. There were debating societies, student leagues, and action and discussion groups across the political spectrum. Despite the efforts of headmasters and teachers to protect and isolate their ivory towers, boys and girls inside schools, as in the greater world, were choosing sides. Esmond's growing opposition to the way the OTC boys paraded and drilled excessively had fueled an early interest in pacifism. On Armistice Day, he tucked pacifist leaflets into the chapel prayer books. He requested and was granted an excuse from participation in OTC activities and, until he ran away, was Wellington's most visible and indefatigable dissenter. Esmond read the Left journals, held a subscription to the *Daily Worker*, and kept a bust of Lenin in his room. Given any subject and opportunity, he'd argue the left-wing position. He had much to say in favor of progressive education and against sexual repression. More often than not, his arguments attacked Mosley and the British Union of Fascists. And though not himself a party member, Esmond liked to try to convert his classmates to Communism.

He was two years younger than Giles, but tended to lead his more scholarly, less impulsive older brother into their "joint rebellion." Esmond was stronger, more assertive, and never at a loss. Giles, with finer features and a more slender build, was perhaps more conventionally handsome. He ran around with a crowd of other handsome comrades. Esmond was beautifully poised when debating politics, but otherwise a sloppy, callow youth for whom the word *frivolous* was an all-purpose put-down, useful in dismissing anything he didn't care to do or didn't know much about. The brothers bickered, though it was clear they adored each other.

Esmond was fifteen when he made his middle-of-the-night escape from Wellington. ("Mr. Churchill's Nephew Vanishes.") He found refuge in a room in Bloomsbury above a radical bookshop, which also functioned as a clubhouse for intellectuals of various Left schools of thought. There he met the fabulous denizens of grown-up bohemia, some revolutionary veterans of assorted international conflicts, and various writers, artists, and dilettantes. At first, being one among these disreputables must have seemed like a fantasy fulfilled. Everyone congratulated him, encouraged his audacity, applauded his courage. He was like a mascot (a characterization that would have driven him into a frenzy, had he believed it). They gave him Craven A cigarettes, tea, chocolates, books, and a camp bed to sleep on and claimed to take him seriously. He met poets and philosophers, and once, even W. H. Auden asked to see the poetry Esmond had himself begun to compose in that milieu. One night, when they were alone together, Auden made a pass at the exciting young pet. Esmond apparently went blind with fury and threw the poet's clothes out the window. As the story made its way around the demimonde, instead of gaining the sympathy he expected, Esmond found he'd lost both standing and glamour. He was considered even more uncouth, a young "barbarian, possibly prejudiced against homosexuals." Decca, who found the story funny, later wrote: "Of course the real reason for E's fury was hurt pride: he thought he'd been asked up because of his intellect, discovered to his chagrin it was for other motives. How many girls have gone through the same?"

Still, he was very young, and after he repeatedly refused to return to school or to their family home, his parents had him arrested. "We have done all we could. He quite refuses to submit to any control," his mother, Nellie, told the judge, who sentenced sixteen-year-old Esmond to six weeks in a remand house for delinquent boys. In 1935, out on his own and scrambling again, Esmond teamed up with his brother to write *Out of Bounds: The Education of Giles and Esmond Romilly.*

»«

IN JULY 1936, several right-wing Spanish army generals staged a coup to overthrow Spain's democratically elected government, plunging the nation into a brutal civil war. Like Giles and others, Esmond viewed the battlefield of Spain as the last line of defense for liberalism, modernity, and democracy. At eighteen years old, he had enlisted in the International Brigades. Back in England, as one of only two survivors of his battalion, Esmond began to write *Boadilla*, a memoir about his experiences in battle.

When they met for that first time at their relative's home for dinner, Decca found Esmond thin and surprisingly short, with "amazingly long eyelashes." He hadn't been back from Spain long. Decca thought herself plump, but photographs reveal a lovely young woman with high cheekbones and a wonderful grin. Esmond's closest friend, Philip Toynbee, described her in those days as "very pretty, incautious and enthusiastic." From their first course to the end of dinner, the couple whispered together. They were hungry but did not note the menu, our heroine and her first love. When he answered yes, he would take her with him to Spain, it was all intensely romantic. Boy with no illusions meets girl with plenty. Who would change whom? Running away was an art form, which Esmond had practiced repeatedly and Decca had dreamed about for years and years.

Decca had fifty pounds in running-away money. She needed a visa and an outfit to fight in. Farve had a charge account at the Army Navy store, where she bought "a brown corduroy ski suit with military-looking jacket and plenty of pockets." Esmond suggested they sew in name tags: Jessica Mitford—*Inglesa*. Next they concocted a story to cover their escapade. Decca's friends, a pair of twins, would write to invite her to visit them in Dieppe, the French town on the English Channel. *Do say you'll come!* the twins chanted in a phony letter written by Esmond. To keep their escape under wraps, Decca and Esmond planned to procure her visa in Paris. For days, she kept up the deception until she and Esmond could meet on the train to France.

Muv and Farve saw their daughter off at the station. Her mother made small talk as Farve tucked a rug around his daughter's knees, to keep her warm. He waved to his laughing child—the rebel with the wonderful smile. She made him laugh, made him furious, too, with all that sulking and insolence. It was February 8. Decca knew her accomplice was lurking somewhere on the train, and she needed all her acting skills just to sit and wait.

They rendezvoused as planned, and on the train, the two runaways drew up a practical budget: visas, cigarettes, pens, notebooks, wine; they wouldn't need much food (Muv had given Decca a hamper filled with delicacies, which they could stretch). Their largest expenditure would be lodging—separate hotel rooms, so they'd have to be thrifty. Soon they were in Paris.

At the Spanish consulate, the couple met their first disappointment. The Spanish consul had been called to London. His assistant said he was sorry, but Señor Lopez was the only one who could administer a visa for Miss Mitford. They followed the consul back to London, and their savings dwindled.

That night, Esmond came to her room and admitted, "I'm afraid I've fallen in love with you." How satisfying that must have sounded, out of the mouth of he who was unafraid of everything: the people in power, tyranny, war. Afraid he was in love! In London, they heard that Señor Lopez had departed abruptly, but surely they would find him in Paris this time. Off they went, mailing cards like mad from France to Decca's family, keeping up appearances. In subsequent hotels, they would register as married, although they were in no hurry to do the deed. Both of them were under twenty-one and would need parental permission to wed.

Decca finally succeeded in applying for a visa, and she and Esmond awaited its arrival in Bayonne, France, on the border of Spain, where an international press corps was gathering.

Fashioning themselves as freelance reporters in Bayonne, Esmond and Decca hunted for news and story ideas. They dogged government officials and tried to get the real scoop from refugees. Many of the reporters and photographers Decca met held passionate commitment to the antifascist cause. Objectivity, she learned, was a luxury; accuracy the truth to aim for. The press corps were young, agitated, eager to talk, and lonely. To Decca, these journalists seemed heroic. She was young and lovely, made tea, took notes, listened to their tales of the front and their stories of home. Finally, her visa arrived and the couple took ship for Bilbao, on the Spanish front.

If their escapade was the embodiment of Decca's ambitions to run away and seek freedom, she could now add a crazy, urgent love. Esmond was a sort of rainmaker, a fireplug—all sex appeal; nabbing Decca Mitford might have been the pièce de résistance of his pirate's life. Once they were out on the road together, it took less than twenty-four hours for their romance to turn Esmond into a devoted lover. She fascinated him.

Decca admitted that she felt "completely, deeply committed." At first Esmond had seemed like a project to be undertaken, but soon she felt ravished. He was "like a star around which everything revolved. A wind, a star, he represented to me all that was bright, attractive and powerful." Later she would also find him "deeply moody."

Because he was young and a bit aggressive, people knew he couldn't be pushed around. But Decca wasn't cowed. He didn't know much about girls, living as he had among men and considering this arrangement normal. So she had something she could teach him. Meanwhile, she thought she understood that his alpha traits were the result of his life on the streets, in the juvenile reformatory, and on the front lines. She saw how he'd honed the ability to trounce his antagonists by both force and guile, and she watched as he out-consuled consuls, out-judged judges, and strategically, categorically, out-snubbed snobs.

During their nights in Bayonne, between bottles of cheap, rough wine, Esmond recounted his war experience. How had he survived—only one of two to do so in his brigade? There was no real explanation. He wasn't more skilled or stronger; nor was his urge to live any more powerful than that of the other young men he fought beside. He didn't believe in destiny. No, neither did she. The bullets just missed him. He was fortunate. Was that it? So random? All those other boys.

She learned a little more about him. He was "a committed partisan of the fight against fascism." He was also completely incapable of making the most basic mechanical gadget work. He could barely open and close a door. "He would get into a fury of frustration with his portable typewriter, the workings of whose ribbon and the shutting of whose case were quite beyond him." It wasn't that he lacked consciousness of the actual lived-in world—the one beyond war and struggle, world politics and passion, love and sex. He knew the present, but the future was unimaginable. That gave him license. Drunk or sober, he could be oblivious, insensitive, irresponsible. Trying to test if a pair of scissors worked, he cut up her best suit. Theirs was a world in which nothing must be owed to the old snares of property and propriety. So much of their life was about untangling the debt they'd inherited.

Esmond and Decca hurtled on at a high pitch. He expected her to bear up under discomfort, and she surprised herself. But before they boarded the boat to Spain, they had their first argument. Sitting in a French café, they saw a man start to beat his dog. Decca begged Esmond to intervene. Instead, he gave a lecture: "What right have you got to try to impose your beastly upper class preoccupation with animals on these people? . . . French people and Spaniards don't give a damn about animals, and why should they? They happen to think people are more important. If you're going to make such an unholy fuss about dogs you should have stayed in England, where they feed the dogs steak and let people in the slums die of starvation." Decca held her ground. Kindness was kindness everywhere, and cruelty was its opposite.

On the short trip across the Bay of Biscay to Spain, Decca became violently seasick. As Esmond nursed her, she observed the "glimmerings" of his kindness. Not an overwhelming endorsement of kindness, "glimmerings," but their passion filled the vacuum. She was far from home on her own; life had a cruel edge, but it was sexy. Life had, she said, "far more the quality of a dream than of a dream come true." Suddenly, they were in a psychosexual crucible, with all the vino and cheap gin they could drink. He had a bitter edge. She had a wicked mouth. Finally, they were just kids.

In Spain in 1937, Decca and Esmond were surrounded by violence; garbage piled up in the street, and there was little food in the noisy, refugee-crowded "grim, serious town of Bilbao." Decca described herself as "bemused, a convalescent barely out of anesthetic after a major operation which had severed at one great sweep of the knife all old ties." She was "trying to get in focus," to "understand the heroism." Esmond's salient characteristics were determination, intelligence, and courage, she said; she had these herself, but just then, she was so dazed that the world had a "sense of unreality."

Esmond was already starting to boil over with the responsibility of their mission, desperately trying to hold it all together and watching the finely drawn outline of himself start to melt. What could he do? He was in love. Meanwhile, Decca was no longer following docilely. They'd just been on the road a few days, and she was coming into herself.

CHAPTER 3

W HAT WERE THEY fighting for? Light in the darkness. They were against the cult of the leader, against conformity, against being pawns in a capitalist game. They were with Spain and against the enemies of its democratically elected government. They were against the flirtation of their own leaders with Germany. (And in Decca's case, her own sister's very real flirtation with Hitler.) They opposed silence in the face of aggression. Esmond wrote:

> I am not a pacifist, though I wish it were possible to lead one's life without the intrusion of this ugly monster of force and killing—war—and its preparation. And it is not with the happiness of the convinced Communist but reluctantly that I realize that there will never be peace or any of the things I want, until that mixture of profit-seeking, self-interest, cheap emotion and organized brutality which is called fascism has been fought and destroyed forever.

In Bilbao, the press corps was tougher, more impatient, filthier. There was less to eat. Decca continued her writer's apprenticeship, observing how journalists spoke and acted, sharpening her own political acumen. She conducted interviews with refugees and bureaucrats and helped Esmond type his freelance dispatches (with titles like "One Night on the Spanish Front").

One day in Bilbao, about two weeks after their elopement, the Spanish proconsul found them and told them that a coded telegram had arrived, addressed to the British consul, who was out of town. Esmond and Decca deciphered it together: "Find Jessica Mitford and persuade her to return." Using the same code, Esmond replied: "Have found Jessica Mitford—stop—impossible to persuade her to return—stop."

When the British consul returned, he was not sympathetic and insisted that Decca return home. Apparently, all hell had broken loose in the Mitford household. Decca's family imagined she had gone to Russia. Then Scotland Yard, the Foreign Office, and the press all got involved. It was front-page news. The headlines blared: "Peer's Daughter Elopes," "Consul Chases Peer's Daughter," "Misfit Mitford Feared Lost." At home, when Farve finally heard whom she had run away with, he said, "Worse than I thought."

The day after the telegram arrived, Decca and Esmond learned that Anthony Eden, the British foreign secretary, was sending a warship to collect Decca. She agreed to meet the ship, but promised nothing further. The consul gave her a lift to the harbor, where she sat in the rain while the ship docked. In time, the ship's handsome captain invited the soaking Decca to join him in his cabin for a delicious lunch. Their menu was to be homey British food, roast chicken and bread sauce, and after weeks of chickpeas and gray bread in Bilbao, the thought of it made her mouth water. She phoned Esmond for advice, and he warned her not to get on the boat. "Have them bring it out on a tray. As a matter of fact, you might bring some of it back here for me." The captain, suitably offended, declined to provide takeout, and Decca went home hungry. Back in Bilbao, another telegram arrived, this one declaring that Decca, still just twenty and still under the age of consent, had been made a ward of the Chancery Court. She would have to have the court's permission before entering a legal contract. This meant they'd be breaking the law, and Esmond threatened with jail, if they wed. The couple intended to get around to marrying, but hearing their plans forbidden moved them at once to a public betrothal.

Over the previous weeks, Decca had harbored a fantasy about bringing Esmond home. She relished the idea of seeing her love in debate with Unity (who would undoubtedly flounce off after a few moments), Diana (whose arguments he'd crush like so much dust), and especially Nancy (a clash of titans!). She had not reckoned on the passion with which Esmond forbade any consideration of this, but she still thought she might persuade him. In the midst of the Bilbao chaos, she daydreamed about life's "normal progression" back in England, "breakfast, lunch, tea, the six o'clock BBC news, and bedtime." But what was normal about Unity's following Hitler around? Or parents who rationalized such behavior? Or Diana's becoming the first lady of British fascism? (Just the year before, Diana had married Oswald Mosley at the Berlin home of Joseph Goebbels, the Nazi minister of propaganda, with Unity Mitford and Adolf Hitler as witnesses.) This outrage in particular galvanized Decca. Esmond liked to recite a poem from Federico García Lorca that contained the line "*No es sueño la vida. ¡Alerta! ¡Alerta! ¡Alerta!*" Life is not a dream. No it wasn't. She and Esmond declared "total war."

The British destroyer's guns apparently not sufficiently persuasive, the consul pulled out his ace. The Spanish government was counting heavily on British facilities to evacuate refugees, but unless Decca left Spanish territory, Britain would refuse to do so. The couple agreed to leave, but only as far as the south of France, where Nancy and her husband, the debonair Peter Rodd, would meet them in Saint-Jean-de-Luz.

Nancy was disappointingly on the side of the grown-ups. She tried to warn Decca of the dangers and discomforts in store for anyone of their class shunned by society. She didn't like Esmond (and later would call him loathsome). His refusal to acknowledge surfaces, to keep up deceptive courtesies (which both Esmond and Nancy knew were fraudulent), and to consider the long view seemed to Nancy almost—horrors!—American. She appreciated some socialist ideals, but his revolutionary (and importunate) nature annoyed her. Worst of all, she simply could not charm him. His castle was impenetrable, defended by secret spells—charms to ward off the charms of charm. He was an authority against authority. Nancy told Decca of the sadness and madness back home in the wake of her elopement. If was as if there had been a death at home. People came around to condole and brought flowers. Muv and Nanny wondered if Decca had enough clothes for the weather.

When Esmond refused to allow Decca to accept her mother's money for a new frock in the midst of antagonism, he was wielding Mitford weapons. The Mitfords' world contained an array of such colorful exceptions.

That there would be a dress budget during total war went without saying. You might take your dress money and give it to Spanish orphans, but to refuse such a gift when offered was churlish. Esmond didn't play with class enemies, and Decca stuck by him.

Mischievously, craftily, wickedly, crazily, Unity kept Decca well apprised of all late-breaking Hitler news. *Der Führer*, she boasted, had invited her to tea, and they had sat alone together for two and a half hours. Unity gossiped about Decca's elopement and reported that on hearing the news, Hitler put his head in his hands and sighed, "*Armes Kind*," poor child. The thought of her name on Hitler's lips must have driven Decca wild. The idea was absurd.

The couple returned to Bayonne, where Esmond resourcefully found work as a translator. After a month away from home, Decca wrote to her mother. "You will honestly *adore* Esmond when you know him & please don't be put off by all the secrecy, the only reason for it was because I wanted to go to Spain with him & I thought you might try & stop me."

Muv's reply was heartbreaking: "My darling, We have been in such agonising suspense about not knowing where you were. Now I have your letter. Esmond will I am sure look after you but please come home. I cannot do more than *beg* of you to return . . . Please write immediately & often as I cannot bear it."

In another letter, Muv guiltily wondered what caused Decca to elope: "I cannot help blaming myself terribly for it all . . . I knew you were unhappy, but the cause of it all was beyond me, except that like many girls you had nothing to do. I ought to have been able to help you more."

In childhood, Decca's threat to jump off the roof had garnered a mere "Oh, poor duck, I do hope she won't do anything so terrible." These letters tell another story. Muv's composure, that parental vagueness much discussed by her daughters, disguised a penetrating awareness. Muv had borne seven children, six of them daughters, every one of them with great and different combinations of desires, requirements, demands. She couldn't possibly notice everything; she had to handle what was in front of her first.

For much of the time, her daughters seemed to entertain and occupy one another. Muv knew their education was never going to be perfect. Nancy had tried art school, but left after a brief time; Unity was asked to leave her school. Who could have said for sure that Decca would have thrived away from home?

Decca's next move after writing to Muv was to inform the Chancery judge handling her case that she was expecting a baby. She sent a letter, the contents of which she never forgot:

> I realize you are my guardian now, but I'd like to point out that I know from reading romances that it will take about a year to extradite me as I haven't committed any crime. Furthermore, the administrators of Bayonne are all Communists and they're all on my side. I think it would be nice if you would give me permission to marry, otherwise I might have a large family before I'm twenty-one, and this I think would be inappropriate, don't you?

In other words, if he forced her to wait, she'd be an unwed mother. After that bombshell, permission to marry was expeditiously granted and Muv came to Bayonne bearing gifts. There was a gramophone from Unity and Debo, a pearl and amethyst necklace from Diana, some books and wedding money. The only other family guest at their marriage was Esmond's mother, Nellie.

Farve was unable to forgive Decca's continuing insubordination. Later, he would cut her out of his will; every clause would contain an "except Jessica." Why? Not for eloping—Diana had also eloped. He could change his mind, but not where Decca was concerned. He perceived her repudiation of class and background as a rejection so final he could never forgive it. Years later, Decca would say, "I knew I was cut out, and I'd have been very surprised if I hadn't been . . . I think it's quite natural of them not to like what I did. I never expected them to."

》《

THE YOUNG COUPLE deposited their wedding money, along with Esmond's advance for *Boadilla*, into a cardboard box and tied it up with a red scarf. Decca as secretary-treasurer would dole out the box's fantastically diminishing contents. While they still had money remaining, Esmond calculated all the odds and angles of boule and blackjack. Then they set off to try their luck at the casino in Dieppe, where he blew the rest of their nest egg in a two-hour gambling spree.

Later that night, as they sat in another French café nursing brandies and contemplating their next move, Roger Roughton, an English friend of Esmond's, entered. A Communist and a poet, Roughton had just acquired a huge, furnished home in London; the property had been left to him as a farewell from a departing lover. He told them they could rent the upstairs flat if they liked for two pounds a month. So to Rotherhithe they would go, after spending part of the summer in Dieppe with the Romilly family. Decca's mother-in-law, Nellie, was solicitous, but Decca didn't trust her and never forgave her for sending Esmond to a juvenile detention center. "The ordinary Mrs. Romilly," she called Nellie behind her back, the nickname a mean, teasing reference to Decca's own higher rank in aristo protocol as an "Honorable." Esmond said he loathed his mother, and it was clear he had little respect for his father. While in Dieppe, the honeymooners went to the beach every day and gambled in the casino every night, where sometimes they'd see Nellie across the blackjack table.

By summer's end, Decca and Esmond were installed in Roughton's four-story building by the London docks. (Their rent included the hire of a housemaid, whom they paid one pound, one shilling, and three pence, monthly.) The newlyweds took over one floor with a kitchen, and the rest of the house became a sort of crash pad for friends, artists, and fellow travelers. Brother Tom visited regularly, the only member of her family whom Esmond would tolerate. They hosted bottle parties, to which guests would bring their own alcohol and which often transformed into a floating gambling den. "Esmond was always trying to pile up enough capital to start a night club, or buy a milk bar, or get a car," said Decca. They hit the greyhound races every Friday, whereupon Esmond "would display the almost touching faith of the inveterate gambler in the dog of his choice." Esmond invited all sorts to the gaming, including Bryan Guinness, Decca's former brother-in-law and once Diana's husband. Guinness remembered how one embarrassing night, he bet recklessly, trying to lose his money to Esmond's "house," but his luck was too good. He kept winning and had to stay late just to lose enough to break even. The loud and boisterous crowd gathered round, unsteady on their feet, running low on cigarettes, but unable to leave. Languid ladies drowsed on their fur coats; Champagne Reds and Parlor Pinks and poets shouted for Guinness to lose his hand, betting he wouldn't. He apologized again when he didn't, and Decca laughed. Even Esmond lost his poker face.

Esmond found work in an advertising firm as a copywriter. Decca soon lost interest in domestic engineering, for which she had little talent. She preferred the world outside the house and took a job as an occasional market researcher. The work entailed collecting public opinion on new products and was based on theories being floated by an American named Gallup. With a small group of women, she traveled to various parts of England and went door to door. For the most part, she liked the sorority, but some of the bitter girls-room intimacies stunned her. Her fellow workers were all older and more experienced. They called her "the Baby," and few of them were aware that Decca would have her own child within the year. Their jokes and cynicism about sex as a weapon—and the men they fooled or fooled around with—seemed like a foreign language about which she knew just enough to feel defensive and indignant. Decca was still in a honeymoon state of mind.

This was the time when Philip Toynbee first entered Decca's life. He had known Esmond in his earlier *Out of Bounds* days, and as a boy had also run away from school. Toynbee straddled two worlds: He was a young Communist still engaged in the upper-class society that Decca and Esmond had rejected. As a friend, he functioned as a sort of spy reporting on dinner-table gossip in the homes of the gentry they all knew and at the comrades' meetings. All three had many a rambling conversation about the Communist

Party (CP) in England. Decca and Esmond recognized the CP's value in the fight against fascism and in its "singleness of purpose," but they didn't join. "In Esmond's view, the British party was at the time overloaded with bourgeois intellectuals, too much off in a corner, isolated from the main labor movement to be worth the effort involved in being a member." They would hear of this or that friend being disciplined for some comment or act of individualism, and they'd feel less and less partial to submitting to CP discipline. Toynbee thought the Romillys simply anti-authoritarian, unless they were the authority. "Philip was forever trying to recruit us in the party," Decca wrote. "The accounts he gave of internal bickering and rigid sectarianism, which he couldn't resist telling in the most amusing fashion in the midst of his recruiting pitches were hardly persuasive." In contrast to Esmond, Decca was always more inclined to bend if and when she wished; she didn't rule out membership, but bided her time.

Decca developed a much more equal say in their marriage. Though she still acquiesced for convenience to the superopinionated Esmond, nothing felt too oppressive. She didn't enjoy hearing how her workmates misled the men in their lives, but she was learning how to organize things in her life according to the way she preferred them. Esmond wouldn't hear of her seeing her family, but she would meet up with Unity without his knowledge. And sometimes, Unity would drive Muv to Rotherhithe when Esmond was out.

In Rotherhithe, they stayed up late with their friends arguing about socialism and Communism, Stalin and Trotsky, anarchy and poetry and feminism, Spain and Hitler and how to play the angles at the greyhound track. They'd all drink and smoke, and every electric light in the house would blaze away while they slept where they'd fallen—on the bed, in the chairs, or wrapped in blankets on the floor—and wake, some to go to work, others to argue more. *Who's for a ciggie? No milk for the tea?* Decca thought that Esmond was a brilliant political philosopher with his "instinctive understanding of subtleties," as gifted as his uncle Winston Churchill. One particularly awed visitor recalls that the young Decca also displayed a "political vision" that made her seem "almost clairvoyant."

Later in life, Decca proudly called herself a subversive. Toynbee recalls the couple during their Rotherhithe period "in an open and declared war against the rich and the established." Through their connections, they would sometimes find themselves invited for dinner or overnight stays at the homes of wealthy acquaintances, and what could be lifted was fair game. On one occasion, Decca returned home with her handbag packed with expensive cigarettes fished from gorgeous glass dispensers. At another house, Decca's every request was granted unquestioningly: more pillows, cigars, chocolates, breakfast in bed. Late in her pregnancy by then, she enjoyed the cosseting. Esmond had to stop Decca (the outlaw, the bandit queen, the saboteur) from cutting down the curtains around their guestroom bed. Such curtains, she thought, would look better in Rotherhithe.

On another visit, this time to Eton, whose geography she knew from her visits to brother Tom when he was in school there, Decca attended the chapel service while Toynbee and Esmond stole thirty top hats from its cloakroom. This more conventional prank might have been viewed as naughty, at worst irritating, if they had just thrown them away out of a balloon, perhaps, or from the top of the Eiffel Tower. But Esmond pawned the hats. They needed the money. "Being good was never conspicuously on our agenda," Decca said.

To what part of their past did they owe respect? To the elders who had sent a battleship to capture them? To the meaningless customs and boring rituals, the surfaces and appearances that had led a guest at a dinner Toynbee had attended to say unreservedly, "we need someone like Hitler over here"? They didn't have much money, and they were used to nice things. They knew that in such houses, there would typically be a surplus of cigarettes, breakfasts, and hats.

It wasn't just the upper classes who judged them undisciplined and immature. Their Communist pals would cluck their tongues, too. As adventurers, rogue and scamp, they wanted to be regarded and commented upon. Sister Nancy called Esmond a publicity hound. Decca would try to explain their freebooting behavior by referring to the "rich vein of lunacy" that ran in her family and the "brutality" in Esmond's past. These experiences "hardly calculated to endow us with an instinct for the highest in humanity and culture."

Theirs was an implausible pace to keep up. They had the hectic energy of youth and the stamina of their convictions. They would meet the coming war with that tough-mindedness they had cultivated on their travels together. Raising a child, free from the bonds of privilege, was going to take another kind of courage.

CHAPTER 4

"**I AM GOING TO** have a baby in January," Decca told Nancy in a letter dated July 1937. "Do you remember poor Lottie's agonies, & I expect it's much worse for humans." (Lottie was one of the family's dogs.) "Some of us do our duty to the community unlike others I could name." For the first time in her life, Decca had something her childless elder sister wanted. "Shall I call it Nancy . . . ? Goodness, I have been sick but I'm not any more now."

Decca wondered if her child would be a boy, and she hoped he would be pretty. Before the baby's birth, she had a dream in which she was trapped in Swinbrook and awoke grateful to find herself back at Rotherhithe, where Esmond and she had made a quiet nest in the chaos. Their baby daughter was born December 20, 1937, and they named her Julia, after sixteenth-century poet Robert Herrick's divine portrait of Julia, "the queen of flowers," in *The Parliament of Roses to Julia*. As a subversive, exalting sensuality in a puritan society, Herrick suited the young couple's taste. Another of Herrick's poems, *The Bracelet to Julia*, spoke to the young mother Decca about new varieties of love:

> I am bound, and fast bound so
> That from thee I cannot go
> If I co'd, I wo'd not so

Nanny Blor offered her services (for which the Mitford parents offered to pay), but Esmond vetoed the idea, thinking Blor would bring too much in the way of Mitford family associations. They planned to raise their child without nannies or governesses or any other such minions of British upper-class family life. Esmond himself had hoped to help out more, but he was the only one working at the time. In any case, as he was "known for his inability to carry a teaspoon from one room to the next," the principal care and welfare of their baby fell to Decca. Julia quickly became, Decca wrote, "the center of my existence."

Decca and Esmond were beginning to feel at home among the brothers and sisters of the Bermondsey Labour Party. Bermondsey was a notable redoubt of radicalism, and its membership "considerably more militant" than that of the official Labour Party. Decca complimented her new neighbors for their "seriousness of purpose." The Bermondsey mob was also fun to be around. She and Esmond attended lectures and joined in conversations, arguments, and radical sing-alongs, which Decca loved. She loved to harmonize, and she particularly loved to belt out a novelty song. (Noel Coward's were her favorites.) Despite Britain's nonintervention policy, which Bermondsey members resented and condemned, they held fund-raisers for Spanish orphans and Jewish refugees from Germany. Decca found the tale of the Bermondsey schoolchildren who had "lined up to boo Princess Mary, symbol of hated charity," an especially appealing advertisement for her neighborhood. She liked their style.

So did Esmond. *Boadilla* had been published in autumn 1937 to good reviews but so-so sales. Still, at nineteen, he had two books under his belt and was confident of his ability to write well and complete his projects quickly. He had plans for a novel, but for the time being settled into work as a copywriter at the advertising agency of Graham and Gillies. Back in Spain, when Esmond had first received his fifty-pound advance for *Boadilla*, he and Decca had thought they might emigrate to Mexico, a world away from the dismal weather, the loss of Spain, and German aggression. But family life was at least for the moment more like a sanctuary than an exile. For a change, they weren't running away or under fire, and they didn't have to justify themselves to anyone. Esmond's job had its amusements; he was good at jingles and jargon. The New Year looked promising. He was earning enough to support the three of them. Perhaps there was some adjustment necessary now that they were outside the limelight. Naturally, the neighbors gossiped about the celebrity couple. There were nice cars parked outside from time to time, and well-dressed toffs going into and out of their house. But it was a good life in its almost ordinariness and one he would hardly have predicted for himself.

Decca, too, was learning the ropes and adapting. It is easy to imagine her out and about, buying the Craven A cigarettes they chain-smoked, a paper from the newsboy on the corner, a chop from a jokey butcher who called her *pet* or *love*. Sometimes, the wives of the "tired, white-faced dockers" would stop on the street and coo at Decca and her sweet baby. She and Esmond had been in the habit of being together all the time. It might have been hard at first to be alone—in her house full of siblings, she had never been alone for extended periods. But Decca adapted and caught up on her novel reading while the baby slept.

Esmond and Decca still liked to have a lot of friends around, but what was once a gambling palace now smelled of diapers. Guests to their transformed casino brought bottles of beer, wine, and liquor; food hampers; and fish and chips wrapped in newspapers. Decca and Esmond shared with their guests and with almost everyone they knew—everyone awake, at any rate—a sense of always needing to be on the alert. Around the Romilly household, there was an enduring brightness, a nimbus of power and energy symbolized by their fabulous electricity bill. Neither Decca nor Esmond understood the social contract in capitalist societies regarding public utilities (like where, when, or how to pay), so they ran up their bill without worry. Other generations of Romillys and Mitfords wasted their fortunes on horses and cards. This all-night parsing of the issues, betting on the future surrounded by light, was another kind of gamble.

In March 1938, while General Franco's armies were crushing the Republican forces in Spain, Hitler annexed Austria and initiated the threats that would soon lead to German occupation of Czechoslovakia. Despite the wretched news from Europe, Decca and her friends were eager to take on what would come. Esmond had anticipated the loss of Spain. He grieved, but like the practical, perpetual motion machine that he was, he forged ahead. They had new plans, hopes, and dreams. If not Mexico, perhaps they could move to Paris, where Julia would grow up "a little gamine trudging to a lycée with books in a satchel." In any case, their daughter would be "born to freedom and May Day parades."

To Decca, those early May Day parades seemed the apotheosis of socialist delight. By the time the May Day march of 1938 came around, there was a feeling in Decca's circle that the fight against fascism would be long and vicious, but that they and their comrades had the courage, the strength, and the determination to beat back any threat. Starting with its throngs in the street, she painted the day of the march—"the entire community turned out"—full of passion and confidence in their solidarity. With people's collective power and dedication, they felt that they could stop any juggernaut. Decca carried Julia, with Esmond and their friend Philip Toynbee arm in arm. The trio sang "The Red Flag," then teased their soberer comrades with altered lyrics—instead of "The people's flag is deepest red," they sang, "The people's flag is palest pink. It's not as red as you may think."

Decca and her friends marched with the Bermondsey Labour Party contingent. It seemed that every antifascist organization and person in London had turned out, thousands upon thousands, and thousands more joined at every intersection—the co-ops, the Communist Party, the Independent Labour Party, all with their flags. The unofficial theme of the day was repeated on banners snaking through the parade: "United Front Against Fascism." The march was good-natured at the start. There were children and baby buggies and flirtations of every variety. It was a long walk to Hyde Park. Along the way, a marcher might rest with a bottle of beer or take off her shoes to cool her feet and wonder at the holes in her stockings. Whole extended families might stop to take tea along the route, amusingly furnished with proper cups and saucers. But the marchers would be wary, too, that Mosley's British Union of Fascists troopers would line the parade route and at some point attack as those antagonists had been attacking each other in a miniature world war for years.

Decca was ready for the Blackshirts to disrupt the May Day parade, and they showed up on schedule, jeering and harassing. There were fistfights on side streets as groups peeled off and then rejoined the march scratched, bruised, and bloody. At some point, Decca saw her sisters Diana and Unity, both statuesque like twin nautical figureheads, up on some prow pedestal or perhaps just standing on cars and above the crowd as they liked to be, waving their swastika flags and giving the Nazi salute. Decca shook her fist back, though they were too far away to see her. She later said she would have gone for them, too, anything to shake their smug confidence, but Esmond and Philip held her back and then threw themselves into the fray. Decca saw a fascist gang armed with rubber truncheons and knuckle-dusters beaten back by the Bermondsey faction. Later, Esmond and Philip would wear their bloody cuts and black eyes as badges of honor.

DECCA'S MOTHER AND sisters Debo and Unity continued to visit when Esmond was at work. They brought gifts and fluttered around Julia, whom Muv thought "too thin." Every week, Decca would bring her baby to one of the Labour Party's free health clinics to be weighed and for a dose of free cod liver oil. Toynbee admired Decca's resourcefulness, her "light-hearted maternal competence." Then Julia caught the measles.

As soon as she had heard of the latest measles epidemic raging through London that May, Decca had visited her clinic to ask about the danger to Julia. The overworked, inundated nurse explained about the contagion of childhood diseases and the immunity conferred by a breast-feeding mother. But a mother could only confer immunity if she had had the disease herself, and Decca hadn't. There was no inoculation. A few days later, both Decca and her daughter contracted the disease. Decca suffered with a high fever for two days. Esmond did his best, with nurses to help, but little Julia caught pneumonia and died on May 28, 1938.

Did Decca blame Muv, who believed in the good body's ability to heal itself? Or Esmond, who had stubbornly refused Nanny Blor? Or herself, for

acquiescing? Nanny Blor might have known what to do. Decca couldn't listen to anyone's sympathy. Philip hadn't wanted to, but one drunken night,
Decca and Esmond forced him to tell them what people were saying at
their dinner parties: It was because they'd exposed their child to the vapors
and stink of the East End. Esmond had been roundly excoriated, while she
was supposedly some kind of pitiable, mesmerized zombie. Their marriage,
strangers and friends alike supposed, would never survive this.

Decca and Esmond left London the day after their baby's funeral. They
wanted to escape and to grieve without the added burden of family solici-
tude. Esmond had made it his business to put a lot of distance between
the Mitfords and them. He knew they would have to run for it before the
women in their black clothes led them back consolingly to the bosom of the
clan. Esmond and Decca agreed they could best console each other if they
got as far away as fast as they could. They made for Corsica, though not
before Decca wrote a polite thank you letter to Debo. "Dearest Hen, Thank
you so much for writing. We are going tomorrow morning, so I do hope you
will write to yr. hen. Please give my love to Muv, & thank her for her letter
& for offering to help with the house, but as a matter of fact Esmond has
already arranged for Peter Nevile to try & let it for us. If any of you hear of
a likely person, would you let him know?"

The Corsican months included many nights of weeping and drinking
and regret. Decca swam in the sea and let herself be fussed over by the
ladies of the Grande Hotel de Calvi, who had heard the whispered gossip. Everyone knew her secret, though no one was crass enough to say it
aloud. They plied Decca with the local delicacies: the sea urchins, strong
Corsican cheese, *figatelli*, donkey sausage, and dark purple wine in ceramic
bowls. Down on the beach, some veterans of the Spanish Civil War had
pitched tents. Decca and Esmond found a refuge among other young radicals. Though they talked of war and struggle, the way they lived day-to-day
was by distraction, trying their best to keep their memories of Spain and
their apprehension of the coming European war at bay, in exchange for a
few hours of peace.

At night, they sat on their veranda or out on the beach with the campers. Someone would roll cigarettes to hand around; someone would play a guitar, point out a constellation, quote a poem. "Murmur a little sadly, How love fled / And paced upon the mountains overhead / And hid his face amid a crowd of stars." There were so many stars. Once in a while, someone would hiccup or change positions with a groan. In the quiet, you could hear another cork being pulled.

Esmond and Decca had expected the loss of the war in Spain, but back in England in a happier time, it had seemed more of a diminishing horizon, twilight into darkness. Here, confronted by the most recent events as told by men and women of the International Brigades (from France, Germany, the United States, and England) who had witnessed them, the horrors of the endgame took shape. They heard about the retreats, the enemy's vast superiority in firepower, tanks, and numbers, and the final plunge in morale.

Some of them, in their earliest idealism, had believed that the example of their conviction—their "willingness to fight and die to prevent the spread of fascism"—would have influence. They believed it might take some time, but even if theirs was an underground current, it had the power to charge others. They had to persuade the leaders of neutral Western democracies to finally, even at the last minute, even in a *deus ex machina* moment, rescue Spain. There were so many lies, so many deaths, such a waste. As they drank their wine around campfires, the veterans on the beach discussed the newest race laws in Germany: laws forbidding Jews from having driver's licenses, owning radios—even owning carrier pigeons. It was public knowledge that the Communists not already in prison were being arrested. Germany military aggression escalated every day. All of this was reported, every fascist act scrutinized in the English and European papers. With so much at stake, the intoxicated veterans of the International Brigades wondered aloud to their English comrades, *Why won't Britain act?!*

》《

WHEN DECCA AND Esmond returned to London in August, they found that the government both counseled circumspection and continued to play down the growing dangers. A few years before, a scare had gone around the East End Jewish community. The rumor was that if Edward VIII hadn't abdicated, he would have cut a deal with Germany to trade Britain's Jews for entente. Decca felt nothing but contempt for the influential aristocrats and elite politicians (among them her relations) in favor of appeasement or a friendly alliance with Germany. "Their furled umbrellas so symbolic of furled minds."

Back from Corsica, with a wider perspective and now unprotected by the happy family's haze that had surrounded them in Rotherhithe, Decca and Esmond set themselves on track. They told one another that the best way to commit to the antifascist cause was to abolish illusions and be single-minded.

They moved to a smaller place in Edgware, to which they were soon tracked by a debt collector demanding action on Rotherhithe Street's huge unpaid electricity bill. Since they were just scraping by, payment of such an enormous bill was "unthinkable." It outraged them (they said only half-jokingly) to think that electricity, which ought to be free, was in fact a privilege. They considered a countersuit and brainstormed a strategy "on the grounds that electricity is an Act of God—an element like fire, earth and air." A "pale, sad-looking youth in the employ of the London Electric Company" paced the pavement outside their house and did his best to tail them to the underground and the shops, but they were light-years ahead of him, donning goofy disguises and skittering past. One day, Esmond might emerge wearing a Groucho Marx mustache, another time in a top hat. Decca would tuck her hair under a worker's cap or wear her starlet dark glasses. It took longer than they imagined for their "tormentor" to catch on, and dashing past him was only fun before they realized how slow and naturally confused he seemed. Then they stayed inside and watched him through their window watching them.

"Esmond had a theory that it was illegal and in some way a violation of Magna Carta to serve process on people in bed," so they nested there for a couple of days at a time. But they also felt besieged, while Esmond skipped work and their larder grew bare. "Obviously, life in England had become untenable, in more ways than one," Decca wrote.

On September 11, 1938, Decca turned twenty-one. She had come to expect nothing much from her family. She saw Debo sometimes. Unity was swanning around with her swastika badge in London, racing back and forth to Germany. She hadn't managed to make it to her niece Julia's funeral the previous May, because just then she'd been arrested in Prague, confidently advertising her Nazi connections in that tinderbox.

But Muv, whose consolation Decca had limited at the time of Julia's death, still indefatigably kept in touch. At her children's birth, Muv had begun a savings account for each of them and deposited sixpence on their behalf every week. When she turned twenty-one, Decca received the balance of one hundred pounds. When she had first heard that she would be coming into money, Decca had experienced one of that traumatic year's greatest pleasures. Her bonanza was enhanced by a certain triumph over her elder siblings, all of whom had invested their own trust funds in one of Farve's crackpot schemes (in this case a treasure-hunting globe that descended the seas and, like the claw in a carnival game, was meant to scoop up precious ornaments fit for a sultan). The globe's inventor had absconded with the Mitford family's investment, so only Decca and Debo had received their trust funds intact. This, thanks to Muv, who despite Decca's childhood pleas for permission to invest her own money, had said that at seven years old, Decca had been too young to do so. Decca remembered feeling envy and fury, so the pleasure of her inheritance when it came, with the process server still pacing outside, was spiked with schadenfreude.

Esmond and Decca spent their hours in bed considering their windfall. They were torn, but instead of paying their electricity bill, they decided to save their money and start a new running-away account.

THEY BOTH WENT back to work—Esmond returned to Graham and Gillies, and Decca took up her job as a market researcher. She traveled to

Southampton with her team, where they spent their days going house to house to interview homemakers about the new convenience products they used. It was hard to concentrate on the desirability of one kind of breakfast food compared with another when on the border of Czechoslovakia, the future of the world seemed so precarious. But it was also exciting to be out on her own earning money again, and sometimes, the housewives Decca met were fascinating in their convictions. A half-dressed woman might throw open her door in the middle of a lover's tiff, or a lonely person might ask her to share some meager meal. There were suspicious types, flirts, and enthusiastic shoppers. Apparently, some people really did care deeply about their cleansers.

It was harder to be away from Esmond at night. She wasn't anything like the baby she'd been on the job before she'd had Julia. Some of the girls knew how she had lost her daughter; they were sweet and gave her the breathing room she needed. But this type of work took being in a certain mood, and she would have preferred to have spent her days in a Lyons tea shop poring over the newspapers. The banner headline announcing the Munich Pact signed on September 29, 1938, quoted British Prime Minister Neville Chamberlain's speech: "Peace in Our Time." There was an eerie placidity that day in the population of Southampton. Where were the outraged crowds? Listening to the radio, Decca homed in on news about the latest wave of refugees. She was shocked to learn that some people, including one young woman in her market research group, took the Munich Pact not as tragedy but as reassurance and with a sense of relief. "Oh—Chamberlain," she said vaguely. "But the paper says he's for peace. That's good, isn't it?" All the stillness seemed such a topsy-turvy response.

Decca liked to move on things. She had so much energy, and much of it was concentrated in her politics. Politics gave her inspiration, but waiting while someone else made the decisions, old men who had gotten so many things so wrong so often before—men like her father—made her feel like jumping out of her skin. The misguided power at the top grated; the apathy and lethargy of the bourgeoisie was maddening.

Decca had never seen Esmond so depressed and restless. His sadness must have been painful for her to absorb since he was naturally so sure of himself. His moods were so intense, and he was unable to let his guard down except with her. On October 9 and 10, 1938, they read in the papers about violent mobs that were led by German storm troopers who shattered the windows in Jewish synagogues, shops, and homes in Germany and Austria. Orchestrated by the Nazi leadership, *Kristallnacht*—crystal night, a strangely poetic name for such terror and anguish—was a German pogrom that signaled the start of a systematic anti-Semitism, leading to the so-called Final Solution. In the days that followed, observers noted the shattered glass layered over the streets, in some places deep as their ankles.

The previous autumn, Decca had been full of hope. Now, the first anniversary of Julia's birth was approaching.

»«

SOMETIME THAT AUTUMN, Decca had an abortion. With five one-pound notes and an address in her handbag, she traveled alone by bus and tube to the East End of London. *Sheila sent me,* she said to the woman who opened the door and who then checked the street for prying neighbors or police. There had been no telephone to reserve an appointment, and if Decca had felt apprehension or dread, she was relieved just to have found the address. Paying her money in advance—five pounds was the going rate that day in the East End for a soap-induced abortion—she was ushered into where the deed would be done. It interested her to find the practitioner no "Dickensian crone," but "an ordinary middle-aged English woman plying her trade":

> At her direction I undressed and lay on a bed. I was a bit surprised that there was no sign of sterilization of the instruments, which she fished out of her underclothes drawer. Never mind, I thought, she knows what she's doing; and she went to work.

The deed itself consisted of the abortionist introducing grated carbolic soap into Decca's womb through a syringe. It was "horribly painful," and after several hours finally induced labor. It was also horribly dangerous for the patient and for the practitioner, the latter risking arrest, imprisonment, and capital punishment. Death by hanging was still the punishment for the crime.

Why hadn't Esmond accompanied her or, at the very least, sent her in a taxi? At the time, Decca and Esmond had been together for nearly two years. Defiant as she may have been to others, it was unusual for her to oppose him, but it would have been even less likely for him to leave her to have an abortion on her own. The idea that this might have been another man's child (a drunken night in Corsica?) is possible but seems unlikely.

Esmond didn't help her find a more sanitary or reliable practitioner, because, as it turns out, he didn't know a thing about it until the procedure was all over and done. Decca made this decision on her own. She may have thought that it was too soon, that they needed to be lighter on their feet, that the world was too vicious a place on principle, or that Esmond would have made these arguments had she asked. Years later, when her oldest living daughter was grown, Decca remembered thinking that Esmond wouldn't have wanted a baby.

When Decca finally told Esmond about her abortion, "he was absolutely furious." She argued that he had taken plenty of dangerous risks in his life. Whom had he consulted before enlisting to fight in Spain? That had been his decision, and this had been hers. It had been horrible, she conceded, but she did what she thought she had to do, and it was long since over; they would have to move on.

CHAPTER 5

*E*SMOND AND DECCA cast their thoughts westward. Earlier, they had considered emigrating to Mexico, but now their shared dream was to reach distant, isolationist, jazzy New York. With the one-hundred-pound inheritance Decca received on her twenty-first birthday, they bought a second-class stateroom on the Canadian SS *Aurania* and planned to stay at the Shelton Hotel in New York City for $3.50 a night. Esmond said that he would return and fight when England "was drawn into a war," but when that war would begin, and even how the allies and enemies would line up, was still unclear. As they embarked in Southampton, England, in February 1939, Unity was busy in Germany, a member of Hitler's social circle. In conversation with the British consul in Munich, Decca's sister "mentioned that Herr Hitler believed that he had been sent by God and that when one heard him say that one believed it too." Of family and friends only Philip Toynbee, Tom Mitford, and Nanny Blor waved bon voyage.

Decca and Esmond held much in common with many others traveling from Europe that February: their age, energy, haphazard education, and eagerness to escape the old country. But in other ways, they were two rare immigrants. Esmond was something of a literary prodigy; as every tabloid headline regarding him trumpeted, he was also Winston Churchill's nephew, the son of the powerful Conservative leader's sister-in-law. Decca, the red debutante, was herself twice famous—for opposing her family's public attachment to fascism and now for being the Mitford girl who got away. The couple's arrival in New York generated a few gossip column items and several welcoming invitations to dine and visit, but nothing that might immediately be translated to real income, which was what they desperately needed.

They came to the United States armed with extraordinary letters of introduction collected in the months before their departure. Decca said that on their very first night in town, they sat in the Shelton Hotel bar and agonized over the best wording for the letters they composed to introduce themselves. "We sat in a dim, plushly upholstered corner ordering dry martinis, absorbing the amazing un-Englishness of it all." They must have felt giddy to have made their escape from London, where they and their friends had come to feel so discouraged. From the other side, America had shone like the big rock-candy mountain, sunshine and peppermints.

They considered their precious list of contacts a lifeline of favors to call in. These were family acquaintances and friends of friends, as well as artists, writers, and even Hollywood moguls, anyone who might know someone who might give them a break. For instance, a letter from their friend Roger Roughton provided the names and thumbnail descriptions of New York residents e. e. Cummings "an amusing and sometimes very good writer, he's an authority on burlesque; politically he's pretty cynical" and James Thurber, who was "exactly as you would imagine him and very kind," as well as Carl Sandburg in Chicago.

At some point, Esmond hit upon Hollywood as a place where he might have strong earning potential, either as the foreign correspondent for the *London News Chronicle* or as a screenwriter. Roughton suggested they look up Walter Arensberg, "an elderly millionaire, very good natured with a magnificent collection of contemporary paintings and a belief that Bacon wrote Shakespeare." He also encouraged them to meet homegrown artists like left-wing actor Lionel Stander, experimental filmmaker Ken McGowan, and Edward Weston, who "is very nice indeed, with a character much like Henry Moore's." In Carmel, "Bloomsbury on the Pacific," the person to see was Ella Winter, "an English communist who was married to Lincoln Steffens. She knows a lot of people in Hollywood and will give you many introductions."

Decca and Esmond knew they needed a reliable form of income that would work in all locales and weather. What had they to sell? They had their inexhaustible energy, the benefit of their intense though brief life experiences. How to use their resources, wit, and prolixity and the accident of their birth to turn the (assumed) American weakness for British aristocracy to their advantage? Someone suggested a lecture tour; others had tried it and made out like bandits.

A letter they received from acquaintance Walter Starkie of Dublin lit a fire under that plan. His advice:

> In America what they want is originality and unconventional ideas. They must always hear something for the first time, if they have ever heard what you tell them before, they look on you with contempt. The easiest prey for the visiting lecturers are without question the Women's Clubs. You should do well with your companions if you give them talks on "England's gilded youth," and "how the British Army gets recruits." You must remember that in some of the God-forsaken towns of the Middle West you and your party will become the sensation of the week. This is flattering at the time, but do not expect them to remember you after you have left because memories like emotions are short lived in U.S.A. There is a great deal of snobbery among American women and you would do well to cultivate it, so I should keep handy your subject "how to meet the King."

Decca and Esmond thought this through and strategized accordingly. They recruited three co-lecturers. Sheila Legg (the same Sheila who recommended Decca's abortionist) would discuss various types of men in her lecture "Men from the Ritz to the Fish and Chips Stand." Philip Toynbee would offer the titillatingly titled "Sex Life at Oxford University" and, as a Father's Day special, "Arnold Toynbee: Historian but First and Foremost 'Dad.'" Decca would draw on her early observations in "The Inner life of an English Debutante." And as manager of the lecture series, Esmond would offer "The Truth About Winston Churchill."

They eventually had to junk the lecture tour idea when all their traveling companions dropped out. The start-up expenses deterred Legg, who couldn't raise her fare to America. Then Toynbee fell in love and promptly lost his hunger to escape England. The world was unpredictable and lumbering toward war, but under Esmond's demanding management, his "fellow lecturers" might have felt themselves already in service. In his memoir, Toynbee later admitted that what he feared was the couple's "undeliberate but crushing domination."

Once Decca and Esmond actually started to meet the Americans they had only fantasized about, they were pleasantly surprised. Decca noted early on that New Yorkers elaborated whenever they had the chance and seemed incapable of giving a simple reply. Americans in general rarely seemed suspicious, didn't hold the couple's youth against them, and actually liked engaging strangers—going as far as to invite them into their homes (an act Decca thought would particularly shock her parents). Such universal friendliness and curiosity melted them. Often, even brief encounters would include the conversational gambit "Do you like America?" which for the couple epitomized the contrast between the two nations. "It would never occur to us to ask a foreigner if he liked England," said Decca. "Because if he did, so what? And if he didn't there would be nothing you could do about it." Still, like other immigrants, she discovered America to be a land of opportunity and consolation. It helped to be adaptable, and she had that gift.

Describing those early days in the United States, Decca saw herself as a carefree cosmopolite, careening from one funny episode to another. Photographs of the time show off her beautiful complexion and eyes. She was always nicely dressed, well coiffed, and merry again like the mischievous child she had once been. Grief didn't play an overt role in her New York character. She was the first to find a job (as a salesclerk in a fancy dress shop), and the balance of power in the couple's relationship shifted accordingly.

The one subject that always remained taboo between Decca and Esmond was Unity. Decca couldn't discuss her anxiety regarding Unity's activities in the months leading up to the war. She despaired when she heard that her sister had ignored all advice to leave Berlin and gone apartment hunting.

(Unity would soon move into a flat vacated by a Jewish family.) For Decca, her "Boud" was a problem like no other. Decca reflected that "perversely, and although I hated everything she stood for, she was easily my favorite sister." Unity said she hated Esmond as much as he hated her, but made overtures in her own delusional way: "My attitude toward Esmond is as follows—and I rather expect his to me to be the same. I naturally wouldn't hesitate to shoot him if it was necessary for my cause, and I should expect him to do the same to me, but in the meantime I don't see why we shouldn't be quite good friends."

On September 3, in Munich, once Unity had recognized that war between Britain and Germany was certain, she shot herself in the head and survived. She had written suicide notes (one note had proclaimed her special love for Decca), along with instructions to be buried with a signed photograph of Adolf Hitler. Decca wouldn't hear this news until two months after the fact. On September 6, Decca wrote to her mother: "I see that in the papers Bobo is in Germany, do tell me if you have any news of her & please send her address as soon as you can so I can write to her. Is she going to stay there?"

ESMOND HAD HOPED to find work in advertising, but despite his celebrity, nothing clicked. They relied on their contacts for little luxuries. Decca was stunned by the New York City heat and delighted to accept invitations to the country estates of millionaires like Mrs. Murray Crane. In her letters, Decca marveled that Mrs. Crane has "fine wirenetting around their windows to keep out moths & slow flies."

The very rich and very Republican *Washington Post* publisher, Eugene Meyer, and his wife, Agnes, lived in "a sort of Winston Churchill-ish atmosphere of other bigshots." Meyer himself, according to Esmond, was "a terrific Washington Big-shot w. an aura of cigars, badly sequenced liquors and huge stomached business friends." He and Meyer found themselves simpatico. They circled one another, each calculating how money might be made from the other's notoriety. Meyer's soon-to-be-married daughter Katharine would herself become a good friend of Decca's. Eventually "Kay," a committed Democrat, would introduce the couple to the young and idealistic New Deal community of Washington, D.C.

In March, after a month's stay at the Shelton Hotel, the Romillys moved to their own small apartment on Christopher Street. Greenwich Village seemed a theater of wonders where Decca found shops full of goods and a store window that Dalí decorated. Soon they adopted a stray cat that would wake them up in the morning by walking on their heads. They started to feel so much at home that they took out citizenship papers. England had begun wartime rationing of food and clothing. Decca sent little luxuries like gloves and canned tuna fish in care packages to her mother.

In early summer, Esmond found a job as an executive with an advertising firm called Topping and Lloyd. This enterprise was a calculated tax dodge, designed to efficiently launder his employer's money, then vanish. (Esmond had wondered why no work was ever required of him, but put it down to the American way of doing business.) For the short term of his employment, the couple managed to save Esmond's weekly hundred-dollar salary while they lived on Decca's more modest paycheck. By then, she had moved on to a job at the 1939 World's Fair selling tartans in "Ye Merrie England Village."

In terms of minutes and hours, Esmond and Decca hadn't had much of a courtship. They had eloped after knowing one another for a few days. While they had always laughed and joked and their sexual attraction was intense, they were also always either fighting a war or waiting for one. In the United States, they were amazed by the degrees of frivolity available for connoisseur and amateur. The pursuit of self-fulfillment and personal happiness was for some Americans a way of life—enshrined in the Declaration of Independence, no less. They were busy that year finding their feet, and along the way, the two of them also became great friends.

EUGENE MEYER BECAME fond enough of Decca and Esmond to become something of a patron. In the summer of 1939, Meyer commissioned the

Romillys to write a series of articles for the Sunday *Washington Post* about their first year in the United States. The job provided some advance money to travel. Meyer ran the series about nine months later under the headline "Blueblood Adventurers Discover America," with a sidebar introducing "Two Youthful Escapists Who Fled to America with a Song in Their Hearts."

The earliest articles were illustrated by cartoons of the couple in action: exclaiming over tea; daydreaming over U.S. guidebooks; persuading the U.S. consul (framed by portraits of Washington and Jefferson) of their commitment, exemplary conduct, and financial stability; and then waving *au revoir* from aboard the SS *Aurania*. Subsequent features included cartoons of Esmond smoking in bed as he fantasized about winged horses winning at the track, and Decca flogging plaids at the World's Fair. The nation was still in the grip of the Depression, and the tiresome and often disappointing rituals of job hunting, employment, and unemployment seemed sparkly and amusing when the working man and woman involved were famous young British aristocrats who seemed to have walked right out of a film comedy.

The first week's feature, in addition to its many illustrations and over-sized photographs, offered a boxed biographical summary of the couple's life-so-far and this additional hearty introduction: "A gay and exciting salute to reality by two front-page young lovers who bought the world for a song and are making their dreams come true in America where slammed doors and empty pockets have only been fun to two top-drawer immigrants."

Esmond had already written many articles, but these were Decca's first publications. She'd honed her brisk, amusing style in letters. In the feature titled "English Adventurers Stalk Job in Wilds of New York," she reported on her job at the World's Fair. In her description of "Miss B," the American manager of Ye Merrie England Village who would "discourse eloquently on the necessity of knowing only the right people," Decca began what would become a lifelong habit of skewering snobs in print. Her job was to sing "the merits of Highland Hand-woven Tweeds." Miss B was shallow and deluded. Sales at the booth were slow, the manager claimed, only because "the best people" hadn't yet found them.

At first Decca had been delighted by her job at the fair. Built to demonstrate "The World of Tomorrow," the fair offered many international delights, including the outdoor cafés of the Swiss pavilion and a television in the RCA pavilion, which transmitted "operas, cartoons, cooking demonstrations, travelogues, fashion shows, and skaters at Rockefeller Center." Outside the Heinz pavilion, hungry urchins stood in line to get the tiny gherkins offered as samples. Then they lined up again, making a day of it. The booth in which Decca worked was a faux "old Scotch cottage with a spinning wheel and handloom," with a "weaver imported direct from Scotland," who was also their barker. "Only 10 cents to come in! It's better than the Billy Rose's Aquacade!" he would shout hopefully, though the Aquacade featured Esther Williams, Johnny Weissmuller, and the opposite of tartan woolens: a wet, refreshing spray. Working the fair in August was too hot, and Decca loathed her boss. Soon, she and Esmond were beckoned by the open road.

》《

THE HEADLINE OF the couple's next installment was "English Adventurers Learn the Hard Way," and following the conventions of a second act, introduces its hero and heroine to a deepening series of obstacles. Unemployed again, Esmond attended bartender school, where he met real salt-of-the-earth types, homegrown and immigrant, and worked hard to gain both his coworkers' and his readers' approval. In a complementary piece, Decca delighted in describing the two of them as gadabouts, flirting with the underworld in the person of an expat racetrack tout.

Decca and Esmond invited Donahue, as they knew him, to their apartment for dinner, and he reciprocated by letting them in on some sure bets. Donahue had a "soft Lancashire brogue" and a line about loving and losing a "lass who worked in a mill in Wigan," as well as a tale of complete financial ruin followed by a miraculous turnaround at the track, once he hit upon a plan to beat the system. Simply put, Donahue bribed jockeys to throw races, and for a very small investment, he offered the young couple an opportunity to share in great rewards. In confidence, he added that his foolproof plan required only that he never be greedy. To Esmond, the humility of the scheme—its nonviolent but low-grade risk—as well as Donahue's implied friendship with Broadway habitués such as writer Damon Runyon and legendary boxer Jack Dempsey, proved irresistible. Decca was amused but more reluctant to gamble away their small savings. Esmond persuaded her with a strategy of his own to con the con: "You see, he's planning to take us for a LONG ride. He's much too important a crook to be interested in some piddling amount. Then when we've won say around $500, we'll simply stop there. The SHORT ride versus the LONG ride, that's what our policy should be."

They invested everything they had. Donahue raised their hopes with a big win on their first horse, but when he never showed up to pay them off, they lost their savings after all. The consequence of that deal inspired some unusually revealing writing. Decca rarely portrayed Esmond as anything less than stoic, but on this occasion, he was angry and vulnerable. He stood in the shower looking "as if he'd been there for hours. Water was dribbling down his face, contorting his expression. 'Don't come near me,' he said. 'Don't touch me.'"

Esmond loved to gamble. Perhaps he believed that fortune favors the brave. He always had so much riding on quick, correct decisions. It was perhaps a talent that had kept him alive in Spain. A little fast money would have alleviated the pressure. They hadn't been in New York long, but all the rushing around—meeting contacts and keeping up appearances—had to have been wearing. Donahue hadn't persuaded Decca to bet a dime, but in those days, for Esmond, she'd have gambled everything.

Decca and Esmond snatched success from the jaws of that anecdote. They knew how to frame a good yarn, and they had friends in the press. A New York gossip column called "Only Human" reported: "If we had such an introduction to England on our first trip over, we'd brew a horrible curse upon the country. But not these two. We've never seen two such healthy-minded gloriously happy people." Or so they may have seemed to avid newshounds, but the Romillys were fed up with New York. Their next feature would announce, "Young English Adventurers Make a Door to Door Tour of Washington," in which Decca records Esmond's "disturbingly successful" career as a salesman for Silkform stockings. With the instant authority of his British accent and deportment imported from Wellington school parades, Esmond would bring the full force of his charm to bear upon an unsuspecting housewife in some prosperous Washington neighborhood. Only a week or so into Esmond's new career, both felt they had to make a supreme effort not to be seduced by the prospect of bigger and bigger commissions. Esmond wasn't actually making much money, but the promise of an elevated income from a job to which he was naturally suited was a temptation they had to escape before it was too late. At the end of two weeks, feeling inundated by Silkform mailings—which steadily trumpeted new products, praised Esmond's talents, and promised more and bigger rewards—they set out for the open road.

During their brief spell in Washington, the couple had reconnected with Eugene and Agnes Meyer and their daughter Kay. In Washington that autumn, the talk at dinner parties was of movies, novels, fashion, and who was having affairs, but world politics was the main discourse. What would it take to move the United States away from neutrality toward a more confirmed antifascist position, and under what circumstances would the United States enter the war? Decca was worried about her brother, Tom, now an officer in the army, and sister Unity's still ambiguous whereabouts.

THE HEADLINE OF the *Washington Post* final installment reads: "Young Esmond Romilly Tries His Hand at Being a Waiter—Is Fired After Two Days." An apparent failure at waiting on people, Esmond tried for a position with a little more panache. He had purchased a used tuxedo in a thrift store and considered working as a maître d'. New Orleans seemed to offer a range of possibilities in the field, so he and Decca procured a used car and headed south. Then, somewhere in Georgia, they missed the turn meant to take them west and just kept driving to Miami.

Decca didn't enjoy the journey as much as she had imagined she might. She found the Southerners she met (friends of friends and others from the list of contacts) "snobbish," and far too indifferent to the poverty of their neighbors. Driving through South Carolina, she and Esmond passed the dilapidated roadside shacks of poor tenant farmers. These she compared to "old, broken-down chicken houses. We couldn't believe people actually lived in them till we saw inside."

Southern Florida offered an immediate contrast, but Decca didn't take to it, either. Miami struck her as garish and greedy. Working as a salesclerk at the costume jewelry counter of a drug store, her impatience increased.

> I had plenty of opportunities to observe the Miamians. They struck me as a humorless, suspicious, narrow minded lot. It was our first experience of a Southern American town. The Negroes lived like a band of ghosts in miserable shacks on the outskirts, their very existence ignored for the most part by the whites. The verbal fire of my co-workers in the drugstore was reserved for use against the Jewish tourists, on whose money the town grew fat, and whose patronage paid their salaries. Many of those with whom we came in contact exhibited a sort of smarmy bonhomie, reminiscent of sugary German *gemütlichkeit*, a front behind which lurked the foulest racism.

They spent days on the beach sunbathing and swimming, but Decca continued to give Miami poor reviews. Despite its purported glamour, it seemed shabby and sleazy. She and Esmond were stuck in an apartment alive with huge tropical cockroaches. Decca eventually came to see Miami as one of those end-of-the-road coastal destinations that attracted outsiders, dissidents, the lost, and the reinvented. Miami was full of characters, and she met them on the beach, in the bar, and at the track. As Decca would note in a letter to Unity (still unaware of her sister's suicide attempt), this Miami was much "like the South of France or Venice, all the people here have got something extraorder about them," even the vapid rich. A couple they met in Palm Beach "have a French butler & although he talks perfect English they insist on talking to him in very bad French for the atmosphere."

They would stay in Miami for six months. In the evening, already exhausted from work at the drugstore, Decca would join Esmond as an employee at the Roma Italian Restaurant, where in quick time he worked his way up from general help to part owner. Eventually, Esmond would run the bar while Decca worked as a part-time bookkeeper and bouncer. She described with great pleasure the bouncer part of her job, in which she'd occasionally be asked to entice intoxicated women out of the restrooms. Esmond also considered Miami "mean, murky and meretricious." For him this wasn't necessarily a bad thing. He was drawn to its Graham Greene sort of tropical intrigue. It was also a great theater in which he could exercise all his considerable talent and charm, a place in which to lose himself. Behind the bar, he would perform characters: a Chicago gangster, a stiff-lipped butler, the sophisticated playboy, and the young immigrant barman, welcoming confidences and dispensing advice. For a while, the nights in the restaurant were an idyll. The Italian meals were delicious, plentiful, and free. Esmond's energy, Decca's beauty, and her sense of fun endeared them to their partners in business, the close-knit, amiable Italian American Chizzoli family. In Miami, the couple established a home and network of acquaintances. Unexpectedly, the Roma became their permanent address.

It may have been the war news in the background or the rumors arriving concerning sister Unity, but as Christmas in Miami approached, Decca had the premonition "that something unpleasant would spring out at us from behind the garish façade of that horribly tinselly town with its maddening eternal sunshine pouring incessantly down." In late December 1939, Decca learned from newspaper headlines that her sister Unity had shot herself in the head, but the bullet had not immediately killed her. Decca's family soon confirmed that Unity had survived her suicide attempt. No one in England knew yet how seriously she had been wounded or that, on Hitler's orders, she had been transferred to a hospital in Switzerland. Every part of Unity's story excited a prurient interest that sold papers. Reporters demanded to know just how close Unity had been to Hitler. Who was funding her repatriation? And how, when Britain and Germany were at war, did an unreconstructed Nazi get to return to England when the lives of so many anti-Nazis remained in jeopardy?

Decca may well have been surprised by the newshounds who had discovered her in Miami, and by their number, but she was hardly inconspicuous. The press descended, hovering outside her house and inundating the restaurant. Reporters insinuated themselves with personal questions and demanded statements. One reporter offered Decca five hundred dollars for an interview; another bid one thousand. A third offered to arrange a transatlantic telephone call "to be recorded & used in a broadcast all over the U.S." At night, sightseers would wander into the Roma and casually ask to meet "Unity's sister." This might have been good for restaurant business, but it made Decca miserable. Not knowing the extent of Unity's injuries, she was at first "terrified" and "grieved" for her sister. She was also worried that her family might see fictitious quotes and think them authentic, when in this instance, Decca had loyally stood with the Mitfords and refused to speak to the press.

In January, hearing the news that Unity had returned to England amid a media circus, she wrote again to her mother:

> Do please write & tell me all news of Boud, it is of course absolutely impossible to get anything reliable from the newspaper reports, & the last few days have been so terribly worrying, all the papers here have been saying the most dreadful things . . . Every paper says something different about Boud & how she became so ill, and it is so awful not knowing *anything*. However I am terrifically glad she is at home now as whatever is the matter with her she must be better off at Wycombe where she can have proper food & Blor & everyone.

Muv withheld Unity's true diagnosis from Decca for several more months. Their mother encouraged Decca to think that Unity had simply lost her memory and suggested that the patient might be well in six months; later, Muv amended the prediction to a year. By March, when Decca exchanged her first letters with Unity, she faced the reality that at age twenty-five, her sister was permanently brain-damaged. Unity would remain childlike and dim for the remaining eight years of her life.

One of the reporters who plagued Decca asked whether it was true, as speculated in some papers, that Unity had shot herself after "a terrible quarrel with Hitler." That rumor if confirmed might have meant that her sister had broken with the Nazi leader and perhaps in the end even become antifascist. (As long as the facts remained unclear, Decca could try to rationalize her sister's behavior. If Unity had recanted, perhaps even Esmond might soften toward her.) Decca must have longed for, if not gentle commiseration, at least some straightforward help in manipulating the press. Esmond was the expert when it came to hustling reporters and finding out what they knew without giving the store away. But he fervently abjured all discussion of his Nazi sister-in-law. "I knew I couldn't expect Esmond, who had never met her, to feel anything but disgust for her, so by tacit understanding we avoided discussing [Unity]." And her own sense of responsibility and antifascist fervor made it impossible for her to express any public sympathy for her sister.

The couple's partnership, built, according to Decca, on "estrangement from our families, the circumstances of our marriage, our constant wanderings about, the death of the baby, all had conspired to weld us into a self-sufficient unit, a conspiracy of two against the world." Decca was rarely inclined to act alone, but she could when necessary. She had proven this when she had an abortion without informing Esmond. During the Christmas crisis, she coped with the press and her own anxieties and grieved for Unity on her own, with only the occasional letter from Muv to offer small comfort. By the spring of 1940, Miami, though it had many attributes of a last outpost, wasn't nearly far enough away to escape their destinies as Romilly and Mitford.

CHAPTER 6

*O*N MAY 10, 1940, Hitler's army invaded the Netherlands, and the day after, Uncle Winston succeeded Chamberlain as British prime minister. A letter from Nellie Romilly arrived containing a great deal more family news, none of it good: Esmond's father, Bertram Romilly, had died of cancer, far more ill than they had known. And then on April 9, while Esmond's brother, Giles, was reporting from Norway for the English paper the *Daily Express*, he had been captured by German troops. Nellie was alone, and although she implied that she was gallantly coping, there was desperation to be read between the lines: What were Esmond's plans, she wondered? She didn't directly ask him when he would be returning to England or whether he intended to enlist, but she seemed to think that he was only in America because Decca wouldn't leave.

Esmond made his decision to train as a fighter pilot. Having fought on the ground in Spain, this time he preferred to be up in the sky. Since the United States had not yet joined the war, he had to enlist in Canada, the nearest Commonwealth nation. The couple sold their interest in the Roma Restaurant, packed up their car, and drove north back to Washington, D.C.

What a ride it must have been: grief and sorrow over Bertrand, anxiety over Giles. Nellie didn't come in for much sympathy; Esmond typically mistrusted her motives. He took her neutral prose as cool manipulation, her tender salutations as sentimental manipulation. But whatever Decca and Esmond thought of her, she was now suffering and alone. The landscape reflected their misery. It stormed for days with almost hurricane-force winds. Driving through flooded towns, they noted the still-intact standards of perverse social norms: whites-only water fountains and hand-scrawled signs announcing NO DOGS OR JEWS ALLOWED. As they taxed their little car to breakdown, they strategized about money. There would be a gap before Esmond's first check from the air force; Decca would need to find a job. She could go through the want ads—but better to comb their contacts. She knew her way around big houses; she was an attractive and energetic guest who lent beauty and a little radical frisson to an occasion. That was the customary exchange for a nice meal or a string pulled for a ticket or visa or job. Decca had repudiated many of the privileges that came with being the daughter of a British lord, but she could still invoke an air of hauteur when it was useful.

"What a contrast to New York!" Esmond wrote from Washington to his friend Peter Nevile in London. "Instead of the rather wearing kind of sophistication of endless radioish repartee, etc. You get a lot of people sitting around talking about a 'social program.'" A young labor lawyer newly arrived in Washington by the name of Robert Treuhaft noted the capital's "very powerful anti-fascist, anti-Hitler spirit." To Decca it seemed the best place to find a job and companions while Esmond was away. She was impressed by the way so many young supporters of President Roosevelt "lived and worked with a crusading enthusiasm." Many of the staff workers in Washington identified themselves as New Dealers (after Roosevelt's policies to revive the economy in the wake of the Great Depression). Decca shared their idealism, collected their literature, and soon employed the local bureaucratic lexicon of *aid schemes* and *benefit packages* and *farm subsidies*.

She and Esmond made the rounds of cause parties and benefits. She was the aristo-renegade who had publically denounced her family's connection to fascism. He was the veteran who had fought in Spain. At the end of May, Decca's brother-in-law, Diana's husband Oswald Mosley, leader of the British Union of Fascists, was arrested and imprisoned for activities threatening the defense of the realm. In July, Diana was also arrested for being a security risk. Nancy Mitford, among others, had secretly informed on Diana. "Not very sisterly," Nancy admitted, but it was the thing to do.

In Washington, among the socialites and smart-setters who tended to lean left, Decca and Esmond found a few new friends. Kay Meyer (later

Katharine Graham, publisher of the *Washington Post*) and Decca found they had a great deal in common. Both had been born in 1917 and brought up in homes patrolled by nannies and maids. As unenthusiastic debutantes, both had veered off the beaten path for girls of wealth and well-positioned families. While Decca had escaped to Spain, Kay went to college, where she became a dedicated New Dealer. Both had fathers who had powerful personalities and extravagant résumés that included dabbling in gold mines (Eugene Meyer's investments had struck it rich, while Farve Mitford's financial experiments had gone bust). Both women had eccentric mothers whose comparative quirks must have supplied long nights of conversation lubricated by that season's fashionable cocktails: Gin Rickeys, Pink Ladies, and Tom Collinses.

Decca had grown up in a house of girls. It had been liberating to escape being next-to-youngest and all the intense scrutiny, sniping, power struggles, and alliances of their sorority. Decca must have felt great relief finding a friend like Kay, a responsive and discerning companion so unlike her sisters. Over the previous few months, Decca had spent a lot of time alone with Esmond, and she adored him, but there was no denying he was a handful. The days were long gone when he had dominated every conversation, but she still often had to fight for an inch, he was so full of opinions. He was quick to take offense when criticized and, at the same time, a harsh critic of others. He wasn't a snob, but he held high standards about the quality of literature a person should read and how to interpret almost everything. In Kay, Decca found an adviser she trusted and a girlfriend in whose company she could relax.

Watching the war arrive and the news in Europe from her crazy Floridian perch had wrung her out. Esmond's resistance to any discussion of her family had made her doubt herself. She knew it wasn't wrong to wonder, to inquire, even to have some sympathy for Unity. To Kay, Decca confessed her fears, scorned fascist Diana and all her works, and described the amazing and contradictory Nancy. (Kay also had an older, accomplished sister who meant the world to her.) All those surface similarities would have meant little if Decca and Kay hadn't clicked as optimistic outsiders, sympathetic to one another's ambition to eschew convention and have brilliant careers as journalists. Kay had recently returned from a stint as a junior reporter on the *San Francisco Chronicle*; Decca admired her experience and education and dreamed of taking journalism classes once she found a job. They shared political convictions—starting with a mutual admiration for Franklin D. Roosevelt and the New Deal. Kay had (like Decca) visited Paris in 1936, where each attended a demonstration organized by the antifascist alliance the Popular Front, an experience that Kay said produced "the most impressive feeling of communal strength I had ever had."

That the Romillys were glamorous, attractive, and temporarily without visible means of support meant they would have to spend their last dime on a hotel or fall back on society contacts (Lord Lothian, the British ambassador, was one). It was a great relief when Michael and Binnie Straight, a wealthy young couple and benefactors of the Spanish antifascist committee, invited them to share their Washington home. Michael was a sleek, Cambridge-educated cosmopolite who worked for the family firm, *New Republic* magazine, which he would eventually direct as publisher. Esmond was more liable to view a trust-fund baby as a prospective meal ticket than a buddy, but Straight's politics provided a partial dispensation. Esmond had the ability to talk people into gambles and risks and outrageous schemes that sounded just plausible, like starting a cattle ranch in Arizona (investment prospectus upon request) or betting the house on Peccadillo in the fourth race at the track. Straight considered Esmond "brilliant, colorful, often hysterically funny, sometimes unspeakably cruel."

Decca treated Binnie, a sagacious nineteen-year-old (whom her friends agreed looked like Alice in Wonderland) like a younger sister. She alternately teased and counseled Binnie, particularly regarding the subject of money. Decca was careful to preserve every dime of her own savings (a necessity, thrift was now also a game at which she excelled), but she had countless opinions about causes to which Binnie might tithe her fortune. Both Straights agreed that Decca had quite a "fine satirical mind." Binnie admired her new friend's independence, nonchalance, and ambition to become a journalist. The younger woman was intrigued by the way Decca coped with her unpredictable husband—this took another kind of bravery. He could be sweet and flirtatious when he turned on the charm, but he would sometimes stomp around the house disturbing the help (whom he nonetheless always wished to befriend). It was maddening to have the Romillys for houseguests. They were sloppy and disrespectful of people's things but if they broke an ornament or tore a curtain, they would fall all over themselves to apologize, promising to repair or replace whatever it was. Even Esmond—no matter how he scowled or snarled—couldn't suppress a certain imprinted courtesy. He was unquestionably gallant, and Decca was marvelously sympathetic.

It was at one cause party that they met Virginia and Clifford Durr, who in 1933 moved from Alabama, following Virginia's sister Josephine (called "Sister" in the Southern style) and her husband, Hugo Black (then a senator from Alabama and soon to become a Supreme Court justice), into the heart of the Roosevelt administration. Cliff was chief counsel for the Reconstruction Finance Commission. Virginia was active in the Women's Division of the National Democratic Committee and was devoted to overthrowing the poll tax: a prohibitive fee imposed at various locations across the South to keep nonwhites and white women from exercising their right to vote. The poll tax, an entirely unconstitutional custom sustained by segregationists and male supremacists, was maintained through threats and intimidation.

The Durrs' home in the graceful suburb of Alexandria, Virginia, just across the Potomac River from Washington, was one of the unofficial New Deal salons. An invitation to an evening there might include sharing a home-cooked Southern meal with government workers, labor activists, and musicologists. At their first encounter, Decca had felt "outnumbered" by Virginia's conversational style and wasn't eager to repeat the experience. Nevertheless, at Virginia's invitation, the Romillys and Straights arrived for a dinner date, the women dressed in hats and heels.

Virginia ushered them in. "Why, I'm so absolutely delighted that you-all could come!" she cooed. Her house was in a state of controlled chaos, the drawing room occupied by a "tangled mass of small children." Virginia, an irresistible hostess and raconteur extraordinaire, launched at once into a set of stories to enthrall her new audience. Cliff, ever the gracious host, poured drinks amid the persistent din.

Between those colossi Esmond and Virginia, it wouldn't have been easy to get a word in edgewise. Virginia had a loud voice, but she was always perfectly polite, correct, and hospitable. She was big-boned with quick reactions. Though sometimes brash, Virginia also had an open and vulnerable side—an appealing way of suddenly cracking a smile. If Decca had been any less confident, she might have felt jealous.

Virginia and Esmond almost instantly developed a strong rapport. Before her acquaintance with the Romillys, Virginia had never met an English person. She was "very much engrossed with him." His impressions of American politics seemed exotic, an "aristocratic . . . upperclass . . . point-of-view." But his assessment of the unsophisticated and his contempt for American politicians (though not Roosevelt) made her laugh. Esmond had a *realpolitik* view of the Hitler-Stalin pact. He "knew it wasn't a real pact, just buying time" for the Russians to build an army to fight the Nazis. To Virginia, "he was a man, not a boy." He felt a similar attraction of like minds. Her age, experience, and breadth of interest gave him the confidence to take a wild gamble. He'd have to leave for Ontario, Canada, in a matter of days, and he was sure Virginia would be the best person to protect Decca in his absence.

He went to be alone with Virginia in the kitchen, where she was cooking dinner. A few comments were made on the savory fragrance, the comfortable feel of home. He had already given her the nickname "Old Virginny" (after the song starting "Carry Me Back to . . ."). Then, as Virginia Durr recollected later, he asked her to look after his wife. "Don't you think you could keep dear Decca while I'm gone? You know the Straights are going up to New York for the weekend and she will be all alone. I'm sure that she will be so lonely. If you will just keep her for the weekend, I can't tell you how much I would appreciate it."

That was what he had wanted? If Virginia had thought his advances were intended otherwise, she quickly recovered. She told him, in case he hadn't heard, that the Durrs had already agreed to house some English refugees, a mother and child who would be arriving soon. The house would be full with the Durrs, their four children, and Virginia's mother living with them: "We're already cramped."

That didn't faze Esmond. "Just keep her until your refugees arrive," he replied. Anything might happen—their transport ship might be bombed, for instance.

Virginia didn't know Decca and didn't want her, but the American hostess could not say this to her guest. He was a very appealing young soldier, but Virginia was no pushover. She had years of hard-earned experience in saying no gracefully. "Well, Esmond," she said. She would have to make this very clear. "I'm terribly sorry, but I'm going to the Democratic Convention in Chicago. I'm leaving almost immediately."

"That will be wonderful. Just take Decca with you," he said.

》《

ESMOND DROVE OFF to Canada, leaving Virginia and Decca just a few days to take one another's measure before they set forth together to the Democratic National Convention in Chicago. Virginia had impressive energy, stamina, concentration, and curiosity, but she was not happy about the added work Decca's company entailed: "I didn't want to take her a bit." Why, she wondered, would Decca even want to attend this inimitably American event? People wore funny hats, drank themselves silly, and took every public opportunity to swell up and boast about their wonderful states, counties, and towns. Virginia didn't plan to be a tour guide; she had a mission, the abolition of the poll tax.

She was planning to drive out with two young New Dealers, a man and a woman. With all their luggage and a two-day drive ahead, Decca would crowd the car. But Virginia couldn't in the end deny a hero of the Spanish Civil War his request, especially not after he had recapped Decca's last year. He told Virginia they had "come to the U.S. to get Decca out of the sorrow she was in over the loss of the dead baby." Since then, her favorite sister—infatuated with Hitler—had tried to commit suicide; another sister had been imprisoned by Britain for Nazi sympathies; another had married in her absence (so she was missing the good things, too); her father had declared he wouldn't see her again; her brother-in-law had been captured by Nazis; her father-in-law had just died of cancer; and her brother was a British officer somewhere in Africa. Now her husband was on his way to become a pilot in the Canadian Air Force, and neither he nor she had ever been to Canada. Virginia agreed. How could she not? That didn't mean she was happy with the situation.

Decca, meanwhile, was just barreling forward. Nobody could say she didn't have grit. She hadn't yet figured out Virginia, whose personal intensity approached Esmond's on the tectonic scale, but she proceeded apace as she had early on with her husband by watching, listening, making herself useful, and being amusing. Traveling to the Democratic Convention sounded like fun—she would hear Franklin and Eleanor Roosevelt give speeches, and she would get to go west, which she and Esmond had often discussed doing together. When she returned to Washington, she might go stay with the Straights or the Meyers, whoever would have her until she got on her feet. She'd find a job. One more factor to add to the mix—she was about three months pregnant. This was the real reason Esmond was determined to see her settled.

As it happened, Decca's pregnancy became the theme of the drive out. She hadn't told Virginia she was pregnant, and Decca knew she was there on sufferance. And though she was good-humored and an enthusiastic traveling companion, almost immediately after they hit the open road, she asked to stop at a restroom. "Thereafter," Virginia said, "every fifteen minutes she wanted us to stop again." Virginia suspected that Decca was coping with something apart from a weak bladder and, at the next rest stop, found Decca throwing up: It was morning sickness. Once the secret was out, it was easier for everyone to enjoy the ride.

Along the way, Decca came to see another America. The Midwest was almost as foreign to Virginia as it was to the Englishwoman. The little towns were waking after the long decade of the Depression. The travelers would have seen abandoned homes along the roadside, the occasional hobo looking for a lift (there wasn't room for a mouse in their crowded car), and miles of fallow fields. But there were also neat little houses, high stalks of corn stretching forever, crowded baseball diamonds, and unexpected swarms of fireflies. Their trip took them from Maryland to West Virginia, into Ohio then Indiana and Illinois. At night, they slumped on one another's shoulders to sleep. Decca sang some bawdy music hall tunes and amused her companions with her talent for nicknaming. The baby she was carrying kicked like a donkey, and since the donkey was the Democratic Party symbol, she started calling her unborn child "dinky-donk" or "little donkey," "Dink" for short.

In Chicago, the other two passengers went their own way, while Decca followed Virginia to the Sheraton, where many of the delegations were staying and where there would be meetings and conferences—fish in a barrel for Virginia to buttonhole regarding the poll tax legislation. The two women's friendship had been accelerated by the compressed nature of the road trip. They had discovered, despite their first impressions, that they were kindred intellectual spirits. Decca, Virginia learned, had a great deal of curiosity and was well informed about the U.S. political scene. Virginia, Decca saw, had a soft center; she was protective and maternal, and if anything, she might be too attentive and worry too much. Decca was suddenly on her own for the first time in her adult life, without husband, parents, or sisters, and she liked the feeling. Chicago was strange, but she had Virginia Durr's guidance.

The first person Virginia recognized in the Chicago throng was her old friend Lyndon Johnson. Since neither Decca nor Virginia had delegate badges, Johnson made them honorary delegates of the Texas contingent. That gave them a base and seats in the sweltering and smelly throng. Virginia worried on Decca's behalf about their distance from the ladies' lavatories in the vast Chicago Stadium. When she confided to Maury Maverick (a congressman and delegate) that Decca was expecting and prone to throwing up, Maverick bowed and chivalrously offered his sombrero, "Madame, use my hat if you need it."

The second day, Decca decided not to risk having to employ the congressman's hat. She fell easily into her trickster mode, in which mild deceptions were second nature. It didn't hurt that "by this time Decca was looking very glamorous and beautiful." She used her accent and appeal to get closer to the floor, and the ladies' lounge, as she later explained to Esmond in a letter: "I went up to an official looking man & told him I was lost & my friends were in a box & the policeman wouldn't let me in; so he said I could sit in his box, & he turned out to be the Secretary of State for Illinois & I sat right behind Mrs. Woodrow Wilson in the best place of all!"

With the convention under way, Decca the Democratic functionary-in-training scouted out seats to observe the resolutions committee meeting. She found a good perch at a table in the center of the room, which confused the pages, who had to ask her to move out of the committee members' seat. The platform plank, Decca learned, had already been hammered out in smoke-filled rooms and this meeting was more like a public performance, but she was still caught up in the atmosphere of intrigue and consequence. She felt that with the New Deal faithful, she was on the winning side. She was for Roosevelt, and her guy was unopposed.

Roosevelt had strategized that the only way to accept the nomination for an unprecedented third term would be if he were to be seen drafted "spontaneously and with unanimous support." Just to make sure the president got what he wanted, Chicago's Mayor Edward Joseph Kelly patched a microphone into the public address system. Decca enjoyed the display of some mild, Chicago-style chicanery when Thomas D. Garry, Chicago's superintendent of sewers, interrupted a message from the president urging the convention to feel free to nominate any candidate. Garry burst out with an emphatic, "No, no, we want Roosevelt!" The convention went on to nominate Roosevelt on the first ballot and Henry Wallace, secretary of agriculture, as his vice presidential candidate.

Decca and Virginia were whisked around on a tour of labor-proud Chicago. Richard Wright, one of the contributors to the *WPA Guide to Illinois*, had just published *Native Son*, which Decca would later read and recommend to her sister Nancy. There were also many amazing Works Progress Administration murals, painted on the walls of schools and field houses all over Chicago, to visit. Everywhere Decca went, her Britishness became a part of the conversation. Virginia Durr was not alone in her fascination. Most Americans had never met an English person. Should the United States enter the war or not? Her husband was an airman? Brave girl! Intended or not, Decca's presence was a case for intervention.

CHAPTER 7

HE HEADLINE ON the *Washington Post* society page of July 27, 1940, read: "War Means Separation for Esmond Romillys." Under the caption "Husband fights for Britain," Decca smiles gamely. Her miniature white straw hat perched fashionably front and forward, its narrow brim tilting toward one darkly painted brow. Her hair is down, midlength—no pompadour—and the shoulders of her short-sleeved, navy blue summer frock are tailored but not overly padded. A white ruffle flounces about her jugular. For this photo, she's buttoned up, stylish but demure, not the look of a girl who would run away to the Spanish Civil War, but more like a tourist available for a delicious cup of tea and a gossip with a congressman, or a debate with his wife at the local library on the folly of American isolationism. Twenty-three years old, so beautiful and plucky, she represented all her sisters—not just the celebrated biological ones, but all the Brits, who were just then enduring the terrible bombing in the Battle of Britain and resisting so superbly.

The rest of that day's society page reported on bridal trips, dinners attended by generals and judges, vacation plans of senators and Egyptian ministers, and the maiden voyage of a new ocean liner christened *America*, which has "among other new features, upholstery and curtains of fireproof material. All the furniture is metal."

On its face, this distillation of prewartime domestic celebrity was awfully sedate. The prewar city that Gore Vidal imagined in his novel *Washington, D.C.* is a wicked landscape of leathery and nostalgic mothers, beautiful and glittering social-climbing daughters, and power-hungry fathers and sons. It's a land of insult and injury, scandal, ambition, deceit, and illusion. In the society pages, *quality* (or *tone*) is the watchword, which explains why

Decca was such a catch. Her history was already well known. Let other papers seek their celebrities in New York and Hollywood. That day, the *Washington Post* crowed, it had Jessica Mitford.

Not just anybody got this treatment. This photograph and the accompanying article composed a deluxe job advertisement (courtesy of Eugene Meyer) announcing Decca's intention to find work in the nation's capital. Her requirements: respectable work at satisfactory pay. Her résumé included keeping the books in Miami's Roma Italian Restaurant, according to the "'Decca Method,' which she invented herself."

Of all the millionaires and socialites she'd encountered, Decca considered Eugene Meyer the most interesting. He was a big-shot financier, a mover and shaker, and a solicitous and affectionate father to his children. He was paternal in his dealings with the Romillys, but not excessively patronizing. Though she heartily disagreed with him politically (he and his wife opposed Roosevelt), he was both "colossally useful" and considerably more amusing than anyone she had met in the Durr crowd (who deplored Meyer and his powerful Republican cohorts). Since Meyer had arranged for Decca to pose for the deluxe job ad in the society pages, she couldn't very well refuse when he invited her to their New York estate in Mount Kisco. She'd have to sing for her supper, but who knew what doors a visit might open.

Mount Kisco indeed proved to be "an absolute riot of anti-New Dealism." It was also a very pleasant atmosphere, full of good food and privacy. Decca was by then an old hand at negotiating varieties of experience. She and Esmond thrived on contrasts. In their first few weeks apart, their letters were one long, rolling repartee. An exchange from Mount Kisco began as Decca described (in menu-worthy prose) a luxurious summer morning, during which she woke

> about 9:30 . . . reached out & pressed the button M (for Maid)
> . . . directed her to press my dress, clean my white shoes & serve
> breakfast. Shortly was served with ice-cold California orange

juice, 1 strictly fresh egg, 4 strips young prime bacon, steaming coffee (special brew) with thick sweet country cream, & jumbo raspberries . . . then lay back relaxing among the pillows while bath was running.

They both knew how lucky she was.

Before Mount Kisco, Esmond's absence had felt exotic and temporary. Now, five months into her pregnancy, she had some new sense of what daily life without him really meant. Esmond was in Canada, enlisted to become a pilot. He was in the war that they'd talked about and seen arriving for all their youth. He was uncomfortable, bored, their two worlds forking away from one another, as must happen with a soldier and the family he leaves. It was more and more important that she write well and carefully, and she wanted to be sure to make him laugh.

»«

WHEN DECCA RETURNED to Washington, locals were bragging about the city's wet, buggy summertime. The capital was built on swamps. Everywhere, jocular interrogators lay in wait, *Hot enough for you?* Best to retreat to some cool spot, drink something refreshing. All good advice, but Decca had to work for a living. She counted her pennies: The bargain of sending a telegram at night "only cost 58 cents for 50 words"; the expenses of her trip to Chicago amounted to sixty dollars round-trip; but still she needed some expanding clothes. There was some good news on the financial front: Upon her return from Mount Kisco, Virginia had met her at the door to say a prospective employer had seen her photograph in the *Washington Post* and telephoned several times.

Decca hoped the job would come through. Beyond that, she would wait to hear from Esmond. If there were a way to join him, she would. Virginia, concerned that Decca was still throwing up a lot, invited her to stay on in Alexandria, "until you get over being sick."

"My plans are completely flexible & I can use this house as a base as long as I want," she wrote to Esmond. "However if you should return here don't let's stay here . . . This house is rather cluttered up with children & old mothers etc."

The first casualty of a new dependent is her privacy. At the Durrs', Decca slept in Clifford Durr's study and she was rarely alone. Virginia quickly got over whatever reticence she might have felt regarding Decca's foreignness. Virginia had a household to run and the anti-poll-tax campaign to organize. There was no time to indulge spoiled aristocrats, pregnant or not. Virginia had sympathy with the young woman's loss and loneliness, which Decca hid well. But there was nobody to clean up after her at the Durr house in Alexandria. Decca asked the Durrs' eldest daughter, Ann, to wash her stockings and underwear, and when Ann refused, Decca laughed and said she wouldn't wear any. Virginia was amazed that her guest had never "learned how to make a bed, never washed stockings or underwear, used a whole box of Lux on her first time. Had absolutely not done 1 single domestic task, never had to, either didn't do it or had servants." But of course, Decca had—she had lived with Esmond for two years, and it fell to her to do something, because he did even less. Their domestic arrangements were typically haphazard. As a housekeeper, she did the minimum. If others were more fastidious about mess, she left them to take charge. She could at the very least make an omelet and could sew on a button.

The senior member of the household—Virginia's mother, Mrs. Foster—ran afoul of Decca early on by criticizing her for taking an unladylike interest in food. From then on, Decca felt free to tease the older woman by "debunking the aristocratic Old South whenever possible." Eventually Decca became a favorite of the Durrs' three-year-old daughter, Lucy. As math and French tutor to Ann, Decca applied inimitable Mitford pedagogy. She would sit beside her pupil smoking a Chesterfield and threaten to "burn her hands with the cig or else pinch her" if she didn't give the right answer. Decca didn't carry out her threat on Ann, but that month, the woman was in a burning mood. She told Esmond that she had pinched and burned Virginia with a cigarette when her hostess had carelessly revealed a secret concerning a mutual friend. There was no report of Virginia's reaction—which must have been impressive.

Eugene Meyer felt responsible for helping Decca find work where her celebrity wouldn't be exploited. His assistant pulled some strings to find her a place in a small, exclusive dress shop called Weinberger's, where Decca would draw her salary mainly from sales commissions. Decca was thrilled to have the job search ended and was in a hurry to earn some money before her pregnancy started to show. She began "Weinbergering" in mid-August and all too quickly exhausted the clothes budget of her closest friends (though she was sure Binnie Straight, who had so much money, might splurge even more on clothing). She trolled society parties at the British Embassy, schmoozed the Meyers' friends, and sought potential clients among the more affluent matrons in Virginia's circle. The commission hustle soon took its toll—for every "American glamour girl" who evinced interest in a dress, she had to endure a dozen bores or the presence of a "rich reactionary." These soirees could leave her feeling "dragged through a filthy mire, they were all *so* awful."

Decca would car-pool to her job in Washington from Virginia's home in Alexandria. The always-crowded car included other commuting neighbors like John Kenneth Galbraith, upon whose "bony" knees Decca would often have to sit. By September, she was already having to squeeze into an ever-more-restrictive girdle to give the impression of a still-slender figure. On the drive home, she would wiggle out of its elastic casing in the car. Sometimes, she would just tear it off in the most convenient spot. "Decca, you have simply got to stop taking your girdle off in my office," Cliff Durr told her.

Back at the Durrs' home in Alexandria, Decca might find Durr relatives and friends from Alabama, Cliff's colleagues and younger protégées in the New Deal administration, poll-tax campaign workers, neighbors, children, and friends of friends. Neighborhood guests might include Dee Dee Walker, an Englishwoman who made a mean mint julep. She reminded Decca of the "staunch" ladies she'd known in England. (Later reports suggested Walker was a spy for British intelligence. One of her assignments was to keep her eye on the Mitford girl in Washington.) Decca was having a wonderful time meeting new people like Pete Seeger and Alan Lomax at the Durrs' parties, but missed Esmond terribly. In the act of drawing as complete a picture as possible for him, she sharpened her own reporting skills.

Marge Gelders was eighteen years old when she met Decca. She thought Decca was "the most beautiful person" she had ever seen. The way people "buzzed around her like bees" impressed her, and Marge concluded, "Decca also had a wicked sting."

Marge had grown up in Tuscaloosa, Alabama, the daughter of two Jewish professors. Her father, Joe Gelders, quit teaching physics and hitch-hiked with Marge to New York City, where he became a labor organizer, and his daughter a member of the Young Communist League. After school, she would hawk the *Daily Worker* on street corners. Her vivacious style, urchin look (complete with worker's cap cocked to one side of her short, tousled hair), and strong Alabama accent made her a top-selling newsie. Marge was on her way to Radcliffe.

Joe Gelders became one of the founders of the Southern Conference for Human Welfare.

At Virginia's party, Decca argued with his isolationist position on the war, but still found him an interesting, principled man. Years earlier, Joe had been kidnapped and brutally beaten by thugs hired by the Tennessee Coal, Iron and Railroad Co. to intimidate and silence his labor organizing. Virginia considered Joe a living saint and always credited him with inspiring her involvement in human rights work.

In September, Decca's twenty-third birthday party spread at the Durrs' featured "fresh curried shrimp & rice, succotash & garden green lettuce salad & hot rolls, followed by the Grand Entrance of a cake." In England, the Royal Air Force had rebuffed the German attack in the Battle of Britain by shooting down more than 185 German planes. Decca felt great relief that now the suffering in England might be lessened, and she also felt less guilt and worry along with some pride. She continued to scrimp and save, occasionally indulging in a little jiggery-pokery. At a Bundles for Britain sewing party, which collected useful articles like canned foods and donated clothing to send to the U.K., hostess Dee Dee Walker caught Decca trying to make off with a package of baby clothes, and demanded she return them, despite Decca's argument that "it might save postage to England & yet still go to a Briton."

Decca insisted she only ever stole from those who could easily afford the loss, and mainly from the very rich Meyers. She had told Binnie—in confidence—about the silk stockings that she'd taken from the Meyer family residence. Binnie told Kay Meyer, and this made Decca cross, but it was no secret that Decca didn't respect private property. When the Straights and the Romillys had shared a house, Michael Straight and Esmond would some- times have ferocious arguments. And one time, after Esmond had accused Michael of being a "bourgeois philistine," he and Decca had stormed out carrying away a load of Michael's "shirts, socks and ties." Kay certainly wasn't surprised to hear that Decca had borrowed a few little things. The American woman had often heard her father recount the speech he'd given once after dinner with the Romillys and others as guests. He had just reached the part about "there is one thing you can say for the British . . . they never steal other people's property," when all eyes swiveled to Esmond, who was filling his pockets with Meyer's best Cuban cigars. Binnie thought it was all amusing. Kay didn't care about stockings or cigars. Decca knew that these very wealthy women could never understand her impulse to relieve them of the things they'd never miss: from each according to her ability, to each according to her need, as the Marxist maxim goes.

By December, no girdle could disguise Decca's pregnancy. She left Weinberger's after the management gently pointed out that her secret had been known for some time. At Christmas, Esmond was finally granted leave. According to Virginia Durr, he "wanted an intense Christmas." He had an enormous appetite for whimsical holiday sweets, and he whipped up funny seasonal cocktails like grog. He wanted the biggest tree they could find and

the biggest goose and took on the job of chief Christmas decorator, string-
ing popcorn and strewing tinsel. One night, he took Decca and the Durr
family out to a French restaurant where there were garlicky snails and frogs'
legs on the menu. Every day, he insisted Decca walk two miles with him for
the health of the baby. Many years later, Virginia would still marvel that she
had never seen "two people more completely in love."

CHAPTER 8

IN THE WINTER of 1940–1941, Giles Romilly was being held in Germany as a prisoner of war. He was ill and hungry and would later write about that "long dead time when German victory arrogantly straddled Europe. The war crawled, signs of change were scant." A continent away, his brother returned from Christmas leave to train as an aviation navigator in Ontario. Esmond hated Canada. It was distinctly not the United States (which fascinated and frustrated him by its stubborn refusal to formally enter the war), but at least it wasn't England, where he anticipated military service under a slew of "ghastly" Mitford relations.

In Washington, Virginia Durr was getting nowhere with her poll-tax campaign. Even her friends complained that her persistent calls were becoming annoying. Her husband, Cliff, complained about his backache. Decca and Virginia's mother were bickering. Virginia, tired of the way her young guest monopolized the bath, was beginning to feel like a "Bloomsbury lodging house keeper." Decca offered to leave, but they really did like one other. And beyond their walls, there was just so much misery. The red-baiters were suddenly everywhere, hating everyone. Mostly, Virginia wanted Decca to make arrangements for her child's birth. The house was very crowded, and it ran best when Virginia, its nerve center, knew what everyone was planning to do.

Before Virginia mentioned the word, Decca had never heard of the medical specialty obstetrics. She'd had her first child at home, in Bermondsey, close to a Labour Party maternity clinic, which provided her with the free and excellent services of a doctor and nurse. She wanted to give birth this time in Virginia's home and hoped to convince her hostess that all one needed was "a quantity of stout brown paper [to cover the bedclothes], boiling water, and a competent doctor."

"Absolutely not," said Virginia. It wasn't just that the demands of her home's occupants would try the patience of even the most accommodating, or that the drama of a young, British aristocrat's giving birth in the second bedroom might push Virginia beyond her limits. Imagine the publicity, the press, the photographers. Decca's life was news. Virginia had her husband's peace of mind to consider, and she had to protect her own children. Then there was the deep current, rarely addressed, that this young woman had lost her first daughter when the infant was six months old. Who knew what the childbirth experience might dredge up? What if something went wrong? Decca offered an alternate plan. Why not set up a crèche in the barn? Virginia insisted that in Washington in 1941, women gave birth in a hospital.

"I hated that idea," Decca said, but she did as Virginia advised and engaged the services of a "highly touted" obstetrician. Decca never liked spending her own money, and once she stopped working, she worried even more over her and Esmond's dwindling resources. Medical care, like electricity and toothpaste, were the kinds of things one should always receive free of charge—and would be provided gratis, in her kind of socialism. She felt trapped by the capitalist, big-shot, patronizing doctor, and eventually she hit on a dramatic way to escape his unwelcome care, which she described years later in *The American Way of Birth*:

> At each visit, for which he charged $5—a large amount in those days—he demanded a sample of my urine. To my absolute fury I discovered that Virginia's sister Josephine, wife of Supreme Court Justice Hugo Black, was being treated by the same obstetrician for menopausal troubles—for which he prescribed injections of the urine of pregnant women at the outrageous cost of $10 per shot. I stormed into his office, accused him of profiteering by selling my urine to Josephine and charging both of us, and told him he was fired forthwith. He seemed astonished, and had nothing to say in his defense.

Though others within earshot might have heard the big-shot doctor say something along the lines of *Thank goodness I've seen the last of her*, Decca exited in triumph. In sacking her specialist, Decca also lost the hospital bed he'd reserved for her. Required now to find an alternative, she went bargain hunting, a skill that came naturally. She applied to Columbia Hospital in Washington, and though it wasn't exactly in the same vein as a Labour Party free clinic, the price at fifty dollars for ten days in a four-bed ward with an ordinary doctor was closer to what she wanted. She was intrigued by the public ward setup and particularly by the nurses, whom she thought

> all v. pretty rather like chorus girls, with a lot of make-up & they stand around chatting about dates etc & two were even playing cards, paying absolutely no attention to the groans & writhing going on all round, except occasionally to say sharply to some screaming woman "Lie down AT ONCE! You're not to sit up. Marie, come over & hold her legs a minute while I fix my hair.

On the day of their daughter's birth, February 9, 1941, Esmond was at Malton, Ontario, in an air-observer course. Of their child's actual birth, Decca provides this in *The American Way of Birth*:

> The anesthetic given there was unlike anything I'd heard of before or since; possibly a short lived fad of the moment. It consisted of hot air pumped up one's rectum, rather agony while being administered, but it must have served its purpose, as I remember almost nothing about the actual birth except for the joyful moment when the nurse handed me the baby, wrapped in pink for a girl.

Over the next few days, a parade of visitors trooped through the ward to pay their respects. She received congratulatory cards and letters, including one from Lady Clifford Tate, a friend of Nellie Romilly's, who offered Decca the use of her house in Nassau for two months. Kay and her new husband, Phil Graham, and Eugene and Agnes Meyer visited, bearing gifts of eau de cologne, baby clothes, flowers, and hampers of delicious food, which Decca shared with her ward mates. *Washington Post* photographers were on hand to record the first days of mother and baby, and from then on, Decca's presence on the ward became public knowledge. "Are you any relation of Hitler's friend?" one of the women in the ward asked. Another new mother, unaware of the Mitford connection, wondered, "Was her baby born with teeth?" Eugene Meyer sat by her bed for a while and said that if she needed anything, she had only to let him know. After he'd gone, Elaine, the unmarried mother in the bed next to Decca's, said, "I was just thinking; wouldn't it be wonderful if President Roosevelt came to see you, do you think he will?"

In the 1940s, new mothers routinely stayed in the hospital for two weeks. Decca felt fine, her daughter was healthy, and after the initial influx of visitors, she had a lot of time on her hands to observe what she interpreted as the class system at work in the behavior of doctors, nurses, and patients in the public ward, and she didn't like what she saw. Decca enjoyed her food on most occasions, but as a new mother, she wanted to be sure that she was getting enough good nutrition to nurse her child. She was convinced that the private-room patients were being fed much better than the women in the multi-bed maternity wards. The longer Decca stayed, the more authoritarian the nurses seemed to become. She thought they didn't pay sufficient attention to the needs of their patients, particularly when it came to pain relief. She bridled at the nurses' disrespect and endeavored to both organize and entertain her ward-mates.

> I became increasingly restive over the callous behavior of the nurses, and devised a punishment to fit their crime, which I unfolded to my fellow patients: "Next time Mrs. ___ rings her bell, I'll count to ten. If a nurse hasn't come by then, let's all wet our beds." It worked beautifully. The bell was rung, I counted, no nurse loomed, and we all swung into action—even Mrs. ___, who in the giggly excitement that swept the ward found herself suddenly able to perform. When

the nurse finally appeared, she was faced with changing all nine beds, eighteen sheets. For the rest of my stay at Columbia Hospital, one had but to touch a bell for a nurse to come flying.

The style of this action recalls Esmond and Philip Toynbee's theft of top hats from Eton a few years before. At that time, they had still been children: two rogues and a nymph, an adventuress and her highwaymen. Decca's "pee-in" was another kind of action, born not of boredom but of indignation. She believed she was defending the weak, using her brain, plotting a tease, and having a laugh—and in all this, she felt her power.

Esmond phoned the hospital nearly every day. Decca adored hearing from him, but telephoning was pricey and simply not enough. Letters could be read and reread. During her hospital stay, they had their first extended disagreement since Esmond had been away. She thought they might name their child Esmé, but he vetoed that. Then, since she had been reading *In Place of Splendour*, the autobiography of Spanish Civil War heroine Constancia de la Mora, she suggested Constancia. In his return letter, he said he was wary of nicknames (like Connie) and nixed Constancia. Then Decca, from a proud, nicknaming tribe, replied:

> How extremely thoughtful of you to decide against Constancia just after I'd filled in the certificate form & got everything arranged. I don't much like Carol for a girl & Ann Carol would be a shade arty don't you think? On the other hand I adore Constancia & don't at all see why it means the Donk will be called Connie any more than I'm called Jessie. We could call her Stan for short (after Laurel & Hardy) or Cia.

He'd done nothing except assert his prerogatives, and she was being impatient. The strain of the distance between them was starting to show. It's hard to always be good. In a subsequent phone call (in euphoria disregarding the cost), they compromised on their child's name: It's "Anne Constancia," but, "If you really want to change it we can," Decca wrote.

In March, Decca packed up her newborn, still called Dinky-Donk for short, and went to meet Esmond in Hamilton, Ontario. She had planned to visit for the weekend, but decided to stay and rent an apartment near his base.

Decca borrowed a pram, and she bathed the baby in a big saucepan. Although the town was full of young women like herself, temporary residents there on account of their soldier husbands, she felt terribly lonely. Esmond visited their apartment as often as he could get leave, one day out of four, but he lived on the base. Decca had been brought up in a teeming household, with a phalanx of sisters, a kennel full of dogs, a parade of weekend visitors, the constant presence of Muv, and Nanny plus rotations of governesses. When her father roamed through the house, he filled the corners, his every mercurial mood noted. Decca would say that she often felt alone in her youth amid the tumult, perhaps a loneliness tied to an adolescent sense of feeling misunderstood by those she counted on most. Her loneliness in Canada was of a different stripe. In New York, on the road, and in Florida, as a dynamic duo she and Esmond had rocketed forward—there were always new things to observe and to adjust to. She had been on her own when Esmond worked in the bar, but he always came home at the end of the day, and if she had been bored, she could have visited him. Besides, she had her own job. She may not have thought she enjoyed anything about her celebrity, but she missed the attention. This was the first time she felt completely without it.

It's EASY ENOUGH to imagine Esmond as the young soldier, sick of any place in which he was a foreigner, alone, moving from one martial environment to another. Canada's winter was long, and he had spent it far from his young wife, missing the birth of his daughter. He'd chosen this path, he studied hard, and he was no sentimentalist, but the war was going badly, and there were deep doldrums. But he was glad to be back together with Decca. They made love, made jokes, made much of their darling child. They danced and sang along with the radio, drank and ate (the remainder of the hampers of delicious, exotic food, courtesy of the Meyers—prewar pâté de foie gras, cornichons, marrons glacé), caught up on the news and family gossip, and planned for their future.

Sometimes, Esmond just wanted to sleep. He was so tired of people telling him what to do. It wasn't easy assembling 197 parts of a machine gun, as he was expected to. She thought she might be able to do it, though, given the chance. It wasn't always easy to submerge her own emotions. Sometimes, she'd been up in the night with the baby, and much as she might have liked to look fresh and be receptive, she sometimes felt aggressive. A soldier's wife had a role to play, she knew, but he wouldn't love her as much if she were less smart or less pretty because she was climbing the walls from boredom. She longed to be with him always, but did they really want to expose their new child to the hardships of travel? This child could not be allowed to get ill. It would help, she knew, to get another job. In Washington, the Durrs' Alexandria home had been crowded, she'd had to fight to carve out a space, but they'd been kind and she had fit in to her satisfaction. From the distance of Canada, it looked like an excellent place to be, if only Esmond could be there, too. He wouldn't be. They would transfer him to someplace in Canada that was even colder and more godforsaken, and then they'd ship him overseas first to England, then to Europe. There was no doubt about that. He was in training to drop bombs.

Decca's letter to her mother in April spoke of the many things she was turning over in her mind.

April 9, 1941. To Lady Redesdale. Toronto. Darling Muv . . . I don't like Canada at *all*, it seems to me like an awful copy of America, & the people are horrid. They are very anti English & anti American but vastly inferior to both. I expect it was quite different where you were, & Esmond says the West is fairly nice where the people are more of Central European rather than English extraction. I'm only staying here 6 weeks unless I decide to go out West when Esmond goes, but it's 2,000 miles away & the Donk might not like such a

long journey so I expect I'll carry her back to Old Virginnie. There
are several English refugees here & I really feel sorry for them (tho
not for those in America as they are very well treated & anyway
America is such heaven).

Decca returned to Washington while Esmond went on to Manitoba
for the final phase of his flight training. In England, her sister Nancy had
been working in a first-aid post; then she had opened up the Mitfords'
London house at 26 Rutland Gate and taken in homeless evacuees. First,
the Mitfords sheltered the family Sockolovsky and, later, other Jewish refugees, most of them Polish. Nancy was brave and graceful under pressure,
a sister to admire. Her observations of those first days of the bombing had
been suitably apocalyptic, but now she had her "sweet refugees." She was
just scraping by, not much of a housekeeper, but she managed the coupons
and the food and fuel. Meanwhile she was writing away—books, articles,
letters. From Nancy, Decca learned that Farve and Muv had become so
deeply divided over their politics that they were living apart. Before the war,
both parents had been champions of Hitler, but recognizing the Nazi threat,
Farve had turned violently against Germany. Muv still defended *der Führer*
as a courteous and maligned friend of her daughters Unity and Diana. To
prove a point, Muv had once kicked Nancy out of her car for making rude
remarks about the German leader. Nancy generally cut her mother a lot of
slack, but now England was in a war against fascism, and the daughter was
fed up with her mother's ignorance.

In her letter to Decca, Muv simply evinced sympathy for the homeless
refugees. "Little D." had turned out in some ways to be as ferocious as
Farve, and Muv didn't want to give this daughter another grudge to harbor.
Times were difficult on all fronts. Her husband was a particular disappointment. He wasn't at all able to bear being around Unity, as she had become
childish, sloppy, and incontinent as a result of her injury. Muv was caring
for Unity in a cottage near Swinbrook House. She had hoped to live with
her daughter on Inch Kenneth, the family's island home in Scotland, but

the area was declared a coastal protected zone and Muv and Unity were forbidden access because of their fascist sympathies. In 1940, Farve stayed on Inch Kenneth for six months. The rest of the year, he lived with Nancy in London. Diana was also in London, detained in the Holloway women's prison. Sister Pam looked after Diana's sons while managing a large farm.

In April 1941, Decca's youngest sister, Deborah, married Andrew Cavendish, the son of the Duke and Duchess of Devonshire, at the Mitfords' London home. Muv covered the windows broken in the Blitz with thick wallpaper that looked just like brocade. The Cavendishes sent up one hundred red camellias from their Chatsworth estate, and the families invited over three hundred guests. Nancy, Pam, Unity, and Tom attended.

In May, Decca wrote to Nancy from Alexandria. She had now spent nearly a year at the Durrs'. She had become independent and much more aware of the way things worked, of her own place in the big picture. She had pretty good judgment and wanted to let Nancy know that she hadn't been wasting her time in America. On the contrary, she'd been acquiring an excellent education. You just had to breathe the air in Washington to absorb political science, social philosophy, and economics. All of prolabor America seemed to find itself at the Durrs' table. A year of dinners there was equal to a graduate degree in organization and administration and campaigning. Decca read every newspaper and magazine she could get her hands on, and her earnest letters show off a growing political acumen. At this point, impressing Nancy with her focus and analysis had become important to Decca.

> The Durrs & most of the people I know here think that at the present time in Washington there is great dissatisfaction with Roosevelt for not moving fast enough, & also for putting Republicans & big business people in key positions. Part of the trouble is that here, as in England, people all want to fight for different things; some for the supremacy of the British Empire & America, some for the destruction of Fascism. Very few people follow Lindbergh, who is

considered a dangerous defeatist. Americans on the whole talk as though they were already in the war, & all think it will be only a matter of months before they are . . .

Decca didn't receive her sister's reply until July 1941. By that time, the Germans had invaded Russia. Nancy didn't spare much time in analysis. She wanted to talk about her new niece. "I think Constancia a heavenly name & I am going to make a will & leave her all my things." And she wanted to talk about Russia. "Up the Reds! Aren't they heaven? Quite my favorite allies."

》《

WHEN DECCA AND Esmond had first come to America, they had spent several weeks on Martha's Vineyard. In those last four days before Esmond would board a troop ship for service in England, they returned to the island together and reluctantly left five-month-old Dinky with Virginia.

Coming in on the ferry from the Massachusetts mainland, Decca and Esmond saw a scene almost identical to the one they had left two years before. In the distance were white sailboats and family fishing boats, swimmers in the water, and umbrellas on the beach. It all looked unchanged, a lost universe, an excellent harbor. They stayed again at the Menemsha Inn, whose every building and path was framed with flowers: pink hydrangeas, blue hyacinths, red geraniums. Their housekeeping cottage had a screened-in porch smelling of citronella, calamine lotion, damp, and the creepy tang of flypaper. There were wood-chipped paths to follow down to the ocean through fields sectioned off by stone fences. The ocean had a wonderful brackish smell, and from the beach you could see the Gay Head Lighthouse beacon. Later that day, they planned to meet their friends Selden and Hilda Rodman for dinner and drinks.

The Romillys had first met the Rodmans on Martha's Vineyard in September 1939, a month after Stalin had signed the nonaggression pact with Hitler. That news had naturally dominated their joint vacation. There was an interesting symmetry to this reunion on June 22, 1941, because Germany had spectacularly broken the agreement by invading Russia, and it became, in Decca's words, "a whole new ball game." The foursome listened to the radio together as Winston Churchill declared, "Any man or state who fights against Nazism will have our aid." By then, they were all used to the thrill of Uncle Winston's oration, but this was a turning point and everyone knew it. England had been fighting alone against the Nazis; now it would be England and Communist Russia: Liberals, Tories, and Socialists all on the same side. All this they discussed and absorbed over local lobster and clams. It was important to maintain perspective, to keep a healthy skepticism, and to have some more blueberry pie and another Tom Collins.

From hour to hour, their time was as full of play as politics. Selden recorded their tennis and their swimming and one raid on a neighbor's ice-box for lemonade. Esmond mocked with tongue in cheek the local "over-abundance of resources. Too many tennis courts, too many beaches, many too many cars and much too much ocean." Once, when they were alone, Selden, who had received his draft notice, asked Esmond if he had any "mis-givings about going on a raid." Esmond answered, "None," and added, "I have no doubt at all that I will survive this war whether shot down or not."

Survival was the theme that Decca and Esmond embraced when they were alone. The future was unsure, but one thing was known: Flyers could survive and had. His brother Giles was by then being treated as a protected prisoner of war. Perhaps he was being considered a hostage to trade. The same thing might happen to Esmond. But those possibilities were all down the line.

Esmond had an almost mystical sense that he would survive the war. Decca had to feel this complete and total belief, too; anything less, any hesi-tation, could tear the fabric. They spoke to give comfort, heart, and courage to one another. Decca would write, "The unutterable blankness of such a separation loomed menacingly for both of us, and we each tried rather unsuccessfully to reassure the other that it wouldn't really be for very long, that soon we should be together again in England." The atmosphere was charged with unresolved questions about their future, but one immediate question, when to join the Communist Party, seemed settled at last. Years later, Decca would say:

> Once the Russians got into the war . . . that to us changed the entire complexion of one's dedication to the idea of Communism. Now we were allies. We never dreamed that capitalism would survive the war. We thought that obviously it would be socialism everywhere, and we would join the Party . . . and we'd bring Dinky up as a Communist.

On the night before Esmond left, the two couples played poker until midnight. In the morning, after a week of fair weather, a nor'easter brought with it fierce wind and heavy rain. Decca stood on the dock watching Esmond board the ferry to Halifax, Nova Scotia, where he would join his ship to England. In a letter written soon after, she told him, "I was so miserable when you left but now feel as though I was recovering from an illness, better each day."

That week, the residents of Washington, like much of the rest of the world, were fixated on the extraordinary events in Russia. The Communist press, as Decca and Esmond had presumed, made an immediate turnaround in its editorial position from opposing intervention to emphatically endorsing it. In Congress, a coalition of Southern segregationist senators filibustered the poll-tax repeal to defeat, to Virginia's great disappointment. Meanwhile, Virginia's mother sank into a morbid depression, and the house filled with the sound of her weeping.

Decca struggled to take herself in hand and avoid indulging in her own fantasies of gloom and doom. There was no knowing where Esmond would eventually be stationed after his initial English posting and how long it would be before she could join him. She wasn't constituted to wait patiently: "My two main preoccupations were to find and to join the Communist Party, and to equip myself to be useful once a member." Her letters were cheerful and illustrate her growing imperative to establish herself. She wanted to escape the "dead-end world of market research, retail selling and the like, and acquire some training."

Returning to her long-cherished idea of becoming a serious journalist, Decca considered how best to ask Eugene Meyer for a job. First, she planned to enroll in a short summer course at the Columbia School of Journalism. Such useful training would go a long way toward helping her "feel much more confident about a possible *Post* job." Esmond was all for it. They had come a long way from the days when he had run the show.

But Decca never did take that journalism course. The way she came to tell it, she had been all set to go until she realized Columbia University was in New York and not the District of Columbia. "By the time I discovered my mistake—and learned that to qualify for enrollment one must have an undergraduate degree—I was thoroughly settled in with the Durrs and disinclined to move." She'd been stymied once more by her old nemesis, lack of formal education. Here, as elsewhere and often, she turned a disappointment into a punchline.

CHAPTER 9

*A*BOUT A MONTH after they separated, Esmond wrote that he was stationed in England. Decca discovered she was pregnant again and started looking for transportation to join him sooner rather than later: "I think it would be more difficult to get a passage if I was huge." They needed money, she had to get a job, but being pregnant meant she couldn't work in dress shops anymore. She left it up to Esmond to decide how much this news would change things. She was in a safe place with reliable comforts, but those weren't the most important considerations. She wanted to be with him. "However the whole decision is yours & whatever happens don't worry about it, but just say what you *really* think because I will be terrifically all right & happy whatever we decide."

Esmond had arrived in Halifax to find himself promoted to officer's rank. He hadn't looked for a commission and considered rejecting it, but was too aware of the time it would take and the tribulations guaranteed if he were to reject the commission. Since school at Wellington, Esmond had been practiced at avoiding the worst excesses of the officer class, and it wounded him to think he'd be automatically lumped in with all the ghastly types he had run away from. His worst scenario materialized soon after he had boarded the boat to England, when a Canadian sergeant preferred not to drink alongside the uppity officer he supposed Esmond to be. But during some late-night poker playing, their long conversation turned to what they held in common. They were, they discovered, fellow travelers on this crossing. In a political sense, both were men of the Left, and in a practical sense, they were passengers on a warship threatened by German U-boat activity in the ocean around (at any moment perhaps even dependent upon one another for survival). They drank some more whiskey and played another game. Fortuitously, their ship dodged the U-boats and made it safely across.

Esmond hadn't been in England since 1939. One great pleasure after two and a half years was finding Philip Toynbee again. Philip and Esmond spent as much time as they could together, sometimes meeting up with other friends from London and their *Out of Bounds* newspaper days.

Esmond missed Decca dreadfully, and whether she should join him was the dominating theme of their correspondence. It was all very confusing, but he was satisfied that she and Dink had a very good place with the Durrs, better than anything they'd find in England, where everybody seemed to be splitting up. On August 17, 1941, he sent her a telegram: "Please don't think of coming over for present as my own plans uncertain. Go ahead with other things instead."

In Washington, the interventionist movement had stalled and all the interesting action that autumn seemed to be on the domestic front. The American labor movement, with its cycle of conflict and negotiations, had seized Decca's imagination. Through friends of the Durrs', she planned to visit the Highlander Folk School in Tennessee, an institution that trained labor organizers through classes like labor history, union publicity, fundraising, and coalition building. To Decca, the school seemed like a once-in-a-lifetime kind of education, an unusually enlightened institution where her passion to become politically involved might be instantly rewarded. It also seemed like the perfect transitional thing to do before she had to enter into another tedious job hunt.

Several days before she was to leave for Tennessee, and a few weeks into her new pregnancy, Decca miscarried. The doctor she consulted said that nothing could have been done to prevent it. In a letter to Esmond, she tried to downplay the importance of their loss and hoped that by displaying a sort of sangfroid, he'd do her the favor of playing along. She assured him that she had been taking good care of herself. "The whole thing is awfully disappointing, but now it has actually happened & the only thing to do is just forget it was ever up."

She set off for Tennessee and returned to a bundle of letters from Esmond full of consolation and concern. Her two weeks away had provided a helpful distraction. She had been struggling all along with the desire to be useful, and at the Highlander School, so many things had clicked. Books, art, action, conversation all fused in the service of basic rights. The labor movement was just the kind of stage upon which she could apply her talents while she waited to join Esmond. There wasn't any money in it, but she would have more patience to wait if she had something useful to do. She wrote that she had come to regret having bombarded him with so many letters on the theme of traveling to England.

Decca reassured him that her sadness had passed. His letters were affectionate: "I am thinking of you all the time, and simply longing to be able to see you again." He added that he was aware that once she returned to England, her life wouldn't be as "fascinating and interesting" and their daughter wouldn't be as safe as she was in Washington, so he was torn and hesitated from letter to letter about whether she ought to come.

He had started flying as a navigator in the air crews, but there were long periods of waiting around, when he'd take the hours to compose a letter to his wife and daughter. He wanted their company, but considered it selfish to take Decca away from the life she had made in America, and he warned her that once he was transferred, she would probably have to live with her ghastly relations, or his. Decca said it was sweet of him to sacrifice the time they might have together for her comfort, but unnecessary. In case he thought she'd grown soft in America, she was as tough and capable as any of the other British women managing with less. Neither wanted to complain or burden the other with expectations.

Decca went back to the *Washington Post*, but even with Eugene Meyer's patronage, she found nothing available in the newsroom or in advertising. The editor was all for hiring bright new talent, but there were the newspaper guilds to consider. He would have to get back to her. Aware that she needed some of the basics, Decca wrote to Esmond to tell him she had enrolled as a beginning student in stenography at the Strayer Business School:

This is said to be the best school of that kind here, & it certainly did look rather fascinating—all bustly & studenty & vigorous & go ahead. You can't think how wonderful it is to have decided on going there . . . I'm convinced it's a really good investment, both for the U.S. where there is a terrific shortage of secretaries & also if I ever come to England, when it would probably mean a much more interesting type job than if one were completely unskilled.

Esmond replied on September 22: "I will never be able to explain how tremendously I miss you." He asked if she had made any further investigations into "safety of passage, various options available, swiftness of trip."

On October 9, Esmond transferred into a light bomber detachment in the East Yorkshire town of Linton-on-Ouse. Now that he knew where he'd be stationed for a while, he told Decca that he still felt their daughter would be safer in the United States, but "if she really frightfully wanted to and it was possible," she ought to look into joining him. Immediately, Decca put in a call to the British air minister in Washington to inquire about passage home. She learned that she might even find a seat "on a bomber." But, this turned out to be false information and she settled back into her life in Washington, still unsure about what Esmond wanted.

>«

By AUTUMN, PHILIP Toynbee had come to think that time and trouble had changed Esmond into a more sensitive, surprisingly empathetic young man. They both thought the thing to do was look to the future. You had to believe that the worst excesses were in the past. Socialism still offered hope and promise. Consider the alternative: the misery, inequality, and injustice that accompanied capitalism. For now, Esmond told Toynbee, "his only political motive was his dismay at human unhappiness." How did this balance with the job ahead, carrying and releasing bombs? Toynbee later remembered how Esmond felt about his military missions:

He told me how once, in a raid over Holland, he had just released his bombs (he was doubtful whether he had ever yet succeeded in hitting a target) when his bomber was suddenly illuminated by a blaze of searchlights. He felt then as if reproving fingers were pointing at him, and as if he himself were a naughty boy suddenly discovered in the light of the larder. But usually he felt no guilt or dismay at dropping bombs, simply because fear entirely submerged any more noble or humane emotion. What he found hardest to bear was the shocking, incomprehensible contrast between the comfortable everyday life of the station and the succession of familiar faces suddenly withdrawn from the mess table.

Esmond was participating in raids at the rate of several times weekly. The worst part about the flights, he told Decca, half joking, "is the take off, piling onto the lorry, dressed up like a stuffed animal, for the ride across the hangar to the plane, treading on someone's hand and upsetting their equipment as you get in. Once 'airborne' the outlook becomes very much better." This letter continues in a more lyrical vein, describing their approach to the target until

the pilot hears the welcoming phrase—"Bombs gone." The night's work is over—except of course for the business of getting through searchlight belts and shells and night-fighter patrols to the coast, and on across the sea to the English coast and home—but the rest is mainly cold and worry and hard work and complicated problems of navigation and hence any sort of description would be out of place in such a highly romanticized account as this.

That letter was more than enough for Decca, who felt it was finally time to force the issue of whether she would join him in England. Perhaps Esmond simply wanted Decca to relieve him of making the decision. For the first time in her letters, she admitted it was demoralizing to be all undecided for months as to what is going to be up. What I mean is, to feel one doesn't know whether it'll be in 6 months or a year or longer . . . So if you find it would be at all possible for us to be fairly near each other in England I would be all for coming as soon as possible . . . darling it is so difficult not being able to discuss it all & find out what you really think about it; I so tremendously want to be with you.

Esmond replied: "I am pretty well settled now . . . and have found out that if you were able to come over, this would be nice to know." Very soon afterward, he sent a telegram asking whether Decca had made any plans for traveling to England. She wrote by return post:

I sent you a cable last night which must have crossed yours . . . I went to see this same Group Capt. Anderson, the one I asked before about the bomber trip. He was v. nice & helpful (tho slightly the befuddled old Englishman type), & said that while there was no longer any chance of going by air (the regulations have been tightened up a lot & they don't take any women now) I could be sure of getting a sea passage sooner or later, within about 3 weeks to 3 months if I put in an application; they are ordinary passages with about the same accommodations as in peace time, only many fewer available as only a few ships take women. He called up the Cunard Line, & it all seemed v. normal.

On November 8, Decca cabled him: "Good possibility ship transport . . . but will come only if you are 100% pro." "Yes," he wrote on November 11, "more than anything else in the world." He had only wanted to spare her whatever hardships might be ahead in England, and had come to realize finally what was most important was that they should be together for as long as it was possible. Whatever hesitation he had felt was in the past; he had only wanted to be sure. But suddenly, the need was urgent. Four of his friends had died that day in a plane crash. He just returned from a mission to recover their missing aircraft. The night was damp and freezing. He had a crushing toothache. He wrote: "It isn't only that I can see that you will be really happy over here in spite of all the factors I mentioned and irrespective of myself. It is also that I am being utterly selfish over the whole thing and want to be with you again."

Over the next week, Esmond went on two missions. He wrote to Decca again. The subject this time was Dinky. Perhaps they ought to leave their child in Washington? That might make it easier for Decca to participate more fully in the war effort, as he knew she had been wishing to do. From the time they were in Florida, Esmond had understood that a person needed to be completely immersed; otherwise, "the whole thing is utterly bleak and pointless." Decca contemplated leaving her daughter with the many friends clamoring to care for her, but not for long. She had made her decision; they would be traveling together.

Finally, there was good news in the world again. The Red Army had recaptured Rostov in the first general offensive of the war in the Ukraine. The Russians had turned the tide of the war. She sent Esmond a cable on December 1, 1941:

LEAVING FRIDAY SO TERRIFICALLY EXCITED DARLING STOP
DECIDED BRING DONK DO WIRE THAT YOU AGREE HOW SHALL I
CONTACT YOU JOURNEY WILL BE VERY COMFORTABLE GREATEST
LOVE=ROMILLY

On December 2, Decca was home with Dinky in Alexandria. Virginia and her children had gone up to New York, where Cliff was scheduled to give a speech. Decca planned to spend two days in New York with the Durrs before boarding a ship with Dinky on December 5.

She spent the morning packing. Downstairs the doorbell rang, and she heard some murmuring, then quiet. Mrs. Foster was crying again. Decca descended the stairs to see Virginia's mother holding a slip of paper. A telegram had come addressed to Mrs. Romilly.

REGRET TO INFORM YOU THAT ADVICE RECEIVED FROM ROYAL
CANADIAN AIR FORCE CASUALITIES OFFICER OVERSEAS YOUR
HUSBAND PILOT OFFICER ESMOND MARK DAVID ROMILLY CAN
J FIVE SIX SEVEN SEVEN MISSING ON ACTIVE SERVICE NOVEMBER
THIRTIETH STOP LETTER FOLLOWS.

She grabbed up Dinky and ran to the house next door. The information had
to be a mistake. Someone had to check the facts, make some calls for her.
Her neighbor Mary Walton Livingston telephoned Virginia at their hotel in
New York, and the Durrs immediately came back to find Decca "absolutely
desolate." Decca kept insisting to Virginia that he must have been rescued
by a ship or submarine—that he was somewhere a prisoner of war. The
Durrs questioned everyone they could find in the Canadian Air Force and
the British Embassy. They learned that Esmond's plane had crashed into the
North Sea on its return from a bombing mission over Germany. A rescue
mission had determined that there were no survivors.

On December 7, 1941, Pearl Harbor was bombed, and the United
States finally entered the war. Winston Churchill came to Washington during Christmas week to confer with Franklin Roosevelt, his cabinet, and the
Pentagon. On Christmas morning, the White House telephoned to invite the
young widow to attend church with Churchill (who was a distant cousin of
the Mitfords as well as Esmond's uncle), the president, and Mrs. Roosevelt.
Decca accepted the invitation, but when two Secret Service men arrived to
escort her to Foundry Methodist Church, no one could find her. Perhaps she
just stepped out for some fresh air and a cigarette. Waiting for her return,
Virginia broke the gloom and announced, "It will take more than two men,
to get Decca into church, even for the Prime Minister of England and the
President of the United States." Later that morning, Decca met up with the
president and company. She was sure there was more to be learned about
Esmond's accident and knew that her Cousin Winston might have access
to more detailed information, which she imagined, could offer hope for
Esmond's survival. Attending the Christmas church service was the price

she would pay. As it turned out, the prime minister had launched a private investigation. He invited Decca to meet with him in a week's time.

On New Year's Day, friends Michael and Binnie Straight drove Decca and her daughter to the White House, where Mrs. Roosevelt was waiting for them, "gracious as she always was." Churchill was just waking from an afternoon nap as Decca was escorted "to his bedroom. He embraced her there. He had nothing on, save for a loose dressing gown."

> He said that his heart bled for her. He strode around the room, rolling off sonorous phrases about the enemy striking with brutal fiendishness at the British home and hearth. Then he remembered that Decca's elder sister was married to Sir Oswald Mosley, the fascist leader. He explained to Decca that he had put her brother-in-law into prison and he apologized for his action. It was the best way to protect him, he said.
>
> "Protect him!" she snorted. "He should be hung!"

Decca later told Virginia that "Churchill had got in touch with the commandant and the land crew that dispatched Esmond's plane to Berlin and the one that guided the plane back, and there was no doubt that Esmond was dead." When she left his room, Churchill sent his secretary after her with a gift of five hundred pounds. It was an enormous sum, which she needed but would not cash for some time, calling it "blood money." Eventually, she would give part to Virginia's daughter Ann, so that she could buy a horse.

In the weeks that followed, Virginia would hear Decca in her room awake and weeping at night. "I would go in there and she would say, 'Oh the water was so cold. The water was so cold.'" After a time, she began to accept the idea that Esmond was dead, but claimed that she would never return to her "filthy fascist family," and held them all responsible.

CHAPTER 10

ROBERT TREUHAFT, CALLED Bob by his friends, arrived in Washington in 1939, the impeccably educated son of worldly Brooklynites. He had moved from New York City to take a job with the Securities and Exchange Commission then transferred to the Office of Price Administration, where he and Decca would meet three years later.

Bob's parents had emigrated from Hungary at the beginning of the twentieth century. Aranka Hajos, his mother, was a smart and stylish milliner. His father, Albin Treuhaft, dabbled in bootlegging and liked the company of fellow gamblers. Albin moved around the New York area, working as a waiter and sometime manager in various eating establishments, looking for his chance to buy into a restaurant. He was subject to a peculiar local myth that may have worked in his favor. Within the Eastern European Jewish immigrant communities of New York, Hungarians were rumored to make the finest pastry chefs and maître d's.

The customary route for Eastern European immigrant Jews working their way up the economy was to start out on the Lower East Side. When the family income increased sufficiently, the road diverged. There might be a walk across the bridge to the Williamsburg neighborhood of Brooklyn or a pioneering effort out in the Bronx. The next step up might be a decent-sized apartment in the two- or three-story brownstones of Bensonhurst. After their marriage, Bob's parents lived in the Bronx, where he and his sister Edith were born. When he was ten or eleven, their family moved into half of a two-family, semidetached house in Bensonhurst.

Bob's social circle was almost exclusively Jewish, but not religious. His only Jewish education was the result of his own curiosity. He attended a Jewish summer camp, which offered instruction and a bar mitzvah ceremony and party at no cost to a boy's family. The event also earned a camper status, which counted for something in the hothouse in which Bob submerged himself for many summers. His parents were also genuinely proud of his initiative. Afterward, he remained as secular as they were.

Assimilation was a creaky process. Bob's encounters with the neighboring Irish and Italian Catholic kids were occasionally antagonistic. Stories abounded of tough streets and little kids with big glasses who lost their seltzer money on the way to the candy store. The only black people he saw were the maids, whom Aranka and Albin, echoing the casual racism of their neighborhood, called "schvartzas." Around the time Bob began New Utrecht High School, his parents' marriage broke apart, leaving Aranka as the only reliable wage earner. Albin had become the co-owner of a New York City restaurant, but his success was short-lived. "He disgraced himself by having an affair with one of the waitresses, financing it with some money that he took out of the receipts." Humiliated, deeply depressed, and more or less bankrupt, Albin went out west to California, where, contemplating suicide, he bought a fifty-thousand-dollar insurance policy, with his children as beneficiaries.

Bob had taken it for granted that as a good student with some ambition, he would move on to one of New York City's fine free public colleges, like Brooklyn College. He had one friend who had become obsessed with the idea of attending Harvard University, and on a whim, Bob also applied. His friend had a case of nerves and blew the entrance exam, but Bob aced his test, and that changed everything. That summer, Bob worked in upstate New York as a camp counselor, while his father returned to New York City. Albin was an ill man and, by autumn, died of cancer. The insurance policy he'd purchased in California made it possible for Bob to pay full tuition to Harvard in the depths of the Depression.

Bob was absolutely baffled by the Ivy League social script. The death of his father—at forty years old—was so recent, Bob had hardly absorbed it. He didn't like his roommates, and he missed his girlfriend. He was surrounded by strangers, most of whom were snobs. A quick study and a lucky guy, he went on to meet aesthetes, jocks, young politicians, poets, lunk-heads, comedians, and the occasional genius. Eventually, he dated Radcliffe girls and went as far afield as Wellesley. He learned to glide, ever alert to how far and how fast he had moved away from Bensonhurst.

Politics didn't particularly interest Bob, and though Harvard offered a thousand ways to be engaged, it was also protected by a powerful ivory-tower charm, which made it easy to stay above it all. He attended some antifascist rallies, but mainly bent his considerable energy toward earning his undergraduate nickname, "Bob, the fun-loving Rover Boy."

After graduation in 1933, he thought he'd go on to medical school, but was stymied by the quota systems commonly used to limit Jewish applicants. Next, he tried law school and was accepted by Harvard Law. Harvard University was offering refuge to intellectuals from Germany and Spain. Refugees were trickling into Manhattan, where his mother now lived. Aranka was in contact with her family in Hungary, and the news there was never good. Through this exposure to urgent political events as played out in his own family and (to some extent) at his college, Bob gradually became more involved in left political causes, but "only in a peripheral way." Later, he'd say, "The only people who were deeply involved or committed were the communists in those days. There was nobody else. I suppose I could have become a Party member. If somebody had asked me, I would have said prob-ably, great, I'd love to. But nobody asked me and I didn't find my way into it. And I think I missed a great deal by not having been involved at the time."

In 1937, Bob traveled with a new Leica camera to the Hungarian village where he had spent an idyllic summer when he was twelve. His plan was to document in how many ways that world had changed. A magazine publisher for whom he sometimes worked had asked if he'd stop over in Germany, to find out what he might about a few photographers who had lately fallen out of contact. Even with his American passport, this was a risky proposition, and Bob had no luck finding the missing photographers. He hadn't needed an actual dose of Hitler's Germany to activate his antifascism, but seeing it certainly concentrated his mind.

Soon after returning to New York, he joined a labor law practice. Its clients included the Garment Workers Union leader David Dubinsky. Despite the idealism of the Popular Front (a loose confederation of antifascist organizations), non-Communist and Communist factions of the Left still disputed every inch of ideological territory. Dubinsky was a passionate trade unionist, with a horror of the Communist Party and a fondness for Leon Trotsky.

Another of the firm's clients was the impresario Sol Hurok, who booked the Ballets Russes de Monte Carlo in venues across America. Bob, properly dazzled by "these beautiful prima ballerinas tripping through the office," was distinctly hospitable. Women liked him. He knew how to show a girl a good time in New York.

》《

BOB TREUHAFT WAS thirty years old in 1943 and eminently eligible, a catch. A charming, single guy with a great sense of humor, he made an excellent living. What's more, he wasn't in the military and he wasn't going to be. He wasn't happy about staying out, but there wasn't much he could do if they wouldn't take him. He had tried to enlist, but was classified as 4-F, or unfit for service.

Bob had suffered his first epileptic episode in college at eighteen: a grand mal seizure, like lightning in his brain. He bit his tongue, and blood had run from his mouth, and when he came to, he found himself surrounded by horrified onlookers. The shock terrified Bob. He felt ashamed at first, to have been so violently transported. These episodes continued at the rate of a couple a year. He suffered convulsions of varying intensity and once fractured his shoulder. Not many people knew. Epilepsy had an aura of mysticism and madness, not qualities an up-and-coming young lawyer cared to publicize, no matter how modern and tolerant his client base. He worked hard, dated around, downed the elaborate cocktails, danced smoothly, and stayed up late debating the state of the world. He was a New York Jewish intellectual, the witty, pragmatic type fond of puns and satire, with an elite, Ivy League polish. He couldn't have been less of a mystic. Still, there was something vulnerable in his nature, a sensibility that moved him to make the most of his time. He took the medications available, but it would be years before he'd find the right combination of drugs to control his condition.

VIRGINIA PROVIDED CARE and refuge for Decca and Dinky for the better part of a year. The Romilly and Mitford families urged Decca in letters and through intermediaries at the British Embassy to return to England, but she refused to consider the prospect. She started to look for work, and when Binnie and Michael Straight offered her their apartment, Decca and her daughter moved to Washington.

Because of the city housing shortage, Decca shared her new home with roommates, all of them "government girls" filling the many war-related job vacancies. She thrived on the chaos and noise of this sisterhood and invited refugees and friends of friends traveling through to squeeze in wherever another cot could fit. A visitor would find bras drying on the umbrella stand and newspapers piled in the sink. The place smelled of nail polish, and the telephone was always occupied. One night, fifteen-year-old Ann Durr was invited to dinner with Decca's roommates and their boyfriends. The older guests drank a lot of cocktails, and after a few, Decca tipped her chair back and then fell all the way, heels over head. (Ann saw that she wasn't wearing underwear, and it occurred to her that Decca still hadn't found anyone willing to wash her clothes for free.) The tipsy guests declared the wayward chair a reactionary tool. In those days, *reactionary* was the prime epithet used by young Lefty women who poured into Washington offices. (Among themselves, the young women might condemn their *reactionary* boss, *reactionary* boyfriend, *reactionary* father.) The word had bite.

Decca arranged day care for her daughter with a kind woman whom she nicknamed Honkert (an encomium from the childhood "Honnish" language she shared with her sisters) and went to work as a receptionist for the British Royal Air Force delegation. Then in September, she found a job at

the Office of Price Administration, a government regulatory agency. It was
fun, she wrote in her first letter to Muv in nine months, in the OPA.

BOB TREUHAFT HAD begun work as a lawyer for the Office of Price
Administration the previous June. He met Decca around the time he was
putting the finishing touches on a regulation that he had written and that
would come to be known sarcastically as the "ban on pleasure driving."
The proposed policy would conserve fuel by limiting all non-war-related
automobile driving. Civilian drivers could still commute to work and use
their cars in emergencies, but were encouraged to use public transportation
and carpool wherever available. This deeply unpopular regulation butted
up against a battery of myths about the American way of life. It challenged
the individualist's legendary mobility, the freedom of the open road, and the
country's love affair with its vehicles. It polarized opinion within the OPA
and spoke to Decca's gathering interest in collectivization—for what she
saw as the social good—above individual desire for success or comfort.

At first sight, Bob thought she was just another stunning girl in the
secretarial pool. Decca was many things, but not quite a secretary. She
had entered the civil service at the "cruel category of sub-eligible typist."
Although her typing skills were subpar, her social skills were prodigious.
She had resourcefully "discovered a marvelous place called the typing pool,
and learned to partake of its life-restoring waters." Her voice, accent, hauteur, and confident presence worked wonders. She'd request multiple proof-
read copies, and the unsuspecting eligible typist would practically curtsy. It
couldn't have been very long before the word got around that a celebrity
was walking among them. Somebody would have seen the photos, read the
articles, heard the rumors. The masquerade didn't last long. Soon she was
applying for a promotion to inspector, a rank for which her deportment was
well suited. Decca was rarely rattled, and rattling others while remaining
impassive—a talent she had cultivated since childhood—was an excellent
qualification for any OPA inspector, who was liable to be cursed and otherwise abused for enforcing unpopular regulations.

There remained one obstacle to promotion, which she easily overcame. The civil service requirement for the inspector job was a college degree. Decca recalled her completion in Paris, at the age of sixteen, of a course called Civilisation Française, so "Graduate Université de la Sorbonne" was true in its way. She later wrote: "Paris was then occupied by the Nazis; it seemed unlikely that the personnel people would check."

Bob was an agency lawyer about to test the new pleasure-driving regulation, and Decca the new investigator assigned to gauge its real-world success. For several freezing autumn nights, they stationed themselves outside an upscale nightclub called the Troika, in the Mayflower Hotel. Most government employees had some kind of waiver to drive on official business, but few could claim exemption for a drive to a nightclub. Apprehending a millionaire would demonstrate that the mandate was meant to apply to everyone, rich and poor alike. And the prospect of nailing a hypocrite made it that much more fun. They were on a stakeout, sharing hot coffee from a thermos.

What did Decca and Bob say over those four or five hours? What had they in common? Both had unresolved relationships with unlucky fathers. Bob had a sister. Decca knew sisters. Did he know she had two fascist sisters? He knew, of course he knew (he'd done his homework). He was really "marvelously funny." She hadn't known that in the Bronx, *toilet* was pronounced "turlett." She thought him dapper and found his background fascinating: Hungary, the ballet, the American labor organizer David Dubinsky. She liked his "slanting, twinkling black eyes." He'd been in Europe in 1937. So had she! In Manhattan in 1939! She, too! They might have met on the street, sat beside one another in the cinema. About the time Decca agreed to a date the next day, they heard a car's tires crunch on the icy avenue in front of the nightclub. Gotcha! She and Bob slid over to confront the car's passengers, the Norwegian ambassador and his wife. (The accusers knew she really was his wife when she made a big fuss about their diplomatic immunity.)

The next day at lunch, Bob and Decca met in the OPA cafeteria. Her thrifty strategy for dining impressed him. "She would pick up a glass of tomato juice and drink it and put the empty glass down on the shelf below the counter; then when we got to the salad, she would eat a salad and put the empty plate down below the counter; and at the end she'd take a cup of coffee and I'd pay for it, and that would be five cents . . . It was a very cheap date." Bob was besotted and rationalized "such frugality"—he might have called it chutzpah to go from policewoman to scofflaw overnight. Steeped in the rogue tradition in which she had come of age, freeloading lunch may have seemed unremarkable, or maybe she was showing off the part of her character that didn't care if she got caught. Before long, Bob was toasting her with this ode:

> Drink a drink to dauntless Decca,
> OPA's black market wrecker
> Where there is no violation
> She supplies the provocation.
> Smiling brightly, she avers
> *Je suis agente provocateuse.*

Soon they were having dinner almost every night, either in Bob's flat or at hers. It was all happening very quickly. Decca wrote to her mother that she'd visit England again when it was possible, but America would be her "permanent home" for all sorts of reasons: She enjoyed her job, and it was a better place to raise her daughter. The one thing she wasn't ready to admit was that she had met someone at work. Even if it seemed a little soon after Esmond's death—not yet a year—she liked him very much.

Bob made her laugh. She was happy for the first time in a long time—awake again, her funny self. Behind her were the dark months of brooding and fearing the future, of weeping and clinging to her child. He was so sweet with her daughter, and twenty-month-old Dinky liked him, too. Ahead, whatever was to come, he was 4-F. He wouldn't be going into the army or overseas. No one could say she hadn't given enough. She brought him to Alexandria to meet Virginia and Cliff Durr. Virginia liked him, but never thought it was a serious affair.

Bob had the advantage of being nothing like anyone Decca had known before. But in her friends' eyes, he had the disadvantage of being so unlike Esmond. How do you compete with a meteorite? Bob just kept going. He was indefatigable. They punned together, their banter good-natured and unsentimental. They were friends, equals—if anything, it was Bob who deferred to a radiant Decca, who was roaring again, singing Maurice Chevalier songs, doing a Charlie Chaplin imitation, pulling faces, making Dinky crow, telling long stories about eccentric aristocrats as distant as myth. Their friendship was inspiring. He was in love with her—of this she was confident. Yes, he did have a reputation. He was a little famous for being in love. Before they had met, there had been a fiancée. There were the ballet dancers from the Ballets Russes de Monte Carlo, who would look him up when they came through town. Bob kept his mother up-to-date on his social calendar:

Dear Aranka, You will be pleased to hear that I have reached one of the pinnacles of social success in Washington, having attended, by invitation, a dance at one of the most exclusive Virginia homes. In fact, it was so exclusive that my roommate, Abraham Glasser and I were the only non-Congressmen or non-Commissioners or non-Directors—and certainly the only non-Aryans, present. In fact, I don't think we will be invited again.

At the end of November, Decca wrote to her mother: "You can't imagine how fascinating my job is . . . I'm now an Investigator, and may have to travel around the country. If so, the Durrs will look after the Donk while I'm away." Decca was restless. There were OPA offices across the United States, and she was attracted to the idea of San Francisco, so far from everything. She did the paperwork, expecting to have months in which to change her mind and plans. With surprising alacrity, Decca's transfer to the OPA office in San Francisco was approved. In December, she wrote to Katharine Graham in South Dakota (where her husband was stationed) to say she thought she'd see her en route, but that letter and others written around that time are ambiguous. She was waiting for some encouraging signal from Bob.

Around Christmas 1942, Bob moved in the wrong direction. He and his roommate Abe Glasser recorded a musical marriage proposal to Glasser's girlfriend on "one of those do-it-yourself phonograph machines." They sang: "Dear Joyce, please come to Washington—Abe wants to marry you; Dear Joyce, please come to Washington—No government girl will do."

Decca thought the boys' caprice fairly amusing until she discovered that loosened by cocktails and infatuated by new toys, they had made other records proposing to other old flames all over the country. Bob sent at least one proposal to an old girlfriend, who didn't understand the joke part and planned to visit.

By New Year's, to Bob's "pleased surprise" and Decca's "deep chagrin," several of the girls showed up in Washington. Decca wrote that she was not invited to their marriage proposal party: "For the first time in my life I was assailed by the bitter, corroding emotion of jealousy." Her feelings for Bob were in a "hopeless muddle." Bob said she suddenly told him that she was leaving. "She claims that she left Washington because I was interested in other girls, that I wasn't going to make up my mind." Meanwhile, Decca had made up her mind to go "as far away as possible, and start a totally new life."

CHAPTER 11

 I N FEBRUARY, BOB helped carry her suitcases (several unreliable-looking bags with torn handles tied with string) and Dinky's tricycle to Union Station. He didn't want her to go. He wasn't sure he knew what he wanted, but certainly not a separation of three thousand miles. The station platform was the stage for a million farewells; swelling emotions, sweet words all were in order. The train corridors were crowded, everything booked solid. The baby, overexcited and tired of waiting, needed to be consoled. Being romantic wasn't this couple's métier; it was far easier to crack wise. "I didn't expect to see matched luggage," Bob said, "but you might at least have gotten matched shopping bags." He took Decca's laughter as an invitation to stand by her seat all the way to West Virginia. It had been hard enough leaving Washington, but here on the train, under the scrutinizing eyes of so many young soldiers, Decca recalled Virginia Durr's maternal cautions. Not that she couldn't take care of herself, but as long as Bob was along, she hadn't had to see herself as a young, British widow.

Hitchhiking back to Washington later that day, Bob realized a guy would have to have a hole in his head to let as stunning and smart a woman as Decca out of his life, if there was anything he could do to prevent it. He understood she had to go, but it wasn't over. She said she wanted to see him again, and they would write. He would follow her west as soon as he could.

On her road trip with Virginia to the 1940 Democratic Convention, Decca had gotten as far as Chicago. She had seen some of the vast nation's byways, lavish forests, and meandering rivers. Now, waking up one morning to behold the Rockies was marvelous. The train carriage was a relatively comfortable place to pass the time with strangers she would never meet again, no commitments required. Sometimes the train was overly hot; sometimes its heat failed and she'd wrap Dinky in all her sweaters at once. Their carriage and the corridors were always smoky. Lending matches and accepting cigarettes from your neighbor were harmless icebreakers, and Dinky—the little charmer—was also a great conversation starter in the dining car. Decca could always find a conversation to while away the restless hours. The long nights were for musing. If loneliness assailed her, she could tuck in the edges of her daughter's blanket again.

Train seats were reserved primarily for travel in the national interest. But that could mean almost anything: families reuniting; couples honeymooning; students, priests, farm-machinery salesmen, high-society dolls, and newspaper reporters all needing to get somewhere for some reason. From coast to coast, men and women from every part of the armed services poured on and off. Businessmen rode the long leg and the short leg to clinch a deal. There were government workers like Decca who labored in the "field" (as the Office of Price Administration designated the area beyond the national headquarters). Some single ladies, older than Decca in black traveling hats, knit or read magazines. Some younger matrons just stared out the window on their way to or back from something they didn't care to talk about. Once a conversation did commence, Decca's accent was always the first line of inquiry. The train ride took three days.

At one point, she met Harold Smith, celebrated in those days as a well-known gambler and entrepreneur. He had recently opened a casino called Harold's Club in Reno. She was going to San Francisco. He had worked the coast, and he knew it was a nice place, but it was old and couldn't hold a candle to Reno. Not only was his little town the divorce capital of the country, but gambling there was legal. Just the place for a new start if that was what a person was looking for. Smith was a heavy drinker, a big gambler, and a crackerjack entrepreneur. He may have known of the Romillys and of Decca from the newspapers. Perhaps he considered her a good investment, with high return potential, or was just dazzled by her. In any case, he offered her a job in Reno at a munificent starting salary. What would her life have become had she taken that alternative track? Not quite as radical a departure as assassinating Hitler, but . . . queen of a crime syndicate? Mob moll with a heart of gold? She graciously declined, leaving Smith somewhere in Nevada to another conquest.

WALKING ALONG THE San Francisco waterfront their first few days in town, Decca saw swarms of enlisted men on their way to meet their transport ships. She passed Red Cross stations where volunteers handed out coffee and doughnuts, perhaps a Women's Army Corps band or a politician on a soapbox barking out bromides about patriotism and faith. Whole families crowded in to wave good-bye. Little children licked lollipops as older kids wove through the crowds on bicycles carrying messages, forgotten articles: shoes, a lost wristwatch, guitars. Wives and mothers tried to be brave or gave up trying and then tried again. Children laughed, cried; girlfriends sometimes a little dizzy from a beer or two staggered on their platform heels, shrieked to their vanishing lovers, *Write!* There were wolf packs of boys without anyone in particular to see them off, most of them on the make up to the minute they headed up their gangplanks. They would give a pretty girl the eye and whistle, and the girls out for a lark with their friends, or whose guy had already boarded, would wave. *So long boys, be good!* And they would wave back. *Don't forget me, even if you don't know me, don't forget.* It must have been hard for Decca, all of these partings a reminder of the day she said good-bye to Esmond. She had stood on the pier at Martha's Vineyard in a terrible lightning storm. It had rained and thundered for days. In San Francisco, even after a downpour, the slant of the earth, the fog, and all the alchemies of meteorology surrounded the city with a golden glow. How he would have loved this city.

Because of San Francisco's reputation as a great liberty town and its location as an employment hub for war work and as a transit port, apartments were at a premium in 1943. Decca was lucky to rent a couple of basement rooms in Haight-Ashbury, which was then a working-class, predominantly Irish neighborhood. Her new home had some boarded-up windows and a complicated, alley-side entry, but one overriding asset. Decca's new landlady, Mrs. Betts, was warm and quirky. She held many homespun opinions, particularly regarding the lamentable state of modern marriage (Mr. Betts had disappeared, leaving her with several young children). Decca was relieved to attach herself to a household with playmates for Dinky and to find that Mrs. Betts was agreeable, for a small additional sum, to feed and care for her daughter while Decca went to work at the San Francisco office of the OPA.

She had only a few days to settle in. Above the city, Decca would have seen skies full of military air traffic. The grocery stores and bakery were rife with rumors about Japanese submarines targeting Los Angeles and Portland. She would have heard of Japanese neighbors, fruit and vegetable merchants whose shops were closed since they had left town or become interned. Even families who had been there forever, she learned, were sent by federal order to internment camps. But few people in the neighborhood asked direct questions, and in keeping with the prevalent mood in the United States, most people she spoke with were shockingly passive about the disappearance of their Japanese neighbors.

Decca inhaled the local newspapers (capitalist and Communist) for news as well as a sense of the local scene. Northern California had a literary constellation completely apart from the East Coast intellectual centers of New York and Boston. The poet Robinson Jeffers lived down the coast in Monterey; John Steinbeck came from Salinas. Prewar Carmel had been "Bloomsbury on the Pacific," home to Edward Weston, Tina Modotti, Judith Anderson, and Isadora Duncan. But one needn't go down the coast to be ravished by beauty, and it was easy to see why it attracted poets (the rakish Kenneth Rexroth reminded some people of Esmond). In the society columns, she read about opera affairs, equestrian events, war benefit balls (stocked with beautiful ingenues who wore the long, fastidiously waved hair of those who didn't need to work), and other high-toned entertainments for class enemies whom she hoped to avoid, but whose names she recognized from Kay Graham's contact list. She tracked down a few of the famous old lefty haunts: Flor D'Italia in North Beach, Izzy Gomez's on the

Embarcadero. "I'm getting to like Frisco a lot, there are the most marvelous restaurants & nightclubs," she wrote to her mother. Meanwhile, she worried that she had made a terrible mistake. More than anything else, she was lonely. One morning, she came down with a fever. Her legs felt so wobbly, for days she couldn't stand.

"Gee Decc, Don't be sick anymore," Bob wrote, "at least while I'm away. You're so wonderful flushed with fever that I feel jumpy at the thought of missing it." His amusing and sexy letters soon become her "only source of real pleasure and sustenance." By the end of March, he told her he planned to quit his job and move to San Francisco.

>«

IT WAS SPRING 1943. There was a visceral sense on the street that the whole war had turned. The six-month-long Battle of Stalingrad had ended in a Russian victory, and a new alliance with the Soviet Union begun. On Decca's street, the plum blossoms were in bloom, and when the young Betts boys played soldier, they could use ripe lemons right off the tree for ammunition. Dinky adored her new friends, and Decca started buying a few pieces of furniture. In her letters to Bob, she captured Mrs. Betts' homespun commiserations. Regarding Decca's mysterious illness, she had opined, "Poor Mrs. Romilly, her throat's gone to her knees." On another occasion, the landlady confessed that the perverse Mr. Betts had somehow "ruined" her bladder. It was a scenario that Bob memorialized in verse: "In a fit of depravity he filled the wrong cavity . . . what's the madder, you ruined my bladder, you took advantage of me."

Decca's first job in the San Francisco office of the OPA (its detractors called it the "Office for Persecuting Americans") was as the only investigator in the Industrial Machinery Section. Just as in Washington, she learned on the job. On one hand, there was nobody to teach her the ropes, and on the other, there was no one to see that she didn't know a damn thing about machinery. She had finally found her way to the rip-roaring West, though,

as she recounted in this letter to her mother: "The office here is very pleasant & I love my work. The other day I investigated a very tough character
called Joe Fontes, a second-hand machine tool dealer, & after I left he called
the office & said he would punch my nose if I came back! I did, but he
didn't."

Decca believed deeply in the economic benefits of price regulation. In
San Francisco as in Washington, the office staff divided left and right. The
radicals like herself, who were for unionization and rent and price controls,
were trying to achieve the extraordinary feat of holding "inflation down
during wartime." The conservatives, she saw as allied with business interests, like the apartment-house owners associations that fought rent control
and undermined compliance.

Decca made her own new alliances—war work had thrown her together
with another young woman her age. Doris Brin Marasse, whose friends
called her Dobby, was short, trim, and focused. The daughter of a Jewish
couple from Dallas, Dobby had discovered Marxism as a sorority girl at the
University of California at Los Angeles. She was one of the first women to
graduate from the University of California at Berkeley with a law degree.
Most impressively, she was the president of the San Francisco chapter of the
Federal Workers Union. Back in Washington, when Decca had enthusiasti-
cally joined her local, her sponsor was Al Bernstein. He had also moved
to San Francisco to work as a senior West Coast investigator, and Dobby
considered him her mentor in all things union. Sometimes after work, when
most of the office had cleared out, the two young women sat on their desk-
tops to smoke cigarettes and gossip. Decca knew Al Bernstein pretty well
as a skillful organizer who had most famously helped unionize the Alcatraz
Prison guards. Dobby admired the way Al stood up to the conservatives
in the agency. He and his wife, Sylvia, held famous parties at their place
in Potrero Hill. Occasionally, their whole apartment house would hold a
party altogether. The downstairs neighbors would make delicious spaghetti
or cioppino, and there would be dancing in the garage. Upstairs they just
played a lot of poker—sometime at high stakes.

Dobby was only dimly aware of the Mitford celebrity. She was unsentimental and not easily awed, so Decca was able to replay bits of her life as she wanted it known unmediated by myth. She wanted to talk about Esmond, and she wanted to talk about Bob. She told Dobby that "she'd been restless and come to San Francisco because she needed a change." Less than two years since Esmond's death, Decca wondered aloud if it was too soon to be serious about this new man, and she preferred to concentrate on her job and union business. She suspected that Dobby was a Communist Party member and inferred her interest (there was some danger in appearing too interested, as one might be suspected as a spy). Meanwhile, Dobby, a member of several years' standing, had quickly sized up Decca as a possible new recruit.

BACK IN ENGLAND, Muv wrote faithfully about family matters. They all had enough to eat, though the fare was plain. Home-baked bread, eggs, and milk. Pam sent vegetables from her farm. She telegraphed the good news when Debo had a daughter named Emma. Decca wrote that Dinky was well-cared-for by Mrs. Betts, and she was feeling at home in San Francisco: "I feel that in my job here I'm working for the cause I always believed in —the destruction of fascism—& that all my friends are working for the same thing, & that I'm really happier than I would be in England. I do long to see you all, & to show you the beautiful Donk, but I think you'll admit that it wouldn't be a good plan for me to come & live at Swinbrook."

As AN OFFICIAL of the OPA and author of the ban on pleasure travel ordinance, Bob could hardly make the case that he had to pursue his lover across the country. Instead, he organized an agency-related trip. Booking a precious seat (no berths available) on a streamliner, he spent much of his time across the three thousand miles working on his marriage proposal to Decca. Had he realized the depth of her interest in him, he would have shaped up earlier. He had never met anyone like her before. Until he started college, he had only ever dated Jewish girls; he hadn't even had any "real connection" with a non-Jewish girl. He wasn't biased. It was always just a matter of *common ground*, as his mother might have said.

THE OAKLAND TRAIN platform was just as crowded as Washington's with servicemen and women and just as hectic, its loudspeaker squawking train numbers. Four months had passed since Decca and Bob's ambivalent leave-taking. This time, neither of them started with a joke. All around them, couples and families and friends were kissing hello and good-bye. Once Bob put his valise down and they stood eye to eye, there was the welcome kiss, the glad-to-see-you kiss, and the clinging, passionate kiss, after which we will draw a veil. As Decca told it, she wasted no time before asking his "intentions." Bob had no need of the persuasive argument he had built over three thousand miles. He had just to declare that he meant to "marry you, and move out here to live."

Crossing over to the city, they found themselves on the Embarcadero. Decca suggested they have a drink at Izzy Gomez's, a restaurant as full of poets and journalists as it was of racing touts. Izzy himself had been having a bonanza year—raking it in after *Life* magazine had named him one of 1943 San Francisco's "most colorful characters," so there were tourists peeking in as well as servicemen on liberty. The decor was all very Barbary Coast: rough plank walls and sawdust floors, the steaks cut thick, and the coarse, local wine potent. Decca would have known some of the locals by then, and Izzy, a romantic, ordered free drinks all around to celebrate the happy couple. From there, the pair went back to introduce Bob to Mrs. Betts and to tell Dinky that Bob would be staying.

CHAPTER 12

A FEW DAYS LATER, Decca, Bob, and Dinky took a bus ninety miles north to Guerneville, the center of the Russian River honeymoon resort area in Sonoma County. The Russian River is particularly beautiful in June. Along the route, there are almond orchards and small vineyards, and horses and cattle graze on yellow hillsides. From the bus windows, the travelers saw California poppies in yellows and reds, wild roses, oleander, groves of eucalyptus and coastal redwoods; nearing the Sonoma town of Petaluma, they smelled the poultry farms operated by the Russian-Jewish émigrés who had settled there. Many of the farmers were comrades, and Petaluma chicken was often the main course at Communist Party affairs.

Before they had left the city, Decca had phoned a couple with a young son whom Kay Graham knew were living near Guerneville. Would they look after Dinky, just for the wedding night? A pleasure, they said, and arranged to meet en route, pulling their car alongside the stopped bus as Decca handed her daughter and little suitcase out the window. She and Bob continued down the road to Guerneville, where they were married on June 21, 1943, by a justice of the peace.

The town of Guerneville still looks much like it did in the 1940s. Many of its resort cottages are made of redwood. They have sun porches, wood-burning stoves, and beach access when the river is low. Resort owners favor cowboy hats and bolo ties and offer homemade meals served family style: fried chicken with gravy, barbequed lamb chops, or beef steak and fresh strawberry, peach, or apricot pie. The day of her wedding, Decca wrote to her mother:

You will be v. surprised to hear I am married to Bob Treuhaft. I
know I haven't told you about him before, so will do so now: I
have known him since about last December (he works for OPA
too, & is an attorney in the Enforcement Division). Since coming
out here last February I was terrifically lonely without him, & he
tried to transfer out here too but they needed him in Washington.
2 weeks ago he came out on annual leave & we decided to get
married. I am tremendously happy & all the bitter, horrible past
months seem to have vanished.

Muv passed the news on to a family circle, which must have been at least
intrigued by the pure normality of Decca's situation. In England, Pam was
efficiently running a farm. Her husband, the scientist Derek Jackson, was
flying for the Royal Air Force. Diana was in prison, Unity recovering from
her suicide attempt, Farve suffering from failing eyesight. Nancy was working in a London bookshop (hunting daily for firewood and fresh eggs—
fresh produce sometimes arrived from Pam's farm). Nancy's husband, Peter
Rodd, was an officer in the army posted to Africa, and her brother Tom was
leading a regiment in Burma. Debo, meanwhile, was adjusting to her new
position as the young married Lady Andrew Cavendish. Her husband, an
officer in the Coldstream Guards, was on active duty in Europe.

HAVING SAFELY RETRIEVED Dinky, the newlyweds returned to San Francisco,
Decca vastly pleased that she had managed to keep their marriage a secret
from the press. Only a few people in San Francisco knew or cared about her
history, and for the first time, she was truly enjoying an extended period of
privacy. Had the news about her marriage leaked, she imagined the papers
"would probably have made an awful stink, especially as Bob is Jewish &
they would have brought out all the old stuff." For his part, Bob intended
to show that he didn't care who knew—he didn't fully understand the need
for secrecy (he hadn't yet seen the Mitford press frenzy), but went along
because it seemed to matter so much to her. He would have been happy to

stand on the rooftops and shout about it. Failing that, he teased in a way he thought only she could appreciate. Returning to the house after "some errands," Bob showed Decca the headline of a tabloid newspaper he said he had picked up. Its bold font trumpeted: "OPA Snoopstress Weds Slide-Rule Boy: Stuns SF." Decca went white, stuttered, and almost fainted before he explained, with "profuse apologies," that this was only a joke page printed for the occasion.

It wasn't often that Decca would admit to being shaken by a tease. They still had so much to learn about each other. Bob had seen her angry before, but never speechless. Though capable in so many ways and quite discreet, Bob was a little tone-deaf early on when it came to applying new gadgetry to their lives. (That phonograph-proposal prank had cost him dearly back in Washington.) Within two weeks, Bob had wrangled moving expenses from OPA and a transfer to San Francisco. He also had a case of galloping poison oak, which Decca discounted with typical sangfroid as some "flea bites."

》《

IN THE WEEKS after her marriage, there were several competing reasons for Decca to accelerate her application for citizenship. The regional office of the OPA had instituted a loyalty ordinance, which excluded resident aliens from employment. Dobby launched an appeal to defend Decca's job. The campaign cemented Decca's friendship with Dobby, who succeeded in persuading national headquarters to revoke the ordinance.

Meanwhile, the Communist Party USA had also introduced a policy that only U.S. citizens could become members. This was part of a greater (and ultimately self-defeating) effort to identify and exclude anyone liable to inform under stress. Poor recruitment risks included anyone subject to the array of weaknesses a Federal Bureau of Investigation probe might discover: unorthodox sexual proclivities or orientation (as identified by the Feds), financial improprieties, mental instability, or lack of citizenship. Such precautions explain in part the straight-arrow character of the war-era rank and file. The FBI had ways of discerning vulnerabilities that some people didn't know they had. As time would tell, even the most stable person might break down.

The final leg of Decca's application for citizenship was her interview. When the immigration official asked, "Why do you want to become a citizen?" she may have thought back to when she and Esmond had first applied for visas in England. America had seemed to them a distant and gigantic country, its denizens "endearingly childish." The House Committee on Un-American Activities, for example (brand-new in 1938), they had thought "bizarre . . . a joke. Imagine a committee on un-English activities. What's that? Not taking tea?" Almost five years later, she bit her tongue to avoid saying, "So I can join the Communist Party." She officially became an American citizen in January of 1944.

Membership in the Communist Party was still a matter of some protocol. Both Bob and Decca, judged of high moral probity (notwithstanding some small concern about whether Decca showed "too much levity toward the Left"), still had to wait patiently to be invited. By late summer, the local Communist membership was thoroughly impressed with both prospective members. Once Decca's immigration interview was over and her citizenship papers approved, Dobby presented the Treuhafts' names to her Communist Party "club," whose approval would allow her officially to recruit them. The motion carried unanimously.

That September, the Congress of Industrial Organizations held its national convention in Fresno, the market center of California's greatest agricultural valley. Since the 1930s, this location had been a flashpoint of the kind of farmworker strikes Decca had read about in her labor history classes and in *The Grapes of Wrath*. Fresno is a hot, dry tinderbox in early fall, surrounded by well-hydrated fields of crops. Further east, yellow hills step to the Sierras. Dobby, attending as a leader of the United Federal Workers local, couldn't wait to take Decca and Bob out on a hike at their first opportunity. She wanted them to see California from a great height, the way she loved it best. Decca didn't want to disappoint her friend, but hiking in the heat wasn't high on her list of fun things to do in Fresno. Decca was at the convention as one of her union's elected delegates. She had been to the 1940 Democratic Convention with Virginia Durr and marveled at those old Chicago pols in action. Now in Fresno, she looked forward to a gathering of "working class heroes," organizers of the 1934 waterfront strike, and American veterans of the Spanish Civil War.

Decca might have wanted to keep a low profile on the Mitford front, but she must also have had a desire to talk about Spain, pride when she would run into someone who knew of Esmond or had read *Boadilla*, euphoria to hear of so many people doing so many of the things she believed in. After the first night of the conference, Dobby invited Decca and Bob (on hand in his new job capacity as a member of the War Labor Board) to meet her in a hotel bar away from the crowd. They'd been looking forward to this, and Decca was glad she hadn't had to hike anywhere to hear her friend "pop the question." "Would you be interested in joining the Communist Party?" Dobby asked. To which Decca and Bob replied singsong in unison, "We thought you'd never ask." Dobby's club had approved their recruitment some months previous, but since everything had to be done in elaborate secrecy, the Treuhafts hadn't known they were approved until this ritual invitation was concluded.

This new commitment demanded a kind of investment that Decca was eager to make. She understood there would be a party line, which she would be required to endorse, and that the kind of defiance or escape she was used to indulging in might result in criticism or chastisement all the way up to expulsion (an unthinkable and terrible outcome). "It was indeed a matter of conform or get out," she said, "but this did not particularly bother me. I had regarded joining the Party as one of the most important decisions of my adult life. I loved and admired the people in it, and was more than willing to accept the leadership of those far more experienced than I."

Whatever the future held, her experience had proved that there was always wiggle room and that a little joke often helped to lubricate a difficult situation. She had no fear, unless it was—as always—of being bored. There were, of course, "bores and misfits in our organization but even these seemed to be to some extent redeemed by their dedication to our cause," she said. On the whole, she was "enchanted by the flesh and blood Communists" she met.

If at first Decca indulged in the romance of the movement, it was all of a piece with being in love again, being happy, watching as the war turned their way. But over the long run, she and Bob would need to exercise the distinctly unromantic dedication, stamina, and discipline. An all-in, modern-day American Communist needed to be physically able to take risks, to withstand the persecution. The discipline this required was not for the faint of heart. Decca was not an innocent, and she wasn't sentimental. She knew of the deceptions and betrayals of the Communists in Spain, as well as their heroism and success in hopeless situations. She knew her Orwell and read Koestler, and she felt she could say her "conversion to Communism was not an instant process, nor did it ever have the profound religious overtones ascribed by ex-Communists to their experience. It developed . . . on looking back, out of the political exigencies of the times," a rich brew including but not exclusive to memory, love, and shared conviction, new friendships, education, and the encouragement of those for whom she now cared most.

She and Bob began attending weekly meetings. So, what was that secret coven like? There was no initiation fee, no blood-letting ceremony, no funny masks or headgear. "We didn't do anything terribly subversive," Bob said. It was just a meeting. What about those notorious cards that Commies were suppose to carry, the ones that gave them their evil power, in the imaginations of the John Birch Society, the Ku Klux Klan, certain congressional inquisitors, and the FBI? Bob did have a card, which was issued to a fictitious name. The name (which he didn't remember after a while) was a joke, the card was a joke, and all the Moscow gold they were supposed to be bathing in was a terrific joke. The local chapters were always short of money, and the greater part of every agenda included how to raise more.

Each week, whoever was able to do so gave what he or she could to aid the defense of comrades caught up in the courts, in loyalty commissions, or suffering from civil rights abuses. There were discussions of benefits, drives, rummage sales, and potluck parties to plan; small committee reports on labor, education, literature, and family issues like the cost of milk and hamburger meat; and sign-ups to carpool to the all-day child-care center at San Francisco State College. There was always a cry for more petty cash to keep the chapter (or club, as they called it) in coffee and pencils and toilet paper. No gathering was complete without some discussion about how to keep the *People's Daily World* afloat.

At some point in the meeting, sometimes even first thing before people got too drowsy, there would be an "educational" period. One week's assignment might be a thudding bore and another's an inspiration; more often, the lesson fell somewhere in between. It wasn't easy to slog through dense theory from Marxist journals while holding down a job or caring for young children, but members prepared as best they could. Bob was used to rigorous study, but for Decca, cramming was a new and thrilling experience. Assigned to read Marx's *Capital*, Decca remembers that "dead tired from the round of work, housework, and meetings," Bob and she would sometimes "read aloud to each other until three in the morning." Even slackers could amuse themselves at meetings by checking out what their comrades wore and who was giving whom special looks. The clubs were anything but salacious, but even in the Puritan churches of Massachusetts, everybody looked. And in these meetings, the members were often young and handsome, of rude health and passionate energy.

Like many of their comrades, Bob and Decca were still government workers, and any hint of membership could bring dangerous scrutiny by the FBI. The Congressional Dies Committee (named after its first chair, Martin Dies Jr.), otherwise known as the House Committee on Un-American Activities (HCUA or, more commonly, HUAC), had as its mandate to uncover just those people who were determined to stay covered. There was something Shakespearean in the doubling that membership compelled: Like men playing women playing men, your true nature only appeared ordinary. Perhaps you thought your membership was nobody's business but your own, perhaps you were proud to proclaim it, but if you wanted to keep your job and your effectiveness, then you had to lie.

In November, Decca learned that her sister Diana and Diana's husband, Oswald Mosley, had been released from prison after three and a half years. By then, Decca had pretty much come to terms with her sister Unity's permanent mental disability and had forgiven Unity to the best of her ability. Diana was another story, and Decca felt a powerful inclination to immediately denounce the Mosleys' release, but there was a glitch. The pleasure she felt in the New World was due in no small way to her relative anonymity. The Mitford sisters were news however you sliced it, and if she wished to renounce Diana and her hateful trappings, she would lose her precious privacy. The dilemma resolved itself when a reporter from the *San Francisco Examiner* tracked her to her desk in the OPA. When the "cameraman," as she described him, ignored her pleas to go away, and proceeded to snap her picture, she tackled him and kicked his camera.

Back in their apartment, while reporters milled outside, Bob and Decca "locked the doors, pulled down the blinds and prepared to wait it out." When she and Esmond had eloped, they had waited out the whole British government, and later in London, there had been that unfortunate electric-company employee who had tried to shadow them. This time, Decca had the redoubtable Mrs. Betts to bring food and bulletins and the next day's *Examiner*, with its story full of outright mistakes. Starting at the top, the headline was just ridiculous—"Sister of Hitler's Nordic Goddess in OPA Job Here"—when, after all, had Unity ascended to Valhalla? Last that Decca had heard, her brain-damaged sister had been helping out in the church kitchen, following the parson around like a kitten. The subhead was cause for further hilarity, but again only down the line. It read "Beauty Hates Nazis," which led Muv to exclaim, "Fancy Little D being a beauty!" According to some unnamed source, Unity had attempted suicide "when Hitler's friendship for her cooled." How could any reporter possibly know that? Far worse, the story contended that Decca had married Bob Treuhaft several months previously in Washington "shortly after Romilly had been killed." Decca had waited deliberately, she had even run away to San Francisco to put some space between them, and now here was this horrible rag, broadcasting lies.

She had already lost her privacy; now she would get to work. Not only was she Oswald Mosley's sister-in-law, but she was also Winston Churchill's cousin and niece by marriage. That cameraman had no idea whom he was tangling with. Esmond might have known instinctively how to use the press, but Bob was no slouch. Together, with the editor of their union newspaper, they mapped out a campaign. First of all, there would be a public letter to Winston Churchill, decrying the Mosleys' release from jail. This document would be an exclusive to the *San Francisco Chronicle*, the *Examiner*'s competition.

> Dear Cousin Winston:
>
> I am writing to you to add my protest to the thousands which I imagine you are receiving against the release of the Mosleys.
>
> Their release is being interpreted in this country, even by the reactionary press, as an indication that there is a real cleavage between the will of the people and the actions of the ruling class in England, and that the Government is not truly dedicated to the cause of exterminating fascism in whatever place and in whatever form it rears its head. Unless the Mosleys are immediately put back in jail where they belong, great harm will be done to the cause of friendship between Britain and America.
>
> My personal feeling is that the release of the Mosleys is a slap in the face to antifascists in every country, and that it is a direct betrayal of those who have died for the cause of anti-fascism. The fact that Diana is my sister doesn't alter my opinion on this subject.

Churchill did not reply to the published letter.

Decca was not alone in her rejection of the Mosleys. On November 23, there was a huge demonstration to demand that the government put Mosley back in prison. The protest brought much of central London to a standstill. Diana, who under the conditions of her release was not allowed to visit London, give political speeches, or meet with fascists, wrote to Nancy that she was disappointed that she couldn't attend.

PART TWO

Dissension has begun to spread in the ranks of the living.

—JESSICA MITFORD,
"ST. PETER, DON'T YOU CALL ME"

CHAPTER 13

IN JANUARY 1944, the Red Army defeated the Nazis to end the twenty-nine-month siege of Stalingrad. The next month, the Allies began their offensive, dropping seventeen thousand tons of bombs on Germany in one week. In Decca and Bob's household, these staggering events paled temporarily beside the springtime invasion of Bob's mother.

Aranka Treuhaft arrived from Manhattan with feathered hats, furs, high heels, creams, and perfumes, to find her son's new wife—when at home—clothed efficiently in workman's overalls and their house in a permanent state of disorder. Dishes went unwashed, floors unswept, meals haphazard, and her adorable new stepgranddaughter left to the care of an eccentric landlady.

Decca's previous experience as a daughter-in-law offered little to recommend it. She held Nellie Romilly in contempt as an unregenerate class enemy. Aranka would work harder to find common ground. Her character was in general more accommodating, but she was no pushover.

The writer Judith Viorst, who would marry Bob's closest friend, Abe Glasser, remembered being told that Aranka had mixed feelings about the marriage. "Upside," said Viorst, "Bob had married an aristocrat. Downside she wasn't Jewish." Bob agreed that Aranka "was rather put out when I married Decca without consulting her, and it took some time for her to accept the idea."

Bob's younger sister, Edith, said that during this period, their mother "demanded a lot from the people around her." Their father, Albin, Edith called a *luftmensch*, someone with his head in the air, in contrast to the energetic Aranka. When Albin's restaurant business had failed in the 1930s, he'd wanted to start all over again in California, but Aranka was "so New York-ish, she wouldn't think of leaving."

Aranka found Bob's radical politics and California home life equally disappointing. After the education he had received, she hoped he would have established a more comfortable, affluent life. It was convenient early on to imagine that Decca's influence was responsible for this dissatisfying turn of events. To Aranka, Bob and Decca's home seemed too wide open, and maybe that was the California way, but there were always too many people of all shapes, sizes, and colors wandering through singing, playing games, eating, and always talking about what must be done. (On one visit, Aranka arrived to find Decca also playing host to the blues musician Huddie William Ledbetter—aka Leadbelly—who was in town to play a benefit. Leadbelly chivalrously camped on the living room floor, while Aranka took the couch.) She may have thought it odd, too, that Bob took on most of the household responsibilities (but she was glad to share her recipes), but since there was nothing to be done, she adapted. Her daughter-in-law, she discovered, was a whirlwind, very persuasive, a natural saleswoman, a quality they had in common, though Aranka preferred the soft sell. When Decca wrote requests for donations to causes, she was virtually impossible to resist. A few years later on a visit to Paris, Aranka found that she was more like her daughter-in-law's sister Nancy, with whom she shared among other things impeccable fashion sense, mutual bad luck in men, and bafflement over the things Decca did.

It was around this time that Decca began to hit her stride as a fund-raiser. This was the adult fulfillment of an incipient talent. Given the opportunity to raise money for the causes she believed in, Decca quickly rose to her club's director of fund-raising. In the future, her organizational zeal would find its zone in activities investigative and journalistic, but for the time being, it was sufficient to be recognized for accomplishing her assignments quickly and well. One of Decca's earliest challenges was to plan a benefit for the *People's Daily World* fund drive. The "coveted prize of a lifetime subscription to the *People's Daily World*" was promised to the comrade who could raise more than one hundred dollars in donations. Decca fully intended to surpass that mark and do so with brio and originality. The party she and Bob would give at Mrs. Betts's would serve notice to the Communist community of the Bay Area that a new *compañera* was on the scene, and she was one of a kind. Invitations were passed along the grapevine to party members and fellow travelers—and a party of this sort always included a few undercover agents in the mix.

Among the guests whom Decca especially looked forward to seeing was Pele deLappe, editor of the *People's Daily World* Women's Pages and creator of "Vicky Says," a daily illustrated column. Pele described Vicky ("Vicky," for *victory*) as "a leggy female who with limericks, exhorted readers to speed the war effort." This featherweight diversion was then under attack by the Communist Party's local Women's Commission, which denounced it to party leadership. Vicky (the curvaceous cartoon sexpot who liked to philosophize from atop her office desk) was "cheesecake," they complained, and ought to be replaced with articles treating women's issues "with more seriousness and concern." Decca considered the Women's Commission a bunch of pious persecutors and vociferously defended "Vicky Says" and its author against their censorious campaign.

Pele deLappe was married to the lawyer Bert Edises, whose firm Bob would soon join. Both women had small children and shared an abiding interest in becoming serious journalists. Pele's first impression of Decca was of a pretty, jolly woman in a one-piece corduroy coverall, which young Londoners called siren suits (since they were easy to slip into on your way to the underground shelters). They discovered a mutual delight in rowdy wordplay and bawdy songs. Guessing that Decca's debut fund-raiser would get raucous, Pele was looking forward to it, too.

Pele was a talented artist in the social realist grain. The daughter of socialists and a native San Franciscan, Pele had been arrested for the first time when she was fifteen, during the San Francisco general strike. Her father, a locally celebrated intellectual and newspaper cartoonist, had turned Marxist before World War I.

Pele's mother was a "New Woman" from the Midwest whose travels in the South Seas gave her daughter that Polynesian first name. As dedicated modernists, the whole family had trooped off to Paris to meet James Joyce. Pele went to study at the Art Students League of New York with Raphael Soyer, Frida Kahlo, and Diego Rivera and, while in New York, fell hard for jazz and the blues. She spent one summer in a Woodstock retreat among artists, mystics, and politicos. These composite adventures led Decca to say that Pele "had the luckiest childhood that I could dream of."

It was a lovely night for a party, as Decca stood at her door ushering in her guests. *Welcome, delighted you've come. Give what you can to the* People's Daily World. *The inestimable Mrs. Betts is on hand to help watch the little ones . . . Dance wherever you like.* Guests had hardly said hello before their debts mounted. *It's crowded in here, shall I take your coat? That'll be a quarter. A drink? Typically five cents, but tonight it's fifty cents, for the cause. Come in, come in, standing still will cost you. Better move around. Five cents a dance. Music too loud? Turn it up? Ten cents, turn it down—no, then how 'bout . . . a dollar!* Decca improvised: *A second drink costs fifty-five cents. Twenty-five cents to refuse a drink; ten cents for use of the lavatory, five cents extra for toilet paper; a seventy-five cents exit fee if you want to leave the lavatory. What'll you give me for soap, for a towel? Extra tax for those leaving before one* A.M. *Come taste this delicious goulash, it's Bob's mother's recipe! One price for the whole plateful. Comrade darling, one more drink? Just five cents. Hah, made you laugh . . . Laughs a penny each.*

They earned upward of five hundred dollars. Pele had a grand time, but it did "raise hackles," she noted, and some comrades reacted poorly to Decca's "lighthearted view." There was no denying a subterranean current of "prejudice against her background," a reaction to the full press "Lady Redesdale syndrome," as some people called it. Sometimes, even Pele imagined Decca "could always fall back on the old family, on the mansion," though doubted she ever would. The last thing Decca wanted was a reputation for being grandiose or prepossessing or as someone with retreat rights to a ruling-class background—even from people who couldn't take a joke. She wanted it known that invoking such elite privilege was out of the question for her.

Her wonderful and terrible party was the talk of the town. The upshot, once word reached the county leadership, was another promotion for Decca, this time as full-time county financial director. The job required her to learn about long-range budget design as well as party planning for the Communist Party membership of the entire city. Anything educational was serious business to Decca, and she bent herself to it, increasing her skills in math and accounting. The hustling and schmoozing came naturally. She rejected the previous generation's techniques as old-fangled and inefficient. For instance, those handwritten notes her predecessor had favored were time-consuming and expensive (form letters were the wave of the future). She also sought new money in unexpected places: Comrades might sell blood or participate in medical trials to test how much pain they could endure. Travelers to a Communist Party convention might even volunteer to escort corpses in coffins. For every corpse, the funeral parlor would pay for the fare of its escort. "Marvelous," Decca said, "if we could line up a few bodies for the delegates."

Decca reveled in being "busy, busy, busy." For a banquet to welcome home Communist Party veterans from the war, she organized a hundred threads at once: "ticket sales . . . publicity, decorations committee, waitresses committee . . . cooking committee." For supplies, she turned to one elder habitué of the county office, a man in whom a life of hard knocks and understandable paranoia had produced "a general air of mystery." Invited to weigh in on the menu, this venerable man silently and economically printed the word *Petaluma* on a piece of paper. Decca understood that "comrades in Petaluma, chicken farmers all, might supply gratis the main course of the banquet," and with all due secrecy, she scratched out her question to him, "broiled or fried?" If only he hadn't egged her on.

IN MAY 1944, Decca gave birth to Nicholas Tito Treuhaft. The accoutrements of an infant added another layer of clutter to the books and clippings
in piles, the table covered with leaflets-in-process, carbon paper strewn, toys
and clothes and groceries stored across their crowded flat. Bob and Decca
decided it was time to find a bigger place.

Bob and she brainstormed a theory of child care that would see them
through the next few years. Their situation with Mrs. Betts had inspired
them to look for live-in help, a baby nurse for Nicky since Dinky was by
then in nursery school. Their new home on Clayton Street had three bedrooms. Nicky's new nurse and her husband would take one room, while
their three school-age children would share a room with Dinky. It was just
the kind of Communist lifestyle that gave Aranka the shivers.

Muv sent her congratulations on Nicky's birth, and surprised Decca
with a sweet note enclosed from Farve, even though they continued to live
apart. Decca hadn't written to, or spoken with, her father for eight years.
His note was affectionate:

> Just to send you my love and every good wish for him and his
> future. Some day, when things are in a more settled state, I greatly
> hope to see you all, and judging from all news and the look of
> things it seems to me there is some prospect that I may last that
> long—I should much like to.

Why did he write to Decca after all this time? Muv may still have had
some influence, passing on their daughter's words of sympathy when Farve
had suffered some eye problems leading to cataracts. Or perhaps Nancy
had—he'd stayed with her intermittently during much of the war, which
was at last turning in favor of the Allies. Farve had always been a powerful man, stubborn and self-regarding. Perhaps his brush with infirmity had
made him nostalgic. If Decca replied to his note, she did not keep a copy.

In San Francisco, Decca was living in the center of the vortex. She had
new friends and a new house and, one month after Nicky's birth, began a
new job as staff fund-raiser at the Oakland branch of the Tom Mooney

Memorial California Labor School. This was an adult education center of the kind pioneered by the Highlander Folk School in Tennessee. It offered courses like History of the Labor Movement, Documentary Photography, and Dance Theatre, as well as free lunches for children. Pele taught a "life drawing class for retired longshoremen and seamen on the beach."

In August, Paris was liberated. September brought Decca's twenty-seventh birthday. She felt fit, but even she had to concede that the twice-daily two-hour commute to Oakland on trains and buses was a bit much. Meanwhile, Aranka had been getting herself in trouble. After a whirlwind romance, she had married a man named Al Kliot, whom she later discovered was still regularly seeing his previous girlfriend. Decca and Bob had been sympathetic when she said she had kicked Al out, but when she took him back, Bob wrote to her and told her that he was puzzled: "We're very much worried that if you don't break with him completely he will do you great harm." Ever in organizing mode, in the same letter Decca wanted to know if Aranka could send her some of her lovely hats as a donation for a benefit at the California Labor School?

When the hats arrived, Bob thanked his mother: "Decca loves them . . . the black one is especially super." He had finally achieved his ambition of joining the law offices of Gladstein, Grossman, Sawyer and Edises. His new firm, he told Aranka, has an "attorney in Reno and can get you a bargain [divorce] about $150."

》《

IN MAY 1944, Earl Browder, at that time the leader of the Communist Party USA, dissolved and then re-formed the organization as the Communist Political Association, a kind of lobbying special-interest group attuned to the needs of Americans who were also Communists, and distancing its U.S. constituency from its origins and international associations. Browder, a Kansan, had a strategy to promote American Communism as an unthreatening political option, an alternate choice on the ballot. In this vision, the social stigma associated with Communist opposition to the capitalist economic system would subside and eventually become unremarkable. While Browder tried to emphasize the links between Communism and American Revolutionary ideals, there was little evidence in the contemporary landscape that Americans would accept any form of socialism.

In Washington, the House Committee on Un-American Activities in 1945 became the first congressional entity established to investigate "subversive" and "un-American propaganda and activities." Over the next decade, the committee and its FBI partners would cultivate fear of a mythic Red Tide that threatened to overthrow the celebrated American way of life—that of unrestricted markets, individuality, and the pursuit of happiness—to impose a cold, collective, and totalitarian regime as in the Soviet Union.

Browder's policy was imaginative, but it couldn't withstand attacks from old enemies outside or a stroppy membership from within. Decca and her friends thought Browder was shelving "the goal of socialism for the foreseeable future." She agreed with his all-out win-the-war goal, but regarding the new Communist policy, she was "secretly disappointed that its revolutionary goals seemed to have faded away."

Then in April 1945, Jacques DuClos, hard-line leader of the French Communist Party, denounced Browder as an "Enemy of the People." As the DuClos letter circulated, some members felt relief; some rolled their eyes. "The DuClos letter" meant stronger ties to Stalin and occasioned very few actual changes in daily life. Decca and Bob saw Stalin as the strong-armed leader of the Red Army, whose main preoccupation would be to rebuild the Soviet Union after a devastating war. Over the coming months, Stalin would begin another bout of purging, and expand the prison gulags. Most people in the West, including Decca, Bob, and their comrades, remained ignorant of these secret, vicious realities. The extent of the persecution would not become common knowledge for several more years. There is some early proof of the Treuhafts' ambivalence toward the Soviet leadership in the middle name they gave son Nicholas. In 1944 "Tito" was the independent Communist leader of Yugoslavia and a thorn in Stalin's side. After the American Communist leadership replaced Browder with the hard-line Stalin loyalist William Z. Foster, Decca noted that for members in outlying chapters, the emphasis was renewed commitment:

> Did I feel we were automatons, blind followers of the Line as handed down from on high? There was an element of that, but it is not the whole picture. Throughout the Party there were intensive discussions preceding these changes; we held meetings that lasted far into the night to study and dissect draft resolutions from the national office, to scrutinize papers submitted by club members, all of which gave me a strong sense of personal involvement in the Party's national decisions.

San Francisco with its balmy breezes, golden mountains, and bountiful tables was an outpost far, far away from Russia, far from France, and far enough from New York. The newly re-formed Communist Party USA, California branch, would retain its own Western sensibility. Though the members were passionate and principled, their community was smaller, their meetings and cultural activities generally more casual and low-key. Among their membership were doctors, lawyers, teachers, scholars, and merchants. Decca could rely on her comrades for child care. They often shared meals. Though families lived separately and members' homes were separated—sometimes by many miles—theirs was an intentional community, and they were committed to it.

JUST A FEW days before the DuClos bombshell, Decca heard that her only brother, Tom, had been killed in Burma. Tom had been good-natured, curious, and a remarkably balanced young man. His natural diplomacy had been by necessity sharpened as the one male sibling to six opinionated and energetic sisters. Since her elopement to Spain, Decca and Tom hadn't exchanged many letters, though the few he had sent had expressed affection. After his death, Diana maintained that Tom had been a member of

Mosley's British fascist party. Decca rejected the claim as slanderous. (In later years, when Oswald Mosley publically returned to the subject of Tom Mitford's political affiliations, Nancy wrote Decca to commiserate: "Have you noted all the carry-on about Sir Os? . . . I'm very cross with him for saying Tud [Tom] was a fascist which is untrue though of course Tud was a fearful old twister & probably was a fascist when with Diana. When with me he used to mock [Oswald Mosley] & he hated Sir Os no doubt about that.")

By May 1, 1945, Hitler was dead and World War II virtually over. To paraphrase Uncle Winston, there had been an end to the beginning and a beginning to the end. The end of the hot war arrived with fanfare and confetti, drunken soldiers covering drunken nurses in wet kisses. In Union Square, San Francisco strangers embraced; there was hilarity, euphoria, reunions, parades, and one more push to pulverize Japan. The cold war was beginning. Along with her friends, Decca moved forward. She didn't like to look back.

》《

ON HIS TOUR of the Inner Hebrides in the 1780s, Samuel Johnson was delighted to find Inch Kenneth "a pretty little island about a mile long and about half a mile broad, all good land." Over the course of his day trip, he walked the gentle hills, prayed in an ancient ruined chapel, and ceremoniously buried some scattered bones.

In 1938, around 150 years after Johnson visited the island, Decca's parents, David and Sydney Redesdale, purchased Inch Kenneth and renovated its single Victorian house of a "vaguely castle-like architecture." They found the island's microclimate hospitable to vegetables and flower gardens and installed some goats, chickens, and sheep. They kept a boat and an old car to drive between the dock and home. Sydney loved the ocean and boats and was unfazed by the island's isolation and its frequent dark and rainy weather. She walked everywhere across its compact terrain, enjoying things in their place—all dainty and far from the chaos of world politics.

It had been a blow when she had been denied this harbor for the first few years of the war. It must have been harder still, once she and Farve separated, to see that he could come and go to the island and that he stayed there with Margaret Wright, who had once been the parlourmaid in the house Sydney and her husband shared. When Farve's cataracts grew worse, he and Margaret left the island for London. As the war wound down, Sydney and Unity were allowed to return to Inch Kenneth, the best place for them to live comfortably and economically. Lord Redesdale had given his son the island sometime earlier, and when Tom died, under Scottish law the property reverted to his sisters. Decca now owned one-sixth of Inch Kenneth.

In May 1945, around the time she first heard of her inheritance, journalists from around the world were in San Francisco to cover the newly emergent United Nations. The international movement for peace, historically pushed to the margins of powerful societies, found a home in the fragile new institution. Decca and her friends saw their own platform reflected in the Universal Declaration of Human Rights, which every member of the new body had voted to accept: The document called for a fair standard of living, medical care, and social justice for all people—"universal and unalienable rights for all members of the human family . . . friendship among nations, racial or religious groups, and the maintenance of peace."

Over the next decade, a gathering peace movement's efforts to ban the bomb would be belittled as naive, crackpot, and dangerously red. But in this potent, nearly utopian moment, San Francisco was as close to a garden of peace as it would ever be, its denizens shouldering the pleasant duty of hosting diplomats and reporters from everywhere.

Among the Communist writers contingent, Decca met Claud Cockburn, who had also reported from the Spanish Civil War. It's not hard to imagine a rollicking night on the town with Decca and Bob and some local comrades and Claude and other war-weary journalist friends, drinking in the Happy Valley Bar of the Palace Hotel. Decca, an authority, thought the Happy Valley Bar made the best martinis in San Francisco "and possibly the world." Pele was amazed at how emphatically English Decca became again around other Brits. She had a grand old time translating Cockburn's often incomprehensible accent for the locals. The United Nations story could put even the most cynical newshound in a good mood. And to Cockburn, what a sidebar! One of those notorious Mitford sisters, now the dedicated financial director of the San Francisco Communist chapter, had deputized him to act on a family matter. She wished with Cockburn's assistance to donate her inheritance of one-sixth of a Scottish island to the British Communist Party.

Decca had found her métier for the moment as a fund-raiser—raising money in dribs and drabs—but here was an opportunity for a spectacular publicity coup. It was a bit far for the San Francisco party to take full advantage, but London members could, why not? How many times did a portion of a Scottish island fall into your lap? They might use it as a holiday resort or a dacha for fatigued members, or to grow vegetables and raise goats, as Muv did. After a certain number of beverages, Decca agreed to give Cockburn power of attorney to speak to the British party leaders and set the transfer in motion. In an article years later, Cockburn summarized the idea: "What could possibly be more delightful to this lifelong enemy of the grown-ups than the mental picture—however unrealistic—of a horde of unbridled Reds cavorting Marxistically on the beaches, rattling the windows of 'the Big House' with nightly renderings of *Hurrah for the Bolshie Boys* and *the Internationale*."

It was a spectacular tease, but there was something else going on. Decca was still reeling from all sorts of conflicting emotions. It was her style to suppress any public display of grief (a "concrete upper lip," Virginia Durr called it). She had absorbed the loss of Esmond, her sister Unity's suicide attempt and resulting brain damage, and her brother Tom's death so late in the war, when it had seemed so sure he would make it through. She had been stalwart through all these traumas and preserved a sort of civility in all her exchanges with her mother, rarely mentioning the political furies that divided them.

To Decca, the island signified her family's culpability in the war. She wanted to punish them to some extent or at least force them to acknowledge "what a criminal thing it was to have supported Hitler and an appeasement policy for England." This wasn't a particularly feasible plan, and eventually her indignation against everyone (except the Mosleys) subsided. They were all too far away.

Several months would pass, and though their encounter lay heavy on Decca's mind, she heard nothing from Cockburn. Back in England, Cockburn met with British party leaders, who were baffled by Decca's donation. He also tracked down Lord Redesdale in Westminster, who persuaded him that Inch Kenneth, so very far away, was the "very small" home of an old lady and a sick girl. By that point, his assignment wasn't much fun anymore, and Cockburn backed away from the project.

Next, Decca tried to sell her part of the island. She told her sisters that she'd be willing to sell them her share or to divide the proceeds with them. Nancy alone recognized the power of such a tease but wondered, "At what price?" The others sisters were angry at Decca's game. Rather than break with Decca, Muv agreed to become her partner and, on her behalf, had the island appraised.

Decca's inheritance and subsequent effort to sell Inch Kenneth were also a matter of great interest to the FBI, whose increasing scrutiny of Decca resulted in a file of her political activities and consequently a sort of log book. The agent in charge had many informers who reported on her membership in the Twin Peaks branch of the Communist Party and her outstanding success in selling subscriptions to the *People's Daily World* and in other fund-raising. She was followed to a picnic, a New Year's Eve ball, conferences, lectures, and classes, but nothing seemed to spark the engagement of her followers like the story of Inch Kenneth. One agent wrote: "XXX advised XXX that the subject stated that she had inherited one-sixth of an island off the coast of Scotland and reported that she in a joking manner stated that she might give it to the Soviet government for a naval base."

When Farve had written at the time of Nicky's birth, he may have thought the time right to end hostilities, but Decca was just winding up. After the Inch Kenneth business, she never expected to see her father again. She told Dobby she hated him for the way he had acted at the start of the war. Decca always claimed that she understood her father's actions, but his rejection hurt her, even when she was older.

Years later, Decca attended an authors' luncheon. Like others of its kind, there was a rubber chicken dinner, some gossip, and some fund-raising. It wasn't until the guests had enjoyed a few drinks, when a fellow author asked Decca to contribute an article to an anthology on the subject of fathers. Decca stormed out. Her hosts might not have known why, but she felt she'd been set up and she was furious.

CHAPTER 14

$\mathscr{T}$HE TREUHAFTS WERE moving to Oakland. Nancy was appalled—New York and Washington, like Rangoon and Bombay, were on a map from which one might return with amusing stories, but Oakland? Decca might as well wear a calico bonnet. Meanwhile, Decca and Bob could hardly believe their luck. The Oakland general strike, which had shut down the city in 1946, had left it with an attractive reputation for socialist dreamers. The Treuhafts found a sweet little house on a tree-lined street on a steep hill near a rose garden. In Oakland, the weather was perfect all year. Bob, a junior partner at Gladstein, Grossman, Sawyer and Edises (or, as Decca called them, "Gallstones, Gruesome, Sewer & Odious"), pulled in sixty dollars a week, and Decca bought her first new refrigerator. Bert and Pele Edises also moved to the East Bay, but up into the Berkeley Hills, where Pele felt utterly marooned, so far from jazz clubs and artists' studios. In her new surroundings, she thought her children too vulnerable and exposed, "looked on as dangerous reds."

Back in Washington, President Harry S. Truman was cleaning house. He'd already dropped the bomb, and now his to-do list read something like this: Assert the victor's role; protect the sphere of influence; keep Soviets from world domination; pick up dry cleaning. He asked Congress to support a global war against Communism and issued a new Loyalty Order, which barred "subversives" from government employment. This version of the order, designed for the cold war, empowered the attorney general to publish a list of proscribed organizations. The definition of the word *loyalty* was assumed to be self-evident. Subversives were an undermining constituency, and membership in any of the attorney general's listed organizations was immediate cause for investigation. Passports, federal loans for housing, and applications to live in federal housing were all subject to a wiggly standard of loyalty.

In October, Bob and Decca's second son, Benjamin, was born. With each of her children's birth Decca's experience had been that much more complicated. For Benjy's birth in 1947, the doctor had induced with "5 big doses of castor oil, 5 Triple-H enemas (so called by the nurses—it stands for High, Hot & a Hell of a lot), and 45 shots of something or other. Also innumerable pills." High-priced hospitals, highly regarded physicians, and technological advances did not seem to make anything go easier. These observations and her lifelong respect for the midwife's skill would become the source material for *The American Way of Birth*, which she would publish forty-five years later.

In the fast-moving postwar economy, midwifery was considered old-fashioned and unnecessary. All across the workforce, women workers were returning home. Madison Avenue ad campaigns featured sparkling new appliances in immaculate kitchens. Model mothers wore high heels and aprons around nipped-in waists. Such was not the style chez Treuhaft, where "the tidal wave of washing and cleaning . . . daily threatened to engulf." Decca had three young children and plenty of volunteer party work to do. Dinky, Nicky, and Benjy came along to meetings and on the weekends would accompany their parents to picnics, benefits, and concerts. She liked their company, but longed for outside work: "For a few depressing months I stayed at home trying to cope." She was like the farm girl who had once seen the bright lights of Paris. In her case, glamour was a full-bodied submersion in subversion. She knew how much she had to offer. She hated being bored at home, surrounded by that particular nightmare called housework.

The theme of Decca's domestic dyslexia was often a source of comedy—her smart and deliberate choice. There was very little reward that she could perceive for superior housewifery. The consequence of excellence in the field was further encouragement, and the concept of virtue as its own reward was distinctly unsatisfying. In the end, cleaning would be like typing. If she had learned to type well in the days when typewriters were clunky with inky ribbons and springy keys, perhaps she would have become a desirable secretary instead of a subeligible one. But then she might have been stuck in the typing pool, working for others, and it might have been just that much harder to imagine becoming the journalist she wanted to be. She had studied and practiced typing, but it wasn't until she was writing her own books that she really mastered the skill. There was also a political component to housework, which Decca might never have fully appreciated if she hadn't spent these several months at home. She hung this quotation from Lenin above her kitchen sink: "Housework is highly unproductive, most barbarous and most arduous, and it is performed by women. This labor is extremely petty and contains nothing that would in the slightest degree facilitate the development of women."

As party members, Decca and her friends felt particularly encouraged to take leadership roles in organizing, fund-raising, and education. She met a roadblock early on when it came to restarting her journalism career. She approached the *People's Daily World* in the hope of training to become a serious reporter. A male editor who saw her as undereducated, lighthearted, and one of the more vociferous defenders of the "Vicky Says" column steered her toward writing for the Women's Pages. Over time, Decca had come to believe (as the Women's Commission had pointed out) that the Women's Pages were "patronizingly stupid," so she resented his implication. She had spent years defying expectations and didn't like to be underestimated. She would periodically freelance for the paper, but she never joined its staff.

》《

IN APRIL 1948, Decca's mother surprised the Treuhafts with a telegram announcing her sudden decision to visit. For years, Decca had been inviting her mother to California, but their reunion had started to seem unlikely—first there had been the war, then Unity's needing constant care; there was little money, and California was so far away. They had continued to correspond faithfully, both their personas on paper reliably airy, comic, forgiving, and controlled. But letters, no matter how intimate or revealing, are just the silhouette of a body. After nine years, how would her mother find her? Decca felt "at once immensely excited . . . and deeply apprehensive." Here she was with three American children, a stay-at-home housewife with Communist books and laundry ankle deep. About all she could do was clean the house with the help of Bob and seven-year-old Dinky (who, family legend held, was something of a domestic prodigy). One day, her daughter returned home from school to find Decca sweeping the stairs from the bottom up.

"You're supposed to start at the top and go down," Dinky advised.

A PHOTO TAKEN at the airport shows Muv looking thin and fatigued. She was sixty-eight years old. Commercial nonstop flights from London to San Francisco had begun just the year before. The journey took twenty-three hours, still a piece of cake after what she'd come through in the past few years. In the picture, Decca looks healthy and pretty and, just months after Benjy's birth, slightly plumper than usual. Decca didn't pay much attention to fashion anymore, but she had obviously dressed with care. It is one thing to imagine one's mother after many years apart, but quite another thing to actually see her. Consternation and apprehension melted into a joyful reunion made sweeter as Muv and her granddaughter became instant friends. In the car ride to Oakland, Dinky asked her just when she planned to scold Decca for having run away. The very idea, Decca said, "set us all to shrieking with laughter."

From the freeways to the bridges through the gorgeous golden city to the Oakland suburbs, Muv was fascinated, curious, and uncritical. She was playful with the children and unjudging of the household chaos. She told Decca she thought the house "wonderful & very pretty" and Oakland's Victorian homes amid Western gardens something "like a musical comedy stage set." Decca was far more comfortable with Muv's disengaged cool than she had ever been. It seemed her mother was "absolutely bent on friendship."

There was some comforting family gossip. Decca found out what she could about Mrs. Romilly and about Giles, who had survived the war as a prisoner in Germany. He had suffered from deprivation and many losses, but seemed to be improving and had recently married. Nancy was a great source of entertainment; there was so much to say. She'd moved to Paris, and she was still in love with a French diplomat, whom she'd met in 1943. His name was Gaston Palewski. He had been the *chef de cabinet* of de Gaulle's Free French government in exile during the war and commanded the Free French forces in East Africa. Nancy called him "the Colonel." There was a character in her novel, *The Pursuit of Love*, very like him. The family thought Nancy's novel was delicious, and they were pleased by its great success. Farve was delighted by the fictionalized version of himself. Everyone agreed there had to be a sequel. The fictional Farve was easier to discuss than the man in reality, though his health was a neutral subject. It was good to know that his eyes had improved. It had seemed for a while as if he'd go blind due to cataracts.

There were still terrible shortages at home—rationing, nationalization—so it was better not to dwell on that subject. *No politics* was the only rule for this visit. Fresh fruit was hard to find out of season, so the lemon trees in all the gardens were dazzling to Muv. She could now make terrific bread, which she demonstrated. Noting that Decca had no adequate breadboard, Muv promised to send her one. Nancy had started sending rice from France, and—teasing as always—she only sent it to people who had good chefs so it wouldn't be wasted. Pam was getting a divorce—imagine! She'd been so good to Diana's boys, taking them in for the duration of the Mosleys' incarceration. There was a definite chill when Diana's name was mentioned, and Decca made it clear she couldn't forgive her sister. ("Wicked Aunt Diana who would melt us all down for soap if she could catch us," is how she described her to Dinky.) Debo had a new title, the Marchioness of Hartington, and when her husband, Andrew, became Duke of Devonshire, she would be a duchess. With all of that, Debo faced her own heartbreak. Three miscarriages, one around the time of Decca's and the others more recently. Unity was sometimes impatient and rude to Debo, often unable to express herself adequately, but Unity always spoke of her favorite sister, Decca, with affection.

After Unity's suicide attempt, the doctors had thought it too dangerous to remove the bullet from her head. Brain damage had made her "strange and childish." Muv cared for her devotedly, but Farve still found her presence hard to tolerate. Other visitors had noted Unity's weight gain and that she often seemed depressed. Unity hadn't been allowed into town during the war, because American forces had been stationed there, but now on good days, she rode her bicycle all over, singing at the top of her voice. A few things gave her real pleasure. She liked to eat and resisted the healthy diet her mother enforced. Church soothed her to some extent. She loved the hymns and liked to visit the parson. She had also found a part-time job, pouring tea at the hospital near High Wycombe, where she and Muv lived when they weren't at Inch Kenneth.

Muv had seen Unity grow more confused in social encounters. She knew her daughter was unbearably lonely. On one visit to see Nancy, Unity had confided in Derek Hill, a painter and friend of her elder sister, that she had joined the Congregationalist Church because after the service, you shook hands and that was "wonderful," since so few people would touch her anymore. They had a few friends who reliably cared for Unity while Muv visited America.

Decca and Muv's reunion featured a new directness and honesty. It had rarely been the form among adult Mitfords to share introspection. Decca was happy by then living with Bob and her children in California, but that other life—the one with Esmond—was not so deeply buried. Decca may have tiptoed around some subjects, but she was more than ready to talk about her first husband. It must have been a relief just to say his name aloud. They discussed Esmond's death early on in the war and Tom's death at its very end. So many of the young men who used to come to their house had been lost or injured, but a few had established themselves.

Muv and Decca discussed Evelyn Waugh's career. He had been in their house often when Nancy and Diana were home. Hadn't Evelyn used Decca's own definition of *sheepish* in *Vile Bodies*, to mean not shy but as beautiful as Decca's pet lamb Miranda? He had dedicated his new novel, *The Loved One*, to Nancy (just as years before, he had dedicated *Vile Bodies* to Diana). Mother and daughter noted that in the first few pages of *The Loved One*, there is a reference to a chap who before the war had defied convention by staying in America and opening "a restaurant with an Italian partner." That same character returned to fight in the war and died as the Nazis invade Norway. Esmond had died over the North Sea, and Giles had been captured in Norway, and Waugh knew them both. Waugh's genius was for the rolling, light, barely there soufflé spiced with malice. It's just possible that Decca read in the character, who set the standard for eccentric independence, a sort of tribute to her husband. Sydney thought it possible. Writers do so often make fiction out of true stories—they mix and match. Nancy's work was proof of that.

What must Bob have thought? Before her mother's arrival, Decca had worried that Muv's anti-Semitism would become an issue. It wasn't. She was courteous and cordial to her daughter's new husband. For his part, Bob couldn't get over the "non-Jewish-motherishness" of his mother-in-law. When he mentioned that the Nixon-Mundt bill then under consideration in Congress would threaten Communist Party members with long stays in concentration camps, she replied, "What a pity. But of course I'm quite accustomed to my children going to prison." Aranka faced with the prospect had said, "How can you do this to me?"

From the pages of *The Loved One*, Muv had gleaned that a funeral parlor was the American oddity no tourist should miss. She and Decca made plans to visit one together, an excursion that would have a powerful influence on Decca's later career. Muv also wished to tour a supermarket. Decca had a refrigerator now, large enough for a small cow. California's hamburgers were like steaks, and its steaks like heifers. Every tomato was as big as the prize-winners in the church fete. To Muv, shopping in the brightly lit and colorful supermarket was like entering some American folktale. Twenty years later, Decca would have a walk-on role as a supermarket shopper in the Herbert Ross movie *Play It Again, Sam* with Woody Allen. In her character's curiosity and wonder at the overbright, overlarge shelves of merchandise, a viewer can imagine Sydney's delight, even the inchoate stirrings of a letter to the *Times*, which Sydney would send upon her return—heartily recommending that this self-service style be encouraged throughout England.

In May, after a month's stay with Decca's family, Muv stopped in New York, where she had dinner with Aranka, an encounter Decca only wished to attend as a fly on the wall. It had seemed so unlikely that those two worlds would ever collide, but now they had and with agreeable results. Aranka admired Sydney as she had Nancy, whom she looked forward to meeting again in Paris.

Soon after Muv arrived home, she and Unity set off for Inch Kenneth. There they resumed old customs. Muv saw to the farm; Unity went fishing. They spent hours sewing and updating their scrapbooks. There were plenty of new newspaper articles to include. Sydney recounted her visit to Decca in detail. One of the things she'd found odd was that in America, people thought it was more important to spend money on a car than on household help.

UNITY WAS HAPPIEST talking about her youth before the war and about her affection for Decca. It was impossible to say when the sisters might meet again. In the United States, there was trouble on the horizon for people of Decca's political beliefs. The party organization was not yet outlawed, but the Taft-Hartley Act of 1947 required all union officers to sign loyalty oaths and swear they were not Communists or Communist sympathizers. Nationally, there was a coordinated effort to cleanse the country of its residual Communist menace. The film industry came under much public chastisement for harboring intellectuals of a presumed pink persuasion. In October 1947, the House Committee on Un-American Activities sentenced ten screenwriters (in what came to be known as the Hollywood Ten court case) to jail sentences for refusing to adequately answer the question "Are you now or have you ever been a Communist?"

Around the same time, eleven leaders of the Communist Party USA were arrested under the Smith Act of 1940 and charged as conspirators. The Smith Act allowed government agents the flexibility to round up dissenters who assembled to protest, or who published antigovernment matter or whom the agents perceived to be in any way advocating or teaching the "desirability, of overthrowing the government" (this extended to the theoretical support of a socialist system of government). The penalties were ten years in prison and a ten-thousand-dollar fine. The U.S. Justice Department intended to crush the U.S. Communist Party by rounding up its leaders and subjecting them to long and expensive trials. In the Smith Act trial, the government's case revealed little evidence of any actual violence or talk of violence, and the case turned on the group's leadership and organizational influence. These were the men who in 1945 had expelled Earl Browder and dissolved the Communist Political Association to reconstitute it as the Communist Party USA. That series of events was at the heart of the government's charge of a revolutionary conspiracy. One of the senior partners in Bob's firm, Richard Gladstein, was a lawyer for the Smith Act defendants and was himself sentenced to six months for contempt of court. Decca organized a rally to support him.

MUV KNEW FROM deep experience how quick and wide the pendulum of politics could swing. She suggested that in a different political season, Decca might come to Inch Kenneth with her children and new husband. (After all, she owned part of the island.) Unity thought she and Decca would probably never meet again. But in any case, her love for Decca "was quite unchanged." When they had said good-bye in California, Decca asked Muv to give her Boud her love. (In the language Unity and Decca invented when they were children, *Boud* meant "pal.")

Not long after Muv and Unity had returned to Inch Kenneth, Unity fell ill with a fever. Because of their isolation and the bad weather, it took a few days before their physician could treat her. He arranged to move her by special chartered boat to West Highland Cottage Hospital in Oban, where she died on May 28, 1948, ten years to the day after Decca's daughter Julia died. She was thirty-three years old. The cause of death as it appears on Unity's death certificate is "Purulent Meningitis, Cerebral Abscess, Old gunshot wound" to the head.

A decade after her sister's death, Decca recognized that understanding her sister's actions might not be possible: "It is perhaps futile to try to interpret the actions of another—one may be so completely wrong." And if this observation seems to dismiss the efforts of most early-twentieth-century art and social science, it also rings true in the wake of grief. Decca nevertheless goes on, as people do, to try to explain: "But it always seemed to me that this last really conscious act of [Unity's] life, the attempt at self-destruction, was a sort of recognition of the extraordinary contradictions in which she found herself, that the declaration of war merely served as the occasion for her action, which would in any case have been inevitable sooner or later."

CHAPTER 15

OON AFTER OPENING his own East Bay law practice, Bob had a full
schedule of cases defending black youths against police brutality. In
those first postwar years, all the Oakland Police were white. A lot of
police officers and prison guards had migrated from the rural South during
the war, and many of them held the mind-set that no matter who or why,
a white man was always superior. Oakland gained a reputation for being a
Western interpretation of a Jim Crow town. Bob's work gave him a front-
row seat witnessing the abuse of power.

Common occurrence on a Friday night was for cops to grab a black
man who had cashed his paycheck in a bar and gotten drunk. "Two policemen would get the drunk into a patrol car, clean out his wallet . . . throw
him into the slammer," Bob said. There were never any witnesses—at least
none who would come forward, and he represented a "sickening number"
of similar cases. Uprooting such corruption in the police department would
have required the commitment of a district attorney willing to investigate
and eventually bring charges. On that front, Bob was politically contravened
and personally challenged for years to come. Playing out a microversion
of right-versus-left national politics, there began a long vendetta between
Bob and the Alameda County district attorney, J. Frank Coakley. Bob's
law practice would bring cases of civil rights violations and police brutality,
which Coakley would invariably oppose. Coakley's was an elected position
(a sinecure, it seemed to political opponents), which he held for approxi-
mately twenty-two years. He was a dedicated conservative with a large support base and the reliable endorsement of the *Oakland Tribune*.

Around this time, it occurred to Bob and Decca that the financial and
emotional expense of her staying home far outweighed the cost of child

care. (The family couldn't rely as it once had on trading accommoda-
tion for day care. As the children grew, their babysitters became more
conventional and expensive.) The party's policy encouraged members to
find employment in a nearby "mass" organization and become a part of
its decision-making process, in schools, hospitals, factories, or stores—
wherever labor organizing might be done. Decca had this in mind as she
considered how to approach her next job. With the indefatigable energy
and the tough hide of a natural reporter, she hadn't given up on becoming
a journalist. She could make cold calls with insouciance, engage strangers to open up, get the inside scoop in a trice. When offered a trial on the
Women's Pages of the *People's Daily World*, she chose to decline. Higher-
ups with clout might have applied pressure on her behalf if they'd wanted
her on the paper's news reporting or editorial staff, but local leaders had
her in mind for a different job. They thought her talents in organizing,
fund-raising, and writing better suited to the local office of the Civil Rights
Congress (CRC).

The national CRC organization was originally formed to protest the
persecution of Communists and to defend the victims of white supremacists.
The East Bay chapter (for which Bob was also volunteer counsel) was dedicated to opposing police brutality. Its defense of the subjects of segregation
and prejudice ran from protesting blackface minstrel shows at an Elks club
to defending youths accused of capital crimes. It also actively opposed housing covenants and protected families moving into previously all-white communities. To do that, it often relied on an integrated bodyguard of young
black activists, inner-city ministers and churchwomen, white professionals,
suburban homemakers, and a corps of volunteer muscle.

Decca couldn't deny the pleasure of being recognized for her talents in
schmoozing, recruiting, and fund-raising. "Nobody made Decca do anything she didn't want to do," Dobby said. "If she hadn't liked it, she could
have left and looked for newspaper work elsewhere." But the CRC and
Decca were made for each other, and she would stay with them for almost
a decade.

Decca joined the CRC as assistant to Executive Director Hursel Alexander, a black veteran organizer who impressed her with his "mesmeric ability to wring the last ounce of effort from those within his orbit." Their office was a pulsar with Decca at her organizational zenith, and according to the artistic Pele, her skill was in "grinding down on people, intimidating, to coax you into doing what she thinks ought to be done."

Alexander's primary focus was to compile evidence of Oakland's police brutality sufficient to persuade a state commission to investigate. He shared Bob's observation "that there was nobody in the [police] department to put any kind of stop at all to the unbridled brutality, hatred really, on the part of the police, toward the Black citizenry here." As Alexander's assistant, Decca was to gather testimonies from victims and witnesses. She was quick and curious and a good listener, going wherever someone would talk and trying to get them to do so on the record. She visited people's homes, met them in churches, pool halls, taverns, diners, jails, and hospitals, and waited in her car outside their places of work. Her investigations took her to the run-down, dingy waterfront of dollar-a-night motels and whorehouses and into the kinds of bars where people went when they didn't want to be found. This could be hard, and it was certainly risky for her and for witnesses who had so much at stake.

To find her witnesses, she would post leaflets around town with attention-getting summaries of the events she wanted confirmed ("Thugs in Uniform"; "Defenseless Negro Victims of Police Brutality"; "It *Can* Happen Here"). As she went along, she taught herself the art of the interview. Eventually, she would memorize her questions, so she would rarely have to look down at her notes and break the flow. She heard tales of assaults, unjustified arrests, and various other humiliations, after which she found it "hard to describe adequately the monstrous beastliness, authority clothed in nightmare garb that our investigations disclosed."

Buddy Green, a young reporter for the *People's Daily World* and CRC board member, would occasionally help Decca set up interviews and often accompanied her. They made an odd couple—the thoughtful newsman from rural Mississippi, who was black, and the funny, energetic English lady, who some people assumed was a war bride. The combination was effectively disarming, like a BBC mystery set in a West Oakland bar. Both Buddy and Decca were autodidacts, and in the hours spent waiting in hope for a witness, each learned a great deal about the contrasting world from which the other had fled. She was a curiosity in the bars, tolerated for her persistence by men who didn't have a lot of energy for humoring white ladies. Maybe she didn't know that getting involved was just the same as painting a target on your back. She did understand, and she commiserated, but this had to stop somewhere. *Won't you be the one?* she would ask. Once, Decca tried to track down an alibi witness by the name T-Bone. Trolling the portside outposts of lost men, she sang her plaintive refrain: "Do you know T-Bone? Anybody here seen ol' T-Bone?"

Decca and Alexander would periodically present their mounting evidence files to the chief of police, a man named Divine, "a singularly glib, smooth-tongued individual" whose behavior was discordant with his name. Alexander kept up the pressure, petitioning Sacramento until finally a state commissioner came to town. Decca wrote that this investigation was, significantly, "the first time in the history of the nation that a specific probe [was] conducted into the overall practices of a major police department toward minority groups." The commission examined the files and heard testimonials from alleged victims, witnesses, ministers, and lawyers, many of whom Decca had wrangled and assembled.

The commission members eventually issued a report that they found only "some degree of truth," a finding that Decca, Bob, and Alexander all considered a grave underestimation. It was also a personal disappointment that they had to carry back to the many others who had shown up and testified. In the red-baiting years ahead, as the presumed link between civil rights and subversion would be hammered home, the Oakland Police's and the CRC's positions would become further entrenched and antagonistic. The Civil Rights Congress would be labeled a Communist front organization, added to the U.S. attorney general's list of subversive organizations. And in the milieu that assured that no good deed went unpunished, the state committee's chief investigator on the Oakland investigation would lose his job for having "cooperated with the CRC."

》《

IN 1949 THE campaign against Oakland's police brutality found its marquee case in Jerry Newson, an eighteen-year-old black shoeshine worker accused of murdering a pharmacist and his assistant. By this time, Alexander had left the Bay Area and Decca was the CRC's East Bay executive secretary. The way Bob told it, one morning over breakfast, they saw the news of Newson's arrest:

> Decca scooted down to the address that the paper gave . . . and found the place surrounded by police. The boy was in jail but the aunt and uncle were there. Decca got in, got through the police, and talked to the aunt and uncle. Police were searching the place for guns and whatnot. She talked to the Newsons and she offered legal help. She didn't know anything about the case, but these people wanted help.

Bob took on Newson's case. The young man's first conviction was overturned on appeal, and two further trials ended in hung juries. In Newson's defense, Bob argued that not only had his client been elsewhere at the time of the murder, but Newson's confession had been forced, and the ballistic evidence offered by the police faked. District Attorney Frank Coakley, with the editorial backing of the *Oakland Tribune* (for whom this case represented a bonanza in sales), pressed for a guilty verdict. When a ballistics expert testified that the prosecution's trumped-up case had no real evidence, Coakley had to dismiss the murder charges.

Bob's law practice was one of the few still willing to defend loyalty cases. Successful outcomes were "few and far between." Once impugned in the public eye as a lawyer who defends Communists or a red lawyer, Bob found his opportunities to defend those accused of nonpolitical offenses (at more competitive rates) radically reduced. In that red-baiting atmosphere, his cases' frequent losses, huge expenses, and short rewards made his law firm a losing proposition.

Despite Bob's limited income, Decca—who had started working part-time for the CRC at a small salary—soon stopped taking one at all. This renunciation seemed proof to suspicious comrades that there was Mitford money available to her, but that wasn't the case. Decca had looked at the books and made an austerity program. If she and Bob lived frugally, they could stretch one salary to cover child care and household expenses.

The family never had a new car, and they had to budget carefully, but the blacklist was ruining others in far worse ways. Decca and Bob were Marxists, and fair pay for work was a central theme. Decca was a vigilant saver, proud budgeter, and smart shopper. As a family, she and Bob took pride in eschewing and ridiculing the must-have materialist possessions advertised. They had more in common with the rationers and budgeteers of postwar Britain. But they weren't made of stone. During the CRC years, Decca's inability to contribute more to the household budget was "a source of nagging irritation" for her. "Bob didn't mind, but I did," she said.

When Aranka first visited the newlywed Treuhafts' home in San Francisco, she had sought to advise her daughter-in-law on a great many practical matters. Bobby needed to be pushed, to set high goals, to make his fortune if Decca was ever to get a fur coat, jewelry, a big house for the children, or a swimming pool. At first, Decca, on her best behavior, listened avidly. But one morning, she'd had enough, and as Bob left for his office, Decca leaned out the window and (to Aranka's horror) yelled after him, "Get to work, you lazy good-for-nothing bum! How do you think you'll ever amount to anything? I want a new coat! I want a car! Off with you!"

By early 1950, Aranka had adapted to her son's unconventional family with some success and periodic lapses. She visited regularly from New York with her suitcases full of food and presents and, as one of their few regular emissaries from the outside world, brought welcome news of Nancy, whom she occasionally saw on her business trips to Paris.

Aranka made a habit of donating to her daughter-in-law's causes, contributing money and, sometimes, lovely hats, which the CRC would sell at benefit garage sales. Through her New York Park Avenue store, she distributed postcards that advertised a very Bob-like poem:

Whatever fashion may decree
Skirts above, below the knee
Topless dress, or dress with bust
Your new *Aranka* hat's a must!

She was an adoring grandmother, though she thought the kids a bit wild. She tried not to dwell on Bob's lost earning potential or to take offense when Decca teased her for her materialism or for babying Bobby. Once, on a visit when the Treuhaft house was full of neighbor children, Aranka lamented, "I sent my son to Harvard he should baby-sit for a longshoreman's child?" Even Aranka laughed when she realized how snobbish that sounded. She and Bob had a jokey, sweet relationship, but Aranka was never quite sure how to break through to her daughter-in-law: "Oh Decca . . . I wish I was black like Jerry Newson and Leadbelly. Then you would love me."

CHAPTER 16

*T*HE REPUBLICAN OPPOSITION'S vile accusations of "twenty years of treason" under Roosevelt (associating New Deal policies with left-wing, un-American ideas) put the Democrats on the defensive. The new Truman administration went all out to prove right off the bat that it would not be soft on Communism. To win elections, the Truman campaign would sweet-talk the Southern segregationists, prosecute Alger Hiss, and hire many more special agents for the FBI.

On February 9, 1950, Joseph Raymond McCarthy, the Republican senator from Wisconsin, gave a speech in West Virginia, claiming there were Communist Party members working in the State Department. McCarthy never felt the need to hold back. Communism was "a conspiracy so immense, an infamy so black, as to dwarf any previous such venture in the history of man." J. Edgar Hoover, the director of the FBI and McCarthy's twin in hyperbole, agreed that here was "the most evil, monstrous conspiracy against man since time began." McCarthy was like a shiny, new forged shield to preserve the status quo. As represented in the media, Communist men were shifty and hairy, women cruel or sexless; both genders brainwashed from childhood to reject God, the blandishments of luxury, and all temptation to be happy. The Communist mind was a sorcerer's mind with vague, extensive powers that the senator from Wisconsin could only hint at.

The bell for the witch hunt officially rung, the roundup commenced. If Communists had, as McCarthy insisted, insinuated themselves into the corridors of power, they might be anywhere, anytime. They could threaten your dear old mother, let your flag touch the ground, and poison your apple pie. They were to be tracked, hunted, cornered then publically shamed and, when possible, made to recant to the satisfaction of the tribunals before which they were required to appear. The consequence of these hearings was to demonstrate a national conformity of thought. Capitalism was not just the economic system; it was the only mental position acceptable for the American Way of Life. Anyway, that's how Decca saw it.

To New Deal liberals like Virginia and Clifford Durr, the senator from Wisconsin was "crazy as a bedbug—just a wild-eyed demagogue." A witch hunt begins in pervasive fear, and as Virginia Durr came to view it, McCarthy "scared the United States out of its wits . . . You couldn't go to a church meeting or to Sunday school that somebody didn't get up and denounce godless communism." Lillian Hellman also weighed in: "You couldn't possibly have guessed, unless you were mentally disturbed, that there would come into being such a phrase as 'premature anti-Fascist.'" "Skin-color blindness" was another sure sign of subversion. The connection was officially articulated by Albert Canwell, chairman of the Washington State Legislative Fact-Finding Committee on Un-American Activities: "If someone insists that there is discrimination against Negroes in this country, or that there is inequality of wealth, there is every reason to believe that person is a Communist."

Cedric Belfrage called the era *The American Inquisition*. *The Time of the Toad* was Dalton Trumbo's name for it. To Hellman, it was *Scoundrel Time*. Virginia Durr called it a reign of terror, but she also called it ridiculous and went on to say:

> Here we were blaming Russia for being a totalitarian dictatorship. We had fought Nazism and fascism and the persecution of Jews. Well, we put ourselves on the forked stick. The whole basis of the cold war was that Communism meant dictatorship and capitalism meant democracy. How could anyone say that capitalism was the best system in the world when the whole southern part of the United States was segregated and Negroes had no rights at all?

McCarthy was livid, avid, nonsensical, and running amok. The times were dire and the threats were very real. Liberals like Virginia defended their Communist friends, but not everyone was as willing to go out on a limb. There were journalists like Murray Kempton and I. F. Stone, both of whom were critical but fair, and the editor and writers for the magazine *Dissent*, who objected to the escalating federal attack on civil liberties in the courtroom and legislatively. There were individuals who spoke out on behalf of the heretics, and many of these defenders were from the same pool as those who objected to the Japanese internment camps during World War II: Quakers and Unitarians and Catholic lay workers and some rabbis who felt unthreatened by deportation.

To people of similar political interests and nonjoiners—who, given some encouragement, might have been natural allies—Communist Party members could seem like stuck-up, impatient, high-handed hacks, unyielding on the righteousness of their position to the point of boring their audience silly (notwithstanding their deadly puritanism). Party members could seem comical in their superauthoritarian approach, a bunch of tin-pot despots. Still, among former members and other kinds of "small c" communists—socialists, Trotskyites, anarchists—had some defenders, on principle.

Party communities varied from place to place, and the Bay Area attracted a noticeably more freewheeling crowd, but they rarely if ever made any institutional effort to mend fences with other lefty factions. An amorphous group of fellow travelers met in San Francisco through classes at the Tom Mooney Memorial California Labor School, at Izzy Gomez's bar, and the Flor D'Italia restaurant in North Beach. Many of these nonassociated reds (some of them artists and poets) who identified with the American rebel tradition of Wobblies (members of the Industrial Workers of the World) and anarcho-syndicalism, considered the American Communist Party a walking antique.

》《

DECCA SAID OAKLAND provided scope for her "subversive nature." She wrote that from the "days of the Truman-McCarthy era, when we first moved to Oakland, I personally enjoyed a sense of hand-to-hand combat with our neighbors, the city's administration, its police department, its monopoly all-powerful newspaper *The Oakland Tribune*, that could only be possible in a city that is essentially a small town grown big, where vendetta can flourish and become all-absorbing." The Treuhafts' "vendetta" with the district attorney, which began with the Newson trial, would become, in Decca's words, "a mutual enmity that flourished and grew over two decades." District Attorney Coakley, who had prosecuted Jerry Newson, was seen to be in the pocket of a local media baron. Decca, the daughter of an English baron, found in this petty warlord's abuse of power a hypocrite made to order. Coakley's ineptitudes begin with an anecdote that sounds like a comedy routine about two lawyers who meet at an Oakland jail. Discovering a hidden microphone in the area where counselors conferred with clients, one lawyer objected loudly. "That mike wasn't put there for you," the second lawyer said. "It was meant for Treuhaft."

Decca found innovative ways to needle Coakley. One day in the *Oakland Tribune*, she saw that there was a house for sale on Coakley's block, an all-white neighborhood. Knowing of a black family (the Guitons) who wanted to buy the house, she persuaded a young lawyer in Bob's firm and his wife (the Saunderses) to front for the Guitons. (This meant that the Saunderses would initially meet with the buyers, but once the sale was in process, the Guitons would purchase the house.) Around that time, Virginia Durr described Decca, when she dressed to impress, as looking like a beautiful, young Queen Mary. Decca went along with the prospective "buyers" to meet the sellers at their home, and in her "best Aranka hat . . . played the part of their English aunt."

In high aristo camouflage, Decca beguiled the snobbish owner. She complimented her hostess on the delicious tea and quizzed her about the neighborhood. This was a very special community, their hostess crowed, very high-quality people. *Our district attorney, Mr. Coakley, chief among them.* Decca was delighted to hear it, and after negotiating down the asking price, they closed the deal.

On moving day, Decca couldn't resist going along to see the previous and real new owners meet for the first time. She recalls how the owner turned,

> her face contorted with tears of pure rage . . . I had betrayed her trust in me; how could I do such a terrible underhanded thing? I asked why, since she had moved out of the neighborhood, it could conceivably make any difference to her whether her house was now occupied by the Saunderses or the Guitons. Because, she said, the neighbors, such lovely people, would feel she had let them down; she would never be able to hold her head up again in decent society. I coldly replied that she and her lovely neighbors were contemptible bigots, and that if she did not leave immediately, I should be obliged to summon the district attorney from across the street to arrest her for disturbing the peace.

Soon after, Coakley put his house on the market and installed his family in a grander home. In the courthouse, he grumbled to another lawyer, "That pinko Treuhaft outsmarted me this time!"

THROUGH THAT CONTENTIOUS time, absorbed and occupied as she was, she daydreamed about visiting England. She wanted to show her past life to Bob and longed for her family to meet her husband and her children. She even considered patching things up with her father (if he would agree not to aggravate things by insulting Bob or her children). It had been such a long time since she'd been there—"home," she still called it from time to time. So in the spring, and with Muv's help, she started to make plans to travel.

"Could you possibly ring up the *Daily Worker* next time you're in London & ask them whether they know of any interesting mass meetings or demonstrations in Paris scheduled for late Sept. or early October?" she asked her mother. Muv replied that she thought she could not, although she would be pleased to help with accommodations.

By July 1950, it looked as if their family trip to Europe would have to be postponed. The McCarran Act passed in Congress, over a Truman veto. It imposed a wide set of discriminating restrictions on the civil rights of Communists living in the United States. Under the new regulations, Communists would be required to register as subversives. They would not be allowed to use their passports. Further legal restrictions dictated where they could work and their use of the U.S. postal system. Veterans with Communist affiliations were refused the right to live in public housing. One clause, authorizing presidential powers in the case of invasion, insurrection, or war, established detention camps where subversives, spies, and saboteurs might be detained. The logistics were secret, but Decca and her friends anticipated a system of deportation like that employed against Japanese Americans during World War II to distant concentration camps.

Under these circumstances, Decca wrote to her mother to explain the postponement of the trip: "I believe there is now a very immediate danger of people being rounded up & jailed here, and of course we wouldn't want to be away if that should happen."

>«

BOB'S LAW PRACTICE was solvent, thanks to the publicity he had received as counsel to Jerry Newson. A steady stream of civil rights and police brutality cases kept him busy. If Decca and Bob felt stigmatized as Communists or sympathizers by the mainstream white community, their work in the area's black neighborhoods included supporters who, Decca said, "empathized with us as members of yet another persecuted minority."

Their work provided them with a special kind of passage across Oakland and the East Bay. Their home was often a fluid, crowded interchange of children and friends of various races and backgrounds. Across the bridge, in San Francisco, such enlightened convergence was more common. Given that connections between blacks and whites were often socially if not legally forbidden, having normal friendship was a tactical and moral triumph.

In January 1951, the Treuhafts moved into a bigger house and bought their first TV. Now, like most of America, they could watch the McCarthy hearings and *I Love Lucy*. Around this time, Decca found another important friend in Barbara Kahn. Ephraim Kahn was the Treuhafts' family doctor. His wife, Barb, was a sophisticated Vassar graduate whose intelligent, dry wit made her "a perfect foil for Decc." Decca called both Barb and Eph "sparkplugs" in the CRC.

Decca had a full, fast, busy life, as characterized by the exclamatories (Rush! Essential! Imperative!) that headed much of her mail. Every day, there were new alerts of leftists under attack, requests for more money needed for defense campaigns, more leaflets to mail, protests to announce, petitions to circulate. She was good at what she did, but she did it all the time and was starting to tire of the routine. It was satisfying to feel competent and useful, but there just wasn't as much adventure as before. Was it that she was older? She was thirty-three. The party was squarely opposed to adventurism, considering it a manifestation of left-wing infantilism. But left-wing infantilism was the spark that lit her spirit from time to time and gave her joy.

Meanwhile, she wasn't getting on with the thing she'd hoped to do— write. She rarely found the time to revise what she might scrawl in a rush, although she took care with her personal letters when she could. Even first drafts seemed pretty good to her. Then one day in her mail, she found an imperative to her liking, which would shortly send her off on an adventure and require that she write seriously.

In Jackson, Mississippi, Willie McGee, a black man convicted of raping a white woman, was sentenced to die. Decca had no doubt that McGee's confession had been forced and his trial unjust and inadequate. When one of Bob's law partners, Aubrey Grossman, went to Jackson as part of a delegation to support McGee's appeal, a group of segregationists had attacked Grossman in his hotel room and then harassed him all the way to the hospital (where he had needed sixteen stitches in his head). Grossman carried home firsthand tales of McGee's case and the brutal mood in Jackson. Mississippi was the new battleground, the center of something magnetic. Decca wanted to be a frontline soldier again, and this was the moment when motive met opportunity. New evidence had come to light: Williametta Hawkins, the accuser, and McGee had had a consensual affair, which she had not wanted to end.

The imperative that Decca received was a request from the CRC's national leadership that she assemble a quota of four women to participate in a nationwide delegation of white women to travel to Mississippi. She was ready to take a leave from local politics and family concerns, and she went all out to comply.

Decca and her friends recognized that McGee's story, like the Scottsboro case (in which nine black teen-agers wrongly accused of raping two white women were unjustly imprisoned) had the potential to move people. With enough support, their campaign could influence policy and result in more civil rights protection nationally. Things were changing. Black soldiers fighting in Korea were rejecting the old status quo and demanding equal rights in the armed forces and back home. More than anything, the McGee case was a human tragedy. Decca spoke to Grossman, read the literature, and wrote leaflets and resolutions, but it was really when she heard McGee's wife, Rosalee, speak that "the realities of Mississippi began to come alive" for her. The CRC set up speaking engagements for Rosalee across the country. In churches, trade union halls, and private homes, her indignation and eloquence moved her audience. Decca thought she was "one of the bravest people" she'd ever met.

By the spring of 1951, Willie McGee's attorneys, Bella Abzug of New York and John Coe of Florida, had tried the case three times, and each trial had concluded with a verdict of guilty. While the defense petitioned the Supreme Court for a stay of execution, the campaign rested on a national call for clemency. Hundreds of thousands of people signed petitions asking for justice, for freedom, for mercy—all of which the governor denied. Decca and her friends believed that by visiting Jackson themselves, they might influence local residents to pressure their governor. They had the optimistic, grand idea that by speaking one-on-one to locals, they might change hearts and minds. The trial had been so tainted, the new evidence so clarifying, that anyone who learned the real facts couldn't help but join the outcry. At the same time, Decca saw their journey as an opportunity to attack the underlying roots of the maddening system of segregation. They would talk about the dual standard of justice in the courts and, most importantly, "challenge the rape myth that every Negro man is a potential rapist and any act of intercourse between races is rape." From the contemporaneous reports that Decca filed about her travels to Mississippi, she and her comrades planned to counter this "cornerstone of jim-crow ideology" by relying on another myth: "the sanctity of white womanhood," which presumed that a respectable white woman was unassailable as long as she played her role and avoided disgrace. The four Communist women intended to disarm their opposition by dressing in distinctly feminine styles (seamed stockings and flowered hats) and acting at first with modesty and discretion.

Even as Hoover's FBI and other scourges warned the citizenry of reds under beds or demons in the dark, Decca and friends dabbled in the language and imagery of the hero's journey. There would be challenges and ordeals. The territory was a dangerous one, patrolled by monsters in Klansmen's sheets. In disguise, Decca and company would stride among an oppressed population terrified by the giants of segregation: Ku Klux Klan dragons and vicious, tabloid trolls. At the time, Decca called Mississippi a "concentration camp of the mind."

Their quest would take them away from families and friends for about three weeks. Bob was supportive, but some of the other husbands complained, seeing themselves as "the real sacrificers."

The women's gallant company included Eve Frieden, whom Decca dubbed "rollicking, jolly" Evie, a voluptuary in contrast to dour, top-rank politico Billie Wachter, whose piety and asceticism made for a female Sir Galahad. Finally, there was Louise Hopson, whom Decca called the "Youth Comrade" and whose quiet character seemed to mark her as the first likely snack for locals.

The four-woman delegation set out with the expectation that the national campaign, as organized, would at minimum provide them basic information describing the state of the trial and assign them some particular project. Collectively, they had only a rudimentary knowledge of the area, so they would need maps, contacts, and, of course, lodging. But when they reached the campaign's first gathering point in Saint Louis, they discovered that the four of them "were the whole delegation, the generals and soldiers of this great nationwide call to action." Decca knew the resources of the CRC were stretched thin across the country, but there were not even leaflets to distribute and no guarantees of protection for anyone.

Decca saw this for the amateur operation it was, but there was something to be said for acting without all the creaky machinery of a big offensive. One could be more flexible and responsive to the situation on the ground, a guerrilla, unless perhaps like Sir Galahad, you had a harder time improvising.

Early on, the fellowship suffered an immediate clash of temperaments. Billie was a local leader and, as such, tried to assert her authority. It seemed she disapproved of gossip, of joking, of incorrect language. Decca thought they might be allowed a little fun; this was a road trip, not a suicide mission. Evie sided with Decca, but "the Youth Comrade said not a word." In any case, it would have been hard to get a word in edgewise.

The four crusaders rode into hostile terra incognita in the full armor of postwar, Southern ladies: lightweight dresses, hats, gloves, and stockings. None of them knew the city of Jackson. This expedition may have felt to Decca a little like going to Spain without Esmond, but she could rely on the memory of his single-mindedness, watchfulness, and craft in their battle against "Klan doctrine." As long as they stayed, there was always the threat of real danger, including (as they would later discover) a police department more responsive to the residents' fear of strangers than the protection of white ladies, no matter how straight their stocking seams.

During the course of eleven days, they would speak to more than 150 people, including ministers, club women, community organizers, and one Nobel Prize winner in literature. They buttonholed teachers at a conference, canvassed door to door, and found somewhat to their surprise that

McGee and his accuser's consensual affair had been common knowledge, not news at all and unlikely to stimulate a popular revolt. Timid voices told the women from California not to shake things up, that in Jackson, they would pacify the monsters in their own way.

Decca was elected the group's scribe, which meant that before submitting her reports to the *People's Daily World* for circulation back home, the group looked them over and offered "collective criticism." But despite Galahad's frequent requests for revision, Decca found the discipline of a deadline and word count exciting. She had been for some time sharpening her writing skills on leaflets, press releases, and memos. Her personal letters were wry and understated for the most part, but her memos florid, full of the L-speak (left-wing political rhetoric) she would later satirize to the hilt.

Toward the end of their sojourn and in an effort to claim some material success, Decca and her comrades decided to take their case to the "King of Yoknapatawpha County." In 1950, William Faulkner was the recent Nobel Prize winner in literature. His position in American intellectual society was nonpareil. After their two-hour chat, during which Faulkner held forth with the women in "murky eloquence," Decca had quotes galore on sex, violence, and race and even a few sympathetic words about Willie McGee. The next day, she returned just to make sure Faulkner approved his wording. What did he think, this master of solitude and sumptuous language, of Decca's well-honed press release? He read the newspapers; he'd been in Britain during the war, so he must have known of the Mitfords. He offered her a drink; she sipped while he read casually, pencil in his hand. A comma from a Nobel laureate is worth something, but he wasn't known for freebies. At their second meeting, Faulkner, either having thought more about it or becoming annoyed by his visitor, said, "McGee and the woman *both* should be destroyed." "Oh, *don't* let's put that in," Decca said, tucking her notebook away. After that encounter, the sisterhood raced home. She wrote to her mother about the entire experience: "We drove a total of 7700 miles, in my new car. It was the most thrilling experience I ever had."

Back from the front, Decca continued to organize. She helped plan another tour for Rosalee McGee, this time with American-born, internationally regarded cabaret sensation Josephine Baker. About three weeks before McGee's scheduled execution, she and others organized a motorcade. This uniquely Californian 1950s mobile protest demonstration included a convoy of about a hundred cars with pennants and banners; the convoy drove around Oakland to the areas where supporters of the campaign lived.

At that time, Decca's friends the journalist Buddy Green and lawyer Dobby Walker (the former Dobby Brin Marasse, now remarried and using her new husband's name), were in Mississippi. Buddy wanted to call a demonstration of other black supporters all across the South to march to the governor's mansion. This visionary project anticipated the march to Selma by fifteen years, but the Communist Party leadership was fearful that Buddy's plan "would end in a massacre" and withheld their support. (Decca, siding with Buddy, felt herself at odds with the party line.) Early on in the demonstration, something went awry, and Buddy was arrested. Dobby's delegation was in Jackson at that time to lobby the governor's clemency board. She and her companions were also arrested, and at their arraignment, they saw Buddy across the segregated courthouse.

Bella Abzug, the future congressional representative from New York, and co-counsel John Coe persuaded the judge to drop charges against the white women if they agreed to leave Jackson by midnight. Dobby and her friends refused to do so unless Buddy and his companions were also released. Once the deal was struck, the women stayed until the Memphis train arrived and Buddy and the others were safely on board. Then Dobby drove back west through Dallas to California. Decca was moved by her friends' bravery.

On May 8, 1951, Willie McGee was executed. In his last letter to Rosalee, he wrote: "Tell the People the real reason they are going to take my life is to keep the Negro down in the South. They can't do this if you and the children keep fighting."

I N 1951, THE Civil Rights Congress was having a bad year. The Smith Act trials (there were several around the country, including one in Los Angeles) had drained its national treasury. The National CRC under its trustees had raised money to post enormous bonds for all the Smith Act defendants, and its trustees were hauled up before the House Committee on Un-American Activities (HUAC) to produce the names of funders and contributors. One of these trustees was the writer Dashiell Hammett, whose refusal to cooperate earned him a five-month jail sentence for contempt at age fifty-seven. Hammett's prison stint broke his health; he died at the age of sixty-six.

At the end of July, on the day the Los Angeles Smith Act trial defense rested, J. Edgar Hoover released a supersecret intelligence report revealing a Communist Party plot to overtake the government and occupy the country. The Los Angeles press ran the story in massive-font headlines for days. It was, as Dalton Trumbo wrote, "not a good time in which to stand trial for a political belief that had been up-graded to treason." Back in Oakland, one of Bob's law partners at the time, Ed Grogan, was at City Hall when he passed two cops perusing the headlines about the revealed secret Communist plot. One cop said to the other, "Do you think Treuhaft really wants to overthrow the government by force and violence?" "Well, no," was the reply, "but I think he's trying to get somebody else to do it."

In Oakland, Decca returned to the routine of family life and her job at the CRC in a time when civil rights were being violated in so many places and ways, it was hard to keep track. Her office was short-staffed, its funds earmarked for national defense campaigns. She'd seen deeds of prowess on the front lines in Mississippi, and if she was in the least bit worried about when she would feel that thrill again, she hadn't long to wait. Her own subpoena was about to be delivered, arriving less than one month after McGee's execution.

By June 1951, Decca and Bob had heard through the grapevine that the Committee on Un-American Activities—the California state version, otherwise known as the Little HUAC—was coming to San Francisco's City Hall. This committee had been active from the early 1940s and, under the chairmanship of John B. Tenney, had supervised the publication of "The Fifth Report," which asserted the Communist infiltration of California's universities, media, and entertainment industries. Tenney himself, straight from central casting, as historian Kevin Starr describes, was "hard-drinking, paranoid, dyspeptic." A touring musician through the 1920s, Tenney had later become president of the musicians' union and earned a night-school law degree. Then he had won a seat in the State Senate. He had begun his political career on the Left and made a radical turn to become "the grand inquisitor of California: an ominous figure in a pinstriped double-breasted suit." Tenney had a particularly Californian distinction as the composer and lyricist of the popular tune "Mexicali Rose," for which the mothers of beginning ukulele players worldwide would curse him. By the time Decca's subpoena arrived, Tenney's overreaching behavior, particularly his habit of wildly accusing so many popular, respected, and wealthy Californians, had sufficiently embarrassed his fellow senators. They replaced him as head of the committee, but the inquisition proceeded, as it would for another twelve or so years.

Since at least one Treuhaft was going to have to stick around to look after ten-year-old Dinky, seven-year-old Nicky, and four-year-old Benjy, Bob went into hiding and managed to dodge the sheriff's deputies. Decca's summons required her to appear on September 11 with the membership list, the names of all contributors, and the financial books of the CRC. Decca had no intention of providing any records to anyone. She originally had a plan to try to bluff her way through, to outsmart the committee with witty rejoinders, but her lawyer persuaded her to take the Fifth: *I refuse to answer on the grounds that it might tend to incriminate me.* No other strategy worked to keep witnesses out of jail. Decca knew that once you spoke, you conceded your rights and were required to answer to related facts or to risk an accusation of perjury, the consequences of which might range from a contempt citation to a jail term. A recent Supreme Court decision made even taking the Fifth an unreliable defense, since "the privilege could not be invoked to prevent the *records* of an organization from being subpoenaed." At any rate, there was nothing the committee didn't already know about the CRC's membership list. The FBI had been watching Decca at work, watching their family house, tapping their phone. The committee had duplicate copies of all the records they needed and a list of all the names.

September 11, 1951, was Decca's thirty-fourth birthday. What better way to celebrate than to appear before the committee in a lovely Aranka hat. The public was encouraged to attend. In San Francisco, the hearing room was sectioned off, with its greater part designated for local conservative groups. The supporters of unfriendly witnesses like Decca typically filled the balcony.

She and Bob had decided that this was an important event for Dinky to attend. "Should I end up behind bars as a consequence of refusing to testify, [Dinky] would at least have witnessed my crime with her own eyes." Decca didn't fear her court appearance, but by all reports, she positively dreaded having to go meet her daughter's grade school principal in order to request her absence. "She was absolutely terrified," her daughter Dinky would remember. (The one time her children would recall her being more frightened was when she saw fire coming from the propeller of a plane they were on.) To Decca's great relief, the principal cast proper opprobrium on HUAC for its disgraceful behavior and sent mother and daughter off with her support.

On the day of her testimony, the prosecutor started with, "Have you ever heard of or read the *People's World*? Have you been director of the East Bay Civil Rights Congress since May 1950? Do you maintain a bank account for the Civil Rights Congress in the Wells Fargo Bank? Is your husband, Robert Treuhaft, legal counsel for the Civil Rights Congress?"

The marquee question was, of course, "Are you now or have you ever been a member of the Communist Party?" To this and all the other questions, Decca took the Fifth. Between committee members and witnesses, there was what by then had become a ritual ceremony of polyphonic call and response, leading to an extended state of restlessness. It was banal and boring or, as Decca said, "irksome" to resist making a witty rejoinder. The committee on its podium was all so dull and self-important. After a while, even Decca grew accustomed to the slow and tedious show. When the committee counselor (perhaps wishing to wake things up) asked her, "Are you a member of the Berkeley Tennis Club?" she replied automatically, "I refuse to answer on the ground that my answer might tend to incriminate me." At first, she hadn't understood the laughter rippling across the chamber. She had thought he'd asked, "Are you a member of the Berkeley *Tenants* Club?" which was a renters union—what was so funny about that? But the image of red Decca lobbing balls in a "bastion of posh conservatism" had awoken the audience and angered the committee. "This witness is totally uncooperative!" the chairman shouted. "We won't have any more of her nonsense! She is dismissed from the stand!"

Her lawyer hurried Decca out of the courtroom, saying, "You got them so rattled they forgot to ask for the CRC records—now get lost, before they come to their senses."

For weeks after, there remained the possibility of Decca's recall. One of the letters she wrote to Muv around that time shows what a lot she was juggling: the CRC's decline, the terrible news about Willie McGee's execution, another Jerry Newson retrial. She wanted to make all this clear to her mother, because also on the horizon was the very real possibility of a visit by sister Debo. "Do tell her to come," Decca wrote. "I'll try to get a few days off."

The only thing was, Decca wasn't sure she would still be home. "We haven't been cited yet for contempt," she told Muv in a letter, "so maybe they will forget about it, but if they can prove it on you it is 6 months [in jail] for each separate refusal-to-answer, and they must have asked me 50 questions which I wouldn't answer."

»«

IN THE CHINESE calendar, 1952 was the Year of the Dragon, and by geopolitical measurements, it was monstrous. Both the Eastern and Western blocs in the cold war conducted themselves like outraged, outsized, vicious lovers, willing to trample anything to get the last word. Paranoid and manic, Stalin would initiate another great purge in 1952. Prisoner numbers in the Soviet Gulag would rise to their historic peak of about 2.5 million. The social cataclysm and psychic terror, the sweeping accusations and petty tattling, the fear of conspiracies and punishments for secret injuries all coming so soon after the war meant, for so many, a peace like a numbing, unstable bog.

In the United States, more people were coming under investigation by HUAC for subversive activities. The majority of citizens in the great state of Wisconsin reelected Joseph McCarthy to the Senate. The hunt for American Communists escalated. Not only were enrolled Communists tracked and investigated, but anyone else who had ever publicly or privately espoused socialism, signed a petition, or attended a left-wing meeting—no matter how long ago—was suspect. Anyone refusing to name the names of others who had attended a meeting or signed a petition risked a prison term on a contempt charge.

The U.S. Department of State officially withheld passports from anyone associated with the attorney general's secret list of subversive organizations. Both Decca in her position at the CRC and Bob as a member of the National Lawyers Guild made the list. In June 1951, the Treuhafts were battling on several fronts. Everyone was under surveillance, even the children. Decca wrote to her mother: "Poor Nicholas got arrested the other day for selling tickets door to door for a Jerry Newson Defense benefit." Decca sailed down to the police station and gave them hell. "The only trouble was Benjamin kept having to go to the loo which rather ruined the delegation."

The Communist Party USA, fearful of the detention clause in the McCarran Act, did "what it was always accused of doing—set up a clandestine apparatus." According to its apocalyptic scenario (with the title

"Five Minutes to Midnight"), select members would go underground to
build a resistance movement. Adam Lapin was one of the editors of the
People's Daily World, and once Al Richmond, its chief editor, was arrested,
Lapin assumed the paper's leadership. In the belief that they had to keep
the presses running in the face of intimidation and persecution, Lapin went
underground. For the next few years, he would edit the newspaper from
secret locations, living under a false name, apart from his family. The severed
families of these revolutionaries were less confident of the plan's strategic
value. Eva, Lapin's wife, might not have believed the country was becoming
fascist, but she stood by her husband: "If Adam felt he had to go I had to
support him." She and her children moved back to New York, where family
and friends could help them. Those would be hard years.

Comrades were coming and going from coast to coast. Nowhere felt
particularly safe. One friend who turned up around that time was Marge
Gelders Frantz. She and Decca had first met at one of Virginia Durr's dinners during the war, when Marge had just started at Radcliffe. She quit soon
thereafter to marry Laurent Frantz, a brilliant law student. Both Marge and
Laurent were party organizers. When Laurent had returned from service
overseas, they had settled in Raleigh, North Carolina, which had originally
struck the Frantzes as an oasis of tolerance. They realized their mistake
when Laurent was refused the opportunity to take the state bar exam. They
were followed around by thugs and harassed on the street. Sick at heart,
they loaded everything into their car and drove west, a family of educated,
persecuted Joads.

Marge's parents had found an inexpensive apartment in the federal
housing complex of Codornices Village in Berkeley. The complex had been
built during the war to house ten thousand migrant shipyard workers. By a
great majority, its occupants were left-wingers, and the area was known for
years as an outpost of successful radical organizing. Marge and Laurent had
gone to bed that first night in Berkeley exhausted and discouraged. In the
morning, they were awoken by trucks with amplified megaphones announcing upcoming meetings for the Independent Progressive Party and the Civil

Rights Congress. To Marge, it was simply unimaginable to have found such a secure harbor.

»«

IN FEBRUARY 1952, Decca's sister Deborah, the Duchess of Devonshire, arrived in California. Decca was thrilled to see Debo, although naturally a bit apprehensive. She hadn't much time to be reflective. Her sister would have to take her as she found her, particularly busy with campaigns to defend the Smith Act victims, integrate veterans housing, and free Jerry Newson. She had been organizing fund-raisers—a picnic for the *People's Daily World* and a benefit Paul Robeson concert.

The sisters, companions in their childhood-invented "Hons" society, had once been very close. They had kept in contact, but missed each other's weddings, the births of their children, and assorted sorrows, including— not to understate the case—a world war. When they were children, Decca had wished to run away to join the Communists and Debo had wished to marry a duke. Early in the visit, the two sisters, with so little of their grown-up life in common, relied on their reminiscences. Decca said she and Debo saw themselves "back in the Hons' cupboard, our secret meeting place at Swinbrook, talking our secret language." Over the succeeding days, although Decca was always very busy, she was excited to show off the world in which she now moved. Debo—judging from the first letters she wrote from California—seemed stunned by Decca's new world.

Decca and friends shared a "fortress mentality," made necessary, they believed, by the way the citizens of that other, parallel America treated them. They felt their community was threatened with annihilation. It was a harsh time, and the political landscape impossible to explain to those not subject to it.

Dukes and duchesses are the top tier of British nobility. Their formal title of address is "Your Grace." The Dukedom of Devonshire holds huge estates in England and Ireland, and the family's possessions include some

of the world's great art treasures, homes, and paintings. Debo, though well
traveled and sophisticated, knew very little of the kind of carefully budgeted
life that her sister was then living. Duchesses rarely cleaned their mansions
themselves (which Decca agreed was one of the title's great benefits); their
food was typically prepared by others; their own and their children's clothes
were washed and ironed for them. Children had nannies and governesses
and sometimes tutors and traditionally were sent away to school. They
were not, as Debo found her niece and nephews, zigzagging with dogs and
companions through their "little suburban house," cheek by jowl with toys
and books and papers and ephemera. Among Decca's set, babysitting was
a community endeavor, and there was usually some drop-in company at
meals—the kids' friends or some visiting comrades. Every space was usually
occupied, every surface covered. At the time of the duchess's visit, there was
another family camping out in the Treuhafts' basement while they house-
hunted in the neighborhood.

February is the rainy season in Northern California, but on fine days,
people often will leave their doors open to the street, and children will run
barefoot in the front yards and gardens. On rainy days, a small house can
feel cozy or claustrophobic. The Treuhaft home sometimes smelled of wet
dog fur, a pastiche of burned pots, children's unwashed laundry, and bus-
tling activists in close proximity. Its odor was particularly irksome to Debo,
who wrote of it to Diana, the one person who would surely have lent a sympathetic ear to the subject of Decca's decline. Decca's beautiful complexion had faded; their sister's American accent was as shocking as the slang
she used. Debo didn't quite know what to think of Bob. And although her
nephew Nicky was "rather sweet," he resembled the urchins in American
movies. Only Dinky seemed salvageable—"she is *heaven*." These impressions Debo later admitted were all at first sight.

Over the course of Debo's visit, both sisters adapted and even enjoyed
themselves to some extent. Amused at times by the gap between their worlds,
Decca wrote to Muv that she loved having her sister around, and introduced her to many friends, "although they couldn't quite make each other

out." The Treuhafts hosted a feast (the ticket of that social season) at which the Duchess of Devonshire was guest of honor. At each table, the guests rose one by one to be introduced. They did it "CP fashion," Decca wrote later, "in which one indicates the area of a person's political work: 'This is Andy Johnson, he's active in the Youth Movement. Phyllis Mander, active in the Peace Committee. Dr. Pierson, active in the CRC.'" The duchess was beautiful and charmed the assembled company (who'd had no idea what to expect) by her curiosity and surprising lack of pretentiousness. Debo could be as funny as her sister and, on Christmas, sent the Treuhafts a formal photo of "herself and Andrew, dressed in ducal robes . . . staring stonily ahead. Under the photo she had written: 'Andrew & me being active.'"

》《

AFTER DEBO LEFT in early March, Decca and the CRC joined a pivotal battle to integrate the suburbs. Northern California had absorbed a huge population during the war, but much of its temporary war housing had become dilapidated. Despite a housing boom, most communities remained segregated, enforced by custom and the malevolent legal clause known as a restrictive covenant, which promised the white home-buyer that his or her new neighborhood would remain exclusively Caucasian.

To Decca, this was the kind of situation for which she'd been training. It wasn't Mississippi, and here on her home field, she was perfectly prepared. When she heard about the Gary family under threat for moving into a white neighborhood in the nearby town of Richmond, she mobilized her telephone trees, her committees, and her publicity. Within an hour, a dozen carloads of black and white volunteers arrived to help protect the Gary family and protest against segregation in California.

Wilbur Gary was a black U.S. Navy veteran. He and his wife, Borece, lived with their seven children in an apartment built to house war workers. They looked for a new home, and when a navy friend offered his house in Rollingwood, the Garys made their move into what had previously been an all-white community. The Board of Directors of Rollingwood immediately issued a letter asserting their right to exclude whomever they wished from their neighborhood and offered to purchase the Garys' home at an inflated price. Their offer was quickly refused.

On the day the Gary family moved to Rollingwood, a few white neighbors joined Wilbur and his two oldest sons inside their new house. They barricaded the doors and prepared for a siege. Outside, an angry crowd gathered to shout and taunt. Decca and Buddy Green walked through the mob, past a few cops who "stood idly by watching the scene." Buddy saw an improvised paper cross burning in the front yard and bystanders "throwing garbage and other things." A reporter on the scene described Borece Gary's response when someone in the crowd shouted, "'Get out nigger or we'll burn your house down.' Facing the mob, she declared, 'If you do, then as soon as the ashes cool, my family and I will come back and live on the empty lot.'"

By that evening, over four hundred people came to Rollingwood in caravans from the CRC, the labor unions, the National Association for the Advancement of Colored People, local churches, PTAs, and civic organizations; they came with petitions to the governor, to the mayor, asking the board of supervisors to provide around-the-clock protection for the Gary family and their home. Constance Gary, who was nine years old at the time, remembered a troop of brave high school students who joined the vigil, friends of her older brother and sister.

Two days after the protests began, a leader in the Rollingwood Improvement Association arrived at the Garys' house "with a petition signed by him and twenty-one other neighbors welcoming the Negro family to their new home." The opposition never had a prayer. What a rare victory it must have been! The thrill was mitigated only by the impossibility of claiming victory for the party's role. Any hint of affiliation with the Communist Party could lose Gary his job. Still, Decca wrote, "we wanted to take credit."

CHAPTER 18

IN 1953, DECCA was often engaged in some project or another to raise money or raise awareness for different causes: a concert to protest unfair deportations; a fund drive for the "Let Citizens Travel" campaign (on behalf of those whose passports had been confiscated or denied); a picnic or a dance for the always-financially-strapped *People's Daily World*. These causes were crucial, but among Decca's friends, the most urgent work that year by far was to stop the executions of Julius and Ethel Rosenberg. For the Treuhafts and other party members, the international campaign to save the Rosenbergs was a family affair.

In 1950, Ethel Rosenberg's younger brother David Greenglass, a low-level employee at the nuclear laboratory in Los Alamos, New Mexico—confessed to the FBI that he had passed secret documents to his brother-in-law Julius Rosenberg. Julius and Ethel were arrested and accused of conspiracy to commit espionage. The case against Ethel was slight, but the federal prosecutor's strategy was to hold her as a political hostage until Julius would make a deal: either to confess and name bigger fish in the conspiracy, or provide enough information to ransom his wife. At their 1951 trial, both Rosenbergs said they were innocent, and would not cooperate. Meanwhile, Ruth Greenglass (David's wife) testified that Ethel had typed the notes containing the state secrets that David had stolen. This putative connection was all the government needed to declare Ethel an active conspirator, as guilty as her husband.

Ethel, it has been generally acknowledged by even avid Commie-hunters, committed a mysterious kind of suttee. She might have saved herself, but would not repudiate her husband or allow others to say she had.

She and Julius understood that their crime was not that of treason, but of being Communists in America in 1953.

In 2008, after Ruth's death, David Greenglass admitted that during his sister's trial, he and his wife had lied under oath. Ethel Rosenberg had not typed any top-secret documents. (In the fall of 2008, Morton Sobol, age ninety-two and an associate of Julius Rosenberg's who had served nineteen years for espionage, admitted that he and Julius had passed on some non-nuclear information to the Soviets. They had done so, he said, before the cold war, when the Soviet Union and the United States had been allies.) Ethel had not participated.

FROM OAKLAND, TWELVE-YEAR-OLD Dinky wrote to Winston Churchill to ask her great-uncle to stop the executions, but he never answered. The cata-strophic outcome of the campaign was, for many of the "red diaper" chil-dren engaged in it, a traumatic lesson in the raw exercise of power. Many of the Rosenbergs' young defenders felt like the traumatized refugees of a sacked army. For some, the experience laid bare the obvious imbalance of power between their parents and the great, threatening, adversarial world in which they made their home, went to high school, and listened to Billie Holiday, Bobby Darin, and Howlin' Wolf. The secrets of the persecuted both terrorized and mobilized them.

On the day of the execution, June 19, 1953, Carl Bernstein, the future journalist, was nine years old. He stood with his family in front of the White House, among

> thousands and thousands of people, the crowd overflowing into
> Lafayette Square . . . Pictures of Julius and Ethel Rosenberg and of
> their sons, solemnly held aloft. A sense of helplessness and doom
> mitigated only by faith, by some desperate belief that nothing as
> terrible as this would be permitted to happen, that some law of
> humanity or the universe would intervene, that clemency would
> be granted at the last moment . . . If the phone rang before eight

o'clock, it meant that Eisenhower had granted clemency. A radio played. Eight o'clock came and went. Then the phone rang. They were dead. At first people wept quietly. Then everyone in the room was sobbing, wailing, and some people got sick. I remember the man on the radio said that all the lights around Ossining had dimmed when they threw the switch.

Pele deLappe was with her new husband, Steve Murdock; her nine-year-old son, Pete; and Decca and Bob's nine-year-old son, Nicky, when they heard the news in the public campgrounds at Yellowstone National Park. Pele described the emotional disconnect: "After a cold two weeks sleeping outside within sight and sounds of bears and the odd moose, we emerged half frozen from the woods in June to face the shocking headline: Rosenbergs executed. How to explain such a horror to two little boys, both of them Jewish? In shock and despair ourselves, we did our inadequate best."

Shortly after the Rosenbergs' execution, Albert Einstein urged "every intellectual called before the committee to refuse to testify, [to] be prepared for jail or economic ruin, for the sacrifice of his personal welfare in the interest of the country's cultural welfare." Witnesses and lawyers tried in various ways to speak or read statements that questioned the hearing process, but the powers vested in the committee meant that few defiant words could be heard above the chairman's gavel.

》《

IN 1953, WHEN Decca was thirty-six, she and Bob received subpoenas to appear before the federal HUAC hearings in San Francisco. Bob had the idea to build his defense around the proposition that in the atmosphere of fear and shame, few lawyers were willing to sacrifice their own practice and livelihood to defend people accused of subversion. In the weeks leading up to his court appearance, he embarked on a case study to prove the point.

Instead of engaging a National Lawyers Guild colleague, he made a list of seven prospective defense counselors. His visits to these men recall the tale of *Goldilocks and the Three Bears*. One attorney demurred on the grounds that he hadn't enough gravitas. Another, silver-haired and dignified, thought he hadn't the stamina. A third, energetic, mature, and confident man said yes, he would indeed take on Bob's case and would relish the opportunity. Several days before the hearing, however, he phoned Bob in distress. His law partner, he said, had threatened to jump out the window if their firm represented Bob in the HUAC hearings. It wasn't Bob's politics; it was the scrutiny their firm would receive thereafter by the Internal Revenue Service. There was always a man from the Treasury sitting in all these hearings, taking notes. The law partner would jump, Bob's would-be attorney said, so fearful was he of a tax audit.

Decca trekked back to her children's school to explain their situation. She and Bob would be testifying before HUAC again. They had no idea what consequences there might be. The teachers she met were sympathetic and assured her that they would "give the kids extra care & attention while the hearings were on."

In their parents' absence, Dinky would cope with the assistance of various neighbors and friends. She was a star student in junior high. "The most strongminded and determined child I ever saw once she makes her mind up, she's just exactly like Esmond," Decca wrote to Muv. Nicholas was also coming into his own. He was the kind of youngster who went into raptures over gadgets, an experimenter. He was quick and quieter than little Benjy, who when his parents were otherwise occupied, feasted on mustard and jam sandwiches.

Decca wasn't called to testify this time, but her subpoena required that she attend all five days of the hearings: a disgraceful spectacle, during which the friendly witnesses "served up more than 300 names."

The committee counsel's first question to Bob was, "Are you accompanied by counsel?" Bob replied that he would answer (as opposed to taking the Fifth) and began to read a three-page statement. Statements were typically gaveled down, and a committee member interrupted with, "You'll have to submit that."

"I am answering the question," Bob pointed out. "I was asked whether I had counsel?" The committee conferred and, to everyone's surprise, allowed Bob to explain what prevented him from securing the counsel of his choice. "What a shameful thing it was that I, a lawyer, was unable to get counsel, and how much worse," he went on, for the unfortunate with even fewer connections and expertise. Bob was, Decca wrote, "determined to reveal through his testimony the full extent to which the Committee had succeeded in terrorizing the bar."

"Everyone was breathless," as Bob read his indictment of the committee and its methods. Afterward, "there was terrific cheering & applause," Decca told Aranka. Her son's testimony had been heroic, and also historic—a rare triumph for any witness to make it all the way through a prepared statement. There would be only a few times, over the course of a great many hearings nationwide, when an unfriendly witness would get the chance to speak honestly, in effect to disprove the perception that he or she was a hostile demon. Outside the courtroom, Bob's friends congratulated him. They hoped this day's work opened a crack in the power of the inquisition. Then they waited like the actors in an opening show to see how the mainstream press would review the performance. Headlines pronounced Bob's testimony "The Day's Stormiest."

>«

ONE NIGHT, DECCA arrived early for a CRC meeting at Codornices Village. She planned to do a little leafleting in advance, as she often did. It was dusk. At first, she would run into workers returning home. Most people were friendly and polite and accepted leaflets. The older folks looked weary. They wanted their dinner. The younger ones had other things on their mind—lovers, friends. Some said they'd think about the meeting; some said they'd come. As the lights in the apartments switched on, Decca could see that she had wandered farther afield. Everyone had gone inside. There was no one else in sight, and it had become very quiet, just the night birds singing. A pleasant interlude between the frantic activity of her day and the meeting that night, which like so many others would start as routine and become something exciting as their discussion grew more heated. You never knew who might show up and how they might change the chemistry. She meandered back toward the lights. The benches in the distance were empty of their usual occupants, kids who sucked endless cigarettes and whistled at the pretty girls.

She didn't see the man who pulled her down to the dry creek bed. It happened so quickly, she didn't scream, and then he had covered her mouth. He was a black man in his midtwenties, unkempt, dressed in a motley arrangement that included a dirty army jacket. He had a crazy, wild look, and he muttered that if she screamed, he'd kill her. She nodded and whispered yes, but asked him, was he a veteran? He had begun to pull at her clothes and told her to shut up. She kept talking, calmly. Had he heard of the case of Willie McGee? She had been to Mississippi. Korea must have been horrible for him. She had opposed the war. He mustn't think she was his enemy. He told her she was crazy. She sympathized with his anger and frustration, she said. Why not come along to the CRC meeting? There would be other women there far younger and prettier. He pushed and clawed and she kept talking. All this took just a minute or two, and her luck held. Above them on the creek side, they heard Bob's voice and others calling out to her. Her attacker pushed her and ran in the other direction. She shouted for Bob.

Soon after, she told her friends what had happened. Her friend Marge Frantz said Decca had "escaped by her wits," and Decca was justifiably proud of herself. Dobby remembered the incident, but Decca hadn't made a big deal about it.

Over the years, the story of her attack mutated according to Decca's audience and the degree of vodka involved. Catherine "Katie" Edwards, Decca's assistant, heard of her "narrow escape" and of Bob's arrival in the nick of time (and her irritation that he hadn't come earlier). Decca told her friend, the young writer and political philosopher Bettina Aptheker, a different version. She said she offered her attacker the name of her friend Billie Wachter (with whom she'd traveled to Mississippi). In the heat of the moment, the reference made sense—Wachter was an activist in the peace movement. Decca thought, if her attacker were a veteran, he too would be sick of war. The point of it all was to keep talking, distract him, and negotiate if possible. In the version Decca told Bettina, she was raped. She heard no comforting voices searching the creek side, she made no narrow escape, and "it was bloody uncomfortable." Afterward, Bettina said, Decca made her way from the creek to the home of her doctor, Ephraim Kahn, who examined her and gave her some kind of shot.

The violence surrounding such an experience must have been terrifying, but there are no letters from the time reflecting any trauma. Kathy Kahn, Ephraim's daughter, knew nothing of that visit, but she too had heard a version of the story, which ended, "'So I told him to hurry up and get it over with, and he did,' or words to that effect in Decc-ese." Decca had always been adept at suppressing horrors or turning them into tall tales.

Peter Sussman, the editor of her letters, "puzzled over the rape story too." The only reference Sussman found was in an exchange of letters years later between Decca and her cousin Ann Farrer Horne. Decca contrasted Ann's indifference to newspapers with her own passion for them:

> I could hardly pry my eyes open in the a.m. were it not for the S. F. Chronicle clattering on the porch; although I admit most of it is not only v. boring but v. forgettable. Once years ago, when I was about 30 & thought I might be dead soon (near-raped in a rather dismal creek . . .) I'm sorry to say that my Last Thoughts (as I thought they might be) were not so much for Bob & children as "I'll never see tomorrow's paper."

>«

DECCA'S SISTER PAM had been living in Ireland, but she traveled a good deal and lived much of the year in Switzerland. Nancy and Diana lived in France.

Debo had vast country estates and a grand home in London and had joined the ranks of frequent flyers for which the expression *jet-setters* would be coined in the decade to come. Decca thought it would be nice to get out of the house. She wasn't envious of her sisters' affluence, but she did think it "*frightfully* unfair" when she heard Nancy had plans to visit Russia.

In February 1954, Decca told her mother the "outlook is gloomy" for any trip to England. She and Bob had applied, but there was little hope of being issued passports. Decca rarely felt she was entirely without options. She asked her Muv to please "ring up Cousin Winston & tell him we just want to come for a visit, no politics, and see if he can't arrange it?" When Bob was in Washington, D.C., on business, he also made a stab at invoking special privilege through Esmond's mother, Nellie. "Winston Churchill's sister-in-law was most anxious to see her grandchild," he told the immigration official, who was unimpressed. An FBI special agent assigned to gather information on Decca was following this story closely. He entered the following into her file:

> Note from clerk to Mrs. Shipley, head of passports. Mrs. Shipley, Robert E. Treuhaft (orange card case now pending) wants to see personally re his proposed trip to England. Says his wife is related to British Churchills (Winstons) . . . told him I didn't know when you would be back or whether you would have time to see him.

The CRC was on its last legs. There was always someone watching or listening. From the trenches, England, where a Communist was just another person with a political tic, must have looked like a fantastic holiday to Decca. Muv wrote back that she couldn't ask that kind of favor of Cousin Winston. She also told Decca that Esmond's mother was dying. In her reply, Decca asked her Muv for some advice on protocol and enclosed a note for Nellie Romilly:

> Thinking to give her a little news of Dinky; but then I thought, perhaps she will construe it as hinting about the will, (if any). Also,

perhaps she is dead by now. Anyway, will you use your judgment as to if it should be forwarded, you might even tell her definitely it is NOT hinting about the Will. Oh dear, life is so complicated.

The Treuhafts' life was circumscribed, but they made the best of things. Decca sometimes missed the city lights and throngs. Although San Francisco had its own sophistication, it wasn't London. Hiking was an inexpensive consolation for friends Pele and Dobby, but the beauties of the vast wilderness didn't hold the same delight for Decca, who had grown up on the more domesticated beauty of the English Cotswolds. When Dobby did manage to get Decca out on an excursion once in the High Sierras, it wasn't a success. Their plan was to camp and hike for seventy miles over two weeks. The nights would be cold and the days often very hot, but it would at least be a relief to leave the struggle twelve thousand feet below.

To save money when preparing for the trip, Decca bought her hiking boots out of two different bins in the Army Navy store and very soon developed blisters on the trail. When she wasn't able to walk anymore, she rode atop a supply horse alongside a mountain cliff's steep drop-off. Decca didn't care for horseback riding, and she didn't like heights. The whole thing was more an ordeal than a holiday. When they returned to the Berkeley flatlands, she and Bob held a party to celebrate her survival. Their guests, invited to attend in hiking clothes, were treated to a commemorative ode that included the line "Nature, nature [pronounced "nate-cha"], how I hate ya."

That spring, McCarthy was in the last stages of self-destruction. The senator accused the secretary of the army and assorted generals and admirals of the U.S. armed forces of "coddling communists" in their ranks. The Army-McCarthy hearings were televised, and marketing geniuses everywhere learned quickly that a sweating, red-faced drunk in a wool suit spewing poison did not project heroic values, even when hunting red devils.

"The tide here seems to be turning somewhat politically," Decca wrote to Muv. The Army-McCarthy hearings had concluded with McCarthy's chastisement. Decca and her friends didn't think the persecution of Communists would end overnight, but, she told her mother, "perhaps in the next few years we'll be able to come to England after all. At least jail & concentration camps look a bit further off now than a few months ago."

In the time leading up to Bob's testimony before the "Beastly Un-American Committee" (as Decca called it), the Treuhafts had taken for granted that they, like others, would suffer more financial hardship. They thought Bob might lose his law practice as others had. Instead, he had become something of a local hero, partly for his testimony before HUAC, but mainly as a stalwart opponent of the Oakland Police Department.

One day, a middle-aged woman came to Bob's law office asking for counsel for her eighteen-year-old son. He'd been arrested on gang rape charges and was being held at City Hall. Bob took the case, but when he arrived to meet his client, the officer on duty told him, "He's not in jail now." After some wrangling, the officer admitted that the young man was in District Attorney Frank Coakley's office.

Bob argued that his client was being interrogated illegally and demanded to be brought to him. The police delayed him with excuses, and as Bob and his client's mother kept vigil outside the district attorney's office, they were joined by other lawyers and civil servants and court reporters. Bob repeatedly knocked on Coakley's door and, through the keyhole, saw the legs of several people, all of whom froze at the sound of his voice (like children playing statues). Eventually, an officer cracked open the door and snarled, *Go away*, as he shoved Bob across the floor to the far railing. Rushing back, Bob crashed his foot through the bottom pane of the frosted glass door and then stuck his head inside in time to see Frank Coakley and other officers of the court vanish out another exit. Bob's client was soon back in his jail cell with a harrowing tale of illegal detention and intimidation. Decca thought her husband a hero for having exposed Coakley in his lair.

CHAPTER 19

I N A LETTER sent on Valentine's Day 1955, thirteen-year-old Dinky informed her grandmother Aranka that she would thereafter be signing her name with two *i*'s, and also that "Nicky has a paper route with The Oakland Tribune now. He gets 19$ a month."

The following afternoon, ten-year-old Nicky was riding his bike delivering papers when a speeding bus hit and killed him instantly. Dinky had been walking home from school when some children who had seen the accident shouted that her brother had been run over. She ran to Nicky and stayed until the ambulance came. Some neighbors had also gathered, and Dinky overheard one woman say, "If Mrs. Treuhaft was home more, this wouldn't have happened." Dinky jumped at the woman, scratching and screaming, until the others pulled them apart.

This was the hour when Decca was driving home from work. Their friends had begun to gather in front of the house, and she knew at once from their sober faces that something was horribly wrong. She rolled down the car window. "What happened, what happened to the children?!" People kept coming over all evening, and the police came to make their report. "Bob was in one room and Decca in another," Dinky remembered. "They couldn't talk to one another." The following day, Decca sent this telegram:

> darling mother nicholas was killed yesterday by a bus while riding
> his bicycle funeral is friday afternoon dinky and benjamin taking
> it wonderfully will write soon going to country for a few days bob
> mother coming please don't worry we are alright our friends are
> with us best love decca

About two hundred people attended Nicky's funeral. There was a big white coffin and flowered wreaths. Pele thought the formality and remote ritual of the event was contrary to the Treuhafts' taste, but neither Bob nor Decca was in any condition to object. Dobby was at the service, too, and afterward accompanied the family to the gravesite in Guerneville, not far from where Decca and Bob had married. Afterward, they held a memorial dinner at the home of some friends near the Russian River.

"Darling Muv," Decca wrote from Sonoma County,

> He didn't suffer, was killed almost instantly. He was one of the sweetest children I ever knew, kind & generous, everyone loved him. His teacher couldn't go to school the next day, she was so upset. Dinky, Benjy & all our friends are making things bearable. Don't worry about us, we are all right . . .

Nicky had enjoyed a sweet nature and inquiring turn of mind that intimated the man he might have become. The December before, he had spent endless hours helping "Low Price Al" sell Christmas trees in a nearby lot. He "never got a cent for all that arduous child labor," Pele said, which led her to fondly call him "No Price Nick." Aranka had felt a special connection to this grandchild, which he had reciprocated. Once, hearing that Aranka would be coming to visit in a few weeks, Nicky made up Benjy's bed with fresh sheets and sent his little brother to sleep in the closet with orders to stay there until their grandmother arrived. Nicky had stayed with her in New York over the previous summer, when they had explored the various science and history museums. He'd been such good company she had planned to bring him along on her next junket to Paris.

Decca's friends marveled at how she coped. They would have understood if she had demonstrated a more public, lavish grief. If at any time she blamed Bob, blamed herself, or raged at her fate, she did so out of sight of friends, who saw her only as "stoic." She drank a lot, but then again, she often did. "Brave Little D," Muv had called her after Esmond died. Decca confided in Pele once and only briefly about Julia, the baby she and Esmond had lost to illness. This tragedy, like that and all the others, had to be borne. She stayed in the house for a month after Nicky's funeral. She had caught a bad flu and then passed it to the children, so there was nursing to keep her busy. Benjy's illness persisted for so long that Bob and Decca began to consider it "unexpressed unhappiness."

Decca buried what she could and railed instead at dramatic sorrow. Her mother-in-law's nature was to be more extravagant in her grief, and back in New York, Aranka wrote a series of letters to Decca and Bob detailing her loneliness and pain. Bob wrote frequently to commiserate with his mother, but Aranka's lamentations tried Decca's patience. The younger woman didn't have the words to console her mother-in-law and felt that her first duty was to Dinky and Benjy. A month after Nicky's death, she wrote to Aranka:

> The only way we can possibly repay all the people who were so wonderfully kind and did so much, is to prove to them that they did help, & one can only do this by living a normal life which includes laughter and happiness—(Anyhow, one can't live any other way—for long)—We have bad problems too, but we are trying to overcome them, as I'm sure you are.

Aranka's other grandchildren might offer some consolation and keep her occupied, Decca wrote, "if you'd let them."

Bob went back to work, but Decca's job had all but vanished in her absence. As much as she wished it could still dig itself out, the Civil Rights Congress had been decimated: attacked as a Communist front, its funding dried up, its national leaders imprisoned, and its members' list lately composed of more agents than Communists. Any one of those spying agents (without hearts of stone) might have recorded in her file, *Subject presents little threat now*. Decca simply hadn't the energy or the optimism to rouse the troops. For both Treuhafts, this was a moment of dormancy, with all happiness deferred. And yet there had to be food for the children, clean clothes, homework. Longing and loneliness were the themes of daily life.

IN MAY, BOB reapplied for their passports, fully expecting them to be denied as usual. Twelve weeks later, the Treuhaft family received these "magic document[s]" in the mail. The occasion was as "unbelievable and stunning as winning the Irish Sweepstakes." After sixteen years, Decca desperately wanted to go home. She wanted to see her family and "was longing to stay as long as possible."

Fearful that the passports had been issued by some mistake, a newly adrenalized Decca planned the family's getaway like a secret military campaign. They immediately booked passage on a French ocean liner, the *Flandre*, from New York. Dinky was sent ahead to stay with Aranka in New York until Decca and Benjy arrived by a later cross-country train. Bob would take a plane, and they'd all rendezvous just before boarding the boat.

This signaled a new turn, something so surprising, unexpected, and good that Decca and Bob's friends, who had shared their grief, now shared their exultation through a series of dinners and parties with cakes in the shape of ships. Bob and Decca would be missed, of course, but who couldn't help but think that if there were a synonym for *miracle* in the Marxist lexicon, it would have to be *fortuitous mistake* or *beautiful escape*. At one of their bon voyage parties, which had been given by the Crawfords (a family of intellectuals and labor activists with ties to the Harlem Renaissance), Decca fell into conversation with their host's daughter. Nebby Lou Crawford "at the discontented age of seventeen was madly jealous of Dinky's good fortune." Decca, feeling sympathetic and enthusiastic now and as always tending to the philosophy of the more the merrier, spontaneously invited Nebby Lou to join her family on their European travels.

It must have seemed a dreamlike excursion, crossing the country again. While eight-year-old Benjy and Nebby Lou amused themselves with endless games of cards, Decca sat alone to contemplate the prospect of her return. The constant battle to make things work had stretched the little money they had. They hadn't much to travel on, but there was still a bit in England in her running-away account. Over the years, she had tried to withdraw the balance, but had always been stymied. Ironic now that it would be there to welcome her home, all the time accumulating interest at Drummonds Bank.

Aranka rushed to meet Decca and company at the New York train station. She had dramatic news. Their friends had telephoned to say a telegram had arrived at the Treuhaft house in Oakland. Dated August 16, 1955, it read

> regret your passport issued in error and validity thereof suspended pending determination your eligibility under regulations. please do not use pending further communication. letter follows francis knight director ppt office.

The government was demanding their passports back, and now there were agents on their trail to retrieve them. Even if they'd imagined that scenario a thousand times, it still must have felt like a cosmic joke when proved true. Bob had jumped on a red-eye from San Francisco and would be there any minute. Meanwhile, they would hide out at Bob's sister Edith's apartment.

Decca recounted their evasion of authorities as a kind of Marx Brothers comedy of mistaken identities and ships' gangways pulled away at the last minute. Everyone must have been operating on a kind of jittery, caffeinated intensity that made them forget everything else but the action at that instant. Decca had a talent for organizing under duress, and she and Bob and Aranka combined their considerable resources to plot a clandestine escape. Aranka volunteered to keep Benjy with her. They couldn't use their tickets on the *Flandre*, since it would be watched. No warrant had yet been served, so as long as they could avoid one and they held their passports, their travel remained ostensibly legal. They looked for any kind of immediate transport. The next day, Bob found the last cabin on the French ocean liner *Liberté*. They were out of money, but generously, Aranka bought them tickets and cabins.

As they pulled out of the harbor, leaving behind the Statue of Liberty, they celebrated their narrow escape with champagne. Out in international

waters, Decca and Bob shed their status of rebels and renegades and felt
for the first time in years unscrutinized, out from under their fortress
mentality.

On the crossing, Dinky and Nebby Lou had their own independent
adventures while Decca and Bob consoled each other. "There were no tears
on the trip," at least when Dinky was around. "We all pushed it away. That
was our family style."

>«

DECCA HAD BEEN away from England for sixteen years. As she reunited
with family and friends, she remarked on how much her contemporaries
had changed while the older people like Muv and Nanny seemed to have
stayed the same. (Perhaps, she said, because they had always seemed so old
to her.)

Debo met them in London accompanied by her young son and daughter. Thus assembled, the company took the monumental trip up to Inch
Kenneth. The train ride showed Decca "the half remembered English
countryside, so green, so rolling, so carefully cultivated, so unlike the
bare brown hills of California." (However much she liked California,
she never thought much of those brown hills.) Muv called this reunion
with her children and grandchildren "one of the happiest moments of my
life," and Decca felt the same. She had succeeded in putting thousands
of miles between herself and the life she had made—which had in recent
years become one of endurance and struggle and then, recently, anguish
after Nicky's death. Her mother knew what it was like to lose a son. On
Inch Kenneth, Decca could slough off some of her burden long enough to
simply accept her mother's comfort and consolation. Later she would say,
"There was something rather amazing about her unreserved loyalty to all
the children, even me! And anyhow, Bob was fascinated by all this, he'd
never seen anything like Inch Kenneth, or my mother's way of life." Muv
would economize by eliminating napkins at meals, but she would send the

rest of her linens, round trip by train, to be laundered by Harrods department store in London. She also "sent dirty banknotes to Harrods' bank to be exchanged for nice crisp new ones."

His mother-in-law's way of life was "an extremely slow one but not uncomfortable," Bob understated in a letter home. "Muv's lonely barren life here is relieved, we find, by six servants (a cook, a housemaid, a boatman and 3 others to take care of the sheep, cattle and goats) the house is large and comfortable (10 bedrooms and 4 modern bathrooms) with substantial outbuildings for servants, live-stock, etc. Also standing on the island are impressive ruins of a fifth century church and graveyard."

For Decca, the place was full of ghosts:

> Everywhere were reminders of childhood, transplanted from Swinbrook . . . the six drawings of us sisters done by William Acton in 1934, framed in dark pink brocade; the carved round breadboards that my mother bought for 2/6 apiece from a Cotswolds artisan; the bound sheet music of songs we used to sing in the thirties . . . Boud's gramophone records of Nazi songs: "*Horst Wessel Lied*," "*Die Wacht am Rheim*"; above all, Muv's scrapbooks . . . arranged by subject . . . press clippings about the family and photographs, one of various weddings, another of family groups from 1904 when Nancy was born, to the mid-thirties, when one by one we went our separate ways.

Leaving the island and Muv (with plans to see her again in London), the company went to Chatsworth, the Devonshires' estate, which Bob described as "very comfortable, just a little bit bigger than Versailles." The house would stand in for Pemberley in a remake of the film *Pride and Prejudice*, inspiring one reviewer to describe Chatsworth as "the size of a small planet."

A greater contrast to the Treuhafts' family life would be hard to imagine. Debo had noted her distress at her sister's domestic life when she had visited Oakland in 1950, and now it was Decca's turn. "I had come back to a different world, and a largely different family," she would write. Looking through Debo's wedding scrapbook Decca found, next to Queen Elizabeth's formal congratulations, her own telegram offering "HONNISH CONGRATULATIONS ON A SUCCESSFUL SEASON'S DUKE HUNTING" Decca had never been one to wallow in Marxist self-abnegation; she was anything but austere. She could delight in a formal garden, an eighteenth-century tea tray, but because of the battles she had so recently fought, it was sometimes hard to relax in such surroundings. She still adored playing funny word games and singing silly songs, but she often seemed humorless to Debo. Sisters may sympathize: Both Debo and Decca shared the anguish of having lost babies. And sisters may judge: The duchess looked at the people's representative and found her short haircut unbecoming, her trousers masculine, and her chain smoking deplorable. The gap between them seemed vast.

Through much of her visit, Decca suffered what she called an agony of ambivalence: "Having taken such pains to get away from them . . . I had longed to see them, yet found myself constrained in their company, awkwardly separated by the twin gulfs of time and outlook. They were wonderful hosts and I was not a good guest." She was ill at ease regarding how her family and friends might treat her husband. Bob, overall smarter and better educated than most of the aristocrats he encountered, didn't care much what they thought of him except in the way it might affect Decca. Of course, he knew he must have been compared to Esmond (who might not have been particularly popular but who had still been one of them). Decca said, "Actually Bob fared better than I did. For him, my family was a hilarious spectator sport."

She and Bob visited the Communist Party headquarters and tracked down old friends like Philip Toynbee. In 1954, Toynbee had published a portrait of the young Decca in his affectionate memoir of Esmond Romilly called *Friends Apart*. She admired his book, and at their reunion, they picked up their friendship, easily teasing and sparring as they had in their youth. Decca was "dazzled by the openness and ease with which the Party functioned in the relatively free air of England." If she felt a smidgen of regret that she had not remained where things were a bit easier, she also recognized that life in California had pushed her to greater adventure and further courage—the House Committee on Un-American Activities had in effect made Decca American.

Decca had been looking forward to her reunion with Giles Romilly. Both she and Esmond had adored Giles. In his youth, he had been a "brilliant, attractive person," and their reunion was a shock to her. He was exactly her age, thirty-seven, but looked twice as old. Life had been difficult for Giles. Decca blamed the doctor who treated him after the war for prescribing the barbiturates to which she thought Giles was "hopelessly addicted."

Nellie Romilly had died leaving Decca and Dinky disinherited. But Giles was sympathetic and wanted to help Decca financially if he could. Meanwhile, the Romillys' lawyer conceded that Nellie had made some kind of error regarding Decca's inheritance, the consequences of which remained unclear. To her sister Nancy, Decca explained, "It seems the Romillies wrote their wills out all wrong and as a result they didn't succeed in cutting me off." Decca claimed she was "inheritance prone" in the way some people are "accident prone."

MEANWHILE, MUV STILL hoped to reconcile her family, but Decca categorically refused to meet Diana. Toynbee asked if she didn't out of "sheer curiosity" want to see her sister again? Whatever curiosity she once had felt had long since soured by the colossal disappointment she felt for the older sister she'd adored. And what about Farve? He told Muv he was willing to meet. He might have enjoyed, among other things, the chance to revisit her audacious effort to donate her portion of Inch Kenneth to the Communist Party—a subject that angered him to the day he died. Decca consulted Bob and Dinky, both of whom encouraged her to see her father, but Decca "wasn't all that keen." Although she said, "I'd have been quite interested to see him. I offered to see him," she stipulated that he not take the opportunity to shout at Bob or Dinky. Muv said those were "impossible conditions" and dropped the subject. Over thirty years later, Decca would say, "When you've had this much of a break, and when you've had this much bitterness going on, there's no real point in exacerbating it."

Lord Redesdale was as mercurial as his daughter was tough-minded. Toward the end of his life, Nancy was playing a parlor game with her father. "Whom would you like best to see coming round the door," she asked.

"Decca," he said.

»«

THE TREUHAFTS WANTED to visit Hungary. Just as Decca felt nostalgia for the prewar Lyons tea shops, where she'd loitered when employed as a market researcher, Bob had a hankering for the tastes and sensations of his grandparents' village. At first, it looked as though he wouldn't get his wish. American Communists had no clout, and the Treuhafts' visas were stalled indefinitely until one small deceit set off a chain reaction in their favor. In casual conversation with the Hungarian consulate in Austria, Bob mentioned that their ward, Nebby Lou, who was Paul Robeson's niece, especially wished to visit Hungary. (This wasn't strictly true—but Robeson *was* a close friend of the Crawford family.) The great singer's celebrity in the socialist world was without peer, and the Treuhafts' ties to his relation resulted in an immediate issuance of the necessary credentials. Decca and Bob felt justified to tell the white lie—certainly all they had done to promote the idea of social justice, and their sacrifices entitled them to see the "living face of Socialism."

Invited to tour model homes and factories, they found those first days exhilarating. Decca wrote an article for the *People's Daily World*, "We Visited Socialism," which reads like a giddy tourist's chronicle. She reported on their tours of a collective farm and a children's railway, the ballet and culture houses. Music and dancing abounded. At one point, Dinky was "whirling away to the strains of 'Song from Moulin Rouge' in the arms of a Hungarian army colonel. At the end of their tour, their hosts asked them to stay on a few days more until the Walt Whitman centenary, which they were surprised to discover was a holiday in Hungary. Then a waiter asked them to deliver a letter to his brother in America, and a young teacher who had implored them to meet her English-speaking husband canceled the appointment for fear of repercussions. A few more such encounters gave them clues to an undercurrent of unease, dissatisfaction, and fear, but the Treuhafts were—as tourists often are—obtuse and apparently unaware of the depth of discontent that would erupt into counterrevolution in less than a year.

While Decca, Bob, and the two girls were driving from Hungary to Paris, Nancy was suffering great misgivings about their visit. She had a settled routine of disciplined writing and, in the French capital, moved within a circle of intellectuals, politicians, and socialites. She feared the disruption of her writing routine and resented the emotional eruption her sister's visit might evoke. "How I dread their arrival," Nancy wrote to Diana.

After two days on the road, Decca and company appeared at Nancy's Parisian home on the Rue Monsieur. Marie, Nancy's housekeeper, had to uncomfortably report that Nancy had taken refuge in England with the duchess. Drama reigned. Decca phoned from Nancy's home phone, and just as she heard her sister's voice for the first time in sixteen years, Nancy hung up on her. She may just have been anxious about seeing her younger sister again and expressed this in diva fashion. Her letters from the period also demonstrate an unsupported fear that the Treuhafts, once entrenched in Paris, would never leave again. Most likely, Nancy was angry that Decca had appropriated her telephone to make what was then an expensive call between England and France. A half hour later, Nancy phoned back "on Debo's nickel," (as Bob observed), and the sisters settled in for an amiable chat.

While Bob and Nebby Lou returned to the United States, Decca and Dinky checked into an inexpensive hotel in Paris and waited for Nancy to join them. Her elder sister had sent Decca fifty British pounds for the books she said she'd taken from Decca and Esmond's flat in London after they had left for America. Decca remembered those "tattered old left-wing volumes not worth 5 shillings," and she was grateful for her sister's generosity.

Nancy was apprehensive up until their actual reunion, after which she was relieved that Decca was not a barbarian or puritan, and Dinky was pretty and well behaved. For her part, Decca was glad to report that her elder sister was still "marvelously good company" and "still funny . . . & is not a fascist or an idiot."

In the end, Decca's reunion with Nancy was a good one, full of escapist occupations and sensory delights. Dinky would watch and listen to her aunt and mother together and wonder at their voices. Nancy's accent was "a combo of plummy tones and very down-to-earth vocabulary." Decca's accent had mellowed over her years in America, but in conversation with Nancy, she spoke and shrieked as before. Decca was pleased to have this last stretch of time before her return to the United States, where she knew the FBI would immediately confiscate her passport as they had Bob's. The sisters laughed about the absurd contrasts in their lives. To the unemployed Decca, Nancy's routine as a working writer held enormous appeal.

CHAPTER 20

As a teenager, Decca had wanted to run away to a London bed-sit, and at thirty-eight, she came to feel as she had long ago at Swinbrook, bored and stymied. In 1956, she dreamed of going to Alabama to join the Montgomery bus boycott. In that case, she needed a new running-away account. She wanted a new job. The turn her life had taken away from idleness and privilege would come to mean nothing if she wasn't occupied. When she, Katharine Graham, and Binnie Straight had stayed up all night in Washington talking about how girls with position and wealth had extra responsibilities to make things happen, she'd had no idea how satisfying it would be to work hard. She could keep busy with hundreds of campaigns, but any socialite might volunteer. After all those years of studying Marxism, she knew it wasn't just a philosophical position. Her own character drove her to oppose unemployment. Certainly, nobody would criticize if she took a little time off; nobody would think her a para-site if she let Bob pay the bills for a while. But she felt burdened that he was the only breadwinner. Hanging around the house held little appeal; her talents lay elsewhere.

In late spring 1956, the advertising department of the *San Francisco Chronicle* hired her to sell classified ads. She told Muv about the funny experience she had after just a week's work, when the shop steward pointed out her name in the union paper as a new hire. He said, "I know it's such a thrill to see one's name in print in a newspaper for the first time." It was a great joke at home that the work she was doing was "highly classified." She was wildly overqualified for the job—she'd book ads, which would run, and then she'd book others. Just as in the CRC, she spent most of her day on the telephone soliciting money, and her manager was impressed with her productivity. She was exceeding expectations, and they were glad to welcome such an enthusiastic new employee. To cap it all, she won several prizes for her achievement in telephone sales. There were new colleagues to meet and coffee breaks when the gossip was about *I Love Lucy*. Best of all, and meager though it was, there was that paycheck. Years later, she confided to her young friend Anthea Fursland, "Money, besides being the root of all evil, is the root of all independence, and it's frightfully important to feel you can earn your own way."

Then, after just twelve weeks, Decca was fired. She'd held the job so briefly nobody really had to explain why she'd lost it. Her manager implied that she simply wasn't qualified. She suspected someone had gone back through old issues of the *Chronicle*, where she'd been reported over the years as an "alleged" Communist or the "red lawyer's wife." Eventually, her union confirmed that an FBI agent had visited management. Decca had the proof she needed that her manager had lied to her, and yet, "there remained a haunting suspicion that possibly I really was unqualified, in which case what was to become of me?"

〉〈

CAST ADRIFT AFTER the *Chronicle* debacle, Decca faced "the blank, awful feeling—at 38, with 40 coming straight along, there you are middle-aged . . . and with no future . . . a sort of dead end." Money was again a constant worry. The incipient civil rights movement would take as much energy as she and her friends could provide, but as a community, they were all battle-fatigued (thanks in large part to the unstinting work of the FBI). Among themselves, they were sometimes punch-drunk, feeling a sense of being rudderless. It was in this giddy state that Decca wrote and, with some friends, assembled *Lifeitselfmanship; or, How to Become a Precisely-Because Man: An Investigation into Current L (or Left-Wing) Usage*. This, her first book, was directly influenced by an immensely popular essay her sister Nancy had recently published titled "The English Aristocracy."

Nancy Mitford was living a soufflé of a life in France, wearing marvelous clothes amid beautiful furnishings, taking off for a few weeks to the
Riviera, to Venice for carnival. She'd worked hard for what she had, and
earned it all by her writing. Her early novels gained respectable readerships,
but *The Pursuit of Love* and *Love in a Cold Climate*, both fictionalized
versions of the Mitford sisters' youth and family life, had become best sellers. They had affirmed her role as the aristocratic socialite "lady" novelist
whose novels were frothy with just enough bite and whose biographies and
histories were original, perceptive, and as amusing as her fiction. From her
perch in Paris, she was positioned to weigh in on the debate in midfifties
Britain on class and language.

In the background of Nancy Mitford's essay "The English Aristocracy"
and Decca's contrasting piece *Lifeitselfmanship* is Alan S. C. Ross, a lin-
guist at Birmingham University, who labored to elucidate the vocabulary
employed by the English aristocracy around the mid-twentieth century.
According to Ross's thesis, the spoken English language in Great Britain
could be divided into two categories: U, which was proper, upper-class
usage, and non-U, which was employed by the rest of the population. For
instance, while upper-class types would say "vegetables," non-U speakers
might say "greens." "Cycle" is non-U for "bike," and "wealthy," non-U for
"rich." In September 1955, when Nancy Mitford launched Ross's findings
into the greater world, she added more vocabulary to Ross's lexicon, and
some attitude:

> The aristocrat can augment his fortune in many a curious manner,
> since he is impervious to a sense of shame (all aristocrats are: shame
> is a bourgeois notion). The lowest peasant of the Danube would
> stick at letting strangers into his house for 2s. 6d., but our dukes,
> marquesses, earls, viscounts, and barons not only do this almost
> incredible thing, they glory in it, they throw themselves into the
> sad commerce with rapture, and compete as to who among them
> can draw the greatest crowds. It is the first topic of conversation

in noble circles today, the tourists being referred to in terms of sport rather than cash—a sweepstake on the day's run, or the bag counted after the shoot.

Another indicator: "Any sign of undue haste, in fact, is apt to be non-U, and I go so far as preferring, except for business letters, not to use air mail."

Decca had the same speech patterns, the same original vocabulary. She too had been bred to an innate U-ness, but by then had spent two decades repudiating those U codes, sometimes even wrangling them to her benefit. She recognized how funny the miscues between the English and Americans could be. Despite the somewhat rarified atmosphere of her Communist fellowship, she still lived in America. Her kids went to public schools, she shopped in supermarkets, watched American TV (not yet commonly broadcast in England), read American newspapers, understood California dreaming and the American way of life. She understood the texture of the protocol and social values of the U world in England. If she could just figure out why anyone would care, she was in a unique position to explain these contrasts and to translate the language of each for the other. She looked around again at the piles of laundry and unwashed dishes and wondered how to mine this raw metaphor.

Decca borrowed her title from the book by Stephen Potter, *One-Upmanship: Being Some Account of the Activities and Teaching of the Lifemanship Correspondence College of One-Upness and Gameslifemastery*, which Bob had read on the boat to Europe. After Nancy's essay on "The English Aristocracy" was published in the United States, the *New Yorker* magazine picked up the thread, publishing a series of letters about quirky diction and syntactical oddities, which amused and inspired Decca. In her essay, she intended "a great send-up of the obscure, convoluted language of the Left," and mocked the verbose, official patois of its bureaucracy. *Lifeitselfmanship* functioned as a glossary of a dying language (Marxism in America), as had Nancy's lexicon of aristocratica. The essays of each sister were tongue-in-cheek with just enough sincerity to make them resonate among their populations, students of the form, or curious outsiders (i.e., government agents in America and social climbers in England).

Among Decca's friends and comrades, her booklet was deemed an immediate, hilarious success. It featured the artist Pele deLappe's "Thurberish" illustrations, inflated Marxist rhetoric, and mock-studious matching quizzes. For instance, "What does one do with cadres?" Decca wrote. "One develops them, trains them and boldly promotes them, poor things." Asked, "How do contradictions get started?" she answers, "They either *stem from* or *flow out* of situations. Sometimes *roots of problems* stem from *contradictions*, a botanical anomaly."

Over two days, Decca and friends mimeographed and stapled together five hundred copies priced at fifty cents each. Decca turned all her considerable organizational abilities toward a promotional campaign. She sent copies to party members and the left-wing press. The project was framed as a benefit for the *People's Daily World*, with all proceeds going to benefit the newspaper, although Marge thought the booklet was "welcomed as something that needed to be done." Decca was still "a trifle apprehensive about its reception," and she had a Plan B:

> Hoping to disarm my readers in advance, I added a check list of appropriate criticisms of the author. These include: Anti-leadership, anti-theoretical, right opportunism, left sectarianism, Rotten liberalism, Philistinism, Fails to chart a perspective and Petty Bourgeois cynicism.

In October, she wrote to her mother: "The extraorder thing about *Lifeitselfmanship* is that the worst offenders love it best (some that is, there have also been a few violent reactions anti it)." In England, *Lifeitselfmanship* was positively reviewed in the *Observer*. Orders came from as far away as Australia. Benjy peddled copies on the local bus, and altogether, they sold over twenty-five hundred copies.

This was in contrast, of course, to her sister's book *Noblesse Oblige*, which Decca presumed to be selling millions. However circumscribed, the

attention *Lifeitselfmanship* attracted gave Decca great satisfaction. She was
making people laugh at the same time that they were taking her seriously.
The most important response was Nancy's, and although Decca had to wait
for it by slow-boat mail (U-mail), it was a good one: "I've been *screaming*
over your pamphlet it's too lovely," Nancy wrote.

Decca's fortunes were changing. In further news from London, she discovered that she would indeed be inheriting money from the Romilly estate.
Her first thought was to travel. The Treuhafts still had not been granted new
documents, but a Supreme Court case in process contested the government's
right to withhold passports from its law-abiding citizens, regardless of their
political beliefs. The Supreme Court had three new justices, so there was
reason for cockeyed optimism.

Then, in late October 1956, Soviet forces crushed the Hungarian uprising,
killing over thirty thousand people. Decca recognized that Stalinist repression
had laid the groundwork for revolt. She acknowledged that the Hungarian
revolt was "originated by workers and students with most justified grievances," but at first her perceptions were colored by personal interests. Her
Jewish relatives feared that an independent Hungary would be a fascist and
anti-Semitic Hungary. They feared the rebels would be joined by fascists,
and they wanted to believe that Russian forces entering Hungary did so to
suppress a fascist coup. In 1956, opposing fascism, the enemy she'd been
fighting since her youth, was still Decca's primary political rationale. She
realized how she had misjudged that geopolitical event, just as she had missed
the nuance on their journey through Hungary the year before. In retrospect,
she could imagine all too well the strains upon the Hungarians they had met.
"One thing was dismally clear . . . Bob and I had entirely failed to perceive the
widespread discontent that must have seethed beneath the surface."

》《

DECCA AND MANY of her friends viewed the Communist Party leadership in
New York as a bunch of out-of-touch hard-liners whose enduring influence

gave the organization "something of the character of an ideological old folks' home." Leaders had not convened a national conference in seven years. Despite rank-and-file requests, they hadn't called a national congress to address either the Hungarian revolt or the Khrushchev revelations—to look into the details of Stalin's many atrocities and the horrors of the Gulag (which had rocked the U.S. party membership). To many members, the congress called for in February 1957 seemed promising, if not exactly the spring of reform.

There remained between five thousand and twenty thousand active American Communist Party members (only the FBI knew for sure). The California contingent to the New York convention elected Decca Treuhaft as one of its four delegates. She was delighted to escape the routine and eager to argue their reform position, which looked to her to be poised for success.

Decca arrived on the East Coast—like many Californians who experience winter only occasionally—with inadequate outer clothes. When a snowstorm threatened, Aranka insisted her daughter-in-law borrow her own mink coat against the cold. Although Decca cared not a whit for the judgmental looks of proletariat fashionistas, the heavy press coverage and phalanx of FBI agents surrounding the Communist Party Congress moved her to camouflage. In a nearby subway stop, she folded Aranka's fur coat into a carrier bag and covered it with newspapers. This, no doubt to the accompaniment of unsolicited assistance and commentary provided by observant New Yorkers: *You'll never get it in that paper bag . . . you're covering that with a New York Herald Tribune? . . . You want ink on your beautiful fur?* Trimmed down to her California frock, bulky paper bag, pocketbook, and briefcase, Decca ran through the snow to the meeting.

The congress, like others of its ilk, opened with a few agitated speeches between endless procedural meetings, while the real meat-and-potato debates were scheduled for prime time. During the day, friends wandered off for reunions, drank coffee, caught up on gossip, and updated the various scandals. Right away, Decca discovered that *Lifeitselfmanship* had made her a minor celebrity. She "thrilled to the praise of comrades from all around the country." This general goodwill toward Decca was a notable exception in the increasingly poisonous and polarized atmosphere. Once the real business of the congress got under way, the two main factions faced off. The California delegation and their supporters opposed the New York–based Old Guard, who defended the Stalinist hard line and status quo.

One of her group's symbolic successes was its motion to change the location of party headquarters from New York to Chicago. This effort to further decentralize the party passed unanimously. Everyone knew it would take more than a motion to move the Old Guard, but when Eugene Dennis, a longtime leader (just out of federal prison after serving a sentence as one of the original Smith defendants), threw his weight behind reform, Decca believed the platform would prevail. She hadn't considered the firepower that the aging leaders could bring to bear on their home turf. They defended themselves aggressively and at every meeting; every panel was fragmented with attacks, counterattacks, accusations, and denunciations. When it was clear that the confused membership could not agree on a new direction, several of the young reformers resigned, leaving the Old Guard in place. The New York leadership response to the subsequent avalanche of resignations was "good riddance."

DECCA LEFT THE convention feeling resolved to quit the party. She had made a fair attempt, but her faction had been defeated. The party had become "stagnant, ineffective." It was "a bore," and "leaving was no great trauma, because the trauma had all come earlier."

For fifteen years, the character of their comrades had been tested. Their friends had survived the worst of the McCarthyism and, for years afterward, still parried spies and bullies. Decca stayed in the party until 1957, after others had left, and after she and Bob had stopped believing in the usefulness of the organization. As long as the witch hunts continued, they hated to think that their old comrades might feel abandoned; some of these friends had been in the underground with its odd tensions and abnormalities, some had endured prosecution and imprisonment. Many had shown gallantry and resourcefulness. "Despite all evident drawbacks, I can hardly imagine living in America in those days and *not* being a member." She would glee-fully refer to herself and Bob as "ex-menaces."

She and Bob wouldn't make a big deal out of quitting; they would just occupy themselves with other things and, in the eventual drift, find them-selves far away. There would be no speeches, no grandstanding or repudia-tion of what had been a driving influence for over half her life. She was already sure she wanted to write more (perhaps repeat the success surround-ing *Lifeitselfmanship*), and she was toying with a new subject. Her friends were always telling her to write down all those Mitford stories. Returning to England in 1955, she had felt the force of that atmosphere, but she needed a point of entry. During a forced sabbatical after the New York Congress, with no job and no long-term political project on the horizon, she began to go through some of the boxes of papers and souvenirs that had piled up over the years. She found a box of Esmond's letters (a relief, since she'd feared them lost), read through them, then wrote nineteen pages of prologue at a white-hot speed.

Decca attacked the idea of a book with serious intent. But how serious a book, she had no idea. Why write another version of something that had been thoroughly covered in Nancy's novels? As it turned out, it was the kind of thing she absolutely loved doing. How would she have ever known if she hadn't plunged in? She'd wake up early and write at the kitchen table before anyone was awake in the "wonderful moment between 5:30 and 7:30, of total calm and quiet." Once the kids left for school, she'd write until lunch-time. When she had some pages, she'd show them to a few select friends whom she called her book committee: First among these was Bob, then Marge, Pele and Steve Murdock (now Pele's husband), and other friends Barbara Kahn, Betty Bacon, and Dorothy Neville.

She had begun, she thought, so that Dinky could have a better sense of her father. Early on in the process, she realized there was another reason.

She had appeared as a character in Nancy's novels and in Philip Toynbee's memoir *Friends Apart*. She had been sketched adroitly by both authors, but what Decca wanted was to tell her own story.

CHAPTER 21

NINE MONTHS AFTER she had begun researching and writing her book, Decca had typical writerly apprehensions and always the same money woes. She had begun sending portions of the book out to editors and publishers with little encouragement on the literary front and none financially. Then one happy day, the promised check from the Romilly estate arrived, around eleven thousand pounds. Decca deposited a couple thousand dollars into what she would call her "frittering account" to indulge her family and her friends, who never had any spare money. She bought clothes for Bob and the kids, a dress for Pele, and an embroidered blouse for Marge. She splurged on a cocktail dress at a fancy dress salon, whose saleslady advised her regarding accessories, "If I were you I wouldn't wear any jewelry with it," to which Decca replied, "That won't be difficult at all." For sixteen years, she had been squirreling away the veteran benefits she had received from the Canadian Air Force to pay for Dinky's education, and now, she had fewer worries on that account for either child. She lent some money to the Durrs, for their daughter Tilla's college tuition. Then she put aside a nice bit for her eventual return to England, whenever that might happen. Sooner than later, perhaps, since the judicial tide looked to be turning, thanks in part to Justice Hugo Black and the new, more liberal constituency of the rest of the Supreme Court (which would eventually overturn a raft of red-scare convictions). When a reporter for the London *Evening Standard* phoned Decca that fall to interview the "American" Mitford sister, the interviewer had been aghast to hear that Decca's passport was still being withheld (as if that kind of barbaric behavior was something you heard about only in connection with the most repressive regimes or in the distant past). Decca had welcomed the publicity; any type of social pressure would help the Treuhafts recover their passports.

After dozens of rejections from publishers Decca took a break from her book and turned her hand to freelance writing. The form flowed with surprising ease. Her first article, about a man in San Francisco falsely accused of rape, was accepted by the *Nation* magazine and, after considerable editing, was published under the title "Trial by Headline." Decca clearly identified with the vulnerable and despised outsider, whose life was scrutinized unnecessarily. (The theme—under the surface—speaks to Decca's own sense of mistreatment at the hands of a press corps that whipped up so many false attacks during the red scare.) As it was Decca's first magazine publication, she was "inordinately proud of it," and the seventy-five dollars she received for her article signaled a turning point that encouraged her for the first time to call herself a writer.

»«

ON MARCH 17, 1958, Decca's father died at Redesdale Cottage, where he had been living with Margaret Wright since his separation from Muv. He had just turned eighty. By that time, Decca and Farve hadn't seen one another for almost twenty years. His death came just at the time she was writing about him, and in her memoir, he is the father of her childhood, bigger than life, eccentric, idiosyncratic, and adored. Nancy had written about their father earlier, as the barely disguised "Uncle Mathew," the father of the Radlett clan. A Farve-like character was central to her novels *The Pursuit of Love* and *Love in a Cold Climate*, and his various quirks and comments would show up in subsequent books. In a letter written in 1950, Nancy noted that their father had an unexpected new interest: He "thinks of literally nothing now but cocktail parties." She added that quirk to Uncle Mathew's character in her later novels alongside this elegiac characterization:

> I had known him so vigorous and violent, so rampageous and full
> of super-charged energy that it went to my heart to see him now,
> stiff and slow in his movements, wearing spectacles; decidedly deaf

. . . Uncle Mathew was only in his seventies but he was not well preserved.

After Farve's death, Decca was worried about how her mother would manage and offered one possibility: "I will gladly share my Fortune with you. I don't seem to be using it up much though I did get some fairly nice clothes." (Muv wouldn't need Decca's fortune; the Redesdale estate would provide for her.) Decca had lived on such a tight budget for so long that her mother and friends were glad to hear that she was using some of the Romilly money to take a road trip around Mexico with Benjy, aged eleven; Dinky, seventeen; and two of Dinky's friends. The travelers would drive around in Decca's DeSoto, then meet Bob in July. Their trip would be an exercise in freedom. Although they would be as closely observed as any other American tourists with a "fortune" to dispose of, they would escape the constant scrutiny of FBI agents. The "tor," as they called it, was a great success. Dinky and friends became amateur mechanics as the DeSoto frequently broke down in areas without service stations. Young Benjy started to seem like a "gay blade or roué" to his amused mother when he spent the twenty dollars Aranka had given him as mad money on high-heel shoes for the hotel maids at Ciprés.

At the end of June, the travelers arrived in Mexico City to discover the news about Decca's Redesdale inheritance. Her father had cut her entirely out of his will by adding the words "except Jessica" after each clause. She answered calls at her pension from newspapers in the United States and Canada once this "non-legacy," as Decca called it, made international news. What was her reaction? the reporters wanted to know. She hadn't been "expecting anything," she replied. The FBI clipped several articles for Decca's file, including this interview with the *San Francisco Examiner*: "It seems a hundred years ago," she said. "My father and I disagreed. I was against HITLER. So I ran away to Spain and joined the Spanish Loyalists. He was pretty bitter about this and we've had no contact since."

Mary Lovell, a Mitford biographer, thought Lord Redesdale "had never recovered from her attempt to hand over part of Inch Kenneth to 'the Bolshies' and was fearful that anything he left her would be given away." Years later, in an interview, Decca summarized her feelings:

> I knew I was cut out, and I'd have been very surprised if I hadn't been . . . I think to most people their parents are absolutely everything up to a certain age, and then very soon they become a complete backdrop, so whatever feelings you had towards them are terribly diffused. It's like birds getting out of a nest. You don't feel bound to them any further, and whatever feelings of bitterness you had you don't dwell on it.

»«

IN 1958, WHILE she continued writing, Decca also continued to mail her unfinished manuscript to editors and agents in the hope that someone might recognize its potential and give her the professional endorsement she longed for. Eventually, she found a writer's agent willing to represent the book. Barthold Fles had a small agency with distinguished clients, many of them European leftists, including Heinrich Mann, Ignazio Silone, and Cedric Belfrage. (He also represented Anaïs Nin.) Fles asked Decca to assemble the typical nonfiction proposal package of "two chapters and an outline." He also discouraged her from showing her manuscript around anymore before it was finished. To Fles, it was "like parading around in your underwear." Bob and the agent agreed. "To prove the point the other day," Decca wrote to her daughter, who was in her first year at Sarah Lawrence College in New York, "Bob came in in his undershorts at breakfast time and I pointed out to him that he made me feel as though I were reading one of his briefs."

The next greatest change in the Treuhafts' daily life surrounded Bob's increasing involvement with the Berkeley Co-Op and his appointment to a co-op committee investigating the formation of a low-cost funeral society. (Co-ops represented a counterculture perspective and spoke to those discontented with orthodoxy or majority dominance. There were famous housing co-ops; later, food co-ops emerged. The funeral co-op was not a new idea, having had a successful run among immigrant groups earlier in the century.) In his work as a union lawyer, Bob had become suspicious of the way union death benefits almost inevitably covered the cost of a funeral, with little surplus. It seemed as if undertakers typically encouraged their vulnerable clients to exhaust their benefits on expensive funerals. A funeral society could offer an alternative service. A family would pay once for membership, and then the association could negotiate for less expensive burials.

Their co-op committee's early research eventually led to the formation of the Bay Area Funeral Society. At first, Decca had teased Bob about his new interest. "Off to meet with your fellow necrophilists?" she would ask him. Bob brought home funeral industry trade magazines, like *Mortuary Management* and *Casket and Sunnyside*, whose somber attention to clothes and cosmetics for "the loved one" appealed to Decca's sense of the absurd. Those magazines were, in any case, irresistible: All the "extras" they advertised added up to so many unnecessary expenses. Cremation, when mentioned at all, was regarded as a threat and greatly discouraged.

Bob encouraged Decca to write an article on American funeral practices. If nothing else, it would provide a helpful introduction to new funeral co-op members. The timing was right. Decca was fed up with her memoir and ready for a break. In her life, she had seen more than her share of death and dying, but here was a kind of way to dominate the subject. The ghoulish and morbid lent themselves most naturally to puns and teases. There were plenty of underdogs here to defend, secrets to uncover, and who wouldn't want to write about morticians? (They were, in her opinion, "a very *lively* group.") Drawing on the funeral trade magazines, which exposed the wilder frontiers of American salesmanship, and Bob's research, Decca went to work.

The resulting article featured a sprightly, no-nonsense narrator who relished delving into the social customs, economic forces, and folklore surrounding the funeral industry. She condemned the high cost of funerals and was lucky enough to get some killingly good quotes, like this from the past president of the Funeral Directors of San Francisco: "In keeping with our high standard of living, there should be an equally high standard of dying." Her work led Decca to this explanation of the industry's cutthroat nature:

> It should be borne in mind that the funeral industry faces a unique economic situation in that its market is fixed or inelastic. There are only a certain number of deaths each year and the funeral directors must compete with each other to obtain their share of the business. The television industry touts the advantage of a TV set in every room; auto salesmen advocate several cars to each family; cigarette manufacturers urge "a carton for the home and one for the office"—but in the funeral business it's strictly "one to a customer," and the number of customers is limited by circumstances beyond the control of the industry.

She concluded by promoting funeral cooperatives as an alternative. These organizations, she said, "have declared war on 'materialistic display'" and are dedicated to the principle of "dignified funerals at reasonable cost."

She sent her article to many of the national news magazines, and all rejected it. Eventually, a small, progressive Southern Californian magazine called *Frontier* bought the article for forty dollars and published it in the November 1958 issue under the title "St. Peter, Don't You Call Me."

DECCA WAS STILL engaged in various political campaigns. She and Benjy attended an NAACP (National Association for the Advancement of Colored People) meeting to hear about the latest activity in the civil rights movement in the South. It seemed to her a waste to have accumulated all that experience in the CRC and yet be so far away from the heart of the struggle. For the time being—at least until she sold her book—Decca knew she had to stay put. Some days, particularly when confronted by another rejection, she yearned to run away again, to go anywhere, to do anything but this routine of getting up to write "at the crack of Bob."

Then in December, the Supreme Court ruled against the government in the matter of withholding citizens' passports. The Treuhaft philosophy was that once you received your passports, you made use of them for as long as they lasted. Decca immediately made plans to return to England, where she expected she might find a more receptive audience for her memoir.

》《

WHEN DECCA AND Benjy set sail for England in April 1959, she had been working on her memoir for over two years. Her agent Barthold Fles had been trying to sell her book, but so far had not succeeded. If Decca felt frustrated by the New York publishing world's lack of interest, she also had to wonder whether the book was really bad or whether the rejections were because of her radical past.

It was hard for someone so used to controlling her own sphere of influence to leave everything in the hands of an agent, capable and kind as Fles seemed. She gathered the names of publishers abroad and considered how to shop her book around London. In the months leading up to her and her son's departure, she threw herself into the discipline of a low-calorie diet, aerobic exercise, daily writing, and domestic chores. "I hope to be completely re-molded as the Chinese Reds say by the time I see you," she wrote to Dinky, who was finishing her first year at Sarah Lawrence. Such moral probity was, of course, utterly dull, Decca admitted. "How much more interesting could I have written, 'Dined at Fleur de Lys, got drunk afterwards, held up a department store.'"

Mother and daughter had a mutually admiring relationship, but the subject of Dinky's education divided them. As someone who had been prevented from going to school, Decca couldn't understand her daughter's discontent with her elite college. Both women were animated and charismatic, with the gift their friends reported to "lift up" others in their circle and the ability (though not extravagantly employed) to wound one another. Dinky frustrated Decca when she affected indifference. She knew how to parry her mother's teasing and where to land her own zingers. In the days leading up to their ship's departure, Benjy and Decca visited Aranka and Dinky in New York. Dinky appreciated her mother's project—which had begun as a gesture of love, in memory of Esmond. The college freshman also recognized its value to Decca as a life-changing occupation, even if she didn't quite see her mother as a famous author.

ON DECCA AND Benjy's second day at sea, the worst storm that year slammed the ocean liner carrying them. The grand decks were spookily abandoned since most of the passengers, in all classes of travel, and much of the crew suffered dreadful seasickness. Whatever was not tied down went whizzing by, including paisley shawls, umbrellas, small dogs, and, as Decca reported, several dowagers with bloodied heads. Decca was never seasick; Benjy was not so lucky.

In London, Decca stayed with her friend Joan Rodker. Their first night, they had dinner with Doris Lessing and Clancy Sigal. Decca found it so pleasant meeting other writers, ex-menaces, and once unfriendly witnesses, that she fantasized about moving back to London permanently. She was also fascinated that so many people from her past had become writers. Like Philip Toynbee and Giles Romilly, many of her English friends either had books in progress or were engaged in some kind of journalism. She ran into Joe Starobin, a blacklisted American writer who edited a trade journal for British dentistry. When he offered Decca $120 for an article, Doris Lessing said she'd introduce her to some top dentists.

With all her considerable energy, Decca launched her campaign to find an English agent and publisher for her still-untitled memoir. Someone, perhaps at the English Communist Party headquarters, recommended the literary agent James MacGibbon. Over a drink, Decca found MacGibbon simpatico, a former party member, and willing to read her manuscript. A few days later, he phoned to say how much he had loved her book. He wanted to show it to Gollancz Publishers, confident they'd like it, too. Meanwhile, he'd been in touch with an American editor, Lowell Thompson

from Houghton Mifflin, and Thompson was already on the verge of making
an offer for the U.S. rights. Decca and MacGibbon met on Monday. The following Friday, after a day spent sightseeing with Benjy, they were walking
into Joan's house from the tube when Decca heard the news.

Gollancz had accepted the book for publication and made an offer of a
sizable advance. It had all happened at a dizzying speed. The English publishers wanted her to complete the book by adding a concluding section.
Now, in chronological order, she had "to gently fire Fles" and delicately
inform her mother that she was writing an autobiography. She told Muv,
"The book is sort of memoirs of my life with Esmond. It isn't quite finished
so I shall have to be working on it like mad at the Island, and later, because
it's got to be finished by the time I leave for the U.S."

Two weeks later, in early May, Muv, Benjy, and Decca left together for
Inch Kenneth, where Decca would install herself in a spare bedroom in the
big old Victorian house on the little island. She was glad not to have sold
Inch Kenneth, and alternated between hours of writing and hosting tea parties with her mother to the "nutty" island society.

Bob joined them in May. They had been apart three months, but her letters to him were full of endearments and promises never to part for so long
again. She was also glad to have a confidant with whom to share her new
work. In California, she had relied on her writing committee and at first felt
uneasy without them. From Philip Toynbee, she had learned "that editors
are a completely new thing here, copied from the United States. Philip said
he had never heard of them at all until recently, and couldn't imagine how
any self-respecting author could let a third person mess around with his
book." Once her book was absolutely finished, she would work with a copy
editor, but she couldn't count on much help before then. "They just don't
work that way in England," she explained to Bob and Dinky in a letter, "but
cruelly leave one on one's own. It does make me a bit sad as I really thrive
on suggestions and help."

Her mother was circumspect and dropped many helpful hints, in particular wishing that "there should be no bitterness in it." Eventually, Decca

let Muv read the first few chapters and was much relieved to find her mother approving and even complimentary, with only a few reservations regarding certain obscure details that it amused Decca to correct. For instance, Muv edited the length of her daughter's appendix scar (*eight*, not twelve, inches) and suggested she not mention the brand of their "foul"-smelling water heater, to avoid a libel suit. Muv admitted she was bothered in places by Decca's portrayal of her as a snob, but in general, she seemed pleased with the book. To her sisters, Decca said she was writing a memoir just about her life with Esmond. She was careful that none of them—especially Nancy, whose approbation she particularly yearned for—would learn how much more of their youth together she planned to cover. All her sisters were mad to read it; Debo even volunteered to edit the revised version. Decca was getting along with both Nancy and Debo so much better than they had at their last reunion. Benjy had won a great friend in his Aunt Debo, and Nancy had come to enjoy Decca's companionship again. Nevertheless, they suffered some nervousness about her memoir. "Oh Hen, I do hope it's not going to be frank," Debo said.

Meanwhile, the island proved a lovely place to write. The food was divine: lobsters, fresh milk and cream from the dairy, and there was always homemade bread. She set up her writing desk in a large room whose window overlooked the sea. It was so appealing that Decca wrote to her daughter with a proposal:

> Here is some exciting news (if it comes off, that is). Bob and I have decided to try to buy the Island from the others—buy out their shares . . . Muv, of course, would live here rent free for the rest of her life or as long as she wants to. A great consideration in making this decision is your feelings in the matter. I know you always wanted to keep it if we could . . . might you be interested (a few years from now) in taking a real hand here, either the farming end or possibly running a summer guest house? With Benj as (un) handy-man?

Nancy told Decca that if their other sisters would agree to sell their shares, she would give her share to the Treuhafts as a gift. Nancy was irritated enough by her father's will and affluent enough to do exactly as she wished. Her recent string of successes had run unabated, and Nancy was quite comfortably set, even without the Redesdale inheritance. Over the previous year, she had published a biography of Voltaire and begun work on her next novel, *Don't Tell Alfred* (and finally divorced her husband, Peter Rodd—to whom she'd been married since 1934). This act of generosity from her unpredictable eldest sister caused Decca to inform her English lawyer "to be prepared to deal with yet another inadvertent inheritance."

BY JUNE, THE deal had gone through. All Decca's sisters, including Diana, had agreed to sell and all had been madly curious about why on earth Decca even wanted Inch Kenneth. In a letter to her mother, Nancy speculated, "Atom base I suppose—you'll probably see Khrushchev arriving any day, to be greeted with jugs of cream by the simple islanders." Decca told her friends that she and Bob thought it a good investment, that Dinky had asked them to do it for Muv, and that it might make a retirement home someday. She and Bob had been struggling for so long, no one who hadn't been there could understand the stress and tension and pressure they'd endured on account of their politics, but on this small island, life was like a dream.

Back in London, Decca and Bob visited their old friend Paul Robeson, whom Benjy and Decca had recently seen in the role of Othello at Stratford. In mid-May, the Treuhafts rented an apartment in the same building where W. E. B. DuBois and his wife, Shirley, lived. Over the past year, there had been a signal shift. Now DuBois and the Treuhafts all had their passports again. DuBois was ninety-one years old. "Can you believe it?" Decca wrote to Aranka. "And absolutely chipper, not a bit deaf, delightfully amusing and conversational. We took them out to dinner last night and he had a martini, wine and cigarettes along with us!"

Before leaving California, Decca and Pele had discussed the possibility of Pele's designing the cover for her book, whenever it might be published. In early June, Decca reported back to the artist in California:

> James MacGibbon was absolutely amazed to hear that you had been commissioned to do the cover. He says this is unparalleled in the history of publishing (getting an outside artist) and specially in the history of Gollancz, as they have a definite and immutable cover style from which they've never been known to vary—title in big block letters, usually black on yellow. So he's terribly impressed, both with you for doing one they liked and with me for having the temerity to put it over on them. I note they have upped the price to 15 gns. (45$) so I do hope you'll go right ahead with it.

There were a few loose ends. First was the sticky subject of a title. She had wanted to call her book *My Life & Red Times*, then settled on *Red Sheep*. However, *Red Sheep* was entirely too ambiguous for the publishers. (The sheep in this case being of the wayward variety, as opposed to its more pejorative sister metaphor, *lemming*.) She parried with *Revolting Daughters*, but Gollancz settled on *Hons and Rebels*. It was not a popular choice. Her mother hated it so "violently," that she wrote to Gollancz to object. Decca worried that emphasizing the aristocratic element more than the leftist one might make it seem too much like a Nancy Mitford production ("cashing in on her stuff").

Finally, there was one more section that still had to be written, "the knotty last chapter." The Treuhafts would spend the next month in France, where Benjy and Bob would enjoy a Riviera vacation while Decca would focus on writing an ending to her life before California. This would be both fanfare and valedictory address (but not an elegy) to "set the record straight."

»«

IN JULY 1959, Decca traveled to Bormes-les-Mimosas with Bob and Benjy. Decca had looked for a place in the South of France to make her final revisions and found the perfect writing retreat by "assiduously avoiding following Nancy's advice," which would have directed her to the more fashionable parts of the Riviera. Instead, in her Michelin Guide, she found the Hôtel Paradis on a street called Mont de Roses. The village of Borme-les-Mimosas, about a twenty-minute walk uphill from the hotel, dates back to the Renaissance. Its homes, perched on narrow, hilly slate streets, are still mostly made of stone or stucco faded yellow or gold-green, and with rust or pink or rose tiled roofs. Hydrangea, oleander, and pineapple palms, and plane trees fill the plazas; scarlet, rose, and purple bougainvillea drapes the stone terraces and springs from the many window boxes along the road that winds up to a chateau at the crest of the hill.

In the guesthouse where the Treuhafts stayed, starfish, fishing nets, and tridents decorated the walls. Decca was happy there. Her hosts were so kind and "all mad about Benj." They couldn't do enough to help her write her book, screening off the salon for her exclusive use and providing her with a typing table and desk. Madame had even surprised her with fresh sardines for dinner the very day she'd mentioned how she'd enjoyed them on previous visits to France.

Every day, Benjy and Bob would leave for the beach and Decca would settle down to write. She had been on the Mediterranean twenty years before with Esmond and pregnant with Julia when she'd first tasted those grilled sardines. In the quiet, the distant past and the recent past all came back. Esmond and Julia had both been gone almost two decades. She had absorbed it. Unity had died, and her father, and Nanny, all blows. And then in 1955, Nicholas's death had come as close as anything ever would to breaking her. But here they were in the Hôtel Paradis, she, Bob, and Benjy (whose suffering at his older brother's death had worried her the most). If some ghosts rose up to threaten, she learned how to suppress them. Her job was to shape this story her way, without soggy sentimentality. She might have felt supersensitive, perhaps seeing and feeling things more intensely; naturally she sometimes felt "gloomy about it," but never for too long. "Life here is even-keelish to say the least," she wrote to her friends the Kahns.

> I get up pretty early (7:30) and stagger up to the terrace for café complet. Then return to our cottage, a private abode in the garden, to start work. Bob and Benj gradually wake up and go down to the beach, about 3 miles away, in our rented car. They bring back lovely salady things and pate for a picnic lunch, also a bottle of wine. By after lunch I am too tight from the wine to settle back to work for a while, so a nap is had. Then an hour or so of work, followed by the evening treat of an apéritif in a cafe near the beach before dinner. Doesn't it sound rather peaceful and even constructive?

After a couple of weeks, Bob returned to his law practice in California. By July 9, the end of Decca's work was in sight, and on July 10, she was able to say in a joint letter to Bob and Dinky: "THE BOOK IS FINISHED! I could scream with joy. Isn't it amazing, I was so terrified it wouldn't be done before time to go—or ever, for that matter—then suddenly everything fell into place and the last chapter is DONE . . . Oh how hard I wish you were both here to celebrate."

CHAPTER 22

O VER THE PREVIOUS two years, Decca had been busy nearly every day with her memoir. By January 1960, the book was in her publisher's hands, and she was restless and impatient. She craved a wider audience, to be remarked upon and influential. Such vicissitudes were still, for the moment, outside her control. Her reputation would be, for the near future, up to strangers, taste-makers, unknown reviewers, and that mysterious "word of mouth." She longed to hear her friends' and family's responses, and felt especially anxious to know what Virginia Durr and Philip Toynbee would think of her portrait of Esmond. Sister Nancy had with characteristic sangfroid requested that Gollancz show her the page proofs, which they had refused to do. "Don't you think that is one hell of a nerve? Honestly she is the living limit," Decca wrote Dinky, who was then in her second year at Sarah Lawrence.

Dinky had returned to Sarah Lawrence, hoping things might improve. Generationally, she wasn't alone in her malaise; the mood at the college remained resistant and slow to change. But elsewhere, the allure of the sophisticated tier of the "silent generation" (which had made a virtue of eschewing public passion) had begun to seem old-fashioned and unrewarding to a new class of students finding its voice, in universities and colleges across the nation.

Decca's customary advice, "hard work . . . in contrast, for instance, to too much self-examination," wasn't the tonic to revive her daughter. As Dinky's letters home became briefer, Decca thought anything worth a try—even introspection. "Darling Dinkydonk," she wrote,

One is only really inwardly comfortable, so to speak, after one's life
has assumed some sort of shape. Not just a routine, like studying
or a job or being a housewife, but something more complete than
all those, which would include goals set by oneself and a circle of
life-time type friends. I think this is one of the hardest things to
achieve, in fact often just trying doesn't achieve it but rather it seems
to develop almost by accident. (Clear as mud, dear, sorry, but I'm
not very good at explaining all this. I do feel there's some truth to
it however.) Usually I don't think one comes by all this at a very
young age. Even after one has, all may be knocked out of shape, so
one has to start over again to some extent—which happened to a
lot of us when the Party and CRC etc. folded, and some of us . . .
went through a lot of suffering perhaps a bit like what you are going
through now.

Decca's letter arrived at the end of January, just as Dinky felt she was
"treading water—waiting for something to happen" to give her a raison
d'être. Within weeks, something did. On February 1, 1960, four black college students in Greensboro, North Carolina, staged a sit-in at a segregated
Woolworth's lunch counter. To Dinky and her friends, this event produced
the radiant sense that their future wasn't yet written. The change might not
come immediately, but here were new signposts that their generation had a
part to play, and heroes to lead them.

In March 1960, *Hons and Rebels* was published in the United States
(retitled for its American audience as *Daughters and Rebels*). Decca received
a complimentary letter from Virginia Durr. The *People's Daily World* review
embraced her for being "in the good company of those who have been investigated by our state Un-American Committee for her consistent devotion to
the progress of mankind." When the highly anticipated letter from Nancy
finally arrived, it was brief and subtle. "I think it's *awfully good*—easy to
read & very funny in parts. A slightly cold wind to the heart perhaps—you
don't seem very fond of anybody, but I suppose the purpose is to make the

Swinbrook world seem horrible, to explain why you ran away from it." Decca deemed it a nice note, which could have been so much worse.

Nancy had more grievances, which she kept from Decca but rehearsed among her other correspondents. She didn't think her sister's book honest. Nancy considered it derivative and dependent on her own work. She wasn't at all happy with the ad copy in the *Observer* that *Hons and Rebels* was "the real-life background to Nancy Mitford's *Pursuit of Love*." To Heywood Hill, Nancy said she thought Bob had "re written it or helped a good deal as it is *his* voice."

To Evelyn Waugh, she confided a similar suspicion: "Clever of you to see the two voices. I am quite certain much of it was re-written by Treuhaft, who is a sharp little lawyer and who certainly made her write it in the first place. The words cash in are never off his lips. (I quite like him but oh Americans)."

Though she thought the book deeply flawed, Nancy unpredictably defended Decca against their other sisters, at least on literary terms. She said Decca probably didn't mean to be "beastly" in her characterization of Derek Jackson, from whom Pam was amiably divorced. Jackson, a scientist who had been a daredevil flyer during the war, was, like all the Mitford brothers-in-law, an outsized character. In the book, Decca referred to Jackson, who spent some of his enormous fortune on racehorses, as a jockey. While the other sisters viewed this deliberate mischaracterization as virtual bomb-throwing class warfare, Nancy was amused. Such examples of selective recollection to Nancy were less important than the various sins of unoriginality, borrowing, and even secret collaboration.

The Mitford family circle had for the most part admired Nancy's novels, which portrayed them as charming, a little daffy, but good-natured. If they hadn't loved them earlier, they did particularly in contrast to Decca's book, which seemed to be a product of nongranted license and overexposure. Decca and her family would read the reviews through different lenses. For instance, while Debo thought Lord Birkenhead's *Daily Telegraph* review discerned the book's "theme song" as dishonesty, Decca didn't see that. She thought his review describing *Hons and Rebels* as a "shameless but most diverting book" was "much the best."

As a writer, Decca was holding the reins to a carriage of skittering horses. While one side of her psyche was worrying about hurting her sisters and disturbed by her daughter's ongoing depression, another side was dancing, leaping, and twirling in the attention and admiration. Far, far away in England, her family was vexed and chagrined. After a while, they would grow used to the book.

At forty, Decca was in demand for her accomplishment. She was granting interviews, being asked to lecture, and appearing on radio and television shows. Instead of simply recounting scandals of English aristocracy, as her hosts intended, she used these new opportunities to slam the FBI, HUAC, and the district attorney of Alameda County. Revenge was sweet. "I soon discovered that as a published author one could get away with almost anything," she said. In New York, she enjoyed some of the perks of being a famous author, reuniting with old friends like Katharine Graham and traveling the writer's interview circuit, where she was an ever-amiable celebrity always ready with a quip. She found that the American way of being interviewed went smoother when the event was preceded by a cocktail or two (or nine, as she reported in one letter to Pele). After a series of encounters with celebrity hosts like Dave Garroway, she took their measure: "all high-powered on the surface, but naive & pretty stupid right below the surface."

At one authors' luncheon in San Francisco, Decca was seated beside a well-heeled woman, her hostess for the occasion and a fan of her work. She had read *Daughters and Rebels* with such pleasure, her new fan gushed. Perhaps, since Decca lived across the bay, they might know some of the same people. The Coakleys, for instance? Decca would have relied on all her early training not to snort at the mention of Bob's bête noir. By dessert and coffee, Decca had told her hostess of the time she had helped a Negro family buy a house on the Coakleys' block, and how the Coakleys, refusing to accept integration in their own neighborhood, had quickly sold their home and moved away. Was that, Decca inquired, how a district attorney, elected to serve all the people, ought to behave?

"But my dear, don't you think it's more Kitty's side of the family, than Frank's?" her hostess asked.

"We are hardly on Kitty and Frank terms with them," said Decca.

>«

IT WAS SAN Francisco Chronicle columnist Herb Caen who gave a suitable name to the influx of young fellow travelers following in the wake of the obscenity trial for Allen Ginsberg's Howl. To the common Beat nomenclature, he added the latest popular suffix: Space had its Sputnik; Mad magazine had its nudniks; now San Francisco had beatniks, with their apparent political apathy and general "wiggly nihilism" (Lawrence Ferlinghetti's term). In 1959, after the San Francisco police began staging "beatnik raids" in North Beach, the interests and attitudes of young rebels turned toward resistance and protest. Writing in Frontier Magazine, Ralph Tyler linked the raids in which "beards, sandals and interracial friendship were all treated as equal threats to the social fabric" to the radicalization of bohemians and beatniks previously apolitical.

That spring the House Committee on Un-American Activities announced that it would hold hearings again in San Francisco. The city had excellent food, beautiful scenery, and freewheeling mores—in all ways, the conventioneer's ideal. For committee members and their supporters, the city also held a sufficiency of hospitable spectators to pack the courtroom seats, indignant Communists (and non-Communist unfriendlies) to parade and interrogate, and, perhaps most important, hungrily competitive newspapers and broadcasters. It was universally acknowledged that the committee had succeeded in doing what it had set out to do—destroy the American Communist party. Perhaps such triumph should have ensured HUAC's position, but the members were realists and knew that to maintain funding and position, they had to keep Commie-hunting as front-page news.

Maybe it was timing, maybe people thought they had better ways to spend their money, or maybe it was boredom. But whatever it was, the increasing number of editorials, political cartoons, and satires in the once unquestioning media proved that the value of the committee's service had been supplanted by its unsavory reputation as outdated and self-serving. (One Herblock political cartoon lampooned an unnamed committee member at a fancy restaurant, plying a blonde with champagne, expense account notebook flapping from his pocket, and "Committee on Un-American Activities" stamped on the hem of his soiled jacket. In the caption, he slurs drunkenly to the reporter interrupting his tryst, "You trying to underm'ne the American way of life?") Abolish the Committee organizations had sprung up around the country, including in Oakland, where Decca and her old friends on the left were joining young people in a new coalition for civil rights. On Saturdays, Decca walked a picket line to protest segregated lunch counters at Woolworth's and Kresge's. Her companions were "Old Lefties" and kids in SLATE, a nascent political party formed on the University of California's Berkeley campus to provide "a meaningful alternative to the status quo." SLATE's engagement in "matters of national and international policy—housing discrimination, the H-bomb threat, apartheid in Africa . . . actively repudiated the apathetic-conformist-silent tag associated with their generation." Decca credited the group's emergence with "a new tolerance for unorthodoxy" on campus.

HUAC sent subpoenas to forty-eight people, including schoolteachers, librarians, and union members. Decca's friend Laurent Frantz was subpoenaed, as was labor leader Archie Brown and Douglas Wachter, an eighteen-year-old Berkeley student and SLATE member. Wachter's outraged friends formed an ad hoc committee to defend his civil liberties, starting with a petition and leafleting campaign around campus. This particular group of students was not going to let the dead hand of the past determine their future or destroy their momentum as they had seen it do to the "Old Left." They were informed, indignant, and unafraid. Even faculty members on campuses were beginning to speak publicly again after years of intimidating loyalty oaths. The university's newspaper, the *Daily Californian*, published transcripts of past HUAC hearings, the contents of which seemed straight out of some square medieval kangaroo court. In a matter of days, over a thousand people signed the petition to support Wachter and to oppose HUAC.

It was Decca's habit to bring her kids along to the hearings. This time, she took her goddaughter Kathy Kahn. They set out that morning without the white cards that functioned as seat reservations and entrance tickets to the courtroom. All witnesses and members of the court always received a few extra white cards for their friends and family, and there were usually a few of these circulating. Decca expected to sail inside as she always had. She was as surprised as anyone that first morning of the hearings, May 11, to discover that the courtroom was already full to capacity. Students from the University of California Berkeley and San Francisco State College had begun lining up outside the City Hall at around 7:00 A.M. to sit in the courtroom area designated for the public. By 9:00 A.M., when the hearings were set to begin, there were at least two hundred people in a line that snaked through the corridor, down the building's steep steps.

The Frantzes arrived early, expecting to walk through nearly empty halls and meet a few friends in the gallery. Instead, Marge was amazed by the presence of all the young college women dressed neatly in skirts and sweaters, the young men in ties. Even the beatniks were neatniks for the occasion. Writing about the constituency of the crowd for a later article, Decca mentioned the presence of some "children of radicals," but most of the student participants came from households they described as "pro-Roosevelt." It was a heterodox mix, which held "by no means uniform hostility toward the committee, or uniform sympathy for the subpoenaed witnesses." Some among the crowd were surely there to "express opposition. But, many others came out of curiosity, attracted by the considerable publicity on campus and in the newspapers. Some were covering the event for the school paper; several British graduate students came as observers of the American way of life and political institutions."

Eventually, a few students were permitted to sit in the unoccupied seats or stand in the back of the courtroom. The committee's chief prosecutor, Richard Arens, started things off by calling a couple of friendly witnesses. His current hobgoblin was that Communist propaganda was being sent through the U.S. mail, and he lectured the jury on its widespread and pernicious influence. He then called Douglas Wachter, whom he planned to portray as the very picture of a young Communist dupe. Arens tried to associate Wachter's poor judgment with postal propaganda, but he couldn't get much traction. In his defense, the poised eighteen-year-old claimed both the First and Fifth Amendments.

From the start, the customary power balance was out of whack, and Arens, a typically agile prosecutor for whom hectoring tripped off the tongue, never hit his stride. From inside, Marge heard those still in line outside the courtroom chanting, "Let us in! Open the doors! Open the doors!" Labor organizer Archie Brown, slated to testify as an unfriendly, agitated from inside: "Let them in to see this travesty! What are you afraid of?" Brown demanded to know why the room had been packed with spectators sympathetic to the committee: "You gave all those people cards— why didn't you give me some for *my* friends?" The students who had succeeded in gaining seats in the courtroom stood and began singing "The Star-Spangled Banner." Outside in the corridor voices in the crowd joined in a rousing chorus of "The Battle Hymn of the Republic." Committee Chairman Francis Walter, stunned by the patriotic hootenanny, gaveled for silence, but the singers persevered. Then Walter ordered federal marshals to eject twelve of the singing students, and the courtroom exploded in partisan crosstalk. Inside the hearing room, it must have felt a little as if the ice floes had broken and spring come to Narnia. At various moments, the old threats seemed to dissolve like dandelion fluff.

Eventually, Arens stopped the proceedings, associating the protests outside with the Communist influence of the very propaganda they had come to investigate. It was all one grand conspiracy to Arens, and the Reds were behind it. When he went out on a balcony overlooking the demonstrations below, there began a chant that he had never heard before in all his years as a distinguished inquisitor: "Jump, jump," the crowds admonished him. "Jump!"

ON FRIDAY MORNING, the Frantzes arrived early again. The previous day had been so unpredictable. After all the excitement, it had been all Marge could do to get the kids dinner and make a few phone calls before collapsing into bed herself. Laurent was scheduled to testify, and he'd stayed up perfecting his speech, which he fully expected to be gaveled down. From the top of the San Francisco City Hall steps, Marge looked out over Van Ness, San Francisco's widest boulevard, and all the radiating streets that converged at City Center, and willed those students to return. She heard them say they'd come back again and bring their friends. But she knew from her own experience that it wasn't easy to sustain a protest. On how many cold days in the past—at rallies and through telephone trees—had she tried to muster the veterans and new recruits? A successful protest was a living, breathing thing, dependent on a web of circumstances: the weather, health, communication. The weather today was perfect, those students robust; they were never off the telephone. She'd try not to feel disappointment. Still, looking down at the empty boulevard, she hoped they would come back. She didn't want to go inside yet and waited another moment, though it seemed longer, when up the quiet boulevard, she saw a few pedestrians loping along the sidewalks. Then came a cluster, with their arms around one another. Then, as if out of Marge's best dream, cresting the hill came what looked like a hundred people, and behind them, filling the road, contesting with the cars, at least a thousand more, marching toward City Hall.

Meanwhile, the committee, delusionally believing it was to their benefit, had allowed loudspeakers to be set up outdoors. As Laurent Frantz's name was called, he was applauded by the audience in the hearing room, by the people in the rotunda and mezzanine, and by the overflow crowd on the thirty wide marble steps to the street. This was now national news, and television crews were setting up their cameras just outside the courtroom as Laurent began to speak and the chairman gaveled him down. Outside the courtroom, the noisy, pumped-up crowd chanted, "Stop the committee," "Go back to the South," "How many lynchings have you investigated?" and "I like freedom—so sue me!" On the other floors of the courthouse, the protest was so noisy that at least one trial had to be postponed.

Again, the police ordered the students sitting on the floor of the rotunda and massed on the stairs to disperse, and this time when they refused, the police aimed their huge, high-powered fire hoses on the protesters. The TV cameras caught the faces of police officers in a kind of battle ecstasy. "You want this?" one cop bellowed as he aimed his water cannon. Anyone still standing was flushed down the stairs by the hoses. Those who could get a grip clung to the banisters. Others were lifted by the cascade and rode the plume of water to the street. Some knocked their heads, and a few lost consciousness. After the water attack, one hundred policemen and an added phalanx of steel-helmeted motorcycle police clubbed, kicked, and dragged the remaining protesters down the marble steps. One news camera caught a cop dragging a student down the stairs by her ponytail. Some students kept their balance for moments before sliding down the steep fall of water; some pulled police down with them. Photos and clips of the day show how high-schooler Danny Grossman, son of Decca's friend Aubrey (slim as a wand in a neat white shirt and black pants) grasped a banister until two immense cops pried his hands off. He dragged both burly officers downstairs with him. That year, on Danny's birthday, Decca paid him this tribute in verse:

> The son of Aubrey can
> Fight like a hurricane
> The shitty committee
> That's called Un-American.

The committee called it a Communist-inspired student riot. Some newspapers dubbed it Black Friday, for the black eye it gave San Francisco; but to the Frantzes and their friends, including Decca, it was the Battle of City Hall.

In the June 1960 issue of *Frontier* magazine, Ralph Tyler, a journalist, reflected on the protest and its consequences:

> What was new—wildly, unforeseeably new—was the thousands of student demonstrators from the University of California, Stanford and San Francisco State College, speaking out as if they had been doing it for years. The sudden appearance of an American generation nobody knew was there.

Looking back, Decca would give full credit to those early student protests for loosening HUAC's grip and holding the abusers of power up to the ridicule they deserved.

CHAPTER 23

*D*ECCA WANTED TO describe what life as a Communist had been like for her in 1950s America, but the subject was too unwieldy or still too close, and she couldn't settle into it. Her interest, much like Dinky's, was thoroughly arrested by the moment they were living. The newspapers were full of the stunning and dangerous, ever-expanding civil rights movement, and she had an idea for an article about how this movement was shaking up entrenched Southern customs. She planned a tour to record "how the southern psyche was faring in the aftermath of the victorious bus boycott," and was offered a two hundred dollar advance from *Esquire* against a six hundred dollar publication fee. She would title it after Nancy's theme "U and Non-U" and call it "You-All and Non-You All."

The chameleon capacity was a happy gift to a good journalist. Decca could claim retreat rights to suburbia when that helped her mission, and she could rely on her contacts and the superfluities of the U-class to open doors when it was expedient. If things worked out, she'd gather enough material to write a book about society in flux and classes in crisis. "Stress the accent," Virginia Durr suggested, "and you'll have the Southern aristocracy eating out of your hand." Mainly, Decca wrote Dinky, she wanted it to be "funny, the moral to emerge by inference."

In May, Decca set off from Washington, D.C.—where she'd been visiting friends—toward Alabama, where she would rendezvous with Virginia Durr. The Durrs now lived in Montgomery, where Cliff had a law practice. Decca's route would take her through Georgia and Kentucky, her dates and destinations incidentally coincided with those of the Congress of Racial Equality's (CORE) Freedom Rides, during which a group of young black

and white civil rights activists defied segregationist laws by sitting together
on interstate Trailways and Greyhound buses.

Decca viewed segregation as a direct continuation of the fascism she'd
opposed since before World War II. What other word described the suprem-
acist mind-set, the intolerance and dehumanization? Traveling across the
South, she rubbed elbows with radicals, devotees of nonviolence, students,
genteel lady observers (whose presence was presumed to lessen the threat of
violence), and no-nonsense testers who followed up to make sure facilities,
once integrated, stayed that way. She had gotten into the habit of studying global conflicts between the weak and strong, rich and poor. Now she
wanted to track the contrasts between outsiders and insiders, urban and pro-
vincial, and the rivalries between enthusiasts—particularly those who sell
and those who buy. She loved word games and dialects, could tell a great
joke, and was most accounts a wonderful listener. These last characteristics describe a universally desirable dinner guest, and when she turned on the
charm, she penetrated the bastions and strongholds she planned to expose.
At a Louisville country club, she wrote of meeting an affluent white couple:

> The conversation turned, as they say, to books, in honor of me I
> think. Mr. Byron said he hadn't read my book because he is a slow
> reader, and consequently does not read any book unless it has been
> condensed for the Readers Digest. Mrs. Byron, on the other hand,
> jerst lerves to read, will go through as many as 3 or 4 books a week.
> Later, of course, the conversation turned to integration. Mr. B. is
> against it (although thinks it inevitable) because it will lead to the
> mongrelization of both races. Like most people in these parts, he
> knows a great deal about horse racing and breeding, and he drew
> rather at length on the parallel about breeding race horses and cart
> horses and the sad results of same. I asked him whether, in that
> case, he didn't think it a bit inadvisable to breed slow readers with
> fast readers, a point that hadn't occurred to him.

Decca went on to Alabama, as did the Freedom Riders, and followed the reports as their various buses were harassed and attacked. At every stop, the young civil rights workers were abused, assaulted, and taunted with threats of rape, torture, castration, and death. One bus was shot at and forced to the side of the road; another set on fire. When Decca asked the white Southerners she met on her journey how this barbaric conduct could still be happening in President Kennedy's America, their rationalizations seemed by turns mystifying, insufficient, and repetitious. (A few brave souls who understood the significance of these events urged her to record them.) The police departments of the various Southern states through which the buses traveled were doing little to protect the protesters. Neither, at first, were the government agents who tracked their activity and took copious notes on little spiral pads. Nevertheless, the Freedom Riders' bravery and persistence made international news. And as their buses approached Montgomery, Alabama, reporters from around the world, including Decca, were on hand to cover the story.

On May 20, 1961, as the Alabama state troopers were escorting the Freedom Riders' bus to the Montgomery city limits, Decca's host Virginia Durr believed there was bound to be a riot, and she pleaded with her friend to be careful. The local police were supposed to meet and protect the young riders from the gathering crowd, but there wasn't a cop to be seen. Cliff Durr's law office was in a building across the street and had a clear view of the bus station. From their window, Virginia and Cliff saw the buses arrive and the crowd erupt. "'Go get the niggers! Go get the niggers.' It was the most horrible thing that I have ever seen," Virginia remembered.

One of the last riders off the bus was Lucretia Collins. All of the riders were overtired and sleep-deprived. Collins had fallen asleep just before their arrival in Montgomery, and she was still a little drowsy as she emerged. Her dreamlike impression of the bus station was of a clutch of people straining at the station door and a reporter with his arms spread as if to hold back the crowd.

John Lewis, the future congressional representative from Georgia, and one of the group leaders had stepped off the bus and begun talking to an NBC television reporter when "a hundred white men and women surged around the bus, swinging metal pipes, sticks, bats, and pocketbooks." Virginia Durr saw people randomly attacked. From within the crowd, Decca saw Frederick and Anna Gach, two local white residents, arrested while trying to protect a black bystander from assault. The police arrived, but the assaults and humiliations continued until the U.S. Justice Department finally sent armed marshals into Montgomery to reestablish law and order.

The Durrs' office had become the central meeting point for witnesses and people escaping the riot. When Bob Zellner, a young friend of the Durrs, arrived, Virginia said that Decca was out there somewhere. Zellner gallantly agreed to bring her back safely. As he recalls, he found her

> cool as a cucumber, taking notes on the corner right outside the office. I was relieved but it turned out she wasn't as calm as she looked. When I clumsily approached her asking, "Are you Jessica Mitford?" a look of pure terror came over her.
>
> "Why do you want to know? Who told you that?" she asked, backing away from me. I finally stammered that Virginia had sent me to get her, frantically pointing over my shoulder in the general direction of the law office. With a great deal of relief, regaining the British jut of her aristocratic chin, she replied, "Well, carry on, we'll go see Virginia and see what we can get into next."

Despite her courtesy to Zellner, Decca was "furious" with Virginia for meddling. She hadn't wanted to be rescued and resented the implication that she had needed to be.

Later Saturday afternoon, once traffic was moving again, Cliff, Virginia, and Decca returned to the Durrs' home on the outskirts of town. Although Virginia, a native Alabamian, urged caution and predicted worse things to come, their guest was impatient to get back to where the action was. The Durrs didn't have a telephone, and Decca wanted at least to phone her press contacts and try to sell the story. More than anything, she was determined to attend the meeting to be held that night at the First Baptist Church. "This is absurd—to be so scared," she told Virginia.

The Durrs lent Decca their old Buick for the night, and she drove to the church with Peter Ackerberg, a white student from Antioch College. Virginia remembers how Decca dressed for the meeting in her "Southern costume—a lovely sort of fluffy green hat with chiffon on it, and pearls around her neck and white gloves and a green chiffon dress."

Outside the church, Decca saw outraged segregationists, freelance hoodlums, vigilantes, and snarling drunks (dressed in their summer riot clothes: men in dirty T-shirts and dungarees, women in sleeveless cotton dresses). They were circling the church to harass the thin line of deputy marshals protecting the church occupants. There were no city police officers, no state guards. Decca had planned to park blocks away and enter the church through a back way, but in the chaos, she had simply parked as near as she could and then with Ackerberg had stridden through the front doors of the church. They were just inside when the mob torched the Durrs' car, down to its frame. Decca and Ackerberg wouldn't learn this until later.

Inside the packed church, it was stifling. The congregation, a cross-section of the African American community—ministers, students, army veterans, teachers, farmers, owners of small businesses, lawyers, church elders, and schoolchildren—had been singing for hours, since the first black families in their church clothes had arrived around 5:00 P.M. Outside, the marshals had thrown tear gas at the increasingly hostile crowd, and the fumes had begun to float into the church just slightly. It stung the eyes, had a terrible sour smell, and made everything even more claustrophobic. All night, people urged one another to keep singing: "Ain't Gonna Let Nobody Turn Me Around," "We Shall Overcome," "This Little Light of Mine." Though there were only half as many people inside as out, every pew was full. There were pockets of chaos inside, but no panic as people rushed to the sinks to rinse their eyes and to the basement and closets to cover and protect their children. Church deacons closed any window still open, which cut down

on the ventilation and spiked up the heat even more. *Help will come*, the
deacons counseled.

Martin Luther King Jr. arrived from Atlanta to address the meeting.
He assured the congregation that the marshals were still in place, but he
couldn't guarantee that their line would hold. This was Decca's first encounter with the Reverend King, and she was impressed by his sangfroid under
pressure. Her companions in the church, particularly those who knew King
or had heard him preach, had more than respect—they loved him and had
no doubt he'd rescue them. She wanted to interview him, but King was
surrounded by an entourage of bodyguards, advisers, politicians, and ministers, and the crisis point was close.

As the Reverend King and Attorney General Robert Kennedy negotiated on the phone to find a safe exit strategy, food was running low and
children fell asleep on tabletops. Governor John Patterson of Alabama was
balky and slow to compromise. The Democratic Party still relied on its
Southern bloc. Kennedy, wary of violating state sovereignty, was reluctant
to call the National Guard to help. Finally, Patterson declared martial law
and activated the Alabama National Guard. These soldiers were also known
as the Dixie division.

Decca watched the newly arrived police and soldiers disperse the mob.
At first, she and others believed that these were their deliverers, so it was
doubly shocking to see these young men—activated by the governor, not the
Feds, and therefore under segregationist control—turn their guns toward
the church and its congregation. Decca and her companions might not have
understood the exact steps invoked in this federal-state minuet, but they
knew they were hostages.

The Durrs listened to the radio news throughout the evening.
Eyewitnesses delivered their reports from inside the church through its one
telephone line. They heard that more federal marshals had been transported
to the area in postal trucks and that U.S. Army troops might be flown in.
That night around midnight, the general of the Alabama National Guard
finally entered the church to address its occupants. Decca noted his words:

"While the mob had been cleared from the immediate vicinity, they were thought to be re-grouping in the dark surrounding streets." Everyone would have to remain inside, said the general, until he deemed it safe for their removal.

It was still steamy at midnight as Decca shared a scavenged meal of matzos and grits (an odd mix but what was on hand) with her neighbors, then stood in line to use the phone in the church basement, her chiffon dress a sticky mess by then. (At some point, she ditched those white gloves for better speed and comfort.) In the one minute allocated to each caller, she reassured Virginia Durr (on a neighbor's telephone) that she and Ackerberg were fine. Someone from the National Guard would drive them home.

Sometime close to dawn, the Durrs heard a vehicle roll into their drive. Virginia had the impression that the general of the Alabama National Guard himself was driving. Ackerberg, Decca's companion, remembered their driver as a more modestly ranked guardsman who had first circled the church looking for the Durrs' Buick. The gentle and conscientious Ackerberg thought they couldn't find their car because they hadn't paid attention to where they'd parked.

Decca was tired but exhilarated. As a journalist, she knew that a great story had fallen into her lap. *Life* magazine agreed to take an article on her firsthand view of the riot at the bus station and the church meeting. Decca's successful work before then had been of a slower and more deliberate nature. She would become better at writing quickly, but beat reporting would never be her strong suit. It was difficult for her to keep her cool and amused voice under the stress of doing the story justice. As she'd begun her tour of the South, it had amused her to identify with the wry and quotable foreign correspondent who writes at a distance. But to successfully draw national attention to the struggle for civil rights, she couldn't afford to be dismissed as an accidental tourist or a frivolous opportunist. She had been lucky to find herself on the spot. In her article, she wanted to do more than inform; she wanted to change minds, move people to act, provoke governments to reform. The word *muckraker* wouldn't be attributed to Decca's writing for several more years, but it described the work she'd do to fortify her position and tell the truth as she saw it. Decca's talent was to write with a light hand; it was the work of her life to combine a humorous quality with serious subject matter. These contradictory demands burdened Decca as she tried to write about Montgomery, and *Life* never published the piece she subsequently wrote. Of Decca's *Esquire* article about the South, published under the title "Whut They're Thanking Down There," Virginia remarked, "All the funny ways she can write were muted because she was so upset and disturbed by the riot. The article was rather good, but it was not terribly funny."

To her hometown papers, however, Decca was the story. The *Oakland Tribune* and the *San Francisco Examiner* reported that she had been one of the fifteen hundred people trapped in the church overnight. Decca's FBI files provided a press round-up of her Montgomery experience and gave the last word to Herb Caen, a columnist for the *San Francisco Chronicle*, in his May 25, 1961, piece: "Author JESSICA MITFORD TREUHAFT had joined the 'Freedom Riders' in Alabama and had to take refuge in a church to escape the wrath of 'Ku Kluxers' . . . 'And only a howling mob,' she adds 'could keep me in church for 12 hours!'"

CHAPTER 24

WO YEARS AFTER *Frontier* magazine published Decca's article on funerals, the *Saturday Evening Post* planned its own feature. Writer Roul Tunley came to California to conduct his research and asked to meet the Treuhafts.

Tunley's article began with a report on a televised debate between funeral industry honchos and "those who feel that burials in this country have reached a pinnacle of extravagance and tastelessness unknown since the days of the Pharaohs." Decca, he called, "the sharpest thorn in the morticians' sides." The topics under debate included inflated prices (Tunley reported that in 1961, funeral bills represented the largest item an average family would ever buy, "excepting a house or automobile") and alternatives to lavish funerals like cremation and co-op societies, for which, he wrote, Mrs. Treuhaft was also a "tireless recruiter." In Tunley's article, Decca at age forty-three appeared an immensely likable and informed champion on behalf of the vulnerable. She was also slightly wacky: an English auntie, fomenting rebellion "over the teacups," not averse to going undercover in "widow's weeds" to ferret out some backroom swindles at your local funeral establishment. Tunley's portrait was an early version of Decca as the crusading eccentric, a characterization that would eventually bloom into "Queen of the Muckrakers" and jolly doyenne.

In June, after the *Saturday Evening Post* published Tunley's article, an editor from the magazine told the Treuhafts that "Can You Afford to Die?" had generated "more mail than they had ever received on anything they had ever printed." The subject's popularity didn't surprise Bob, who thought a book about American funeral practices would also be a surefire hit. First, Bob encouraged Tunley to expand his work, but once the writer demurred (he said he had another subject in mind), Bob suggested to Decca that she write the book. The project would demand a lot of research and a certain sensibility—in fact, Bob thought it cried out for his wife's special talents. Decca said she would write it on the condition that her husband agreed to help. The timing was right. The Romilly inheritance would enable Bob, after years of penny-pinching, to take a sabbatical. In his absence, Bob's law partners, including family friend Dobby Brin Walker, could be relied on to keep their now moderately successful practice stable. As the book began to take shape, an FBI special agent assigned to monitor Decca's activities filed a note to say the Treuhafts were plotting a joint venture, worth keeping an eye on.

DECCA'S CURIOSITY ABOUT funerals came naturally. Her childhood room had overlooked a cemetery. The younger Mitford daughters, Debo said, "were forbidden to watch funerals, which of course made them more fascinating, and we always did. Jessica and I once fell into a newly dug grave, to the delight of Nancy who pronounced that we should have bad luck the rest of our lives." Very little bad luck attended the early days of Decca's book about funerals. She was soon absorbed in her research, delighted by the details she could excavate in her own living room by turning the pages of trade magazines where she found editorials like "Children's Funerals: A Golden Opportunity to Build Good Will."

In the journal *Casket and Sunnyside*, she was delighted to discover "New Bra-Form, Post Mortem Form Restoration, Accomplishes So Much for So Little." "They only cost $11 for a package of 50. Shall I send some?" she asked her goddaughter Kathy Kahn. Meanwhile, Bob spent a good deal of time in the library at San Francisco College of Mortuary Science. He'd do more, she told Kathy, "but he keeps saying they only maintain a skeleton staff there over the holidays." On a research visit to Forest Lawn Cemetery near Los Angeles, Decca marveled at their February and March specials: "Thus making it worth one's while, I suppose, to 'pass on' during one of these months!"

She and Bob already had a title, and it was a beaut: *The American Way of Death*. This was direct from Howard C. Raether, the unsuspecting mortuary executive who, with the boosterism of an industry with no natural enemy, pronounced, "Funerals are becoming more and more a part of the American way of life."

The American way of life—such a capacious concept. In America, one could become anyone, rise to anything, go anywhere. Who better to comment on the irony than two ex-red menaces, themselves persecuted for unorthodox or impossible ideas? The Treuhafts may have been temporarily outmaneuvered, but now they would tell the world about the consequences of materialism, consumerism, commercialism, and rampant capitalism. Comparing extravagant funerals to the excessive and unnecessary ornamentation on Cadillacs, that international symbol of American triumphalism, Decca threw down the gantlet. "It's a racket," she exclaimed. "Why can't we have funerals without fins?" Despite this arbiter-of-taste theme, there is about the emergent book very little of the puritan judge.

Decca reassembled her book committee, which as a group decided from the outset "to go for the jugular and expose, not the occasional miscreant, but the profiteering and monopolistic practices of the industry as a whole as exemplified by its most respectable and ethical practitioners." One of the book's most important themes would be questioning why so many American morticians insisted on embalming for hygiene. This procedure they held to be necessary and sanitary—another superior product to eliminate those germs that bedeviled Americans in daily life and (when the morticians could sell it) the hereafter. As Neil Brown, president of the San Francisco Funeral Directors Association, told Tunley, "I'm not concerned with what they do in England or France, any more than what they do in the Congo. In this country *everybody* can be embalmed. It's the American way."

Embalming was an art with its most particular connoisseurs and aficionados, accessories and products like Tru-Lanol Arterial Fluid. One testimonial that Decca came across was written by a satisfied customer to describe a very difficult case: "'69-year old woman, was 40 hours in heated apartment before being discovered . . . after 4 days of Tru-Lanol treatment, all was OK.' He adds wistfully, 'I wish I could have kept her for four more days.'"

Decca thought her readers would appreciate the offbeat direction her work was taking. Having confidence in her material meant she could follow the thread of an outré subject like embalming where it led. She was particularly amused by the attention paid by the champions of embalming to the importance of a "Beautiful Memory Picture." This embodied the philosophy that the deceased would essentially be best remembered as a rouged and powdered doll. Decca satirized the theory (which seemed to her absurd), but it wasn't an easy one to pry loose. Affluent Americans were generally advised not to view a body (even minutes after its death) unless embalmed, because that last imprint might obliterate all preceding memories. The argument didn't make sense, but it was a tenacious one that folklore reinforced and the funeral industry exploited.

The favorable reception of the first hundred pages by Decca's friends had been encouraging. When she sent these pages off to her British and American publishers (the same companies that had brought out her memoir), she anticipated some grumbling regarding the embalming chapter. Instead, she was shocked to hear that her British publisher didn't like the chapters at all. Her agent James MacGibbon thought the work such a "bad and ghoulish joke" that he couldn't represent it and resigned. Decca's American publisher, Lovell Thompson at Houghton Mifflin, didn't care for the book's tone, either. His suggestion was that she cut out the "foolishness," which led her to this defense:

> I'm more and more beginning to see the subject matter of the book in this way: it illuminates in weird, gruesome and distorted fashion many of the crazy things about our society. For example, it is true that advertising has become madder and more outlandish over the years, and the Practical Burial Footwear people are only doing for their product what other advertisers do for theirs. But the fact this practical footwear is destined for the dead is what exposes

something rather terrifying about their whole outlook. The point of all this is that the book will try to be one of protests, not just against high costs, but against something more sinister: destruction of standards, taste etc. (This is what one hopes will *emerge* from the book, rather than being explicitly stated.)

Decca and Bob had a Plan B. They decided they would rather change publishers than alter the book's tone, or if it came to it, a Plan C, in which they would mimeograph the manuscript and sell it themselves as they had with *Lifeitselfmanship*. They were used to working in an inky mess outside the system, and though the fruits of mainstream success could be enjoyable, such success wasn't necessary. In any case, that scheme proved irrelevant when Decca's new agent, Candida Donadio, negotiated a better deal with thirty-year-old Simon and Schuster editor Robert Gottlieb, whose guidance seemed to Decca "like all the members of my Book Committee rolled into one."

》《

IN JANUARY 1962, segregationists in the South were firming up their defenses. In Alabama, the white riot at the Montgomery bus station had not resulted in a single conviction. Bull Connor, who was police chief in Birmingham at the time of the event, was running for governor on a platform that included acquiring a pack of "police dogs to sic on any freedom riders who ventured into Alabama."

From its new national offices in Atlanta, the Student Nonviolent Coordinating Committee (SNCC pronounced "snick") dedicated many of its resources to voter registration, and students and community organizers began to make their way south to work for them. It was typical for segregationists to accuse these community activists of Communism. There had been a great deal of discussion at the top levels of the mainstream civil rights movement concerning whether to accept the support of radicals and progressives (any of which might be perceived as Communists). The NAACP leaders were concerned that such alliances would slow its progress. NAACP membership was typically older and more cautious, while the students at SNCC were more often urgent and passionate. They had something new to add to the careful design that their elders had plotted. It was their time, and not only would the SNCC leaders fail to be intimidated by the Ku Klux Klan and its political surrogates, but they wouldn't countenance the deceit of the red hunters.

Just as SNCC had pondered the public perception of ex-menaces, so did Decca's book committee. Was this finally the right time for Decca to declare that she had been a Communist? It was a sticky question, which hadn't been relevant to her previous book. Anyone who had read *Daughters and Rebels* would have known she was a lefty, but apart from family controversies, she hadn't had to defend any particular political position. By 1962, the country had distanced itself from the mad McCarthy years, but *Commie* was still a curse word. Khrushchev was perceived as the very model of a totalitarian leader: Dissidents were being shot trying to escape from East to West Germany, and the Bay of Pigs fiasco had done nothing to rehabilitate the reputation of socialism in the United States. At the same time, spies, world domination, and atomic annihilation were increasingly the subject of satire in cartoons and pulp fiction, in movies and on TV. Boris and Natasha were klutzy. If *The American Way of Death* had enough momentum to really challenge it, the funeral industry would have something to gain from discrediting the Mitford-Treuhaft past.

Decca decided it was only fair to prepare her new publishers, so she came clean to Robert Gottlieb. From the first, she'd found her new editor simpatico. He might have been young and full of himself, but he wanted to take risks. The admiration was mutual. Asked by filmmaker Ida Landauer to explain Decca's appeal, Gottlieb said, "She has all her wits about her and most people have no wits at all."

Decca found Gottlieb unsurprised by her disclosure, which must have felt like a jolt to her. So many people, herself included, had worked so hard for so long to keep their affiliations secret. Perhaps it was simply that the intellectuals in Gottlieb's generation assumed that most of their elders "were now or once had been [Communist]." In the same interview with Landauer, Gottlieb assessed Decca's party membership: "Essentially she did it for a tease. I don't think she would have been quite so ardent a communist, if she hadn't known that quite so many people would be upset because she was one."

>«

DINKY ROMILLY WAS in her final year at Sarah Lawrence. She'd joined the new left National Student Association, and the more Dinky became interested in the civil rights movement, the less interested she was in her studies. Decca, who had spent much of her life lamenting her lack of formal education, who had been thrilled the moment her daughter stepped into kindergarten, and who had saved all the checks from Esmond's veterans' benefits in a college fund for Dinky, was not easily reconciled with her daughter's conclusion that college was irrelevant.

On a research tour of the Midwest, Decca continued on to Sarah Lawrence to see if she could sort out the situation. She had an awkward discussion with her daughter's academic advisers, whom she could not move to count Dinky's activism as college credit. Dinky was twenty-one years old. She had inherited her mother's brains and beauty and her father's single-mindedness. Once she had awakened to a sense of purpose, she could capably defend her position, but on this occasion, no words could persuade her mother, who insisted Dinky complete her degree. Decca was "livid" when her daughter withdrew from college just weeks before graduation. In May, mother and daughter boarded a train back to Oakland. For three days as the train traveled west, they glared at each other across their roomette. In her daughter's eyes, Decca could not "make the comparison" to her own rebellious youth when she had defied convention by running away. In Oakland, Dinky observed that her parents, who had always lived so frugally, were now "besotted by money." They left her to find a job and stay with fourteen-year-old Benjy, while Bob was off to Moscow for a peace conference and Decca went to Inch Kenneth to finish her new book.

Muv was ailing, and this would be Decca's last summer with her mother. The drawing room in which she wrote overlooking the sea was a serene refuge after the preceding few months. There was just one small glitch in the supplies department—she was by then used to equating bouts of writing with hard drinking and complained that though there was sherry and wine around dinnertime, there was "no real booze." Before leaving California, her physician and friend Eph Kahn had presumably told her that cutting back might be a good thing. "I don't think so," she wrote to Barb, Eph's wife. "I know I'd get more done on the book if I could have a good stiff drink in the p.m."

The greater interruption was her discovery of a cache of letters addressed to Esmond and Decca Romilly at Rotherhithe Street—covering the period when they had run away. Three of these, all posted from Germany, told three versions of one episode before the war. Her mother had written: "Had tea with Hitler. He is very agreeable and has surprisingly good manners." Debo's teenaged perspective of their tea party included "Delicious cakes. Bobo [Unity] gets quite different when she's with him, all trembly and can't take her eyes off him." Unity's letter said: "Tea with the Führer. Muv kept talking about home-made bread and asked if they couldn't pass a law in Germany making it illegal to take out the wheat germ."

As chief landowner, Decca did try to participate in island life, though the bloom was off that rose. When her mother invited some guests to dinner—guests whose major characteristic was "freedom from fear of being boring"—she learned "exactly how to import ponies from Iceland to Scotland and train them to carry dead stags." Educational, she admitted in its way. "In fact, should I ever be faced with this exact problem at some future time I really do think I'll know just how to do it."

FOR DINKY, OAKLAND had compensations. There was a new militancy on the nearby Berkeley campus. The SLATE group, begun around the time of the anti-HUAC hearings and other New Left groups, proliferated. Among these was a branch of the National Student Association so that Dinky could pick up where she left off. At a SNCC support group, she met SNCC leader Charles McDew. They started a romance, and by the end of summer (once she found a reliable neighbor to look after Benjy), she joined him on his travels. She would eventually wind up back in New York City and moved into a fifth-floor walk-up in Greenwich Village, not too far from the apartment Esmond and Decca had occupied. In 1962, Greenwich Village was a place where a person could share a cheap apartment, where outsiders gathered, and where artists, "ex's" and red-diaper babies felt at home. It existed as it had for generations, in sharp contrast to uptown, not least for its role as incubator of underground arts and its hospitality to love affairs between men, between women, and between people of vastly different incomes, different marital statuses, and different races. In that last category, Dinky was just one of many people whose interracial relationship would have been dangerous in another state. She loved her new neighborhood. It didn't matter that she had only one dress to wear to work—she'd wash and dry it every day. She worked as a receptionist in the day and for SNCC at night as an office worker.

On February 1, 1963, SNCC held a fund-raiser at Town Hall in New York and the glitterati of the civil rights movement were all invited. Among them were Harry Belafonte Jr., Eartha Kitt, Marlon Brando, and Bob Moses, leader of the voting rights initiative. Former Freedom Riders John Lewis and James Forman (the new executive director of SNCC) came from Atlanta to attend. "Who is Constancia Romilly?" Forman asked around the office. He had read and admired the paper Dinky had researched on Lowndes County, Alabama. When they met, Forman told Dinky that her education and skills as a writer and an editor could be put to greater use in Atlanta, the civil rights movement's organizational center. James Forman was a professorial-looking man, large and rumpled. He had the good teacher's motivation to instruct and document and lugged around a clunky reel-to-reel tape recorder to preserve the exact words of people whose stories he believed others needed to hear. He was writing a book, he told Dinky, and needed help transcribing all those tape reels.

Decca and her daughter didn't harbor grudges. She was proud of Dinky's resourcefulness and intrigued by her hip and sophisticated downtown life, but typically (as generations mandate) a beat behind. In June, when Medgar Evers was murdered, Decca wrote to commiserate with Virginia. They discussed the great number of students now going south to work for the civil rights movement in voter registration and in Freedom schools, and Decca wrote that her daughter was among those "chucking her job and going to work for SNCC" (or, she added, "SNCCing her job and going to work for Chuck?"). This was old news to Virginia, who told her that Dinky was already in Atlanta and that Dinky's new boyfriend was Forman, who had separated from his wife. Seen from most angles, their romance wouldn't be easy. Bob told Dinky he "feared the Klan would come around. He had nightmares about that."

CHAPTER 25

I N THE SPRING of 1963, Decca went to New York to consult with Simon and Schuster's marketing team about *The America Way of Death*'s battle plan. The publishing house knew it had a hot property. The team, including editor Robert Gottlieb, shared Decca's amused and irreverent attitude toward undertakers in America. If things went as they hoped, a new breeze would blow the proprietary aroma of embalming fluid out to sea. Charmed by Decca's voice and intelligence and the reasoning of her argument, readers would view the passion and insistence of the funeral industry's status quo not just as old-fashioned but as con artistry. At their New York meeting, they had a whole spectrum of tactics regarding "how to get the book attacked as subversive and me attacked as a red (surprising how little trouble they are going to have in this regard, I was thinking to myself), how to stir up the John Birch Society to go for us. Goodness you'd have roared." She wrote to Bob of interviews, photographs, television appearances, and broadcast debates on their itinerary. "All these special letters and special approaches did so remind me of CRC."

In May, as her publicity team met, Decca heard that at age eighty-three, her mother had died on Inch Kenneth, with four of her daughters around her. Muv had followed her daughter's adventures and occupations, collected articles and photographs, and logged these in great scrapbooks. She'd been proud of her children. They had all shown resourcefulness, courage, originality. Muv had even applauded *Hons and Rebels*, though it had caused her discomfort. Decca had tried to balance the impact of the most offensive English reviews, which had ridiculed Muv for her upper-class hauteur and political obtuseness, with more sympathetic comments culled from the U.S. press, and she had sent these over the last year of Muv's life, like so many mitigating valentines.

Decca was grateful for Nancy and Debo's descriptions of her mother's funeral: the Scottish pipers and special hymns. She still felt lonely and far away, but parsed the details with a connoisseur's mind. The beautiful flowers that she heard covered her mother's grave reminded Decca of the beds from which they'd been gathered on Inch Kenneth. These she compared with the assembly-line floral tributes so often imposed on American mourners, as part of their funeral package. Her mother's death and funeral may have been much on Decca's mind, but it was her habit to bury grief in work. Her bête noire had recently become the floral industry's connivance to add expensive wreaths (sometimes including withered flowers) to increase the mortician's bill. There was something fascinating and bizarre in the custom by which a larger wreath showed greater respect and greater sympathy. The book's publicists planned to exploit this custom; they ordered a giant wreath as centerpiece of their booth at an upcoming booksellers convention. Another green and red wreath would show up on the jacket of the book's first edition.

THE SUBJECT OF a joint byline had yet to be resolved. From the start, Decca and Bob assumed they would share author credit for *The American Way of Death*. Decca was always lavish in her praise of her husband's work. Bob was a "*marvelous* editor." He wrote bits and pieces, and his research was central to their mutual project. "You see," Bob said, "Decca doesn't like research. She won't even go to the library. I did that and also the fieldwork because she didn't like going into mortuaries either." Decca conducted the interviews and narrated the book in her own voice. Bob assured her that he didn't feel jealous or deprived. In the end, the question of credit was settled by the agents and publishers, who advised Decca that co-written books never sell as well.

As expected, in the months leading to *The American Way of Death*'s publication, the funeral industry began publishing updates, warnings, and defensive strategies. Decca played curious and accommodating. After one shopping excursion to Forest Lawn's gift shop, she inquired about the old English-style designs on some of their merchandise. Her inquiries befuddled the funeral industry, from front-desk clerks to souvenir manufacturers to the undertaker's apprentice. What sort of person challenges the veracity of a quotation on an ornament? Why did it matter that the inscription on the gift ashtrays featured an invented coat of arms and phony French words? Everyone had a living to make. Some people found comfort in the twenty-five-cent ashtrays (also attractive as wall mounts) to be found in Forest Lawn's gift shop, or the items wouldn't sell as well as they did. At first, the industry's representatives replied with good old common sense. Then warnings appeared in the trade press, but the more they fomented, the more prepublication orders for Decca's book soared.

IN EARLY AUGUST 1963, the Treuhafts held a party on Regent Street to celebrate the book's publication. Bob made chicken paprika for "thousands." Despite their advance warning, the morticians and company hardly knew what hit them. Their first line of defense was to try to smear Decca by association. Wilbur M. Krieger, managing director of National Selected Morticians, said Decca unpatriotically wished to "substitute communist, Russian-style funerals for our fine American ones." A right-wing journal called *Tocsin* said she was attempting "to bury capitalist America's funeral customs." The mortuary trade journals accused her of ruining business, and some Bay Area morticians simply called her "the devil."

Decca had decided that once the charges about her past began to surface, she would neither confirm nor deny her previous affiliation with Communism. Although she had long since left the party, a simple denial would not be possible, since it would leave the impression that the premise of such a question was legitimate.

On October 15, Congressman James Utt, whose Southern California district included Forest Lawn Cemetery, denounced Jessica Mitford and her book on the floor of the House of Representatives. In addition, he objected to the CBS documentary *The Great American Funeral*, which was closely based on Mitford's research. "While hiding behind the commercial aspects of the mortician and the cemeteries and mausoleums where our dear departed friends and relatives are commemorated, she is really striking another blow at the Christian religion," he read into the Congressional Record. The *Washington Post* reported that Decca called the accusations a "Red herring," or a diversion from the true crime at hand. After this free publicity, her publishers released a list of the cities that she planned to visit on her national book tour.

The FBI agents who seemed to have become rather complacent regarding the Treuhafts' activities over the previous few years scurried to make up for lost time. They produced a secret report, which summarized several critical events in Decca's life, eloquently concluding that she had "lapsed into a steadfast condition of noncooperation."

Decca's book would become a best seller, and she would make news for months. After six weeks, it would be supplanted in the number one spot on the *New York Times* nonfiction best-seller list by John F. Kennedy's book *Profiles in Courage.*

There were protests and letters of opposition to Decca's appearances, and a bomb threat in Boston. Attacks on her past politics and objections to the way she treated her subject were counterbalanced by the encouraging crowds who came to hear her speak and read, and the approval she encountered for questioning the status quo. She vastly enjoyed her popular success, not least of all because such a thing would have seemed impossible ten years before. "I think that only those who have been, as I was, a target of the Truman-McCarthy-era assault on radicals can appreciate the feeling of decompression on having one's work accepted at its face value."

Her touring strategy was to "make thousands of jokes in succession." In this, she was helped by the high-profile preservation of Lenin's corpse in Red Square, which held the record for "long-term viewing," and by Khrushchev's famous cold-war threat to capitalist adversaries, "We shall bury you," which, she said, made Forest Lawn mad since he was "muscling in on their territory." Talk show hosts tried to red-bait her, but she would turn the situation to her advantage. When she was in Denver, a gloomy funeral industry representative declared, "I could put you away for $150." Decca snapped, "Sorry, you're too late. Other undertakers have offered to do it for nothing, as long as it's soon." The success or failure of Decca's book was finally a matter of choice, of taste, of the pocketbook. There was little traction for the attacks against her—and though they continued, its sales increased. "Unfortunately for the undertakers," Decca wrote, "it would seem there is little popular support for the theory that a 'fine funeral' is America's first line of defense and the highest expression of patriotism."

Decca had previously experienced fame as notoriety. The response from most readers, apart from right-wingers and the funeral industry, was admiration. She was instantly the expert, the authority on all things funeral. Almost every day, there were articles in the press, more requests for appearances, and political cartoons on the subject. Decca's droll charm made her an immediate favorite on the interview and lecture circuit. And all this attention translated to money: "Benj is angling for a $2 weekly increase in his allowance," Decca wrote her mother-in-law, Aranka:

> I've already done a couple of daring things, such as to buy a salad bowl (to replace the beat-up old wooden mixing bowl we've been using) . . . Oh yes and Bob Gottlieb said: "Do you want some money? You've only to say the word, you know, you don't have to wait for the royalty report with the way things are going." So I said what a smashing idea, do send loads.

In the past, she'd been used to staying in hotels that were "total fleabags," but her new publishers booked her into a fancy suite at the Boston Ritz, complete with an enormous basket of flowers. "It was thrilling . . . I danced around the room," she said.

Evelyn Waugh wrote that Jessica Mitford's book was funny, but its author did not have a "plainly stated attitude to death." Decca asked her sister to pass along a message next time she saw Waugh: "Tell him of course I'm *against* it." Decca's sisters gave generally positive reviews.

Decca's book was about the exploitation of the vulnerable, the absurdity of fast-changing styles in postmortem fashions, and the mechanism that reinforces the perpetuation of profit. Here was the capitalist system as represented in the phony-baloney funeral racket. The go-getters of the 1950s had taken off their hats and gotten down to business. Waugh, who had become more religious over the course of his life and had converted to Catholicism, read her book through the lens of a tut-tutter. Mitford chroniclers Jonathan Guinness and Catherine Guinness (Decca's nephew and great-niece) saw *The Loved One* as Waugh's dual attack on America's "materialist denial of death and rejection of its religious implications." Decca's book, by contrast, demonstrated that religious implications are more often used to make a killing in the marketplace. Decca was distinctly unconcerned with the "spiritual aspects of death," which she associated with Christian and Jewish theology. However, one of the great joys she experienced in the whirlwind year was of the clergy defending her position, and she went all out to "exploit that newfound respectability." Several subsequent articles containing "occasional references to the spiritual aspects of death," were, she admitted, "a bit specious coming from me, as the undertakers may have divined, but there was nothing they could do about it."

In its review, the *People's Daily World* reliably ascribed the crisis in funerals to the corrupting system of free enterprise: "It is bad enough keeping up with the Joneses in life, but it is even more tragic to try to keep up with the Joneses in death." On the political right, the conservative *National Review* sincerely congratulated Decca for exposing "the whole ghoulish paraphernalia of the death trade." But once the editors, including William F. Buckley, discovered her political history, the publication rescinded it endorsement and, to the delight of Decca and the whole book committee, attacked her as a "crypt-o Communist."

Eventually, the trade magazines began to refer to a gadfly named "Jessica." Sometimes, they'd regard her as a dilettante who got everything wrong, who was hardly worth so much attention. Other times, she was a pernicious and damaging influence. The single-name treatment was at once a snide dismissal and acknowledgment of her fame. Decca considered it a mark of distinction, like "Zsa Zsa" or "Liberace."

In the year after her book was published, Decca was swamped with letters. Some were fan letters, but others were messages of complaint and of forlorn hopes. Among other more amusing consequences of her success was the way the Mitford name became "synonymous with cheap funerals." For a while, the "Mitford style" came to mean the "plainest and least expensive funeral," and a "Mitford," the cheapest coffin available. Years later, reviewing a revised edition of *The American Way of Death*, A. Alvarez would compare the book to another "masterpiece of black humor" appearing that year, Stanley Kubrick's film *Dr. Strangelove*. Each "made fun of the sacred cows of the time with an equal glee." Alvarez wrote that in 1963, "death was on everybody's mind." In November, after the assassination of President Kennedy, Robert Kennedy had to choose his brother's coffin. RFK had read *The American Way of Death* some months before his brother's death, and he was to some extent influenced by it. He chose the slightly less expensive one.

》《

In July, Decca traveled to Inch Kenneth. Without her mother and without a book to write, she found its cold, drizzly remoteness, which had kept her inside at her manuscript on previous visits, demoralizing. She and Bob were still laird and lady of the isle, but the prospect of retiring there one day, now that she had a career at home, seemed unlikely. Wandering through the island house, Decca had discovered another hamper filled with old letters all neatly organized by Muv. These included details of their mother's campaign to get Diana out of prison; letters from Tom to his parents from school, and from his days as an officer, when he was a young cosmopolite who traveled with a tuxedo in his luggage; and "a lot of sad things like Tom's first hair when it was cut, in a teeny envelope." She gave the lot to Debo, who had inherited their mother's family scrapbooks.

In the summer of 1964, Benjy was enrolled at a French college near Lyons, and on her way to visit her son, Decca stopped in Paris to see Nancy. This was their first time together since *The American Way of Death* had been published, and Nancy congratulated the best-selling author, teasing her about her new-made fortune and proudly pronouncing her *un chacal des cimitières* (a graveyard ghoul). Decca liked to joke that "Nancy was dressed by Chanel and I by J.C. Penney," but on this occasion, both sisters swept into an exclusive fashion house for a splurge. It was as celebratory a holiday as Decca would ever spend in her sister's company. On one afternoon, Nancy pulled together some left-wingers for a day's entertainment, and on another, in an unexpected show of intimacy, she took Decca to have lunch with Gaston Palewski, her French lover.

For her part, Decca "loved Nancy's company." In later years, she'd say, "I suppose I never knew her very well. In childhood the age difference between us was too great to permit of much companionship." In later years, theirs was more of an "arms-length relationship." But pleasing—or at least impressing—her oldest sibling may have been one of the driving forces of Decca's life. It wasn't Nancy's way to show vulnerability or obvious sentiment to Decca, but during this encounter in Paris, Decca came at last to see Nancy at close range. The older sister was scrupulous and courteous, droll, sometimes icy, sometimes generous. If her words were occasionally wounding or her conduct sometimes waspish, Decca took pleasure in their shared history, in her sister's expert authorial advice, and in their rare confidences. Outside the family, their relationship looked very different. In Decca's friend Marge Frantz's opinion, "Nancy treated Decca like shit."

Once Decca had left Versailles, Nancy wrote of Decca to Debo: "Oh dear, I regard her as Muv's greatest failure, she is such a clever person & completely uneducated so that one keeps running into a wall when talking to her."

»«

MAGAZINE EDITORS KEPT after the author of *The American Way of Death* to write features. Her magazine workload included articles for *McCall's*, *Vogue*, *Esquire*, and *Holiday*. She didn't much care for the deadline life, but she liked the attention. She read several local and national papers every day. Long after she had left the Communist Party, she was still receiving the *People's Daily World*. Decca had earned her lifetime subscription back when she and Bob were first married and she'd won the prize at the benefit party they had thrown on Clayton Street. Bob joked that "they'd have to produce a death certificate to get rid of it."

Early in the year, an editor at *Show* asked her to write an article about the upcoming film *The Loved One*. Decca had once been in the running to write the film script (as had both Luis Buñuel and Elaine May), but director Tony Richardson had settled on Terry Southern, an author with reliably irreverent credentials. Indeed, the advertising campaign for Richardson's film announced it had "Something to Offend Everybody," which warmed the cockles of Decca's heart.

Decca was a personality in the Bay Area, a national figure whose field was the American funeral, a role often disputed by rival experts inside and outside the industry. Invited to speak on a panel at Albion College in Michigan, Decca first had to endure the lecture of a Dr. Oman, who among his other credentials listed "psycho-dramatist." He defended the undertaker's worthy profession and, with Decca in his sights, issued a warning to all dilettantes. Anyone who dared "meddle with these deep-seated desires of the American people in the care of their dead had better go slowly as force of public opinion is so powerful it will sweep him into oblivion." When Decca took her turn at the podium, she was able to assure Dr. Oman that, actually, meddling had swept her "out of oblivion."

What she liked best was getting up to her elbows in muck. A perfect opportunity came with a commission from *McCall's* to investigate an Arizona spa (or "fat farm," as they were popularly called) where affluent women went to get massaged, indulged, and flattered into losing a few pounds for great amounts of money. The Maine Chance spa seemed made to order. Her subject was extravagance and the expense of beautifying. The organizing idea was in the contrast: political muckraker entering the ante-room of Oz, where pretty maids all in a row would treat her to those secret ministrations typically reserved for the upper class. It was an absurd assignment. "How do I go about getting accepted?" Decca had asked her editor, who replied, "Oh come *on*, you know better than that." No one could argue with her aristocratic credentials.

In the days long before youthful body worship made gym membership universal, and surgical work on aging faces ubiquitous, the Maine Chance spa seemed both a refuge and a quaint warehouse for trophy wives and old warhorses alike, battling the inexorable tide. Decca was forty-eight and had complained little of that sense of superfluity some women her age come to feel. She'd been an acknowledged beauty in her youth and was always striking. She wasn't vain, but she was carrying a few extra pounds she wouldn't have minded losing.

In the article, she described a guest's week at the Maine Chance, lampooning its bizarre mix of servility and sadistic domination, the dietitians and nurses and physical fitness instructors who wrapped, pummeled, and fawned upon their wealthy clientele. Her article takes the form of a diary, in which she sounds slightly uncomfortable throughout, reaching for a brisk tone but bored. Perhaps Decca was too discreet or too concerned with keeping her cover, to look behind the mud mask of the class enemies at their most vulnerable, half naked, and half starving. Perhaps *McCall's* diverted her from including the intimate confessions of her spa-mates. In the end, it wasn't the kind of meddling she liked to do. The piece might have seemed explosive for a ladies' magazine, but it read rather like a soggy éclair. Still, she lost five pounds.

》《

DECCA'S INTERSECTION WITH the counterculture of the 1960s was inevitable. She had a lot at stake in preserving a self-identity as a radical and subversive. The last thing she wanted was to freeze into a respectable house writer somewhere. Defiance and flamboyance were the hallmarks of the youth counterculture. Hadn't she and Esmond been "linked together by mutual amorality which at moments approached the sublime"? At least that's what one reviewer had said after reading *Hons and Rebels*. Decca was interested in the influence of drugs but not necessarily in experiencing them. The major theme of the new generation of political activists was anti-authoritarianism, which, for Decca, struck the right chord.

"Vietnam," she wrote, "nags unbearably . . . That awful, hopeless feeling of being dragged along into destruction, and nothing one can do to stop it." The FBI files pinpoint the first time Decca spoke out publicly about the war, at a rally to raise money for the Free Speech Movement defendants:

> Jessica Mitford Treuhaft was the first speaker at the August 20, 1965, rally at 400 North Point, San Francisco. She was introduced as a socialist and an individual with socialist ideas, and her speech subject expressed sympathy for FSM Defendants. She mentioned U.S. government policy on immigration and passports and asserted that Democracy did not exist in the United States. Subject indicated her opposition to U.S. policy in Vietnam.

Decca was asked to join various committees to end the war, but considered organizations for "old folk," like Women for Peace, "a touch too sappy." At one meeting of the Jeanette Rankin Brigade, a women's peace organization, the only interesting moment was when she made "Hazel Grossman cry by saying that Women for Peace had become a fearful drag." One committee she refused to join was against "wicked toys" for children. "I can't bear to join," she wrote Debo, "because I know I should have rather longed for a model H-bomb if they had been about when we were little."

She remained more interested in the radical, media-savvy tactics of the young. In 1966, the antiwar organizer and radical Jerry Rubin was subpoenaed to give testimony at one of the last HUAC hearings. Like many witnesses before him, he had found the term "un-American activities"

mystifying and, to illustrate his unique dedication to the American enlight-
enment, showed up dressed in the uniform of a Revolutionary War soldier,
straight from Valley Forge. The committee replied with a grumpy sputter.
They'd seen many things in their time on the bench, but this was a new kind
of insolence.

Warren Hinckle III was a San Francisco *flâneur* in his twenties, editor of
the new radical magazine *Ramparts*. Decca and he were both leftist journalists
and outsized characters, and they liked each other. "Hink 3," as Decca called
him, had come up through a hard-boiled apprenticeship on the *San Francisco
Chronicle*. He wore a patch over one eye and had a "swashbuckling" way
with words. Decca was by then one of the Bay Area's best-known investigative reporters. Younger writers gravitated to her orbit, and her imprimatur
had clout. When she was in the neighborhood, Decca liked to hang around in
the magazine's office, where the "level of chaos," Hinckle said, defied "sum-
mation outside of the analogy of an underdeveloped country."

At a *Ramparts* cocktail party, Decca and Bob found themselves face-to-
face with one of the FBI agents who had scrutinized their family and tapped
their phone a decade earlier. William Turner recognized Bob's voice across
the room. They had never actually met, Turner told Bob, but he had been
one of a seven-agent squad who had listened in on the Treuhafts' bugged
telephone. Turner confessed that they had mainly heard kids gossiping and
playing records. The encounter was bizarre and comic, but it was also a
relief to hear that what they had imagined had been happening was real. By
then, Turner himself had become a whistle-blower, and they all had a drink
together.

RAMPARTS MAGAZINE WAS unpredictable and subversive, just the kind of
thing Decca liked. Her connection to the magazine came in particularly
handy once Bob and she decided to sell Inch Kenneth. Hinckle offered her a
free, prominently placed advertisement announcing the sale of her Scottish
island in exchange for her accepting a listing on the *Ramparts* masthead as
contributing editor. Advertising was expensive, and Decca liked a bargain.

The two-page *Ramparts* spread was a romp. "The idea of actually owning an island proved irresistible to many among the misguided in the *Ramparts'* audience," Hinckle wrote. After Inch Kenneth was successfully "unloaded" to Andrew and Yvonne Barlow, he and Decca brainstormed other fund-raising schemes. In one, Decca and her friend Sonia Orwell would visit "the ranking capitalists of the land, affording them the treat of having high tea with two women of the classy, intellectual left, wherein the captains of industry would be charmed into buying space in a publication that was enemy to their cause."

It was a goofy scenario in which Decca would masquerade as the type of indefatigable upper-class Englishwoman she'd known growing up. Her clowning impression of a Swinbrook type (just this side of camp) was reserved exclusively for American audiences. She had begun playing the daffy British auntie, dressed up in her best Aranka hat, in the late 1940s while fronting for black home buyers. (Later, she donned her widow's weeds as a costume to scout out a swindling mortuary.) It was a role she loved to act, which opened doors, disarmed opponents, gave her incomparable leeway as a journalist, and led Philip Toynbee to caution anyone who thought to underestimate her that Decca's "dithering manner concealed an iron will." Hinckle's scheme to employ Decca and Orwell as emissaries into the bastions of power never progressed. Her fund-raising skills were suddenly required nearer to home.

In June 1966, Bob Treuhaft had decided to run against their longtime adversary, Frank Coakley, for district attorney of Alameda County. The politics of the area had shifted to the left, and Bob thought Coakley vulnerable on issues of police brutality, racial bigotry, and corruption. In any case, the very thought of a chagrined Coakley was catnip to Decca, who would serve as Bob's campaign manager. They'd have a laugh she promised Aranka. Of course, Coakley still had the *Oakland Tribune*, which would pull out all the stops to smear Bob, but the Treuhaft challenge would make Coakley work harder than he had at a campaign in years. When Decca told Nancy of Bob's political aspiration, her sister inquired, "Darling, is the

District Attorney the man who puts the rope round your neck while puffing a huge cigar?"

Coakley was reelected, but Bob's campaign carried most of Berkeley and the black population of Oakland. "It was all worth it," Decca wrote, "and stirred many a lovely stink in these parts."

CHAPTER 26

CCORDING TO HER friend Marge Frantz, "Decca loved parties and she got high very quickly. She liked to drink and carried around her own flask of gin." There were frequent mentions of Decca in Herb Caen's society column in the *San Francisco Chronicle*: She ate dinners with a crowd at good restaurants, club-hopped, and often ended her evenings at Enrico's in North Beach with a Vov or an Irish coffee. She loved to sing cabaret music, especially novelty songs. One of her party pieces was "Grace Darling," an English folksong about a brave lighthouse keeper's daughter who saved shipwrecked sailors. Her voice, pummeled over the years by thousands upon thousands of cigarettes and mellowed by booze, was a surprisingly warm alto, more versatile than her audience expected. The song, about which she'd later write a book, told a sensational heroic story; there were thrills and chills, ghastly violence in the threatening storm, and morbid sentimentality in its verses. The chorus of "Grace Darling" demanded a hearty sea-chantey shout, which she'd invite her audience to join:

> Help, help, she could hear the cry of the shipwrecked crew
> But Grace had an English heart and the raging storm she braved
> She pulled away o'er the rolling sea
> And the crew she saved.

The parties, which Decca and Bob frequently threw, were each famous, one-of-a-kind convergences. Her house on Regent Street was like Rick's Café in *Casablanca*: Young and old, hippie and square, exiles, gamblers, lovers, singers, dancers, fighters, and hard drinkers all found one another. As in her early days with Esmond, her door was still open to artists, revolutionaries, socialites, radical journalists, factory workers, poets, insurance agents, longtime Commies and their children, old friends, and old farts from England. Even the occasional Tory made the scene at Decca's. "People who amused her, odd fellows, who didn't agree with anybody," goddaughter Kathy Kahn said. "You could construct a whole friendship at those parties, and never see these people in other contexts." Union legend Harry Bridges was a frequent visitor, as well as old friends like Eph and Barb Kahn, Eva and Adam Lapin, and Marge and Laurent Frantz. Decca's parties were always a good place to catch up. Laurent had become involved with the Sexual Freedom League and would later move in with Miriam Patchen (the former wife of poet Kenneth Patchen). Marge was studying for a master's degree in history and had fallen in love with Eleanor Engstrom, a librarian at Berkeley. Eva Lapin had completed a degree in social work, and Adam Lapin, no longer a reporter for the *People's Daily World*, was writing travel books, one about Alaska, and another a guide to San Francisco, for which Decca had written the introduction. Like Marge and another old friend, Pele, Barb Kahn had been an original member of Decca's writing committee. Barb worked part-time, and it seemed to Decca that her old friend's world was more or less circumscribed by "a lot of boring community work like PTA and Planned Parenthood." She teased Barb about her large house and shiny household appliances. She also counted on Barb's advice, though, and it was to Barb that Decca wrote many of her funniest letters.

Some of the other guests were still in the Communist Party, including Bettina Aptheker, Pele, their old friend and Bob's law partner Dobby (with her third husband, journalist Mason Roberson), and longtime editor of the *People's Daily World* Al Richmond. Herb Caen was a friend and frequent guest at Regent Street. So was the estimable writer Kay Boyle. Boyle lived in San Francisco and taught college there, but her reputation as a literary lioness reached back to the 1930s. Another friend, Herb Gold, had arrived in San Francisco in 1960, joining Oakley Hall, Lee Litwak, and Don Asher, to make up the small core of San Francisco's postwar novelists. That Gold's

work, and those of his cronies, was published by major New York houses
set them apart from the younger countercultural literary heroes, poets, and
playwrights, who were exploding like Catherine wheels all over town and
who were represented mainly by Lawrence Ferlinghetti and City Lights
Bookstore. To Herb Gold, the Treuhafts' "house on Regent Street was more
fun than going anywhere else." Decca provided plenty of food and plenty of
booze. Guests sneaked in their own drugs. Decca didn't take drugs herself,
but she was curious and noted the way LSD was spreading everywhere.
Marijuana, she would write to Nancy, "makes one love everyone, they say.
[Allen] Ginsberg said it made him feel very sympathetic to Lyndon Johnson.
I wish they would invent a Loather's Drug."

What did they talk about, these swarms of guests? The 25,000 U.S.
troops sent to the Cambodian border; the 448,400 U.S. troops in Vietnam.
The four hundred thousand protest marchers from Central Park to the
United Nations and how the newspapers always underestimated the numbers; the latest speeches by Martin Luther King, Stokely Carmichael, and
Dr. Benjamin Spock; the first U.S. air strike on Hanoi. Across the bay, a
fuss was being made over flower power. *Did you know there were Gray
Line "hippie" tours of Haight-Ashbury? Have you heard Janis Joplin at the
Fillmore? Seen Nina Simone in concert?* They'd discuss the local crises, like
when Dinky's dog Koko was accused of repeatedly "munching" children on
the block and the outcry included a complaint to the police. *Were his days
numbered? Could he even be adopted? What about fencing in the backyard?* Nancy had written to advocate forcefully for Koko: "There must be
so many American children, surely some of them could be spared?"

At this point, Decca was going back and forth to England routinely.
What did her friends there think about the riots in Chicago? her American
friends would ask her. Why can't the Brits understand that the word *negro*
has been consigned to the dustbin of history? The people Decca knew over
there all seemed fascinated by the Black Panthers and their fashions: berets
and bandoleers, the way the Panthers paraded with their guns in plain sight.
(*Can they do that? Yes, with a license.*) Huey P. Newton, the Black Panther

leader, had been telling friends that Bob was a childhood hero of his for his defense of Jerry Newson, whose case Newton had followed from the time he was a kid in West Oakland.

There was a lot of small talk and gossip. Someone had succeeded, someone had failed, someone had a brilliant idea, someone had been neglected, someone had seen something never seen before: at a gallery; on *The Smothers Brothers Comedy Hour*; in a wild, psychedelic poster with curvy writing. They'd heard a song, heard a rumor. It was a time of marvels, new designs, new figures of speech: "far out," "out of sight," "hassle," "right on," "power to the people." Decca chain-smoked to her heart's content, gossiped to excess, ate party treats that were sweeter or saltier or fattier than routine fare, drank without inhibition.

Planning a sensational party takes a dedicated hostess. Decca was charismatic, self-assured, and unflappable. She gave parties because they were fun, a kind of service, and she was really good at it. Like a great stage director, Decca had a flair for analyzing social currents. She worked the room as diva, belle, English auntie, battling avenger, witty salonist. She listened carefully, roared at jokes, drank too much, and scattered compliments prodigiously. She might make one friend feel special by announcing his accomplishments and qualities to the assembled company, and another by retreating to a back room for quiet confidences.

At the Regent Street parties, guests found Bob just as funny as Decca but "quieter." Bob would stay on the outskirts as Decca held court. In those days, when political, social, and personal liberation was wreaking havoc on a lot of marriages, Herb Gold thought the Treuhafts seemed "the most bonded couple," but without any obvious "sense of intimacy." Gold flirted as much as the next middle-aged male novelist, but he never felt a sexual vibe from Decca. She was not flirtatious. She had enjoyed two successful marriages and seemed content. Bob "enjoyed her fame and he was gracious and smart enough not to compete." Adam and Eva Lapin's son Mark thought Bob and Decca had a wonderful relationship. As a red-diaper kid, he saw the spectrum of party marriages and thought they were universally fraught, the dynamic usually "strong women, men with their heads in the clouds." Marge Frantz thought Bob could be a "cold fish," but other women found him sophisticated and attentive, and he could always make a girl laugh. Parties are the stage for flirtations, and if Decca presided at the center, Bob was never bored or unoccupied at the margins. He liked the company of women.

While Gold talked to Bob "about law cases," Gold and Decca "talked about writing, not literature. She liked to talk about money, agents." Gold speculated about Decca's consistent good humor: She was, he thought, "metabolically cheerful—self-medicated with alcohol, and protected by an adoring husband."

Decca was nearly fifty years old, but she held to the dreams of her youth and often made new friends, many of them younger by decades. At Sonia Orwell's home in London, she first met the writer Maya Angelou. Theirs was a friendship that would deepen and thrive and sustain Decca and would come to equal the love and affection she felt for her sisters. But it provided at times even more immediacy, intimacy, and intellectual justice. They respected one another without childhood wounds or armor. They played Scrabble and Boggle and sang show tunes and folk songs and would occasionally treat their friends to a grandly over-the-top recitation of "The Cremation of Sam Magee," both their deep voices dramatically quavering on the line "The Arctic trails have their secret tales that would make your blood run cold."

In the past, Decca had sometimes found the limelight beastly, but at her parties, she basked in it. She and Bob had achieved local fame for their hard-won accomplishments, and these celebrations were another way to share the wealth. "The thing I'm most afraid of in life is being bored," she told Mark Lapin. For Decca and Bob, planning parties, throwing parties, even postparty anatomizing, was a way of keeping their marriage interesting. Through the 1960s, the Treuhafts' parties gave a lot of people pleasure, while reserving their hosts a ringside seat on the increasingly youth-centric counterculture.

Decca was as desirable a guest as hostess. For her fiftieth birthday, her friends held a party on a ferryboat on the San Francisco Bay. They served a whole roast pig, and the entertainment included a Chinese dragon dance and fireworks. "It really did take the edge off the dreaded entry into Old Age," she wrote.

》《

IN 1967, THE Mitford sisters then living in France and England had among themselves a scandalous piece of gossip about Dinky and James Forman. Debo first informed Nancy that she'd heard from Sonia Orwell, who'd heard the news:

> The inevitable has happened. Dinky is going to have a baby by a black man . . . the ghoulish & so surprising part is that Bob and Decca MIND . . . I am horrified about them minding because it is such a reversal for them, & old Hen is so set in her ideas & so proud that to admit minding must be truly dread. I wish I knew what they mind, & can only think it must be that they don't much like the man.

Nancy was languid in her response: "Is he *the* foreman or is he called foreman?" Decca wrote to clarify that she was not in the least unhappy with recent tidings: "Mrs. O. slightly mis-reported me." Her concern was not the pregnancy but that Jim and Dinky still had no plans to marry. "I only said that now, if someone says 'Would you want yr. daughter to marry a Negro?' I could answer, '*Rather.*'"

Decca and Bob now called Forman their "common-law son-in-law." They weren't happy that Forman was still married to another woman, an arrangement that didn't disturb Decca's sense of propriety as much as raise fears about her daughter's financial security. Decca always minded issues of money and independence. She never objected outright to her daughter's arrangement, but she did complain to her friends. She didn't think he was much of a writer, and as an ersatz husband, he exploited her daughter. She told Marge that Dinky did the greater share of housework and that her contribution to Jim's book wasn't fairly compensated or acknowledged. Herb Gold said Decca and Bob both held "a lot of anger" against Jim. Benjy saw a different story at home. When his parents spoke about Jim's work, "they were impressed by him and liked what he was doing."

Decca would not denounce Jim directly to her daughter, but she fell into the habit of mean teasing, mainly about Dinky and Jim's failure to wed. Mother and daughter's quarrel escalated until Dinky and Decca "had a knock-down drag-out fight." Dinky made it clear that her mother would have to keep her snide remarks about marriage to herself in the future. Decca argued hotly but conceded in the end. She wouldn't risk losing her daughter's friendship or contact with her new grandson, James Robert Lumumba Forman, born June 1967.

A SOON AS Decca landed the subject for her next book, the public announcement appeared in Herb Caen's column and was duly entered into Decca's FBI files as follows: "Caen mentioned subject after describing her 'as one of our leadings citizens.' He stated that subject was writing a book on DR. BENJAMIN SPOCK'S upcoming trial."

She would attend and then write a book about the court case of the famous baby doctor whose work counseling young men to avoid the draft had resulted in an indictment for conspiracy "to disobey the draft law." A few obstacles seemed certain. Most important, she'd have to unknot all the legal threads of the federal conspiracy laws. The six defendants— Mike Ferber, Dr. Spock, Marcus Raskin, Mitchell Goodman, and the Reverend William Sloane Coffin Jr.—had never all met together before their pretrial discussion with lawyers to plan their defense. Her job would be to illustrate the human cost when political dissidents were linked by thought.

The Boston court setting, the upright, well-meaning, and courteous defendants, did not at first promise much drama, but time would tell. She would have to learn as she went, write on the spot, turn it around quickly, and publish while the verdict was still relevant. Decca thought her new project fascinating, though others, Nancy for one, might rule it a bore.

In the spring of 1968, Decca was visiting New York City with Dinky and grandson Jamie when President Johnson announced that he wouldn't seek reelection. By the time Decca left for Washington to start research on her book, Martin Luther King had been assassinated. She'd hoped to interview counsel at the Justice Department and independent journalists like Andrew Kopkind and I. F. Stone, but both were too busy covering the revolution that week. Decca described the city after it had endured days of rioting: "Washington was rather extraorder, and beastly; what with the curfew, and rather dense smoke, one couldn't get out much." She went from there to Boston, where the riots had also spread and student strikers had occupied Harvard.

As the trial of Dr. Spock began, the world outside seemed tilted off its axis. Decca tried to do the necessary research. On June 5, 1968, Robert Kennedy was shot. Aranka's husband, the unreliable Al Kliot, died the same week. Decca hadn't had much to do with Al, but here was another loss, and she hated to see Aranka suffer. It did feel rather like the war again, the way people were dying horribly, disappearing.

Conspiracy laws are baroque and labyrinthine. The government does not have to prove that anyone did anything illegal, just that he or she agreed to commit a crime. Decca wanted, in 1968, to take this post-HUAC, New Left moment to speak against the use of conspiracy laws as an historic weapon that would attack the American Left and stifle dissent. Bob helped her out with some research, and together they wrote this summary: "The law of conspiracy is so irrational, its implications so far removed from ordinary experience or modes of thought, that like the Theory of Relativity it escapes just beyond the boundaries of the mind. One can dimly understand it while an expert is explaining it, but minutes later it is not easy to tell it back."

The defense dismissed the conspiracy idea as irrelevant. "Spock and Coffin particularly were demanding (and I think expecting)," Decca wrote, "a confrontation with the Govt. on the legality of the war, and hence of the Selective Service Act." The defendants welcomed a public debate on the Vietnam War and the draft. They shared the belief that the United States was acting "in violation of international conventions" and was responsible for the "bombing of noncombatants, wanton destruction of civilian dwellings, and the use of torture in interrogation of prisoners."

To the government prosecutors, trial court was not the place to debate the legality or morality of the Vietnam War. Decca had expected the antiwar movement in Boston to remonstrate and make a louder fuss. But Boston remained cool, proper, and dignified, following the lawyers' preference to keep a sense of decorum. Decca thought this strategy wrong and old-fashioned. She appreciated Spock's position that "the people in power are nothing to fear," but did he have to be so serene about it? She labored to give the characters some drama, but it wasn't easy. She tried color when drama flagged: Describing Judge Francis Ford's courtroom, Decca quoted the *London Times* expression of "vaguely lavatorial." During the trial, she made friends with other reporters, including Dan Lang of the *New Yorker*. "Dan has a low threshold of boredom and mercifully enlivened each day with his restive sotto voce comments: 'Jessica would you ask the bailiff to close the door? I'm afraid if I ask him he'll think I'm trying to avoid the draft.'"

THE JURY RETURNED guilty verdicts for five of the defendants, and as they filed their first appeals, Decca feared that the public's interest in the trial soon would fizzle and her book suffer the same fate. Fizz was that most ephemeral of qualities. It was what characterized the best of sister Nancy's books—delicacy combined with a funny sort of disinterest (an oblique glance that nothing escaped). Too much handling, worrying, attention, or time could flatten the fizz, turn a thing either campy or cold. Writing *The Trial of Dr. Spock* had been "a very, very uphill job," she wrote Virginia Durr. Even Bob's review was unenthusiastic: It was "a workman like job but not up to your best standards," he said.

In August, she may have wished to drop the whole enterprise and go cover the 1968 Democratic convention, but she stayed in Oakland and wrapped up her book. By then she understood, along with everyone else who was paying attention, that the nature of the antiwar movement had changed into something considerably more militant—even the pacifists were more aggressive. *Revolution* was the word, and from her perch in Northern California, it certainly looked to be the deed. She and Bob had seen revolts rise and fall, but this one had a different energy; its subliminal voice saying *let yourself go* was so seductive. In her fifties, Decca could recognize the thrills and euphoria as well as the certain danger ahead for her young friends. As a Communist, she had been labeled a subversive, but as Bob liked to point out, they were always law-abiding. Decca had scoffed at some laws; she might have indulged her renegade nature by walking out on a bill or dressing down a snob, but as a Communist, she had simply represented the antagonist in that chapter of America's war on dissent.

Here was an entirely new generation, unpredictable and crazily brave in its own way. They were willing to stop the daily world to stop the war— get in the way of commuters, interrupt the workday, even block train tracks. In Chicago, one seventeen-year-old protester had jumped on the back of a burly policeman and ridden him for several blocks before the cop had shaken her off, busted her head with his nightstick, and arrested her. In the provocative teases, anti-authoritarianism, and other antics of the Yippies (a group of radical and theatrical hippies whose more famous members were Jerry Rubin and Abbie Hoffman), Decca recognized shades of her own subversive nature. At *Ramparts*, she shared a masthead with Black Panther leader Eldridge Cleaver, the author of *Soul on Ice*. She cheered the witty way that political tricksters Hoffman and Rubin manipulated media coverage. Their energy and passion spoke to her and brought back that distant moment, during the Spanish Civil War, when she, Esmond, Philip Toynbee, and their friends thought young people might stop fascism forever. Here was another chance, and she was a living bridge between those times.

CHAPTER 27

I N March 1969, Decca and Marge Frantz attended the end of the
conspiracy trial of the Oakland Seven. Alameda County District
Attorney Frank Coakley had indicted the seven leaders after a
Stop the Draft protest march to the Oakland induction center, with conspiracy to commit a felony. His primary evidence was an audiotape recording
of the Berkeley campus rally, which had occurred the night before the demonstration. However, instead of proving the pernicious influence of these
particular leaders, it did the opposite—capturing an event that was in the
"great tradition of open, democratic meetings." When the jury members listened to the tape, they heard dozens of people representing views across the
political spectrum: geniuses, visionaries, and boors among them. In the end,
so many people—including "opponents of the demo"—had addressed the
rally that the prosecution could not prove that the leaders they'd charged
had conspired at anything. The atmosphere in that courtroom offered a terrific contrast to the Boston Spock trial.

Visiting an Oakland courtroom meant that Decca was on her home
patch. If she wasn't a legal expert, she was certainly a celebrity pundit
on conspiracy trials. At one point, the judge even asked to meet her; they
spoke of the mystifying knot of statutes and regulations that composed the
canon of conspiracy law, agreeing that its many ambiguities had "got to
go." After the jury acquitted the Oakland Seven, the judge chastised the
District Attorney's office for wasting jury time and taxpayers' money. This
rare triumph for antiwar activists represented "a kind of low-water mark
for prosecutors." It made a nice change. The district attorney's team had
been beaten fair and square and embarrassed, too. Coakley had been outmaneuvered, and Decca was delighted.

IN MAY, DECCA went to Paris to visit her sister Nancy, then sixty-five years old, whose terrible back pain had been diagnosed as a degenerated spinal column. Worse news revealed a mass on her liver. Nancy was housebound, and pain kept her in her bed during most of Decca's stay.

It had been just a year since the French student rebellions of 1968, and the consequences must have been visible—though perhaps slightly less so in tony Versailles, where Nancy lived. In Paris, red banners hung from windows and fluttered on rooftops. On the Left Bank, hippies swaggered in full plumage, philosophers and militants disputed in the cafés, the neighborhoods around the university still seethed, soldiers carrying guns seemed to be everywhere; anything might still happen. Before she'd grown ill, Nancy Mitford had kept a journal she called "A Revolution Diary," noting that one of the leaders of the French student movement, Danny Cohn-Bendit (whom she called "Bandit") was "very reminiscent of Esmond Romilly—a bounding energetic little anarchist giggling from time to time but not making jokes which one might have liked."

Decca didn't take much note of the postrevolutionary moment in France. She arrived from Berkeley, where such images had come to seem normal. Instead, the domestic routine in her sister's household, keyed to the season and hour, was all-absorbing. She looked for ways to help Nancy. It was necessary to pay attention, to adapt, which she did with gratifying results. She walked, she said, a "slight tight-rope—between going up to her room too much, with the attendant danger of either tiring her or boring her . . . and not going up enough, danger of seeming to neglect."

For Decca, Nancy's life in Versailles conjured "another planet, another century." At first, Decca had waded in, thinking she might help increase efficiency around the place by suggesting that their food be delivered in bulk, rather than purchased daily, and that Nancy's doctors visit her at home. These innovations were so un-French they hadn't a chance in hell. But contemplating them, submerging herself in this entirely other world, afforded Decca a real break from politics, her own children's dramas, and her literary life, particularly *The Trial of Dr. Spock*. She "rather lost interest in the book, in all the worry over Nancy." The book was in the hands of its editors, publishers, marketers, and reviewers, and there was nothing she could do at that point.

Nancy's live-in housekeeper, Marie, ruled their home. At seventy-five years old, Marie sometimes required assistance and might assign Decca various tasks like walking to the farther market stall for the better butter, the fresher potatoes, the superior cut of meat. After shopping, Decca might be put to work weeding the poppies and peonies. There were parsley beds, lettuce beds, roses, and lavender. Sometimes, when Nancy felt well enough, she would join Decca outdoors. In the evening, Nancy, Marie, and Decca might gather around the television to watch soap operas or the French presidential debates.

Afternoons, the other sisters would "swoop in," and there would be "nothing but rapid-fire jokes," Decca wrote to Aranka. To Virginia, she said, "Even when N. was in the worst pain she still managed to shriek, it is her way of life." Decca's friends were curious to know how she got along with sister Diana, whom she hadn't seen or spoken to for thirty-four years. The Mosleys' Temple de la Gloire was about twelve miles away, and Diana a frequent guest. In advance, Decca had written to Debo, "who was the go-between, the manager of it all, and said that . . . of course I'd never dream of being unpleasant in the presence of [Nancy], so it was made clear [Decca and Diana would] discuss the situation with Nancy, and what pills she was having—the usual sick-bed talk. And not a word of politics."

"Diana and I are getting on . . . rather well, actually," Decca wrote Marge. "That is, whilst cutting the grass round the irises I forbore to say I was giving the irises *lebensraum* [or living space, Hitler's justification for territorial expansion] although it came into my mind. In other words, all efforts are bent to Nancy's welfare, & that's all we talk about if we're alone together." After so long, Decca thought Diana looked like "a really marvelous statue that's been left out in the rain for a long time. She was so beautiful still, yet ravaged, but only ravaged from old age." Diana seemed to think the only great change time had wrought upon Decca was in her voice.

Nancy's prognosis was grave. Decca alone of the sisters thought she should be told, but she was overruled by the others, who believed Nancy would lose interest in the book she was then writing, since work had always been the thing that gave her energy. To Decca, it seemed "a sort of awful betrayal not to tell the truth." Once she was home, she wrote to Debo to restate her belief: "I do feel most terrifically strongly, and must stress this point Hen very much, that it is now verging on wicked not to tell Nancy, in view of Dr. Evans' report. Because don't you see, it's awful enough to get such news when one is feeling fairly OK & strong; but if it is delivered very late in the thing, when one was completely weak anyway and in much pain, so much harder to bear, I should think. Now might be the time."

>«

In August 1967, *The Trial of Dr. Spock* was published. The early reviews were respectable (not a rating she relished), but as she feared, its fizz factor barely registered. Decca's identity in the movement was tied to her role as a radical journalist. In the literary world at large, the confiding, personalized tone of new journalism was the ascendant trend. Radical journalists and new journalists shared a legacy of social criticism, but radical journalists had a politically left agenda and were more often associated with the counterculture press. (Further left, writers for the underground newspapers were starting to call themselves revolutionaries.) The tone of the radical journalists was less confiding and more defiant. Their work was objective because they said so, and it offered an alternative to what they viewed as the false objectivity of a controlled and biased mainstream press.

Subjects for investigation were everywhere, flying past fast and furiously, but the better-paid writing jobs on Decca's work calendar were light features and celebrity interviews. All had a highly anticipated quirk factor that often depended on the tension of some trendy subject in contrast with her background. These paid assignments were often so frustrating that in

October, Decca asked Marge, "Shall I give up writing & take Laurent's massage class, instead?"

Once the trial of the Chicago Eight began, it was clear that this was the trial Decca should have covered. Its defendants, charged with conspiracy to induce a riot at the Democratic National Convention, included Tom Hayden (who had slept on Virginia Durr's living room floor as a civil rights worker in the early 1960s) and other leaders of the antiwar movement—David Dellinger, Abbie Hoffman, Jerry Rubin, Rennie Davis, John Froines, and Bobby Seale, then chairman of the Black Panther Party. The trial had villains and heroes (among the valiant ones, defense lawyers William Kunstler and Leonard Weinglass, who each received sentences for contempt), fools and knaves. It attracted intense press scrutiny for its contrasts: an ancient, anachronistic judge, a humorless prosecutor, Rubin and Hoffman (the two Yippie comedians), and a sequence of celebrity witnesses, including Norman Mailer, Phil Ochs, and Allen Ginsberg (who "Omed" on the witness stand). All the chatter and tomfoolery of the early part of the trial could not prepare anyone for the moment when Seale, denied the opportunity to conduct his own defense, was ordered by the judge to be expelled from the courtroom. Marshals carried him back into the room, bound to a chair with a gag in his mouth, still demanding his right to defend himself. In the following moments of silence and profound shame, Seale's codefendants, along with their lawyers, jumped up to protest.

In her book on the trial of Dr. Spock, Decca had wished to show how the government historically used conspiracy law to silence its opposition. Dr. Spock and his fellow defendants had hoped to use their trial to demonstrate their loyalty to fundamental American ideals by attacking the legality and morality of the war on a public stage (material in support of which they'd never been allowed to enter into the evidence). The trial of the Chicago Eight was, as the Smith Act trials had been, about big ideas held by dissenters who threatened the status quo. Hoffman said theirs was a "state-of-mind trial"—they were "charged with carrying certain ideas across state lines." The Chicago trial did what Dr. Spock's could not, theatrically contrasting a celebration of life and youth with a militaristic culture of death. The eight defendants weren't interested in maintaining decorum; their support increased with their defiance. It was farce, melodrama, and *Grande Guignol* in the instance of Bobby Seale, whom the government could not silence without the clumsy accoutrements of tyranny.

The end of 1969 brought convictions for the Chicago Eight (all would be eventually overturned). That December, also in Chicago, a squad of police carrying machine guns broke into the apartment of twenty-one-year-old Black Panther leader Fred Hampton and shot him in his bed. The police called it a gun battle, but forensic evidence pointed to a murder and one of many actions initiated by the FBI as part of the counterintelligence program known as COINTELPRO.

In September 1970, a memo from the director of the FBI to the assistant attorney general, Internal Security Division, requested a review to determine whether (in the face of burgeoning rebel movements: antiwar, black liberation, women's liberation, gay liberation) it was still good value to continue assigning agents to observe the ex-menace Decca. The review affirmed unequivocally that her case "should be continued." An attached page announced: "Subject one of speakers at National Guardian sponsored public meeting, attended celebration of release of MORTON SOBELL, gave support to Black Panther Party during 1968–1969. Is currently working on a book about prisons."

》《

IN 1970, SAN Francisco was still absorbing scads of young people. Haight-Ashbury was in decline, but to its young émigrés, that meant cheap rent and easy-to-find drugs. Politicos and apoliticos made their accommodations; they shared garish, painted Victorians, rice and beans, and their mattresses on the floor. Even the most oblivious "*freek*-child" would throw on her glad rags and parade in the day's demonstration against the war in Vietnam. The surliest Socialist Workers Party member knew a Sunday in Golden Gate

Park meant he'd probably lose a battle to a tambourine and end up with his shirt off in the sunshine. Most hippies and radicals agreed the music was still in ascendance; so were hallucinogens and the underground press. In the Bay Area, there were several underground papers, of which the *Oracle* was the most celebrated for its psychedelic design. The *Berkeley Barb* was starting to actually make money, thanks to the brilliant stroke of its editor, Max Scherr, to charge money for its sexy personals. The *Berkeley Tribe* was an earnest, seat-of-the-pants organization with a devoted radical staff and following. There was an acknowledged small-press revolution going on in the early 1970s. The little magazines and niche books introduced hundreds of new poets and titles like *How to Make Your Own Moccasins* and *The Anarchist Cookbook*, both of which landed a devoted readership outside the mainstream.

Decca, who was accustomed to the well-capitalized publishing houses of New York and London, was established on the commercial end of the bohemian spectrum. She didn't have a daily column like other influential journalists, although she was offered one as a sports writer for the *Chronicle*. (Despite her knowing next to nothing about sports, the idea was that in order to keep Decca around, they would publish her wisecracks on just about anything. But when her first question to the section editor midway through the summer was, "When does the baseball season start?" everyone involved reconsidered.) Her latest projects and antic personality kept her in the news—she could enjoy the let-it-all-hang-out attitudes of the younger and emerging literati, but her work ethic was that of the disciplined veteran professional, no matter how much she drank.

Bob's law firm was as busy as it would ever be, defending Black Panthers, professors, students, community organizers, hippies, and dissidents of all stripes. So, when a seventy-two-year-old woman approached him with the complaint that she'd been conned out of some money spent on a correspondence course for writers, she stood out in vivid contrast. A widow on a fixed income, she had originally welcomed the nice young salesman, who had told her about the Famous Writers School, where she could study on her own time at home and receive personal guidance from best-selling authors. She had signed on, but then had second thoughts about the expense involved. When the Famous Writers School refused to return her money, she consulted Bob Treuhaft, famous in Oakland for tackling fraud.

When Bob summarized the case for Decca, she felt she'd heard this cri de coeur before in her conversations with the victims of funeral swindles. There were different promises involved, but the consequences of a con could leave a person feeling small and silly. The facts as they began to unfold showed that only 10 percent of Famous Writers School students completed their course. Those who had paid in advance but wished to withdraw were threatened with legal action if they demanded a refund. Still, the controversy surrounding it would never have gone so far and so fast if Decca's first efforts to place an article about the Famous Writers School had not been met with some reluctance on the part of the editors of the *Atlantic* magazine. The publication had been accepting ads from the Famous Writers School for years. Yes, the editors agreed, perhaps the writing course was unethical, and they shouldn't endorse it in the future. However, they wrote to Decca, "wouldn't it be equally unethical to publish a piece blasting them!!!" (The exclamation points are hers.)

"I am *furious*," Decca told everyone who asked. She had seen these kinds of shenanigans from people in power before. The funeral men had tried to quash her book, tried to suppress her articles, to silence her by red-baiting and other smears. She did not take kindly to threats of blacklisting or, in this case, blackballing in the writing world. The whisper of suppression was, to Decca, like the inspiring breath of an avenging goddess. Exposing such cruel deceptions appealed to the muckraker and gadfly in her prime.

Decca had her pick of publications, but the *Atlantic* editors soon patched things up to her satisfaction, and the magazine featured "Let Us Now Appraise Famous Writers" in their July 1970 issue. The project, Decca said, gave her "more pleasure from start to finish, than any other," and in its composition, she was able to apply all her reporting techniques. Her interviewing style was to be well prepared and self-assured; she enjoyed the chase. She asked graduated questions, from kind to cruel. It was her "special stroke of genius" to extract quotes that were less carefully cultivated or well thought-out and, as a result, were more revealing, funny, and sometimes embarrassing. Decca liked to call them "spontaneous and true."

On a big article like the one on the Famous Writers School, she rarely worked alone. Her friends helped out by posing as aspiring writers passing along the feeble reports they would receive from their correspondence school tutors. The Famous Writers School ads proclaimed that a rewarding career awaited the well-trained scribe, and it all started with the completion of an aptitude test, which one could find on the inside cover of a matchbook. "Of course, the whole thing is a terrific fraud," she wrote to Aranka.

Bennett Cerf, one of the Famous Writers School guiding faculty, was among the most important figures in English-language publishing. He was also president of Random House, which owned Decca's publisher, Knopf. As editor of Nancy's most famous book, he had come up with her book's title, *Love in a Cold Climate*. That the highly placed Cerf endorsed and profited from what Decca called a swindle only made him more desirable quarry, and her interview with him is the article's pièce de résistance. Decca asked Cerf how he could countenance both promising and charging so much to vulnerable idealists. Settling into a confiding chat, he agreed that sometimes, a beginning writer's expectation was inflated, but in addition to producing publishable writers, their enterprise was to draw attention to their public-spirited guiding faculty, whose confidence in education and opportunity was well documented. As leader of the Famous Writers School faculty, Cerf also enjoyed the media attention. "I'm an awful ham," he said. "I love to see my name in the papers." As to the mail-order school's material success and future, this depended on "a very hard sales pitch, an appeal to the gullible." Realizing at once that the vulnerable idealists in his audience could be offended by the word *gullible*, Cerf asked Decca not to quote him. "Would you prefer to paraphrase?" she asked. He offered a long-winded alternative, to which Decca replied, "Sorry I don't call that a paraphrase. I shall have to use both of them."

The finished article read as if it were written by the bloodthirsty Addison DeWitt crossed with the staunch Honoria Glossop. (Or is she, as Alexander Cockburn suggests, a kind of "Aunt Dahlia"? Readers of P. G. Wodehouse may take their pick.) Decca called the finished article "one of the clear-cut successes however temporary of my muckraking career." Its publication in the *Atlantic* magazine busted the organization. The school's guiding faculty would briefly suffer the public mortification of cartoons and comedians. Its stock would plummet and plunge the enterprise into financial ruin.

On September 21, 1971, Decca wrote to Nancy: "Wasn't it sad about Bennett Cerf croaking. I felt v. put out about that, as it takes almost as long in my experience to make satisfactory enemies as satisfactory friends, and there he's not. By the way: those Famous Writers have gone bankrupt. I wish one cld. sink the prisons as easily."

》《

HUEY NEWTON AND his friend Bobby Seale had started the Black Panther Party as a local organization in Oakland. Seale was in prison in Chicago, and Newton, convicted of killing a policeman, was serving his sentence in California. The campaign to "Free Huey" during his trial and appeals process had turned the charismatic leader into a national icon. In Newton's absence, the acting chairman of the Black Panther Party was David Hilliard, whose leadership skills were underwhelming compared with the airy Newton, the inspirational Bobby Seale, and the brilliant Eldridge Cleaver, then in exile in Algeria. Hilliard, like Newton, had grown up in Oakland and knew of Bob Treuhaft's defense of Jerry Newson. He also knew Decca to be an outspoken supporter of the Panther program. (In a letter to Virginia Durr—who had expressed concern that SNCC had rejected nonviolence to support the Black Panthers—Decca wrote: "I know in my heart of hearts that if I was their age and their colour I'd be with them 100%.") When French writer and political activist Jean Genet came to California to speak for Huey's defense campaign, Hilliard knew who to call. Would Decca hold a benefit honoring Genet at her house for the Panther Defense Fund?

Decca had just begun research on her next book about the American prison system, and here, dropping into her lap, was this fascinating French author, jailbird, and outlaw. His subjects were sex and violence, coercion and liberation. He was extrovertly gay and opposed to American imperialism and creeping stupidity. Her dear friend Maya Angelou had even performed in a Genet play in the early 1960s off Broadway in *The Blacks*. The ideal guest! Her own French was quite good, but they'd have an interpreter on hand. The Panthers, Hilliard said, admired their French comrade-in-arms, though they'd had some trouble communicating.

Genet or "this cat," as Hilliard called him, had peculiar hygiene, which the sartorially disciplined Panthers tried to accommodate. Genet's biographer, Edmund White, said the writer "slept in his clothes, seldom bathed, and lived on a diet of Gitane cigarettes and Nembutals." Genet was delighted to accept when Hilliard offered to suit him out in brand-new clothes for the Treuhaft affair. The FBI got wind of Decca's party almost as soon as she had set the date: March 20, 1970.

White described the days before Decca's party. At a Los Angeles fund-raiser hosted by Dalton Trumbo, Genet had an enjoyable conversation in French with Jane Fonda. The following morning, Genet awoke, separate from his traveling companions. He was in some kind of chateau—he didn't know where—and when he couldn't find a Francophone, he called Fonda. To find his coordinates, she said, he should go outside and describe the swimming pool, which he did. "You're at Donald Sutherland's. I'll be right over," she said. The next night, Genet appeared at a party at Stanford, where Ken Kesey showed up high as a kite. *Ramparts* had provided a translator, who had her work cut out for her when Kesey exclaimed he was "wearing green socks, can you dig it? Green socks. They're heavy, man, very heavy."

The party at Regent Street was wall-to-wall people. Herb Gold guess-timated around 150 guests. To him, the party was "like a street fair," with

newspaper hawkers sidling through the crowd, and advocates of one campaign or another circulating with petitions to be signed and requests for
money. There was plenty to eat and plenty of wine for the growing crowd,
which was, according to young Berkeley resident Jan Herman, composed
of "Bay Area radicals, politicos, artists, poets, journalists, professors and
other high-minded riffraff." In the backyard, the smell of marijuana drifted
around small clusters of newly made friends. The company was noisy with
laughter and quarrels, reunions and denunciations. Gold remembers a fight.
Not everybody knew about the guest of honor. Some, like Jan Herman,
assumed the party was "to hear the latest news and to rally the troops, raise
money, and generally show our solidarity with the leaders of the antiwar
movement." Stew Albert and his girlfriend Judy Gumbo, a Yippie and wom-
en's liberationist, were already ensconced with a glass of wine when Hilliard
and "Field Marshal" Donald Cox arrived with a couple of bodyguards. The
Black Panther cohort wore matching military-style jackets ornamented with
glittering red Mao badges, and "Free Huey" buttons. Black berets sailed
upon their spherical Afros, and the men wore dark glasses indoors, which
was customary. They were at once forbidding and beautiful to see, and with
their arrival, Albert noted a distinct lowering of spirits.

Decca welcomed everyone with a few laughing words and a drink. She'd
had some doubt about whether Genet would show, but Hilliard assured her
he was on his way. Hilliard and his guard settled on a large couch and
murmured to each other through the subsequent announcements and short
speeches, before the main event.

Cox warned the Yippie couple that things might get nasty. Hilliard, he
said, was in a bad mood. In his own reconstruction of the evening's events,
Hilliard admitted his "fuse" was "already short" and he was anxious to
protect the Panthers' financial interests (meaning contributions to Huey's
defense fund) once people from the antiwar movement started making
speeches about Vietnam and donations started to flow.

Genet arrived in a red convertible with an entourage including an interpreter, Newton's lawyer Charles Garry, and several conspicuously armed

Black Panthers. Decca was justifiably pleased by the crowd she'd mustered on such short notice. Leading Genet through the crowd, she said, "Isn't it nice that so many people have turned out to hear you?"

"All people are nice," Genet replied, "until they start talking politics."

The Frenchman was very short, and there followed some brief discourse between hosts and bodyguards concerning whether he ought to stand on an ordinary chair, with the result that Bob left to track down a stepladder.

Genet spoke persuasively and with great feeling. He believed the Black Panthers to be in the persecuted vanguard of a resistance movement and Huey Newton a prisoner of war. Concluding his remarks, the author agreed to take a few questions. A professor from one of the local colleges jumped to his feet. "What do you think we should *do*?" he asked.

"*You* ask *me* how to counteract racism in America? Asinine!" Genet grumbled. "I'm from France."

Perhaps considering the level of inquiry, Genet stepped down. Having such a large and attentive audience, Bob Treuhaft suggested that Tom Hayden follow up with a few comments about the Chicago Eight trial, which had ended the month before. Hayden lived in Berkeley; he had just returned home after three weeks in jail. As Hayden ascended the stepladder, David Hilliard booed. This was a Black Panther's fund-raiser, and Hilliard meant to keep the focus. "Why is Hayden free while Bobby Seale's still in prison?" he shouted. As Hayden described his own sense of outrage about Seale's shackling during the trial and continued imprisonment, Hilliard continued to bait and boo. Hayden, who looked to Jan Herman "composed as a turtle," still resisted a public quarrel.

To some in the excited crowd, Hilliard's antagonism seemed to represent the widening crack in the movement's black and white alliance. "The alliance between black revolutionaries and their white supporters had begun to fray," wrote Stew Albert. "Some white radicals were keeping their distance from the Panthers' headquarters; partly the sandbags and automatic weapons put them off."

Hilliard may have wished to appear decisive before his foreign guest, or he was just superbly pissed off. Whatever his reason, the acting chairman launched a gallon jug of wine toward Hayden. But his aim was bad, and instead, he struck Jane McClure, a twelve-year-old girl who was sitting on the floor by her father, poet Michael McClure. Instantly, the news rippled out to the outer reaches of the house and stretched with each retelling: The child was wounded; the child was nearly beheaded; the unarmed poet was facing down Hilliard and his bodyguards. Bob, who had stepped outside for a moment, reentered to see Jane McClure sobbing and many of his guests shouting and streaming out the doors. (Some of them expected a guns-blazing showdown.) Stew Albert saw Genet sitting "in the midst of madness, quiet and smiling . . . The old, balding gangster might just have written the script. When people started shoving he jumped to his feet with a boxer's stance."

The police had been called, someone said, and although that wasn't true, the stoners in the backyard stashed their pipes and joints. Michael McClure was comforting his frightened daughter, whose head gash was treated by a doctor in the crowd. "It's always the children who get hurt in wars," the poet was heard to remark. As the Panthers' red convertible sped away, Decca took her turn on the stepladder.

Thank you, she said crisply to the remaining, scattered guests. *The party is over. Thank you all for coming . . . Everyone go home now. Do come again.*

Radical Chic, Tom Wolfe's satire of a high-society fund-raiser for the Black Panthers hosted by Leonard and Felicia Bernstein, appeared in *Harper's* magazine in the summer of 1970. The Bernsteins' Manhattan apartment provided the setting for Wolfe's report on a meeting of left-leaning socialites and intelligentsia and beautiful Black Panthers trolling for windfall profits. The objective of both the Bernsteins' uptown evening and the Treuhafts' bash was to raise cash for the Panther defense. Some guests who made the scene at Decca's refer to its radical chic vibe, to emphasize how *distinctly of its time* the event was. The main connection between the two parties was the prominence of Field Marshal Donald Cox. In Wolfe's article, he appears at center stage as the initially bewildered then cagy Black Panther spokesperson. Decca didn't record her response to Wolfe's article. She enjoyed the party at her house and was happy to move on from it.

PART THREE

By now adrenalin was flowing, easily the most effective stimulant for the muckraker.

—JESSICA MITFORD, *POISON PENMANSHIP*

CHAPTER 28

I N 1970, *TIME* magazine—then a hugely popular and widely circulated weekly—proclaimed Decca "Queen of the Muckrakers." The coronation was a double-edged sword. In the national news, the contrast between her background as a baron's daughter and her current gritty occupation made good copy, but Decca considered her reputation as a writer more than ever dependent on tireless investigations and exposés.

In February, Dinky and Jim Forman had a second son, Chaka Esmond Fanon Forman. In 1972, they moved with two-year-old Chaka and four-and-a-half-year-old James to Detroit, where Dinky attended nursing school. The couple's relationship, after almost a decade together, was fraying, and as it worsened, they separated. Dinky graduated with an R.N. degree, but she was an unemployed single mother and at her "wit's end," when Decca and Bob sent airfare for Dinky and her sons to join them in London. This was the time leading up to the publication of Decca's prison book.

In *Kind and Usual Punishment*, which was published in 1973, Decca argues that the California penal system is a sham and failure. Its goals "to protect the public, rehabilitate the prisoner and act as a deterrent to further crime" were all fraudulent since "they never mention punishment and that is the only thing it really does." Midway through her research, she learned of abusive experiments involving drug trials on California prisoners. This was "hot stuff," she wrote to Robert Gottlieb, which "nobody seems to know." She ran with the subject in an article for *Atlantic Monthly* under the title "Cheaper than Chimpanzees" and then revised the material into a chapter of her forthcoming book about prisons.

The prison subject matter demanded stamina and a new kind of aggression. She interviewed staff, administrators, guards, and prisoners, in the process becoming a writer "more proud of sticking pins in those people she thought deserved it than being a prose stylist." Her longtime editor Robert Gottlieb would eventually describe her best muckraking as the work of a "ruthless gutter fighter." This description he meant as a compliment, and she appreciated it. "To be a muckraker," she replied, "means you'll fight on using any means at your disposal."

Around that time, on any number of shows, a television interviewer, cigarette in hand, would lean in and confidentially inquire, "Miss Mitford, *Time* magazine has crowned you 'Queen of Muckrakers.' Is that a title you're willing to accept?"

To some, she'd say the title gave her misgivings, since she had long since repudiated that kind of noble rank and status. Or, "I don't think of myself as a muckraker . . . One just falls into these articles." (Later, she would say she "rather loved" her new title: "If they were going to mention me at all I'm glad it was as a Queen.")

But how, the interviewer might cajole, could a muckraker possibly be objective?

"I really don't understand what objectivity means," she'd reply. "I'm not terribly in favor of balance. (I may be unbalanced myself.) I believe in being fair and never distorting the facts." She told another interviewer on the same subject of objectivity: "It's difficult but one must be exact."

"Miss Mitford, what about Bennett Cerf?" came one question.

"I'd got him," she'd say with some pride.

Shouldn't she have resisted publishing material that he had requested be off the record? Wasn't she flirting with unethical journalistic behavior?

She never got flustered. "This hard heart," she'd confirm with a smile, "felt then and feels now, not the slightest compunction for having recorded his words as spoken."

The reporter Doug Smith wrote an editorial on Decca's muckraking (which she thought got her "dead to rights"):

Miss Mitford is artful and—in one sense—thorough. She interviews and quotes everyone who, intentionally or unintentionally, reinforces the position she is espousing. Those who make a strong case for the other side get shorter shrift, and are always placed on the defensive, leading the careless reader to conclude that there is no other side or none that is morally defensible. But that is in the nature of muckraking. Miss Mitford herself probably makes no claim of "objectivity," her journalism is personal and passionate.

To Decca, journalism was a subjective practice and the discipline of sociology a lot of "bosh." Yet as a famous prison reform activist (or in the words of some prison administrators, "our greatest know-it-all"), Decca was invited to bring her experience to bear as a "distinguished professor of Sociology" at San Jose State College. As part of the hiring process, there was paperwork to complete—including a loyalty oath and a request for her fingerprints. Decca looked these over and showed them to Bob, and they both had a good laugh. There was nothing in her contract to require such an invasion of privacy.

Her lecture class, called The American Way, was oversubscribed, and she arrived on the first day to find her lecture hall mobbed by students wishing to add or observe, day visitors who were both well-wishers and oppositional, curious fellow faculty, and members of the press. The lecture class was standing room only, so Decca played to the balcony. She had prepared assiduously for her two classes (the other a small seminar called Muckraking), imagining them as a cross between Mardi Gras and dinner at Swinbrook. She was unbuttoned, confiding, and passionate. As an unexpected bonus, her students would receive a real-time object lesson in confronting power that would be far more influential to those who were paying attention than anything in the course work.

After she'd been teaching for three weeks, the dean reminded Decca that she had neglected to sign the loyalty oath and file her fingerprints. In a series of casual conversations with her colleagues and the dean, she learned that everybody signed in those days. It was a meaningless hoop to jump through, and when Decca replied that little on earth would induce her to sign such an oath, the dean cautioned that her professorship was in jeopardy.

The stalemate between Decca and the administration remained in effect through the fall semester. Her classes were popular and packed. She and her students formed a mutual admiration society. The dean, however, pushed by higher-ups who resented Decca's public resistance, failure to conform, and defiance of authority (all the things that made her Decca and, by extension, such a popular teacher), said sign or else. She refused again and, in mid-December, heard that she would not be rehired for further classes.

At the beginning of Christmas break, when an embarrassed dean appeared before Decca and her class (packed to the rafters) to announce that she had been "de-hired," the class erupted. Students shouted, *We want Jessica!* They thumped on the tabletops and paraded around the lecture hall. At one point, Decca asked for attention and declared, "They'll have to pick me up bodily and toss me out to keep me from teaching!"

The day of her de-hiring was the day Patricia Holt (a publicist at the time, but later the editor of the *San Francisco Chronicle Book Review*) had scheduled a meeting with Decca to drive her to Los Angeles for a series of interviews about *Kind and Usual Punishment*. Holt received a call saying that Decca's class was mobbed and surrounded by police. So might they reschedule? (Holt would continue to try. The next time, the publisher had to cancel. The third time, there was a strike in Hollywood and Decca wouldn't cross a picket line.)

James P. Degnan, a young journalist, was writing a profile of Decca. Not a Decca sympathist, he described the scene after the dean's announcement satirically as the "gallant little Englishwoman fighting the fascist bully." Later, sitting beside Decca as she drove on the Nimitz Freeway, Degnan observed, "Her hair is thin and of a peculiar filing-cabinet gray. She wears thick, gray, gogglelike horn rims, behind which blink the famous Mitford eyes—eyes a British writer once described as 'blue and cold and crazy.' Glancing at her profile I notice a triangle of white, delicate flesh under her chin."

In Degnan's portrait, Decca was a battle-ax who couldn't open her mouth without declaiming some annoying witticism. "From a distinguished professor to extinguished professor in three short weeks," she told him. And later, "Do come to class . . . We're having some convicts in."

Off in another ring, Bob was at work with Decca's legal team combing through the regulations surrounding loyalty oaths. The press was mad for tales of her latest rabble-rousing, and she did interviews nearly every day. She was a gold mine for the college paper, which was solidly in her camp against the trustees of the university. Her lawyers argued that fingerprints were not a statutory requirement. When Decca suggested that she might be willing to substitute toe-prints, a student silk screen crew ran off hundreds of posters with the slogan "Jessica Thumbs Her Toes." As Decca's lawyers fought to reinstate her salary, they agreed with the court's request that she allow her fingerprints to be kept in a sealed envelope in the court's custody. The winner of the case, whether the trustees or Decca's team, would be awarded the envelope and its contents.

Degnan and a goodly proportion of the Bay Area's population waited with Decca for the judge's decision. A TV cameraman Degnan interviewed said, "Every time she gets a chance she tries to stick that goddamn book [*Kind and Usual Punishment*] in front of the camera." Degnan was scathing in his description: "With malice towards all, Jessica handles the college officials—just as she handles the undertakers and just as she handled the late Bennett Cerf."

For her supporters, Decca's performance represented the kind of happy news that reinforced Berkeley's view of itself as a liberated zone, and Decca their principled and comic champion. When asked about the progress of the trial, she would sing (to the then-well-known tune made famous in the Disney movie *Snow White and the Seven Dwarfs*), "Some day my prints will come."

San Jose Superior Court Judge William Ingram ruled "that the university's fingerprint requirement was unsupported by any 'validly adopted statute, rule or regulation' and was therefore legally unenforceable." Asked what she'd do with her fingerprints now that they were returned in their envelope, Decca told a television reporter she thought she might "cremate them, put them in an urn, donate them to the University and take a tax deduction for their value." The final ruling in the case occurred in January 1974. When questioned, the trustees' attorney had to admit that Decca still had not been reimbursed for her semester's work.

"Pay the lady her money!" ruled the judge.

After this instructional drama, Decca would be invited to teach at Yale, where she found the elite students too often reticent to spring for the jugular. She apparently had more luck inspiring Degnan. "Jessica succeeds in bringing out the worst in the officials and their lawyers," he wrote. She trapped "them into saying and doing things that show them up as increasingly petty and stupid, as far worse than they are." Degnan was a frenemy, and in her tradition, he went for the throat.

NANCY MITFORD DIED in 1973, at the age of sixty-six. Decca hadn't attended Nancy's funeral, but ten years later, Decca would combine a visit to her sister's grave and to Swinbrook in a magazine article about the changes that had occurred there since her youth. Nancy's ashes were buried next to Unity's. About her eldest sister's grave, she wrote:

> Nancy's favorite symbol, part of the Redesdale coat of arms, was a mole couchant. My sisters decided that this would be an appropriate decoration for her gravestone. Wishing to employ local labor, they hired the services of a nearby stonemason . . . the result is a wonderful flight of fancy. If we linger we can hear the comments of tourists: "what's that supposed to be? A flying hippopotamus? How Nancy would shriek with laughter, could she only hear them!"

》《

IN 1975, ARANKA died quietly overnight in her New York apartment. Decca's exposure to Aranka's world of Jewish New York had been as important an education about America as anything she'd experienced in her own émigré life. In tracking Decca's escape from her past, few episodes are more revealing than the times she spent in Aranka's house, enjoying a New York City Sunday brunch. Once, Bob returned from the deli with unsatisfactory cold cuts. "This he sold you for three dollars a pound?" Aranka exclaimed. "You should take it back and throw it at his head!" Aranka, as a savvy New Yorker, knew that no deli counter guy would dare to short her. Her son, though, had left all this behind. Fighting for the rights of blacks and Communists, Bob, Aranka implied, still didn't know when to speak up for a fair portion of pastrami. Aranka's cultivation of her wildly unconventional daughter-in-law had resulted in the unexpected benefit of a glamorous extended family. Both Aranka and Decca were immigrants to the United States. Both were ambitious working women. Early on, their views on money had divided them, but as that subject became less fraught, their relationship grew comfortable and fond. After their forty-year correspondence, Decca had to wonder, who now would be so indulgent of their little family matters; who would remember Nicky as she had?

Remembering Nicky and telling the truth about the past would be Decca's hard-fought project over the next several years. In October 1975, Decca had the opportunity to do just that, as Herb Caen announced in his newspaper column:

> Radical chic marches on! Oakland's Jessica (Decca) Mitford is off for five weeks at idyllic Villa Bellagio on the shores of Italy's Lake Como, there to work on a book as the guest of—the Rockefellers. "I simply wrote to the Rockefeller Foundation that I'd like a grant so I could put together something on the fun of being a radical in the 1940s and 1950s and I was accepted," she says in her little girl manner.

Some writers' retreats like Yaddo are designed for creative artists, but the luxurious Bellagio attracted international scholars, whose high intellectual aims seemed to Decca hand-in-hand with their exaggerated self-regard. One fellow resident was Gerda Lerner, an academic from California, who had been a member of the Communist Party during the same period that Decca was a member. By rights, they'd have had a lot to talk about, but Decca dismissed her as a "grim feminist who talks sociologese." Perhaps she was still irritated by Lerner's part in the group that had scorned her friend Pele for writing the saucy "Vicky Says" column in the *People's Daily World*. In any case, Decca was bored and restless, and she childishly indulged in some mean teasing: inviting the professor's friendship then freezing her out until Lerner was "thoroughly muddled."

Decca called her new book *A Fine Old Conflict*, a title Robert Gottlieb told her he loved since she saw her life as a conflict and herself "in adversary position against all comers (including him)." (The book's title was a monde-green, a word or phrase that in mishearing, a person mistakes for another. "'Tis the final conflict" was the original lyric in "The Internationale," but as a child, Decca misheard those words as "a fine old conflict.")

Decca designed her book to alternate between her political adventures and the continuing story of her family life with Bob and their children in California (with occasional Mitford interludes). Early on, she had learned that persuasion was a lot easier when you were amusing, and her style was to treat hardship with humor. It was what her readers had come to expect and what she felt confident providing. It was fun to consolidate the legend of her poor housewifery—all part of the shtick. As was her distracted parenting: "I'm afraid I was a rather rotten mother to Dink & Benj as I was totally preoccupied with CP politics when they were growing up; so while I was fond of them, I didn't pay too much attention to them when they were little." Dinky, who was in a position to know, doesn't think she suffered from dramatic parental neglect. Part of the enduring family myth was that Dinky raised her brothers and organized the household. This was true to some extent, but Dinky remembers her mother making dinner every night and an intimate, reliable family life. So maybe Decca just liked the *idea* of being negligent, a sort of fantasy for a superachiever.

At Bellagio, perhaps Decca's biggest battle was resisting the blandishments of sentimentality, and she invented a tough protagonist, more like the author in 1975 than the resourceful young mother she'd been. Even in beautiful environments like Inch Kenneth or Lake Como, there was no avoiding the misery that came with remembering certain events. She told herself it was cowardly to duck "some of the *unutterably beastly* experiences" and wrote to Bob:

> As you have probably fathomed, I'm in some distress about the whole thing of Nicholas—I really can't bear to face the agony of his death in this book. So I thought I almost might just say that? Even in the foreword (which I know you say I'm always talking about but never do, but I will, I will)—something like "our adored son Nicky was born in 1944, killed in an accident at age 10, I am still too sad to write about him so have left him out."

Bob advised several approaches, but Decca found it impossible to call her son back, just to say good-bye again. She couldn't find a way to write about Nicky or about their family suffering in the aftermath of his death. And in the end, she doesn't mention Nicholas in *A Fine Old Conflict*.

For a writer, the past is malleable; it's material. The present is far less forgiving, and though she was writing about her children when they were young, concern for their adult lives interfered. Benjy loomed as Topic A. His behavior had become increasingly unpredictable, and she'd grown increasingly frustrated at his unwillingness to let her help.

Her youngest son had always been fast and funny. Going to high school in Oakland in the 1960s and having famous radical parents required imaginative flights of adolescent rebellion. He had entered St. John's College, but dropped out to bum around in the counterculture. Still in his early twenties, Benjy was inspired to become a piano tuner, an arcane occupation that combined hard work, close study, skill, sensitivity, and concentration. Without its tuners, the music of the world went awry. Bent on learning from musicians and craftsman and masters in the field, he traveled across

the country to apprentice at piano factories. In New York, he tuned for
Steinway's Concert Department. Eventually, he would repair and tune pianos for virtuosos like Vladimir Horowitz and Glenn Gould. The work was
fulfilling and he was good at it, but he had severe mood swings. In the early
1970s, he started experiencing longer-lasting bouts of mania characterized
by brilliant ideas, relentless energy, and unexpected behavior that exhausted
and mystified his friends. Back in the Bay Area, he was diagnosed with a
manic-depressive condition.

Years earlier Pele's son Peter had been diagnosed with schizophrenia and,
since then, had spent much of his life in institutions. Decca had consoled her
friend after a doctor assessed Peter's condition as "schizo-genic-frenic," or
in lay terms, mentally ill by virtue of bad parenting. The theory only caused
more pain, outraging Pele and reinforcing Decca's view of psychiatry, which
was a "really extreme prejudice in those years," Dinky said. "My mother
didn't think much of a person's chances if they had to go to a psychiatrist."

Bob and Decca looked into behavioral programs that might help their
son. Decca heard that lithium promised some relief, but Benjy refused their
assistance. "At the time," he said, "I was militantly pro-mania. Lucky for
myself, unlucky for my friends."

WHEN *A FINE Old Conflict* was published in 1977, Decca speculated that
Debo "skipped 9/10 of the book (all of the Calif. etc bits) because she
thought them boring." That response was the reverse image of the opinion of her old comrade Aubrey Grossman, who was bored by the sec-
tions about the British Mitfords. Al Bernstein told his son Carl he thought
Decca had trivialized "the whole experience of having been in the Party,
reducing it to almost farcical anecdote." Other ex-menaces, including
Marge Frantz, admired the book as "something that had to be done," but
A Fine Old Conflict did not find the affectionate following that her first
memoir had.

In 1977's San Francisco the cultural gap may have been between
disco and punk, but the larger world was still divided between the era's

superpowers, the Soviet Union and the United States. Benign and indulgent as most critics were, there remained the sense that as an American Communist, ex or not, one owed the world an explanation. Some reviewers called Decca myopic or naive. *Time* magazine coined the expression "transcendental blitheness." Why, critics asked, did Decca stay in the party as long as she did? Few asked why one couldn't denounce Stalin and all his works and still be an American Communist. Decca and her "sharp turn faction" friends tried in their fashion to achieve such political balance, but the air was already out of that balloon.

Writing *A Fine Old Conflict* had coincided with an English surge in Mitfordmania, or the Mitford industry, as the sisters came to call it. Diana's husband, Oswald Mosley, was writing his memoirs, and author David Pryce-Jones was researching a biography of Unity. Decca read the Unity book in manuscript form. It was "incredibly upsetting," she said to Sonia Orwell, "but then what else could it be?" After Pryce-Jones published his biography of Unity Mitford in 1977, Decca tried again to address what might have propelled Unity and her in different directions. Reluctantly acceding that "sibling rivalry—horrid phrase . . . probably did play a part," she suggested that "the Zeitgeist of the thirties . . . the cause of anti-Fascism . . . and the socialist reconstruction of society" probably influenced her more. Pryce-Jones interpreted the divergent paths that Decca and Unity took as "one experience but two outcomes, opposed in externals though in fact complimentary." Decca found this all very interesting, but took exception with his assertion that as 'thousands simultaneously stampeded along the highway to Moscow and Madrid, she [Unity] had taken the turning to Germany, their mirror-image." In *A Fine Old Conflict*, she argued against his assertions:

> Would that there *had* been a stampede along the highway to
> Madrid, a gathering of the anti-appeasement, anti-fascist forces in
> sufficient numbers to compel the governments of England, France
> and America to take an early stand against the fascists—It would
> have changed the course of history.

Later, in reply to all those who said fascism and Communism were two sides of the same coin, Decca would customarily quote Philip Toynbee's review of Pryce-Jones's book *Unity Mitford: A Quest*, "Stalinism may well have been almost as horrible as National Socialism; the motives which led young men and women in England to become fascists and Communists respectively were very different indeed." By her actions, Unity declared she'd rather die than live in an imperfect world. Imperfection inspired Decca, who deliberately and intensely chose life.

CHAPTER 29

THE VARIOUS VERSIONS of how history would record the Mitfords in the Pryce-Jones book and others was dividing Decca from her siblings. She objected to what she saw as her sisters' attempts to control or contain Pryce-Jones's book. She disapproved of Debo's choice of biographer for Nancy. Decca considered Selena Hasting too tepid and tried to enlist the stronger literary stylist Sybille Bedford for the job (Bedford demurred). Mainly, Decca wanted her sisters to pay attention. "I bloody well don't see why she [Debo] is self-appointed arbiter of all that goes on re the family," Decca wrote their cousin. "Esp as I am 3 years older than she is." After a terse letter from her sister Pam, which implied that Decca had taken one of the family scrapbooks (found at Inch Kenneth and archived at Chatsworth) to supply Pryce-Jones with rare photos, Decca's relationship with all her sisters hit its nadir. During the so-called scrapbook flap, her grievances as a sister conjoined with injuries harbored as a writer. She was enraged—hadn't she earned the right to be considered the literary consultant in family matters? Pryce-Jones was a good writer precisely because he wouldn't be controlled. Still, she loved Debo devotedly. Decca had never bothered to hide her casual attitude toward theft (those chocolates at the Palace!), and she wasn't ashamed of a little justifiable jiggery-pokery. She might have been capable of taking the scrapbook or charming a proxy into doing it—but if she had, she probably would have admitted it and laughed about it. A year after its disappearance, the scrapbook turned up near where it had been lost. She would eventually call the episode ridiculous. (How they had behaved like "Victorian old ladies in their late old age, bickering about a lost album.") But one day, in the middle of the drama, Bob had come home from work to find Decca in tears, at the prospect of being alone in her old age, in cruel exile from Debo. It was only the second time her husband had ever seen Decca cry.

Work as always was the writer's panacea. When one book ended, another began. Decca first considered writing a defense of James Dean Walker, who had escaped to California from Arkansas, where he'd been convicted of killing a policeman. His supporters claimed that Walker had rehabilitated himself and that extradition back to the brutal Arkansas penal system would be a certain death sentence. The book project dissolved at some point into articles and op-ed pieces and a barrage of letters on Walker's behalf. In one such exchange, Decca (by then an expert on prison reform) presumed on her earlier connection with Hillary Rodham Clinton, then wife of the Arkansas governor.

In the summer of 1970, Hillary Rodham had interned for Bob Treuhaft's law firm. She'd been a diligent young lawyer from Yale whom the Treuhafts had known only from a distance. When her fame increased, the office gossip was mainly along the lines of, *Who knew?* Decca wrote to ask Rodham Clinton's support to end Arkansas's demand for Walker's extradition. The future first lady, senator, and secretary of state gave assurances that there were changes under way in the Arkansas prison system, to which Decca replied, "Obviously I applaud many of the changes you enumerate. If I am skeptical of such concepts as 'American Correctional Association standards' (page 2, para 1 of your letter) you must forgive me; I had my fill of those alleged standards when researching *Kind & Usual Punishment*." The rate at which such changes would inch their way through the political system, though admirably designed for some future date, might still feel "rather a long time to those confined in the prisons."

ONCE THE SCRAPBOOK flap was resolved, Decca took a trip to Chichester, England, with Debo to see the latest manifestation of Mitfordmania—*The Mitford Girls* (a musical based on the sisters' youth) in its out-of-town run. On stage, Decca and Esmond sang and danced through their elopement:

ESMOND: When we hit Bilbao
          They'll wonder where we are from.
DECCA: In my attaché case
          My running away case
          I'm going to leave a space
          For an incendiary bomb!

The Mitford Girls didn't make it to Broadway, but it demonstrated a version of history that had staying power. Despite all she had written, the most entertaining part of Decca's story continued for English audiences to be the poor little rich girl running away. Decca might be a heavyweight in the United States, but would she always be a featherweight back in her old hometown? She'd made her case in *A Fine Old Conflict*, but the daily life of a U.S. Communist was an esoteric curiosity in England. It would take an awful lot of doing to change opinion that had become legend and presumed history. An opportunity to state her version of the story came along soon, when a young man from the north of England hitchhiked across America to California to meet her.

In 1978, Kevin Ingram was twenty-two years old. He had discovered Esmond Romilly's memoir, *Boadilla*, while researching his university thesis on the Spanish Civil War. After graduation, he tracked down Romilly's widow to declare his interest in writing a biography about the war hero and author of *Boadilla*. Decca was charmed by Ingram's youth and enthusiasm and impressed by the research he had already completed, and she came to believe he had the political sophistication and sympathy to portray Esmond. To encourage his project, she invited Ingram to visit Regent Street. Once the young writer arrived, he moved in for about five weeks. Decca's friends called him "the boy in the attic."

Most days, they'd settle in for a conversation about Esmond and Decca's youth. She showed him her photos and souvenirs and the war-era letters she and Esmond had exchanged. He showed her his writing. Decca found him appealing and adventurous in the spirit of Esmond. Ingram found her attractive and kind. She said she had only two rules for the book's author: that "it would be in no sense another spinoff of the Mitford industry" and that it would not be "the kind of biography that makes out the subject to be saintly and wonderful."

During their daily conversations, Decca, now sixty-one, was smoking heavily, "three packs a day," Ingram noted, and she was always "slightly out of breath." Several times during his stay, she suggested that he nip out for a bottle of vodka, which she liked to sip after her morning coffee. Decca told Dinky that she had begun drinking at twelve years old. In Ingram's estimation, she went through "a liter bottle of vodka in one and a half days." Then, "in the evening she'd have a Jack Daniels or two."

Decca imagined that Ingram's book would offer a bracing contrast to the musical comedy version. She provided him with contacts and introductions to old friends, and he impressively delved into their early lives. At the British Library, he read through Esmond's mother's novel *Misdeal*, written under the name Anna Gerstein. Decca had heard about it but never read it. (He sent her some pages, which she called "ghastly.") From England, Ingram also wrote to ask Decca what she thought he might make of some uncorroborated stories.

She replied, "I've never written a biography (only autobiogs, alas!) . . . But if I was doing one, I think I would chuck in all such reminiscences for what they are worth—whilst being extremely careful NOT to indulge in pop-psychologizing, so boring & often patently untrue, as to why . . . & let reader draw own conclusion."

In 1979, Decca consolidated her reputation as an investigative journalist in a book whose first title, *The Making of a Muckraker*, she discarded as "hopeless" on the advice of her young friend Nora Ephron. Released as *Poison Penmanship: The Gentle Art of Muckraking*, it provided behind-the-story commentary. In her introduction, she combined the remarks of fellow writers Nicholas Tomalin and Murray Sayre to advise young journalists on several key tips for success: "rat-like cunning, a plausible manner, and a little literary ability," to which she added "plodding determination and an appetite for tracking and destroying the enemy." Writing to Philip Toynbee, she admitted the project had been fun to do, but its research was "spurious," and the impulse behind it crassly commercial. Decca transmits her delight in writing the book—particularly regarding her tougher interviews and hard-won access to subjects central to her best stories. Most instructive are those serendipitous, transforming moments that she seized and that made her a muckraker.

In 1980, Dinky and the "'oys" (as Bob and Decca called their grandsons, nicely conflating London slang and Yiddish) moved to Atlanta from New York. James was twelve, and Chaka nine. Dinky had been working as an emergency-room nurse at Bellevue Hospital. In Atlanta, she worked in the emergency room at Grady Memorial Hospital and met Terry Weber, who worked for the telephone company in various jobs, including lineman, cable splicer, and operator. Terry, the divorced father of a six-year-old named Ben, was originally from New York. In the 1960s, he had been active in the antiwar movement and, like Dinky, had been drawn south to work in the civil rights movement. They married in June.

"If my parents believed in God, Terry would have been a Godsend," Dinky said. Decca and Bob both adored him. Hearing that Terry had been raised in a Jewish family, Bob joked, "I'm glad she's found a nice Jewish boy but what's he doing climbing up telephone poles when he should be going to medical school?" Dinky and Terry wanted to have children together, and after Dinky suffered a miscarriage, she had a consoling conversation with her mother about the miscarriage Decca had suffered in Washington, D.C., when Dinky was about six months old. Decca also discussed the abortion she had had, without Esmond's knowledge in 1939, before they left England. "I didn't tell Esmond," Decca said. "To tell would have made it more traumatic."

The wedding of Terry and Dinky, Decca wrote to Debo, went off without a hitch. The bride looked beautiful. Bob had bought champagne in bulk and wandered among the guests, uncharacteristically slugging it down straight from the bottle. Decca was tremendously glad to see her daughter and grandsons emerge from what had seemed to her a rather "thin" time, after Dinky's separation from Forman.

A hot Atlanta afternoon might not have been the first location to come to mind when Decca and Esmond had once considered their infant daughter's wedding day, but a happier, more utopian world than in that place and time—with its potluck meal, folksinging, dancing, unlimited champagne and cake and where the distinctions of race and religion were just normal and went unnoted—would have been difficult to imagine. Decca felt overheated in her long-sleeved and high-collared mother-of-the-bride dress, but she joked and sang with family and friends. On that lovely day, if she had stumbled on an FBI agent hiding in the bushes, she might even have brought the poor misguided wretch a lemonade.

》《

In October 1981, Decca casually mentioned to an acquaintance that she and Bob were planning a cocktail party for Joanne Grant, a writer and filmmaker who was in San Francisco to receive an award at the San Francisco Film Festival. Grant was the former assistant to W. E. B. DuBois and was married to Victor Rabinowitz, a movement lawyer (partner to Leonard Boudin, whom Decca had come to know during the HUAC trials and later as legal counsel for Dr. Spock). Twenty years younger than the Treuhafts, Grant, who was biracial, had met Dinky and James Forman through her own work at SNCC, but she only knew Decca distantly. The Grant-Rabinowitzes lived in New York, but the East Coast and West Coast worlds of leftist lawyers intersected at various National Lawyers Guild conventions. At one of these conventions early in the decade, Bob Treuhaft and Grant met and began an affair. Their romance would have been in its earliest stages when Decca held her cocktail party. She had no idea at the time, and she wouldn't learn about it for several more years.

Decca had always known that Bob liked the company of women. The same friends who marveled at the companionate nature of the Treuhafts' marriage noted how Decca would grow excited and fretful "if Bob was out of her sight too long." She wanted to be with him, but she also wanted to know what he was up to. If she suspected him of having affairs, she told no one. Once, when Pele confided her suspicions of her husband Steve's infidelity, Decca replied, "Oh he's perfectly splendid, you're imagining it. He's a dear old thing." Pele concluded, "It was as if she didn't want to get too involved in identifying with my problem because it ruffled things up."

In 1981, Decca was sixty-four years old. Bob was sixty-nine. Bob did less courtroom work and traveled more as an advocate for international human rights. He still prepared dinners for multitudes, and together the Treuhafts were still considered A-list guests at parties, benefits, and political or literary events. They spent nights at home playing marathon games of Scrabble or Boggle, into which they might rope any casual visitor. After almost forty years of marriage and twenty years of fame, there was no question of their drifting into a tranquil retirement. They both cultivated drama, though Bob's ways were quieter and more mysterious. For Decca, family and political battles remained a constant source of excitement. The couple had long since accommodated one another's routines. She read and wrote all day, with breaks for lunch and drinks, and she liked to stay in her housecoat or pajamas until it was time to get dressed to go out at night. She had just published two books, and in her subsequent publications and letters, she sparred with friends and fans about writing, in discussions that kept her edges sharp. To the visitor, she appeared fulfilled, a woman in her prime. If she felt misery, loneliness, or doubt, she didn't whine. What she did do was drink, excessively. She was a hardy, heavy drinker of vodka, mainly, quite aware of her habit but uninterested in stopping. She'd say to a visitor, "My daughter tells me I'm an alcoholic. Well, I don't really think there's anything bad about that . . . Thinking of all my friends who died, and none of them died a glorious death . . . so what's wrong with this?" Chain-smoking was far more vexing and the habit she struggled to control.

When Philip Toynbee died in 1981, Decca had reason to apply those theories of biography she had once recommended to Kevin Ingram. She

compiled the eulogies and obituaries written about her old friend for
a privately published volume. When no biographer happened along, she
expanded these into a memoir. By focusing on the parts of her life that
intersected with Toynbee's, she would have another go at the way people
viewed their youth together. How, in fact, did one write a biography? "Start
with *the*" was advice she commonly gave to amateurs. Then "chuck in all
sorts of fragments, memories, images, remembered lines as into an enormous soup." One standard of originality was sister Nancy's book *Madame
de Pompadour*, about which critic Raymond Mortimer said her "narrative
style is so peculiar, so breathless, so remote from what has ever been used
for biography. I feel as if an enchantingly clever woman was pouring out
the story to me on the telephone." But, Philip? All that scrutinizing, all that
gin, all those all-night debates about the least little thing, all passionately
important. She complained about it to her publisher:

> Toynbee memoir proceeds at snail's pace, what a bore. Sometimes
> I wish that a) he'd never been born, b) never died, c) never left all
> those diaries for me to extrapolate from, d) never had all those
> wives & children for me to not step on the toes of.

Decca's version of Toynbee, the philosophical and charismatic journalist,
is of a mischievously brilliant, sometimes clumsy, childhood friend (who
hardly ages and never seems separate from Esmond) and whose adult
choices she regards indulgently, at a distance.

In his last years, Toynbee cultivated an interest in spiritual matters and
joined a rural commune. Decca didn't understand these pursuits, and her
effort to explain what attracted him never lifts off. Toynbee had a much better understanding of Decca. Certainly, his talent for portraiture was superior, especially concerning her:

> [Decca] has a strong element of genuine and unabashed frivolity in
> her nature. Whenever confronted by any emotion which threatens
> to become deep—or turgid, she would feel—she dances away from

it in a sort of panicky jitter of comical derision. Since she is the only genuine female clown that I know—not just a wit but a total comic performer—her company is always exhilarating; occasionally exasperating . . . On certain occasions when I have begun to speak with great intensity about some issue which is dear to me but alien to Decca she has suddenly pushed my elbow sharply upwards so that my arm has been raised high above my head as if haranguing a multitude.

Philip was one of the few people to ever see Decca clearly, and in writing about him, she produced her favorite book. *Faces of Philip* doesn't change the common view of Decca and Esmond as rogue and scamp. She'd have to see whether Ingram could make that case.

As Esmond's biographer turned up new Romilly-related facts, another literary event gave Decca a shot at replaying history. In 1983, her old friend Michael Straight published a book called *After Long Silence*, in which he admits that as a young man in the late 1930s, he was the only America student recruited into the Cambridge spy ring. This meant that he was working for the KGB (or Soviet Secret Service) when Esmond and Decca shared his and Binnie's apartment in prewar Washington. Straight admits he was unsuccessful at the spying game and was abandoned by the Communist International (Comintern) organization early in his career. He kept his secret quiet for forty years, through employment in several high-level political appointments, including deputy chair of the National Endowment for the Arts during the Nixon administration. In March 1981, he was publically outed by the English newspaper the *Daily Mail*, after which he wrote his own account.

Reading Straight's book forty years later, Decca was surprised by her old friend's weird status as a deeply covered spy, of which she had been unaware. The account to some extent also explained why, when they had once been such good friends, Straight had cut her out of his life after Esmond's death. Straight's life had been much more complicated than she'd imagined. And though he had in his autobiography written of who he had been in his youth and what he had believed in, in Decca's opinion, he hadn't really succeeded. She recognized that if there were to be a more satisfying explanation forthcoming, it wouldn't come from him. Decca thought he might have conducted himself differently, come to different conclusions. In any case, she wanted him to know she had still been "riveted," by his revelations, adding, "I, of course, should have loved to be a spy; but nobody asked me."

>«

DEEP IN THE Reagan era, Decca was on the road lecturing about prisons, funerals, and the Old Left and protesting the U.S. government's intervention on the side of the Nicaraguan Contras against the Sandinistas. In 1984, when she was sixty-seven years old, Decca joined a women's delegation to visit El Salvador and Nicaragua. It was a demanding tour, hot and crowded with day trips to observe revolutionary collectives, cultural centers, and political events. During the trip, Decca suffered a minor stroke, which "caused temporary loss of feeling in her right hand, and a permanent weakness in her left leg." From then on, she'd rely on Catherine "Katie" Edwards, her new full-time assistant, to organize and help manage the details of her career as writer and celebrity speaker. Although Decca was slowed down by her stroke, this only meant starting a new book that might be neither "indictment nor an exposé," an affectionate treatment of her favorite ballad and party turn. *Grace Had an English Heart,* a benign foray into historical research, posed an opportunity for Decca to remark on what she'd learned of image and celebrity. A reader familiar with the Mitford sisters would have compared the emblematic role Grace Darling played in her day as a sort of Victorian "It girl" with the emblematic roles the Mitford sisters played in their nation's psyche.

While Decca was recovering from her stroke, Kevin Ingram made a return visit. His mother had knitted Decca a multicolored blanket, which he presented with his finished manuscript. The blanket was as endearing as the book, now called *Rebel: The Short Life of Esmond Romilly*. Decca found it to be "SURPRISINGLY good," and urged just two further additions. Why not add a lively personal note about how Ingram had first discovered Esmond and then hitchhiked cross-country to visit her? To give it a bit more status, he might also include a foreword written by Peter Stansky, an eminent scholar of the Spanish Civil War. She had already arranged that part, and once Ingram agreed, it would be a cinch to add. Katie saw that Decca adored Ingram and that Decca was disappointed when he wavered. He told her he was happy with what he had written, "happy that he'd finished it." Perhaps she'd already weighed in so much on all aspects of the book, that her influence over the "style of work may have become too strong." Decca thought Ingram was foolish not to take her advice. She had hoped to influence the way history would regard Esmond, but had also hoped to sway Ingram—a surrogate son—in a way she found all but impossible to do with her own son.

BY THE EARLY 1980s, Benjy had moved out of state and was keeping his distance. When Decca received a "SANE and AMUSING" letter after a long silence, she believed her son had turned a corner. "You know how desperately worrying he was (manic depression-wise)," she wrote to Robert Gottlieb. "Well he's been absolutely OK for more than 2 years, despite adamant refusal to go the lithium route. He is so smashing when he is his dear self, so you can imagine how v. delighted we are. But it is a bit puzzling—how that dread disease came & went; he was approx. 28 when it all started, is now 33."

One night during Ingram's stay, Decca and Benjy had a titanic quarrel at Regent Street. She demanded to know how he could be so sympathetic and sensitive on one hand and then "dreadful, and absurd," when his "disgusting manic episodes" came upon him. She said she had believed his episodes were behind him. It was this feeling of being sideswiped that drove her fury. Weren't there remedies? Wouldn't he listen to anyone? He said she didn't understand what treatment meant or what it was like in those "snakepits," where "they shoot you full of thorazine and lithium." Is that the life she wanted for him?

Once Benjy slammed out of the house, Decca wrote him a letter. She was still furious. They had a guest staying, she told him, Esmond's young biographer. She couldn't possibly introduce them, since "you wouldn't be remotely interested in anybody but YOU." By then, she was exhausted, and her tone became more conciliatory: "Dear Benjy, you are hardly ever out of my thoughts . . . it goes without saying that if you should ever tire of the manic condition & wish to get back to ordinary life, which wld. doubtless require some sort of therapy, we would absolutely stand behind you & do all possible to help."

As Ingram was preparing to go to sleep, he found a letter face up on the bedroom table, written by Decca and addressed to Bob. Not for his eyes, but he sneaked a look. She said she was trying to give up vodka and that she'd found out about Bob's affair. Ingram put the letter back down on the nightstand and hoped no one would come looking for it in the night.

Decca had discovered Bob's affair through the gossip of mutual friends. For someone who had rarely doubted herself in the past, the circumstances were devastating. Dinky said, "Bob's affair was very very painful to Decc in a very deep bedrock way." Decca, wishing to wound Bob, had subjected him to hotly emotional sessions that she called her "X-exams" (or cross-examinations). She ridiculed his girlfriend as "the Loved One" and relished descriptions of Joanne as a snob "only interested in meeting people she conceived of as important." Bob was still very fond of Joanne, and there were several false endings to their relationship, which Decca associated with lies and the "SQUALOR of it all." During the time of her affair with Bob, Joanne had managed to keep their secret from her husband, Victor Rabinowitz. Decca planned lacerating letters to her rival and exposés to Rabinowitz, but did not send them. She was disheartened but agreed with Bob to make an effort to repair their marriage, "given persistence & good will (no snappishness on my part; a modicum of lying on his)."

By the end of August 1984, Decca would believe they had begun to restore their old relationship, but she still had to wonder "if it was easier & less painful for him to give up J. than for me to give up smoking?"

CHAPTER 30

AT THE END of the 1980s, Dinky, who had been working as an emergency department specialty nurse in Atlanta, went back to school to earn a graduate nursing degree. Terry, who had been a working for the phone company, also returned to school to earn an advanced teaching degree. He would eventually head the mathematics department at an alternative public school. Their youngest sons, Ben Weber and Chaka Forman, were in high school, and James Forman attended Brown University in Providence. Dinky and Terry moved to New York in 1991, into a Lower East Side building that Bob and Decca had bought in 1968, a while after the sale of Inch Kenneth.

In the Bay Area, Benjy remarried. His four-year-long first marriage to Sue Draheim, which "began in a cocaine storm, ended in [1984] in a manic storm." His new wife, Jungmin Kim, born in Korea, was a piano-tuning associate. Their marriage lasted for only a few years and was over by the late 1980s. Decca had liked Sue, but she never felt much rapport with Jungmin. During this time, Decca and her friends marveled over the romance of twice-divorced Pele and fellow artist Byron Randall, both of them in their seventies. They had moved together to Sonoma County, where they lived a blissful idyll in the refurbished chicken coop they had converted into an artist's studio.

As the 1990s began, Decca launched into research of what would be her final book, *The American Way of Birth*. Reporting on historic swindles and the overselling of technology, Decca decried the corporate nature of modern obstetrics and championed the practice of midwifery. Her book argued for a national health-care policy, in sympathy with her old acquaintance Hillary Rodham Clinton, whose effort to reform American medical care was scuppered in Congress. In 1992, Decca wrote a letter to *Harper's* magazine, objecting to author Christopher Lasch's attack on Rodham Clinton's contention that children and adolescents in the justice system deserved the same rights as adults:

> And why not? Say I . . . Has Mr. Lasch ever talked with the mother
> of a black nine-year-old accused of stealing a dollar from a white
> playmate? Who was whisked off to juvy and there incarcerated for
> six weeks pending a hearing? Whose frantic mother would gladly
> have bailed him out, engaged counsel, sought witnesses, all to no
> avail?

In 1993, for a "Diary" column in the *London Times* magazine, Decca repeated the announcement originally published in the *American Spectator* that "Hillary Clinton had interned in the law firm of Bob Treuhaft . . . husband of England's most famous red snob Jessica Mitford." In her version, Decca added italics: "*Nobody can yet say how much of Mitford-Treuhaft rubbed off on Hillary during her summer internship in 1970.*" Decca was sure that more would be made of Hillary's internship, and it surprised her when no witch-hunt-style scandal was whipped up. Decca's friend, the novelist Diane Johnson, said, "I think Decca probably (wishfully) thought working for Bob T. was more radical, hotter stuff, than it was by the time Hillary worked for them." (There is some anecdotal evidence that the information collected about Hillary's internship was suppressed by Republican operatives during the first Bush campaign and presidency, in the belief that smearing Hillary would backfire.)

Every morning, Decca would work on some writing project—a chapter, an op-ed piece, an article—motivated by "anything which sniffs of phoniness or misplaced earnestness." In the early days of the fatwa against *The Satanic Verses*, Decca went around wearing a button proclaiming "I am Salman Rushdie" to protest the Islamic clerics' threats on the author's life. Alexander Cockburn (son of Claud) reported on a lecture Decca gave—in defense of the First Amendment—based on her recent investigations into pornography:

There had, she said, been "a man with a most enormous penis, perched on a motorbike with a woman. I said to Bob, 'That looks frightfully dangerous.'" Then she started raising questions about working conditions in the porn industry, industrial comp. and other important aspects of the situation.

In her own family, she was equally determined that nothing should be suppressed. She cherished her friendship with Debo, but chided her gently when the younger sister, as executor of Nancy's estate, withheld ("banned," in Decca's words) some letters their niece Charlotte Mosley was editing for publication. These included "some v. catty items about me & Bob, many more about the royal family":

> You shouldn't have done that, Hen. The whole point of letters is to reveal the writer & her various opinions & let the chips fall where they may. Censoring them for fear of offending the subjects is in my view absolutely wrong.

(Charlotte Mosley doesn't remember "showing Decca any letters with catty remarks about her and Bob." Debo did ask Mosley "to take out some of Nancy's jokes about members of the royal family because they were about their appearance. [Debo's] view was that it was fair to criticize people for the way they behaved but not for their looks.")

There were plenty of times when Decca's friends and family wished she would allow her own self-censor a bit more leeway. Her writing day began with a 6:00 A.M. coffee, shortly after which she'd start sipping "delicious" vodka. Almost everyone she'd known as a young woman had hit the bottle, and certainly all writers drank. According to Katie Edwards, Decca told her young friend that "before an interview a drink made her think better, it calmed her nerves, clarified her mind." In her seventies, Decca felt less and less inclined to indulge uninteresting company, attend boring events, or hide her impatience on that score. Sometimes when Decca was drunk, wit and cruelty would combine. She could lash out at old friends, as she did against Barb Kahn at one dinner party. She was unpredictable, sometimes an impossible dinner guest, telling the same story for the tenth time. When she did haul herself out for a special occasion, she might mock the speakers, sometimes sending her dinner companions notes reading, "Help I'm trapped at this ghastly dinner." Once, at a benefit for abortion rights, after many testimonials, the photographer Barbara Hall remembered how Decca, by then a bit bored by the company but enjoying the wine, casually addressed their table, "Have I ever told you about my abortion?" She began by describing the "grisly details" and concluded, "Of course we were going to America, and it was terribly inconvenient to be pregnant."

In 1992, *Harper's* asked Decca and other public intellectuals to write a short essay about abortion, and composing this piece stirred her memory. Fifty years earlier, when Decca had her dangerous soap-induced abortion, she hadn't known there was a choice to be made between the care provided by a hush-hush upper-class doctor and a backstreet abortionist. She didn't ask her sisters for help, and she wouldn't tell her husband beforehand.

"An obvious omission," Decca wrote to Robert Boynton, an editor at *Harper's* magazine, "is that I don't say why I wanted to have an abortion in 1938. However, I don't want to go into that—too complicated."

This letter's casual phrasing discourages further inquiry. Perhaps because of her reputation or age, no further questions were asked. (Who was going to quiz this distinguished and famously caustic seventy-five-year-old woman who had made it clear she didn't want to talk about the reasons for her abortion, for just a few more details?) Half a century later, in the days of the Clinton-era culture wars, Decca described her horrid experience and ended with this advice to younger women: "So get your safe, legal abortion and don't feel guilty about it. But don't forget that there are those who want to turn the clock back to the barbaric days of illegal abortions."

In 1992, in the months preceding the publication of her book *The American Way of Birth*, Decca gave Boynton an interview. She was typically irreverent and challenging:

"I don't think I'll get death threats the way I did when I wrote *The American Way of Death*," she says with a trace of disappointment in her voice. "I expect the AMA will try to discredit me. The undertakers I wrote about were a quite isolated bunch so nobody much cared about them, but doctors are loved by everyone and have a huge PR machine to keep it that way. They are bound to fight me—I should hope."

The American Way of Birth had a short span of literary success, and its controversy was less than universal, but its influence was strong among the midwives and nontraditional medical practitioners, whom Decca always championed.

OVER THE NEXT couple of years, Decca had several falls and broke bones in her arm and leg. These accidents, she admitted, "were prob. due to being more than tiddly at the time." She had a blood test, which came back "grossly inflated with alcohol"—a diagnosis of cirrhosis of the liver. She still confided in Dinky that there were worse ways to go. Dinky and Terry were settled in New York City, where Dinky worked at the emergency room of Bellevue Hospital. She would later specialize in pain management. If Decca had initial questions about her daughter's choice of career (wishing her daughter had chosen something more "intellectual"), she had long since been impressed by Dinky's achievement and come to depend on her daily advice. According to Kathy Kahn, "eventually Decca thought that Dinky was the strongest person in the world."

Decca had another accident when she was wearing what she called her glad rags, long culottes. She had already been drinking a lot, and she tripped, badly fracturing her leg and requiring immediate surgery. Afterward, as she was coming to, Decca looked up to see Dinky sitting by the hospital bed. "I've ruined your life," Decca said.

"Of course you haven't," replied Dinky. "You've ruined your life. You're the one with the broken leg." Decca's doctor said she had to speak to the addiction specialist, who told her she was an alcoholic and would have to enter a program. Decca said, "Doc, the cure sounds worse than the disease."

Dinky tried to find a nontraditional twelve-step support group, but her mother insisted she could stop drinking on her own. She wrote Debo: "I know I wouldn't be any good at it—all that appalling Frank Talk etc."

"At least find a partner," Dinky said.

"You're my partner," Decca insisted.

Dinky agreed to do what she could, but she had to return to her family and job. They spoke on the phone frequently and exchanged letters. In one letter, Decca described "a time aeons ago Pele & I both decided to give up smoking & agreed to be buddies if in dire need, we'd ring each other up. Usual advice was to 'Dash to the drinks closet & pour a huge vodka or scotch.' So I expect YOUR advice will be 'Dash out & get a pack of Chesterfield non-tipped'?"

"I've gone on the wagon," she wrote to her sister Debo. "I just decided to completely stop, nary a drop of anything, even wine at dinner. What decided me was the trouble I've caused Dinky and Bob, *terribly* tiresome for them having to scram about looking after me."

Decca seemed to think that she'd have enough work to distract her from drinking and in fact planned to update *The American Way of Death*. After much negotiation beginning with a 1984 investigation by the Consumer Protection Bureau of the Federal Trade Commission (FTC), the funeral industry had been required at last to adopt "standard fair practices." It had been a long fight, but for the muckraker, there was still more to do. Decca had become fascinated by the funeral industry's new corporate nature, as represented by Service Corporation International (SCI), a company that owned chains of funeral parlors, flower shops, and cemeteries in Australia and England. In the United States, SCI had a growing share of the U.S. trade. In the months following her surgery, she planned a trip to the company's U.S. headquarters in Houston.

Decca began her revision of *The American Way of Death* with a new research assistant, Karen Leonard, and the working title *Death Warmed*

Over. Robert Gottlieb signed on, and Decca hoped that Bob would muck in, too, but he resisted. That book had made them affluent and shadowed their lives for thirty years. The subject would never be exhausted, but he chose to avoid it for the time being. Leonard brought youth and enthusiasm to the project. On her first day of work, she arrived to find that Decca had broken her ankle. Her new employer excused herself after five minutes to go to a doctor's appointment. On Leonard's second day of work, Decca had to run off to "cut a Rock and Roll record"—not one of Decca's witty remarks, but rather the truth, which answered the question, what do you do after you've become an institution? For Decca, who loved to sing and play and entertain, the answer was to join a kazoo band at the age of seventy-eight. In San Francisco, musician Kathi Kamen Goldmark had first invited Decca to sing lead vocals with a backup band at a literary talent show. For the occasion, they called themselves Decca and the Dectones. Decca showed up in a spangled dress. Among her numbers, she sang "Mean to Me" and wiped away crocodile tears with a pair of men's boxer shorts.

After their debut performance, they went on to perform at the fortieth anniversary of the *Paris Review* and at a benefit for the *Nation* magazine at New York's Town Hall. Of all Mitford's legacies, her most joyfully arcane has to be her recording of the Beatles' song "Maxwell's Silver Hammer" and "The Ballad of Grace Darling" for the "Don't Quit Your Day Job" Records label. Her wavering voice, once quite good, had deteriorated to a comic croak. (Writer Cynthia Robbins, one of the backup singers, described Decca's range tongue-in-cheek as reaching "profound depths . . . which only bullfrogs could duplicate on a clear night.") In an interview with rock journalist Ben Fong-Torres, Maya Angelou said that Decca "doesn't have a lot of musical acumen. But on the other hand, she has the courage, the concentration, of somebody about to be executed in the next half-hour."

Decca was having a blast and didn't care what anyone thought. Some of her friends worried for her. Katie Edwards thought there was an unsavory aura of exploitation about Decca's late performing career. In the audience at Town Hall, Gottlieb was embarrassed enough to exclaim, "Can't you make her stop?" She hit some notes, took a pass at others, but was always vivacious.

Bob was enjoying Decca's new career. He drove her to gigs and gathered other stalwart friends, many in their seventies, to hear her perform, to sing along, and to lend moral support. As a way of celebrating her first record release, Bob and Goldmark set new lyrics to the tune of "Grace Darling":

> T'was on the ground of Swinbrook, there dwelt an English maid
> Pure as the air around her, of danger n'er afraid
> A prisoner of the nursery, as bored as she could be
> So longing for adventure, she split with Romilly—and—
> She sailed away o'er the rolling sea, over the waters blue
> "HELP, HELP!" she could hear the cries of a cause so true
> Decca was very smart, integrity she craved
> She pulled away o'er the rolling spray, and her life she saved.

Decca and the Dectones had plans to record an album of more "inappropriate songs for special occasions." She taped a couple of ribald music hall songs with Maya Angelou, but travel was becoming more difficult. One aspect of this escapade that Decca loved in particular was that her recording profits would go to her son Benjy's new endeavor: Send a Piana to Havana.

In San Francisco, Benjy had studied piano rebuilding with Victor Charles, a piano maker and composer. When Charles died, Benjy inherited twenty-eight thousand dollars, which he spent on a piano for musicians to use in Cuba. He saw the piano delivered and, while in Cuba, observed that the U.S. embargo had produced a crisis in Cuban music. There were very few pianos in good condition, and for these, the embargo had made replacement parts almost impossible to find. The strings on many of the older instruments had rusted through, and the Russian pianos that had arrived before glasnost were almost all infested with termites. In 1995, Benjy began his campaign to collect donated pianos and transport them to Cuba. He organized a cohort of tuners and goodwill travelers to accompany each shipment. Decca may have complained bitterly from time to time about Benjy's unpredictable behavior and her inability to help him, but she and Bob were terribly proud of his project, tickled by its originality and purpose, and delighted by his defiance of the U.S. embargo.

In October 1995, Decca was invited to a seminar of morticians in Northern California. She wrote to her friend and then literary agent Frederic Hill about the experience:

> Needless to say I was absolutely astonished at being invited. Visualize the emotions of a five-year-old being told he's going on a trip to Disneyland, or a teenager given a role in a Hollywood movie; that's how I felt in anticipation of this incredible treat—hobnobbing, or networking to use a more modern expression, with undertakers, casket manufacturers, vault men for two whole days . . .
>
> After my talk, the first question set the tone: "How much money did you make from *The American Way of Death*?" "Absolute tons," I answered. "So much I can't even count it—it made me fortune." Audible groans from the crowd. "Next question?"

After the seminar, Service Corporation International, having heard that she'd made some disparaging remarks about the company, sent her a letter to warn her off further such transgressions. This, of course, she found absurd and inspiring. A lawyer for SCI condescendingly suggested it would not be to her advantage to "cast SCI in a bad light clothed in wit and humor." Decca toyed with these amateurs:

> I'm extremely anxious to get the facts straight about SCI: its history, its goals, its philosophy. I wish to avoid using "baseless gossip and rumors" in my book, and should certainly appreciate it very much if you would point out the "wholly unsubstantiated innuendo and, in some case[s], outright falsehoods" that you refer to, so that these may be corrected in the finished book.

By that time, Decca had been on the wagon for almost a year. Edwards thought perhaps she wasn't as chatty, but there weren't many other obvious changes in her conduct. Then in June, Decca began to cough blood. The diagnosis was lung cancer, which had spread to her brain and her bones. To her visitors over the next few days, she seemed philosophical, without noticeable fear, and curious about dying. Her assistant Karen Leonard saw Bob "panic-stricken"—as was Benjy. They turned to Dinky, who came out immediately to help arrange Decca's care, which began with daily radiation to preserve brain function. Decca wrote to Debo: "Doesn't hurt at all plus I get marvelous pain pills *and* blue cheerup pills."

Bob encouraged Decca to eat and drink whatever she wanted, and after one trip to the hospital, she returned home to find he had filled their refrigerator with chocolate mousse. Vodka didn't taste as good, and she didn't drink again. She seemed undeterred in those first few weeks after the diagnosis, confident that she could complete many of the projects she'd set for herself. She made plans to travel to see her sister and friends in Cape Cod and England. "Possibly late autumn or even Xmas so don't come here. But DO come to me funeral, about 9 months or a year off accdg to the Dr."

Her situation, she wrote to Debo, was "so much better than just being hit by a car or in a plane wreck. At least one can plan a few things with the help of marvelous helpers who are absolutely smoothing every path here, so it's sort of a nonstop party, all my favourite people flocking by. So why worry? Did I tell that when I went to register at hosp name of Jessica Treuhaft the social worker said 'Are you by any chance related to the piano tuner?'"

Over the past few years, Decca had made some effort to put her accounts in order. She had never paid much attention to money management. She had once conscientiously taken Dinky on a tour of the various places she'd stashed bundles of cash around the house, after which they had driven to several banks where Decca had multiple accounts. Now, she gathered some of her cash and began to give it away to her friends while she still could. She and her new health-care assistant, the musician Lisa Pollard, would make

up lists of friends whom Decca wanted to see, and these they would invite
to a series of dinner parties.

Decca had written two memoirs of her life, and she had few regrets. She
still enjoyed the fight, still possessed the power to "denounce wonderfully."
She did not whine. She asked some friends to make sure to sue the Federal
Trade Commission on behalf of consumers. Most important, she had to
explain to Dinky and Benjy why she had decided to leave Nicky out of her
books; this she did in a letter to her children:

> I know it must seem v. odd that in writing *A Fine Old Conflict*
> I sort of airbrushed Nicky out of it entirely, not one mention of
> him—although he was such a star & hugely important factor in
> our life. Bob Gottlieb (editor of Fine Old C) understood, I think—
> or anyway, raised no objection—when I explained that to re-live
> his death (which one has to do, if writing about a person) was a bit
> more than I cld bear.

Late at night, when she couldn't sleep, Decca spoke about the past.
There were always more stories to tell. She was emphatic about her love for
sister Debo. Several years earlier, when a graduate student Anthea Fursland
had written her Ph.D. thesis on Decca, Decca complimented Fursland on getting most of her relationships right, but added to her impression of Debo:

> We adored each other as children (even though when she was small
> I used to be rather horrid to her). Ditto as teenagers. As she was
> completely apolitical there were none of the complications as in
> the Boud/Diana situation; just enjoyment, jokes, non-stop Honnish
> poems and songs.

Naturally, she and Debo had quarreled, but Decca dearly loved her youngest sister. In early July, the sisters exchanged faxes about ways to get funding for the Send a Piana to Havana campaign, Dinky's superior medical
expertise, and dates for their next reunion. She also wrote that Bob was
"being marvelous."

At 3:00 A.M. on July 10, 1996, Decca couldn't sleep and wrote a letter
to her husband of over fifty years:

Bob—it's so ODD to be dying, so I must just jot a few thoughts—
starting with fact that I've SO enjoyed life with you in all ways.
Isn't it rather amazing how we ever met in 1st place—and thinking
back to absolutely everything . . . Mainly, of course, you've been
incredibly GOOD to me all through life and have TAUGHT me more
than I can say, not to mention being incredibly kind & forgiving
of faults such as Impatience. I must say I'm glad it's me first as I
v. much doubt I'd bother to go on much if it was you. Also there
really is a small bonus—I wonder if you agree? In knowing ahead
of time so one can think things out a bit (not just finish book—you
know what I mean). Back to us meeting in Washington. What on
earth would have become of ME if we hadn't. And wonderful Nicky
(actually I do think of him most days, now aged 52) when Mrs.
King told the children her skirt had blown up at Wild Cat's Peak
& Nicky saying "Did the wild cats peek?" You & Dink, whole
relationship over the aeons—goodness what a lucky thing you liked
each other almost from word Go. Not quite; I think she rather
looked away from you at the very beginning, to my worry. But
that soon stopped, & I can skeke imagine a better friendship than
you/her. As for Benj—hasn't he turned out amazingly well lately?
So now, about you. You've got the children & Oys all of whom
adore you, but you'll need someone—I mean you've got all those
household skills, cooking etc., pity to waste don't you agree? Be
thinking of someone agreeable. You won't have to as they'll come
flocking I bet. I do have some ideas but fear to mention for fear of
annoying or being intrusive, none of my business you'll say. On
separate page, am putting down about money. Yr loving Wief

The cancer progressed, and less than two weeks later, in her bedroom at
home, Decca showed Karen Leonard that she couldn't hold up her arm. Her

speech was more or less slurred, and she was weak, but she could understand. In the hospital, the nurse checking her in asked various questions, including, "Can you tell me who the president is?" to which she answered, "That's not my fault!"

AFTERWORD

The point is I just write as I see things. I do have a funny bone.
There's really nothing more hilarious than the funeral industry.

—JESSICA MITFORD, INTERVIEW WITH
IDA LANDAUER, *PORTRAIT OF A MUCKRAKER:
THE STORIES OF JESSICA MITFORD*

EFORE SHE DIED on July 23, 1996, Decca organized the details of
her cremation or, in the mortuary jargon that she both loved and
deplored, attended to her "pre-needery." She chose Frank Rivera
of Pacific Internment Society (whom she knew as the "most hated funeral
director in California" for his defiance of funeral industry leaders and practices) to dispose of her earthly remains. Decca's ashes were dispersed into
the Pacific.

During her last months, undertakers had vied for the opportunity
to "do" Jessica, but none of them expected a good-bye note. That privilege alone belonged to Robert Waltrip, president of Service Corporation
International. In a communiqué sent posthumously by her assistant, Decca
encouraged Waltrip to pick up the tab for all "goods and services" associated with her funeral. She considered this a fair exchange for the free publicity she had provided, and she kept the bill low just to show it could be
done ($475.00, including "$15.45 for the cremation container"). After that
thrifty cremation, there were two boisterous memorial services in packed
houses (first San Francisco, then London). Some people choose music or
readings in advance; Decca designed a comic protest to surprise and lift the

mood. She had long theorized that the speakers at funerals too often relied on the word *but* to combine excellent sentiments with inferior ones, so in her final weeks, Decca secretly charged some friends to object should any of her eulogists wander that way. When a speaker early on in the San Francisco memorial innocently invoked the offending conjunction, her avenging angels rose to protest, and no more *buts* did he bruit.

Once, during an interview, Decca had jokingly expressed a desire for a horse-drawn hearse to carry her corpse. She came to regret those remarks, since her humorless adversaries only flouted them to prove her inconstancy. To her family and army of friends, however, it was a good joke, and knowing how she really would have loved a funeral cortege they arranged one for her.

As the congregation emerged into the lucid San Francisco afternoon, they saw at the curb six black, magnificently plumed horses waiting to draw an ornate and polished antique hearse filled with Mitford memorabilia. A driver in full livery, including top hat, scrambled into his seat. A band of musicians assembled to precede the hearse, and Lisa Pollard on solo saxophone followed behind. As they proceeded along the waterfront, the band played songs in honor of Decca, among these "When the Saints Go Marching In," "Amazing Grace," and "The Internationale."

ACKNOWLEDGMENTS

I AM GRATEFUL TO Decca's children, Dinky Romilly and Benjy Treuhaft, for their generosity of spirit and openness of mind; Peter Sussman, magnanimous editor of Decca's letters who gave me sage advice; Decca's designated literary executor Marge Frantz, Pele deLappe, Dobby Brin Walker, Eva Lapin Maas, Virginia Durr, and Gerda Lerner, all of whom are American treasures. Thanks to the second generation: Ann Durr Lyon, Lucy Durr Hackney, and writers Tilla Durr, Mark Lapin, Leah Garchik, Sally Belfrage, and Nora Sayre for keeping the flame; and to Katie Edwards, who knew everything and was unfailingly helpful.

Thanks to leading Mitfordologists Charlotte Mosley and Mary Lovell; to Kevin Ingram for his indispensable biography of Esmond Romilly; to filmmakers Ida Landauer, Stephen Evans, and James Morgan, whose many interviews with Decca and friends (conducted for their film *Portrait of a Muckraker*) were tremendously valuable; to the late, great Stew Albert; to Jovanka Beckles for her research of the Gary family story; to Cedric Belfrage for his masterpiece *The American Inquisition*; and to Taylor Branch, Jo Freeman, Anthea Fursland, Diane McWhorter, Laura McCreery, Victor Navatsky, Elena Poniatowska, Kevin Starr, Patricia Sullivan, Robert G. Larsen, Philip Toynbee, Robert Rosenstone, and Edmund White, all of whose work was essential to this book.

The following people kindly offered interviews and stories: Peter Ackerberg, Judy Gumbo Albert, Bert Albert, Eugene Albert, Bettina Aptheker, Steve Coats, Carole Cuenod, Lillian Engel, Eleanor Engstrom, Jeff Eliot, Doug Foster, Constance Gary, Herbert Gold, Kathi Goldmark, Tom Hayden, Tanya Harrod, Robert Gottlieb, Danny Grossman, Barbara Hall, Alex Heard, Patricia Holt, Diane Johnson, Kathy Kahn, Wendy Lesser,

Karen Leonard, Lisa Pollard, Bart Schneider, Dugald Stermer, Judith Viorst, and Michael Waite.

I appreciate the help of friends at Centrum, Hawthornden, the Carmargo Foundation, Yaddo, and the Sundance Foundation and numerous librarians: Ohio State University's Rebecca Jewett; University of Redlands' Sandy Richey; and the staff at the San Francisco Labor Library, the Harry Ransom Humanities Research Center at the University of Texas at Austin, the Berkeley Historical Society, the Voices of Feminism Oral History Project in the Sophia Smith Collection at Smith College, the Tamiment Library at New York University, and the British Library. At the University of Redlands, the Creative Writing Department's cheerful and indefatigable Starla Strain and a brigade of student workers have assisted me over many semesters, beginning with Emily Sernaker, David Smooke, and Rachael Severtson, and everyone at the UoR who helped me obtain funds for travel, editing, and a sabbatical, Chris Deyo, Nancy Carrick, Philip Glotzbach, and Barbara Morris. Thanks to special researchers Erica Brody and Jessie Wick.

Thanks to Decca's extended family Edith McKelvey, Terry Weber, Olga Feher, James Robert Lumumba Forman, Chaka Esmond Fanon Forman, Benjamin Daniel Weber, Zsófi Melani Treuhaft, and Isidore Robert Treuhaft, and to the fourth generation: Chaya Lillian Forman, Sakai Esmond James Forman, and Emeka David Chaka Forman. To friends and family: Erin Auby Kaplan, Susannah Crawford, Denise Davis, Karen Derris, Brian Evenson, Patricia Geary, Joan J. Hall, Kelly Hankin, Simon Barker, Laurel Ollstein, and presiding angels Debby and John Hanrahan, Judy Hatcher, Jack Hayes, Joanna Howard, Gregory Lehmann, Andrew Tonkovich, Judy Tschann, Dwight Yates, Victoria J. White, Richard D. and Mary Anna White, Thomas R. White, Emily Wick, Elizabeth Wray. To Dorothy Albert, Agnes Amdahl, Bert Albert, Richard Brody, Jane Cohn Brody, Special Correspondent Lauren Brody, Robert Brody, Philip Brody, and Warren Brody. To Lillian Albert Brody, Steve Brody, and Anna Brody; I miss them. Thanks to Elena Engel, without whose comfort, support, and San Francisco home I would never have dared to continue. To my husband,

Gary Amdahl, and to my muses Alphie, Ole, and Masha, without whom I might never have started.

Thanks to publisher Jack Shoemaker, editors Roxy Aliaga and Patricia Boyd and everyone else at Counterpoint Press, and to my agent, Martha Kaplan.

I am particularly grateful for the assistance of the People's Writing Committee: writer, filmmaker, and WIHU comrade Jenny Shepherd; historian Michael Wilson; novelist and editor Alisa Slaughter. Furthermore, to Regina White, who deferred other things to help get this book right, for her tireless and formidable work as researcher, fact-checker, editor, and friend. Finally, to Esmond Romilly, to Bob Treuhaft, and at last to Decca, fondest love.

NOTES

ABBREVIATIONS

PEOPLE

Benjy............. Benjamin Treuhaft

Debo .... Deborah Mitford (Cavendish),
Dowager Duchess of Devonshire

Diana .... Diana Mitford (Mosley)

Dinky............ Constancia Romilly

ER .... Esmond Romilly

Farve............. David Freeman-Mitford,
Lord Redesdale

JM................. Jessica Mitford

Muv .... Sydney Bowles Mitford,
Lady Redesdale

NM .... Nancy Mitford

RT................. Robert Treuhaft

UM............... Unity Mitford

SOURCES

AFOC........... *A Fine Old Conflict*

AWOB.......... *The American Way of Birth*

AWOD......... *The American Way of Death*

DECCA .... *The Letters of Jessica
Mitford*

H & R   *Hons and Rebels*

OSU .... The Mitford Collection,
Ohio State University

PP................. *Poison Penmanship: The
Gentle Art of Muckraking*

TM-LBSS...... *The Mitfords: Letters
Between Six Sisters*

CHAPTER 1

5   "Dear Madam": JM, interview, *Portrait of a Muckraker: The Stories of Jessica Mitford*, produced by Stephen Evans, Ida Landauer, and James Morgan, KQED, 1990 (DVD and VHS).

5   "Bank of America": Ibid.

5   "I was never at all": Ibid.

5   "spare shillings": Ibid.

6   "uncompromising air": Ottewell, *Literary Strolls Around the Cotswolds and the Forest of Dean*, 72.

6   "lunatic asylum": JM, *H & R*, 2.

7   "The others bored me": NM, *The Water Beetle*, 14.

7   overstimulating: JM, *H & R*, 4.

7   "are you planning to go back to Spain?" JM, *H & R*, 121.

8   "having smuggled": JM to James Forman Junior, 20 July 1992, in *Decca*, ed. Sussman, 663.

8   "restless, unformulated": JM, *II & R*, 35.

9   "We think with joy": Lovell, *The Sisters*, 188.

9   "beastly Fascists": JM, *H & R*, 68.

10   "Unfortunately, my will to live . . . bitterly regretted my lack of courage": JM, *H & R*, 96.

10   "still loved Boud": JM, *H & R*, 72.

10   "freezing shadow": Ibid.

11   "God bless Muv": Lovell, *The Sisters*, 104.

11   "about great movements in England": JM, *H & R*, 63.

11   "irreverent outpourings": JM, *H & R*, 32.

12   "a little jiggery-pokery": JM, *H & R*, 12.

12   "an abortive attempt at running away": JM, *H & R*, 75.

CHAPTER 2

14   "joint rebellion": JM, interview, *Portrait of a Muckraker*.

15   "barbarian, possibly prejudiced against homosexuals . . . have gone through the same?" JM to Merle Miller, 3 November 1971, in *Decca*, ed. Sussman, 436.

15   "We have done all we could": Ingram, *Rebel*, 98.

15   "amazingly long eyelashes": JM, *H & R*, 121.

16   "very pretty": Toynbee, *Friends Apart*, 98.

16   "a brown corduroy ski suit": JM, *H & R*, 131.

17   "I'm afraid I've fallen in love with you": JM, *H & R*, 136.

18   "completely, deeply committed . . . attractive and powerful": JM, *H & R*, 126.

18   "a committed partisan": JM, *H & R*, 140.

18   "He would get into a fury of frustration": JM, *H & R*, 140.

19   "What right have you": JM, *H & R*, 141–142.

19   "glimmerings": JM, *H & R*, 144.

19   "far more the quality": JM, *H & R*, 147.

19   "grim, serious town of Bilbao": JM, *H & R*, 147.

19   "bemused, . . . all old ties": JM, *H & R*, 147.

19   "trying to get in focus . . . understand the heroism": JM, *H & R*, 148.

19   "determination, intelligence and courage": JM, *H & R*, 133.

19   "sense of unreality": JM, *H & R*, 149.

CHAPTER 3

21 "I am not a pacifist": ER, *Boadilla*, 196.

21 "Find Jessica Mitford": JM, *H & R*, 150.

21 "Have found Jessica": Ingram, *Rebel*, 156.

22 "Worse than I thought": JM, *H & R*, 159.

22 "Have them bring it out": JM, *H & R*, 154.

22 "normal progression . . . and bedtime": JM, *H & R*, 147.

23 "*No es sueño la vida*": Federico García Lorca, "*Ciudad sin sueño*," in *Poet in New York* (New York: Grove Press, 2008), 62.

23 "total war": JM, *H & R*, 155.

24 "*Armes Kind*": JM, *H & R*,159.

24 "You will honestly *adore* Esmond": JM to Muv, late February 1937, in *Decca*, ed. Sussman, 24.

24 "My darling": Muv to JM, 23 February 1937, OSU.

24 "I cannot help blaming myself": Muv to JM, 3 March 1937, OSU.

24 "Oh, poor duck": JM, *AFOC*, 6.

25 "I realize you are my guardian now": JM interview, *Portrait of a Muckraker*.

25 "except Jessica": Lovell, *The Sisters*, 456.

25 "I knew I was cut out": Anthea Fursland, *Jessica Mitford: A Levinsonian Study of Mid-Life*, Berkeley, California: Wright Institute, 1996, 146.

26 "Esmond was always trying . . . dog of his choice": JM, *H & R*, 173.

28 "singleness of purpose": JM, *H & R*, 176.

28 "In Esmond's view . . . being a member": JM, *AFOC*, 20.

28 "Philip was forever . . . were hardly persuasive": JM, *FOP*, 25.

28 "instinctive understanding of subtleties": JM, *H & R*, 165.

28 "political vision" that made her seem "almost clairvoyant": Dr. William Kurt Wallersteiner to Decca, 5 December 1980, OSU.

29 "in an open and declared": Toynbee, *Friends Apart*, 112.

29 "Being good was never conspicuously on our agenda": JM, *FOP*, 29.

29 "we need someone like Hitler over here": JM, *H & R*, 165.

29 "rich vein of lunacy . . . humanity and culture": JM, *H & R*, 280.

CHAPTER 4

31 "I am going to have a baby . . . I'm not any more now": JM to NM, July 1937, in *TM-LBSS*, ed. Mosley, 108.

32 "known for his inability": JM, *H & R*, 264.

32 "the center of my existence": JM, *H & R*, 182.

32 "considerably more militant . . . seriousness of purpose": JM, *H & R*, 177.

32   "lined up to boo": JM, *H & R*, 177.

33   "tired, white-faced dockers": JM, *H & R*, 177.

34   "a little gamine": JM, *H & R*, 182.

34   "the entire community . . . as red as you may think": JM, *H & R*, 178.

35   "Too thin": Lovell, *The Sisters*, 259.

35   "light-hearted maternal competence": Toynbee, *Friends Apart*, 115.

36   "Dearest Hen": JM to Debo, 31 May 1938, in *TM-LBSS*, ed. Mosley, 88.

37   "willingness to fight and die": Rosenstone, *Crusade of the Left*, 314.

38   "Their furled umbrellas": JM, *H & R*, 185.

38   "unthinkable . . . tormentor": JM, *H & R*, 190–191.

38   "Esmond had a theory . . . more ways than one": JM, *H & R*, 191.

40   "'Oh—Chamberlain": JM, *H & R*, 186.

41   "depressed and restless": JM, *H & R*, 188.

41   "An ordinary middle-aged": JM, "She's Come for an Abortion: What Do You Say?" *Harper's*, November 1992, 49.

42   "he was absolutely furious": Dinky, interview by author, January 2007.

CHAPTER 5

43   "was drawn into a war": "Only Human," *New York Daily Mirror*, 20 April 1937.

43   "mentioned that Herr Hitler": Pryce-Jones, *Unity Mitford*, 224.

44   "We sat in a dim, plushly upholstered": JM, *H & R*, 201.

44   "an amusing and sometimes": Roger Roughton to JM, 28 January 1939, OSU.

44   "he's an authority on burlesque" . . . "He's exactly as you would imagine him" . . . "an elderly millionaire" . . . "who is very nice indeed" . . . "an English communist": Ibid.

45   "In America what they want": Walter Starkie to ER, 23 November 1938, OSU.

45   "Sex Life at Oxford University": JM, *FOP*, 36.

45   "The Inner Life": JM, *H & R*, 194.

46   "undeliberate but crushing domination": Toynbee, *Friends Apart*, 155.

46   "Do you like America? . . . one could do about it": JM, *H & R*, 205.

47   "perversely, and although": JM, *H & R*, 261.

47   "My attitude toward Esmond is as follows": UM to JM, 11 April 1937, OSU.

47   "I see that in the papers": JM to Muv, 6 September 1939, in *Decca*, ed. Sussman, 32.

47   "fine wirenetting round their windows": JM to Muv, 2 or 3 August 1939, in *Decca*, ed. Sussman, 32.

47   "a sort of Winston Churchill-ish": Ibid.

47   "a terrific Washington Big-shot": ER to Peter Nevile, 5 July 1939, OSU.

48   "Ye Merrie England Village": JM, *H & R*, 226.

49   "Blueblood Adventurers . . . Song in Their Hearts": ER and JM, "Blueblood Adventurers Discover America," *Washington Post*, 28 January 1940.

49   "A gay and exciting salute": *Washington Post*, 28 January 1940.

49   "discourse eloquently on": JM and ER, "English Adventurers Stalk Job in Wilds of New York," *Washington Post*, 11 February 1940.

50   "the best people": Ibid.

50   "operas, cartoons, cooking demonstrations": Ian Baird, "Television in the World of Tomorrow," *Echoes*, winter 1997; and Ian Baird, "Television in the World of Tomorrow," Baird Television Web site, RCA page, at www.bairdtelevision.com/RCA.html.

50   "old Scotch cottage": ER and JM, "English Adventurers Stalk Job."

50   "weaver imported direct": Ibid.

50   "soft Lancashire brogue" . . . "lass who worked": JM, *H & R*, 218.

51   "You see he's planning": JM, *H & R*, 216.

51   "As if he'd been there for hours ": JM, *H & R*, 220.

51   "If we had such an introduction": "Only Human," *New York Daily Mirror*, 20 April 1937.

52   "disturbingly successful": JM, *H & R*, 220.

53   "snobbish": JM to Muv, 23 November 1939, in *Decca*, ed. Sussman, 34.

53   "old broken-down chicken houses": Ibid.

54   "like the South of France": JM to UM, January or February 1940, in *Decca*, ed. Sussman, 39.

54   "have a French butler": JM to TM, 24 December 1939, in *Decca*, ed. Sussman, 35.

54   "mean, murky and meretricious": Ingram, *Rebel*, 199.

54   "that something unpleasant": JM, *H & R*, 270.

55   "to be recorded": JM to Muv, 11 January 1940, in *Decca*, ed. Sussman, 38.

55   "Unity's sister": JM to Muv, 26 February 1940, in *Decca*, ed. Sussman, 40.

55   "terrified . . . grieved": JM, *H & R*, 273.

55   "Do please write": JM to Muv, 11 January 1940, in *Decca*, ed. Sussman, 38.

56   "a terrible quarrel with Hitler": JM to Muv, 1 February 1940, in *Decca*, ed. Sussman, 38.

56   "I knew I couldn't expect Esmond": JM, *H & R*, 274.

56   "estrangement from our families": JM, *H & R*, 261.

CHAPTER 6

58   "What a contrast . . . about a 'social program'": Ingram, *Rebel*, 195.

58   "very powerful anti-fascist, anti-Hitler spirit": RT and Larsen, *Robert E. Treuhaft*, 26.

58   "lived and worked": JM, *H & R*, 252.

58   "Not very sisterly": Lovell, *The Sisters*, 325.

60   "the most impressive feeling": Graham, *Personal History*, 78.

60   "brilliant, colorful, often hysterically funny": Straight, *After Long Silence*, 141.

60   "fine satirical mind": Ibid.

61   "outnumbered": JM, *H & R*, 254.

62   "Why I'm so absolutely. . . small children": JM, *H & R*, 256.

62   "very much engrossed . . . Muckraker Interviews": Virginia Durr, interview, *Portrait of a Muckraker: The Stories of Jessica Mitford*, produced by Stephen Evans, Ida Landauer, and James Morgan, KQED, 1990 (DVD and VHS).

62   "aristocratic . . . upperclass . . . point-of-view": Ibid.

62   "he was a man, not a boy": Ibid.

62   "'Ole Virginny' . . . appreciate it": Durr and Barnard, *Outside the Magic Circle*, 138.

63   "We're already cramped": Ann Durr Lyons, interview with author, telephone, February 2010.

63   "Just keep her until your refugees arrive": Ibid.

63   "Well, Esmond . . . take her with you": Durr and Barnard, *Outside the Magic Circle*, 138.

63   "I didn't want to take": Ibid., 139.

64   "come to the U.S. to get Decca": Durr, interview, *Portrait of a Muckraker*.

64   "Thereafter . . . stop again": Durr and Barnard, *Outside the Magic Circle*, 139.

66   "Madame, use my hat if you need it": Ibid.

66   "by this time Decca was looking very glamorous and beautiful": Durr, interview, *Portrait of a Muckraker*.

66   "I went up to an official looking": JM to ER, 25 July 1940, in *Decca*, ed. Sussman, 51.

66   "spontaneously and with unanimous support": Chicago Historical Society, "Parades, Protests & Politics in Chicago: The 1940 Democratic Convention," www.chicagohs.org/history/politics/1940.html.

CHAPTER 7

69   "among other new features": "Liner's Maiden Voyage to Be Stag Party," *Washington Post*, 27 July 1940.

70   "'Decca Method,' which she invented herself": Dudley Harmon, "War Means Separation for Esmond Romillys," *Washington Post*, 27 July 1940.

70   "colossally useful": JM to ER, 26 July 1940, in *Decca*, ed. Sussman, 54.

70   "absolute riot of anti–New Dealism": JM to ER, 29 June 1940, in *Decca*, ed. Sussman, 55.

70   "about 9:30 . . . reached out": Ibid.

71   "only cost 58 cents for 50 words": JM to ER, 25 July 1940, in *Decca*, ed. Sussman, 53.

71   "until you get over being sick": Durr and Barnard, *Outside the Magic Circle*, 139.

72   "My plans are completely flexible": JM to ER, 25 July 1940, in *Decca*, ed. Sussman, 53.

72   "learned how to make a bed": Durr, interview, *Portrait of a Muckraker*.

72   "debunking the aristocratic": JM to ER, 6 August 1940, OSU.

72   "burn her hands": JM to ER, [undated] September 1940, OSU.

73   "Weinbergering": JM to ER, 2 August 1940, OSU.

73   "American glamour girl . . . all *so* awful": JM to ER, 8 September 1940, in *Decca*, ed. Sussman, 63–64.

73   "bony": Durr and Barnard, *Outside the Magic Circle*, 151.

73   "Decca, you have simply": Ann Durr Lyons, interview by author, February 2010.

74   "the most beautiful person . . . a wicked sting: Marge Frantz, interview by author, November 2005.

74   "fresh curried shrimp": JM to ER, September 1940, OSU.

75   "it might save postage": JM to ER, 10 January 1941, OSU.

75   "bourgeois philistine . . . shirts, socks and ties": Straight, *After Long Silence*, 141.

75   "There is one thing you can say": Ibid.

75   "wanted an intense Christmas": Durr, interview, *Portrait of a Muckraker*.

76   "two people more completely in love": Ibid.

CHAPTER 8

77   "long dead time when": GR, *Privileged Nightmare*, 88.

77   "Bloomsbury lodging house keeper": JM to ER, late January 1941, OSU.

78   "a quantity of stout brown paper": JM, *AWOB*, 5.

78   "Absolutely not": JM, *AWOB*, 5.

78   "I hated that idea . . . highly touted": JM, *AWOB*, 5.

78   "At each visit, for which he charged": JM, *AWOB*, 5.

79   "all v. pretty rather like": JM to ER, 12 February 1941, OSU.

79   "The anesthetic given there": JM, *AWOB*, 5–6.

80   "Are you any relation of Hitler's friend?" JM to ER, 12 February 1941, OSU.

80   "Was her baby born with teeth?" Sussman, *Decca*, 72n.

80   "I was just thinking": JM to ER, 13 February 1941, in *Decca*, ed. Sussman, 73.

80   "I became increasingly restive": JM, *AFOC*, 27.

81   "How extremely thoughtful": JM to ER, early March 1941, in *Decca*, ed. Sussman, 76.

81   "Anne Constancia . . . change it we can": JM to ER, [2 March 1941?], OSU.

83   "Darling Muv . . . I don't like Canada at *all*": JM to Muv, 9 April 1941, OSU.

84   "sweet refugees": Mosley, *Love from Nancy*, 104.

85   "The Durrs & most of the people": JM to NM, 20 May 1941, in *Decca*, ed. Sussman, 79.

86   "I think Constancia": NM to JM, 9 July 1941, in Mosley, *Love from Nancy*, 111.

86   "Up the Reds!" NM to Violet Hammersley, 12 July 1941, in Mosley, *Love from Nancy*, 113.

87   "a whole new ball game": JM, interview, *Portrait of a Muckraker*.

87   "over-abundance of resources": Ingram, *Rebel*, 218.

87   "misgivings about going on a raid": Ibid., 217.

87   "None . . . shot down or not": Ibid., 218.

87   "The unutterable blankness": JM, *H & R*, 282.

88   "Once the Russians got into the war": Fursland, *Jessica Mitford*, 132.

88   "I was so miserable": JM to ER, 26 June 1941, OSU.

88   "my two main preoccupations . . . acquire some training": JM, *AFOC*, 27.

89   "feel much more confident": JM to ER, 26 June 1941, in *Decca*, ed. Sussman, 80.

89   "By the time I discovered": JM, *AFOC*, 28.

                              CHAPTER 9

91   "I think it would be more difficult": JM to ER, 1 August 1941, in *Decca*, ed. Sussman, 81.

91   "However the whole decision": Ibid.

92   "Please don't think": ER to JM, 17 August 1941, OSU.

92   "The whole thing is awfully disappointing": JM to ER, 16–19 August 1941, in *Decca*, ed. Sussman, 82.

93   "I am thinking of you ... fascinating and interesting": ER to JM, 22 September 1941, OSU.

93   "fascinating and interesting": ER to JM, 22 September 1941, OSU.

94   "This is said to be the best school": JM to ER, 14 September 1941, in *Decca*, ed. Sussman, 86–87.

94   "I will never be able . . . swiftness of trip": ER to JM, 22 September 1941, OSU.

94   "if she really frightfully wanted to and it was possible": ER to JM, 9 October 1941, OSU.

94   "on a bomber": JM to ER, 4 October 1941, OSU.

94   "his only political motive": Toynbee, *Friends Apart*, 163.

95   "He told me how once": Ibid.

95   "Is the take off": ER to JM, 5 October 1941, OSU.

95   "the pilot hears the welcoming phrase": Ibid.

96   "to be all undecided": JM to ER, 29 October 1941, OSU.

96   "I am pretty well settled now": ER to JM, 11 November 1941, OSU.

96   "I sent you a cable last night": JM to ER, 9 November 1941, OSU.

97   "can see that you will be": ER to JM, 11 November 1941, OSU.

97   "the whole thing is utterly bleak and pointless": Ingram, *Rebel*, 232.

97   "LEAVING FRIDAY SO TERRIFICALLY": JM to ER, 1 December 1941, in *Decca*, ed. Sussman, 92.

98   "REGRET TO INFORM YOU THAT": Ingram, *Rebel*, 232–233.

98   "absolutely desolate": Durr and Barnard, *Outside the Magic Circle*, 140.

98   "It will take more than two men ": Lovell, *The Sisters*, 104.

99   "gracious as she always was": Straight, *After Long Silence*, 141.

99   "He said that his heart bled": Ibid., 166.

99   "Churchill had got in touch": Durr and Barnard, *Outside the Magic Circle*, 141.

99   "blood money": Sussman, *Decca*, 49.

99   "I would go in there and she would say": Durr and Barnard, *Outside the Magic Circle*, 141.

99   "filthy fascist family": Durr, interview, *Portrait of a Muckraker*.

CHAPTER 10

102   "He disgraced himself": RT interview with Robert G. Larsen in 1988–1989 in *Robert E. Treuhaft: Left Wing Political Activist and Progressive Leader in the Berkeley Co-op: Oral History Project*, Berkeley Historical Society, 1989, 12.

103   "Bob, the fun-loving Rover Boy": Ibid., 16.

103   "only in a peripheral way": Ibid., 12.

103   "the only people who were deeply involved": Ibid., 12.

104   "these beautiful prima ballerinas": Ibid., 20.

106   "ban on pleasure driving": JM, *AFOC*, 32.

106   "cruel category of sub-eligible typist": JM, *AFOC*, 32.

106   "discovered a marvelous place": JM, *AFOC*, 32.

107   "Paris was then occupied": JM, *AFOC*, 30.

107   "marvelously funny": JM, *AFOC*, 33.

107   "slanting, twinkling black eyes": JM, *AFOC*, 33.

107   "She would pick up a glass": RT and Larsen, *Robert E. Treuhaft*, 27.

108   "such frugality ": Ibid., 27.

108   "Drink a drink to dauntless Decca": JM, *AFOC*, 33.

108   "permanent home": JM to Muv, 31 October 1942, in *Decca*, ed. Sussman, 93.

109   "Dear Aranka, You will be pleased": RT to Aranka Treuhaft, 28 December 1942, OSU.

109   "You can't imagine how": JM to Muv, 24 November 1942, in *Decca*, ed. Sussman, 95.

110   "one of those do-it-yourself": JM, *AFOC*, 39.

110   "Dear Joyce, please come to Washington": JM, *AFOC*, 39.

110   "pleased surprise . . . hopeless muddle": JM, *AFOC*, 40.

110   "She claims that she left Washington": RT and Larsen, *Robert E. Treuhaft*, 28.

110   "as far away as possible": JM, *AFOC*, 40.

CHAPTER 11

111   "I didn't expect to see matched . . . shopping bags": JM, *AFOC*, 42.

115   "I'm getting to like Frisco": JM to Muv, 16 March 1943, OSU.

115   My gratitude to Kevin Starr for drawing the waterfront so beautifully in *Embattled Dreams, California in War and Peace, 1940–1950* (New York: Oxford University Press, 2002).

115   "Gee Decc, Don't be sick anymore" RT to JM, 24 March 1943, OSU.

115   "only source of real pleasure and sustenance": JM, *AFOC*, 45.

115   "Poor Mrs. Romilly": JM, *AFOC*, 51.

115   "ruined . . . took advantage of me": JM, *AFOC*, 46.

116   "The office here": JM to Muv, 16 March 1943, OSU.

116   "inflation down": RT and Larsen, *Robert E. Treuhaft*, 36.

117   "She'd been restless and come ... too soon": Doris (Dobby) Brin Walker, interview with author, August 2007.

117   "I feel that in my job here": JM to Muv, 28 June 1943, in *Decca*, ed. Sussman, 99.

117   "real connection": RT and Larsen, *Robert E. Treuhaft*, 12.

118   "marry you and move": JM, *AFOC*, 52.

CHAPTER 12

120   "You will be v. surprised": JM to Muv, 28 June 1943, in *Decca*, ed. Sussman, 111.

120   "would probably have": JM to Muv, 21 July 1943, in *Decca*, ed. Sussman, 112.

121   "some errands": JM, *AFOC*, 57.

121   "profuse apologies": JM, *AFOC*, 57.

122   "Why do you want to become a citizen?" JM, *AFOC*, 63.

122   "endearingly childish": JM, interview, *Portrait of a Muckraker*.

122   "bizarre . . . a joke": Ibid.

122   "So I can join the Communist Party": JM, *AFOC*, 63.

122   "too much levity toward the Left": Pele deLappe, interview by author, October 2008.

123   "pop the question": JM, *AFOC*, 63.

123 "Would you be interested in joining the Communist Party?" Doris (Dobby) Brin Walker, interview by author, August 2007.

123 "We thought you'd never ask": JM, *AFOC*, 63.

123 "It was indeed a matter of conform or get out": JM, *AFOC*, 67.

124 "bores and misfits in our organization": JM, *AFOC*, 66.

124 "enchanted by the flesh and blood Communists": JM, *AFOC*, 66.

124 "conversion to Communism was not": JM, *AFOC*, 16.

124 "We didn't do anything terribly subversive": RT and Larsen, *Robert E. Treuhaft*, 30.

125 "dead tired from the round . . . three in the morning": JM, *AFOC*, 71.

126 "locked the doors, pulled down the blinds": JM, *AFOC*, 59.

126 "Fancy Little D being a beauty!" JM, *AFOC*, 33.

127 "Dear Cousin Winston": JM to Churchill, 24 November 1943, in *Decca*, ed. Sussman, 114–115.

CHAPTER 13

131 "Upside," said Viorst, "Bob had married": Judith Viorst, e-mail to author, 27 February 2008.

131 "was rather put out when I married": RT and Larsen, *Robert E. Treuhaft*, 12.

131 "demanded a lot from the people around her.": Edith Treuhaft, interview by author, February 2008.

131 "*luftmensch*": Ibid.

132 "so New York-ish": Ibid.

132 "coveted prize of a lifetime": JM, *AFOC*, 75

133 "a leggy female who": deLappe, *A Passionate Journey*, 36.

133 "with more seriousness and concern": Lerner, *Fireweed*, 264.

134 "had the luckiest childhood": JM, interview, in *Introduction to Interview with Jessica Mitford*, ed. deLappe, San Francisco State University Labor Archives.

134 "raise hackles . . . she ever would": Pele deLappe, interview by author, October 2006.

135 "Marvelous . . . for the delegates": JM, *AFOC*, 96.

135 "busy, busy, busy": JM, *AFOC*, 88.

135 "ticket sales . . . publicity": JM, *AFOC*, 88.

135 "a general air of mystery": JM, *AFOC*, 85.

135 "Petaluma": JM, *AFOC*, 86.

135 "comrades in Petaluma" ": JM, *AFOC*, 87.

135 "broiled or fried?" JM, *AFOC*, 87.

136 "Just to send you my love": Lovell, *The Sisters*, 386.

137   "life drawing class for retired longshoremen"": Pele deLappe, interview by author, October 2008.

137   "he was puzzled": RT to Aranka Treuhaft, 7 November 1944, OSU.

137   "We're very much worried": RT to Aranka Treuhaft, 3 December 1944, OSU.

137   "Decca loves them": RT to Aranka Treuhaft, 30 November 1944, OSU.

137   "attorney in Reno and can": Ibid.

138   "the goal of socialism": JM, *AFOC*, 64.

138   "secretly disappointed that": JM, *AFOC*, 65.

139   "Did I feel we were automatons": JM, *AFOC*, 66.

140   "Have you noted": NM to JM, 15 November, 1968, *TM-LBSS*, 521.

142   "What could possibly": JM, *AFOC*, 149.

142   "concrete upper lip": JM to Aranka Treuhaft, fall 1957, in *Decca*, ed. Sussman, 172.

143   "what a criminal thing": JM to Muv, 21 May 1946, in *Decca*, ed. Sussman, 125.

143   "At what price?" NM to Diana, 25 May 1946, NM, *Love from Nancy*, 165.

CHAPTER 14

145   "Gallstones, Gruesome, Sewer & Odious": JM, *AFOC*, 98.

145   "looked on as dangerous reds.": Pele deLappe, interview by author, October 2006.

146   "5 big doses of castor oil": JM to Aranka, 21 October 1943, in *Decca*, ed. Sussman, 126–127.

146   "the tidal wave of washing": JM, *AFOC*, 103.

146   "For a few depressing months": JM, *AFOC*, 103.

147   "Housework is highly unproductive": JM, *AFOC*, 104.

147   "patronizingly stupid": Lerner, *Fireweed*, 262.

148   "at once immensely excited": JM, *AFOC*, 150.

148   "You're supposed to start at the top and go down": Marge Frantz, interview by author, July 2007. This is a frequently told JM story. Peter Sussmann also records it in *Decca*.

148   "set us all to shrieking": JM, *AFOC*, 151.

148   "wonderful & very pretty": JM, interview, *Desert Island Discs*, BBC Radio 4, 9 August 1977.

148   "like a musical comedy stage set": Ibid.

148   "absolutely bent on friendship: Ibid.

149   "Wicked Aunt Diana": Dinky, interview by author, May 2006.

150   "strange and childish: JM, *AFOC*, 154.

150   "wonderful": Pryce-Jones, *Unity Mitford*, 270.

151   "opening 'a restaurant with an Italian partner'": Waugh, *The Loved One*, 17.

151   "non-Jewish-motherishness": JM, *AFOC*, 153.

151   "What a pity. But of course": JM, *AFOC*, 153.

151   "How can you do this to me?" ": JM, *AFOC*, 154.

153   "desirability, of overthrowing the government": Alien Registration Act or Smith Act of 1940.

153   "was quite unchanged": Lovell, *The Sisters*, 413.

154   "Purulent Meningitis, Cerebral Abscess, Old gun-shot wound": Pryce-Jones, *Unity Mitford*, 276.

154   "But it always seemed to me": JM, *H & R*, 274.

CHAPTER 15

155   "Two policemen would get": RT and Larsen, *Robert E. Treuhaft*, 46.

155   "sickening number of similar cases": Ibid.

156   "Nobody made Decca do anything": Doris (Dobby) Brin Walker, interview by author, August 2007.

157   "mesmeric ability to wring the last ounce": JM, *AFOC*, 105.

157   "grinding down on people": Pele deLappe, interview by author, August 2007.

157   "there was nobody in the [police] department": RT and Larsen, *Robert E. Treuhaft*, 45.

157   "Thugs in Uniform". JM, *AFOC*, 108.

157   "hard to describe adequately the monstrous beastliness": JM, *AFOC*, 108.

158   "Do you know T-Bone?" JM, *AFOC*, 122.

158   "a singularly glib, smooth-tongued individual": JM, *AFOC*, 109.

158   "the first time in the history": JM, *AFOC*, 111.

158   "some degree of truth": JM, *AFOC*, 111.

159   "cooperated with the CRC": JM, *AFOC*, 112.

159   linking civil rights and subversion: Nora Sayre brilliantly covers this in *Previous Convictions*.

159   "Decca scooted down to the address": RT and Larsen, *Robert E. Treuhaft*, 48.

159   "few and far between": Ibid., 47.

160   "a source of nagging irritation": Fursland, *Jessica Mitford*, 148.

160   "Get to work, you lazy good-for-nothing": JM, *AFOC*, 140.

161   "I sent my son to Harvard": JM, *AFOC*, 142.

161   "Oh Decca": JM, *AFOC*, 143.

CHAPTER 16

163   "a conspiracy so immense" . . . "the most evil, monstrous conspiracy": Thanks to Cecil Belfrage for first putting these side by side in *American Inquisition*, 119.

164   "crazy as a bedbug": Durr and Barnard, *Outside the Magic Circle*, 206.

164   "scared the United States": Ibid.

164   "You couldn't go to a church meeting": Ibid., 202.

164   "You couldn't possibly have guessed": Lillian Hellman, *Scoundrel Time*, 75.

164   "Skin-color blindness": Belfrage, *American Inquisition*, 131.

164   "If someone insists that": Sayre, *Previous Convictions*, 267.

164   "Here we were blaming Russia for being a totalitarian dictatorship": Barnard, *Outside the Magic Circle*, 284.

166   "Subversive nature": JM, *Why I Live Where I Live*, OSU.

166   "days of the Truman-McCarthy": Ibid.

166   "a mutual enmity that flourished": JM, *AFOC*, 121.

166   "That mike wasn't put there for you": JM, *AFOC*, 121.

166   "best Aranka hat": JM, *AFOC*, 124.

167   "her face contorted": *AFOC*, 125.

167   "That pinko Treuhaft outsmarted me this time!": Ibid.

167   "Could you possibly ring up the": JM to Muv, 25 June 1950, in *Decca*, ed. Sussman, 135.

168   "I believe there is now a very": JM to Muv, 20 August 1950, in *Decca*, ed. Sussman, 137.

168   "empathized with us as members": Horne, *Communist Front?* 19.

169   "a perfect foil for Decc": Dinky, interview by author, February 2010.

169   "sparkplugs": JM to Maya Angelou, 9 August 1980, in *Decca*, ed. Sussman.

170   "the realities of Mississippi": JM, *AFOC*, 163.

170   "one of the bravest people": JM to Muv, 23 September 1951, in *Decca*, ed. Sussman.

171   "challenge the rape myth that every" . . . "white womanhood.": JM (as Decca Treuhaft), "The Case of Willie McGee: A Fact Sheet Prepared by the Civil Rights Congress," 1951.

171   "concentration camp of the mind": JM, *AFOC*, 178.

171   "the real sacrificers . . . rollicking jolly": JM, *AFOC*, 166.

171   "the Youth Comrade": JM, *AFOC*, 166.

172   "were the whole delegation": JM, *AFOC*, 172.

172   "the Youth Comrade said not a word": JM, *AFOC*, 166.

173   "murky eloquence": JM, *AFOC*, 182.

173   "McGee and the woman": JM, *AFOC*, 182.

173   "We drove a total of 7700 miles": JM to Muv, 2 April 1951, in *Decca*, ed. Sussman, 139.

174   "would end in a massacre": JM, *AFOC*, 186.

174   "Tell the People the real reason": JM, *AFOC*, 194.

CHAPTER 17

175   "not a good time in which to stand trial": Trumbo, *Time of the Toad*, 92.

175   "Do you think Treuhaft really wants": JM, *AFOC*, 216.

176   "hard-drinking, paranoid, dyspeptic": Starr, *Embattled Dreams*, 301.

176   "the grand inquisitor of California": Ibid., 303.

177   "the privilege could not be invoked": JM, *AFOC*, 200.

177   "unfriendly Witnesses": JM, *AFOC*, 213.

177   "Should I end up behind bars": JM, *AFOC*, 200.

177   "She was absolutely terrified.": Dinky, interview by author, January, 2007.

177   "Have you ever heard of or read": JM, *AFOC*, 202.

178   "Are you . . . a member of the Communist Party?" JM, *AFOC*, 202.

178   "irksome": JM, *AFOC*, 202.

178   "I refuse to answer on the ground": JM, *AFOC*, 202.

178   "Are you a member of the Berkeley *Tenants* Club?" JM, *AFOC*, 203.

178   "bastion of posh conservatism": JM, *AFOC*, 203.

178   "This witness is totally uncooperative": JM, *AFOC*, 203.

178   "You got them so rattled they forgot to ask for the CRC records": JM, *AFOC*, 203.

178   "Do tell her to come . . . few days off": JM to Muv, 23 September 1951, in *Decca*, ed. Sussman, 141.

179   "Poor Nicholas got arrested": JM to Muv, 6 June 1952, in *Decca*, ed. Sussman, 142.

179   "The only trouble was Benjamin": Ibid.

179   "what it was always accused of doing": Belfrage, *American Inquisition*, 163.

180   "might not have believed the country was becoming fascist" Maas, *Looking Back on a Life in the Left*, 65.

181   "back in the Hons' Cupboard": JM, *AFOC*, 158.

181   "fortress mentality": JM, *AFOC*, 116.

182   "little suburban house": Debo to Diana, 8 February 1952, in *TM-LBSS*, ed. Mosley, 277.

182   "rather sweet": Ibid.

182   "she is *heaven*": Ibid.

182   "Although they couldn't quite": JM to Muv, 6 June 1952, OSU.

183   "CP fashion . . . in which one indicates": JM, *AFOC*, 158.

183   "herself and Andrew, dressed in ducal": JM, *AFOC*, 159.

184   "stood idly by watching the scene": JM, *AFOC*, 129.

184   "throwing garbage and other things": *Albion Monitor*, 9 October 1995, www.monitornet/monitor.

184   "'Get out nigger or we'll burn your house down'": *People's Daily World*, 7 March 1952, quoted in Jovanka Beckles, "The Gary Family of Richmond: Fighting

for Equality and Standing for Their Rights (1952)," 22 September 2008, www.smartvoter.org/2008/11/04/ca/cc/vote/beckles_j/paper2.html, 5.

184   "with a petition signed by him and twenty-one other neighbors": Beckles, "The Gary Family of Richmond," 8.

184   "we wanted to take credit": JM, *AFOC*, 131.

CHAPTER 18

186   "thousands and thousands of people": Bernstein, *Loyalties*, 102.

187   "After a cold two weeks": deLappe, *Passionate Journey*, 44.

187   "every intellectual called": Albert Einstein, quoted in Leonard Buder, "'Refuse to Testify' Einstein Advises Intellectuals Called in by Congress," *New York Times*, 12 June 1953

188   "give the kids extra care": JM to Aranka, 5 December 1953, in *Decca*, ed. Sussman, 146.

188   "The most strongminded": JM to Muv, 5 December 1953, in *Decca*, ed. Sussman, 143.

188   "served up more than 300 names": JM, *AFOC*, 207.

188   "Are you accompanied by counsel?" RT and Larsen, *Robert E. Treuhaft*, 98.

189   "You'll have to submit that": Ibid., 99.

189   "I am answering . . . whether I had counsel": JM, *AFOC*, 214.

189   "What a shameful thing it was": RT and Larsen, *Robert E. Treuhaft*, 99.

189   "determined to reveal through his testimony": JM, *AFOC*, 213.

189   "Everyone was breathless": Aranka, 5 December 1953, in *Decca*, ed. Sussman, 146.

189   "there was terrific cheering & applause": Ibid.

189   "The Day's Stormiest": Sussman, *Decca*, 105.

190   "escaped by her wits": Marge Frantz, interview by author, July 2007.

190   "narrow escape": Katie Edwards, interview by author, December 2006.

191   "it was bloody uncomfortable": Bettin Aptheker, interview by author, August, 2008.

191   "So I told him to hurry up": Kathy Kahn, e-mail to author, 23 November 2008.

191   "puzzled over the rape story too": Peter Sussman to author, e-mail to author, 21 November 2008.

191   "I could hardly pry my eyes": Sussman, *Decca*, xiv.

192   "*frightfully* unfair": JM to NM, 6 October 1954, in *TM-LBSS*, ed. Mosley, 278.

192   "outlook is gloomy": JM to Muv, [no date] February 1954, OSU.

192   "ring up Cousin Winston & tell him": JM to Muv, February 1954, OSU.

192   "Winston Churchill's sister-in-law": Ibid.

192   "Thinking to give her a little news": JM to Muv, 25 October 1954, in *Decca*, ed. Sussman, 149.

193 "Nature, nature": Doris (Dobby) Brin Walker, interview by author, August 2007.

193 "The tide here seems to be turning": JM to Muv, March 1954, OSU.

194 "perhaps in the next few years": JM to Muv, February 1954, OSU.

194 "beastly Un-American Committee": JM to Muv, 23 June 1954, in *Decca*, ed. Sussman, 147.

194 "He's not in jail now": RT and Larsen, *Robert E. Treuhaft*, 89.

CHAPTER 19

195 "Nicky has a paper route": Dinky to Aranka Treuhaft, 15 February 1955, OSU.

195 "If Mrs. Treuhaft was home more, this wouldn't have happened": Dinky, interview by author, January 2007.

195 "Bob was in one room . . . they couldn't talk to one another": Ibid.

195 "darling mother Nicholas": JM to Muv, 16 February 1955, in *Decca*, ed. Sussman, 149.

196 "Darling Muv, . . . He didn't suffer": JM to Muv, 23 February 1955, in *Decca*, ed. Sussman, 149.

196 "never got a cent . . . No Price Nick": Pele deLappe, interview by author, October 2007.

197 "unexpressed unhappiness": JM to Aranka Treuhaft, February 1955, OSU.

197 "The only way we can possibly": JM to Aranka Treuhaft, 7 March 1955, OSU.

197 "if you'd let them": Ibid.

198 "magic document[s]": JM, *AFOC*, 221.

198 "unbelievable and stunning as winning the Irish Sweepstakes": Ibid.

198 "was longing to stay as long as possible": Fursland, *Jessica Mitford*, 153.

198 "at the discontented age of seventeen": JM, *AFOC*, 223.

200 "There were no tears on the trip": Dinky, interview by author, January, 2007.

200 "the half remembered English countryside": JM, *AFOC*, 227.

200 "one of the happiest moments of my life": Muv to JM, 26 March 1956, OSU.

200 "There was something rather amazing": Fursland, *Jessica Mitford*, 156.

201 "Sent dirty banknotes to Harrods'": Lovell, 439.

201 "an extremely slow one but not uncomfortable": RT to Aranka Treuhaft, 1 September 1955, OSU.

201 "Muv's lonely barren life here is relieved": RT to Aranka Treuhaft, 1 September 1955, OSU.

201 "Everywhere were reminders of childhood . . . we went our separate ways": JM, *AFOC*, 231–232.

201 "very comfortable, just a little bit bigger than Versailles": RT to Aranka Treuhaft, 16 September 1955, OSU.

201   "the size of a small planet": Lane, "Parent Traps," *New Yorker*, 14 November 2005, 101.

201   "I had come back to a different world": JM, *AFOC*, 228.

202   "HONNISH CONGRATULATIONS ON A SUCCESSFUL SEASON'S DUKE HUNTING" JM, quoting herself to Pele deLappe and Steve Murdock, 25 September 1955, in *Decca*, ed. Sussman, 156.

202   "ambivalence": JM, *AFOC*, 235.

202   "Having taken such pains . . . not a good guest": Ibid.

202   "Actually Bob fared better than I did": Ibid.

202   "dazzled by the openness and ease": JM, *AFOC*, 236.

203   "brilliant, attractive person": JM to Eddie Romilly, 12 August 1967 OSU.

203   "hopelessly addicted": JM to Virginia Durr, 18 August 1955, in *Decca*, ed. Sussman, 369.

203   "It seems the Romillies wrote their wills": JM to NM, 2 May 1957, in *Decca*, ed. Sussman, 167.

203   "inheritance prone," "accident prone": JM to Muv, 4 June 1958, in *Decca*, ed. Sussman, 175.

203   "sheer curiosity": JM, *AFOC*, 229.

203   "wasn't all that keen": Fursland, *Jessica Mitford*, 156.

203   "I'd have been quite interested to see him. I offered to see him": Ibid.

203   "impossible conditions": JM, *AFOC*, 20.

204   "When you've had this much of a break": Fursland, *Jessica Mitford*, 156.

204   "Whom would you like best . . . Decca": NM to JM, 3 August 1972, in NM, *Love from Nancy*, 519.

204   "whirling away": JM, "We Visited Socialism," *Peoples Daily World*, 17 February 1956.

205   "How I dread their arrival": NM to Diana, 8 September 1955, in *TM-LBSS*, ed. Mosley, 287.

205   "on Debo's nickel": JM, *AFOC*, 247.

206   "marvelously good company": JM, *AFOC*, 248.

206   "still funny . . . & is not a fascist or an idiot": JM to Pele deLappe, Steve Murdock, and Bob and Dorothy Neville, 29 October 1955, in *Decca*, ed. Sussman, 158.

206   "a combo of plummy tones and very down-to-earth vocabulary": Dinky, telephone interview by author, March 2010.

CHAPTER 20

207   "I know it's such a thrill": JM to Muv, 13 May 1956, in *Decca*, ed. Sussman, 163.

207   "highly classified": JM, *AFOC*, 265.

208   "Money, besides being the root of all evil": Fursland, *Jessica Mitford*, 226.

208   "there remained a haunting suspicion": JM, *AFOC*, 265.

208   "the blank, awful feeling": Fursland, *Jessica Mitford*, 159.

209   According to Ross's thesis: See NM, "The English Aristocracy," in Noblesse *Oblige*, ed. NM, 27.

209   "The aristocrat can augment his": Ibid.

210   "Any sign of undue haste": JM, *Noblesse Oblige*, 41.

210   "a great send-up of the obscure, convoluted language of the Left": Pele deLappe, interview by author, October 2008.

211   "What does one do with cadres?" JM, *Lifeitselfmanship*, reprinted in JM, *AFOC*, 326.

211   "welcomed as something": Pele deLappe, interview by author, October 2006.

211   "a trifle apprehensive about its reception": JM, *AFOC*, 269.

211   "Hoping to disarm . . . Anti-leadership . . . anti-theoretical": JM, *Lifeitselfmanship*, reprinted in JM, *AFOC*, 333.

211   "The extraorder thing about": JM to Muv, October 1956, in *Decca*, ed. Sussman, 163.

212   "I've been *screaming* over your pamphlet": JM, *AFOC*, 270.

212   "originated by workers and": JM to Aranka Treuhaft, 14 October 1956, OSU.

212   "One thing was dismally clear": JM, *AFOC*, 272.

213   "something of the character of an ideological" JM, *AFOC*, 276.

214   "thrilled to the praise of comrades": JM, *AFOC*, 277.

214   "good riddance": Sayre, *Previous Convictions*, 373.

214   "stagnant, ineffective": JM, *AFOC*, 279.

215   "Despite all evident drawbacks": JM, *AFOC*, 117.

215   "wonderful moment": Fursland, *Jessica Mitford*, 168.

CHAPTER 21

217   "If I were you I wouldn't wear any jewelry," "That won't be difficult": JM to Aranka Treuhaft, fall 1957, in *Decca*, ed. Sussman, 171.

218   "inordinately proud of it": JM, *PP*, 40.

218   "thinks of literally nothing now": NM to JM, 8 August 1950, in *TM-LBSS*, ed. Mosley, 270.

218   "I had known him so vigorous and violent": NM, *Don't Tell Alfred*, 14.

219   "I will gladly share my Fortune" JM to Muv, 19 March 1958, in *Decca*, ed. Sussman, 174.

219   "gay blade or roué": JM to Aranka Treuhaft, 8 August, 1958, OSU.

219   "except Jessica": JM, *AFOC*, 146.

219   "She hadn't been expecting anything": Fursland, *Jessica* Mitford, 170.

219   "It seems a hundred years ago": This quote from Decca from a *San Francisco Examiner* article was one of many clippings that the FBI kept in its files on

Decca. The FBI introduced this clipping with this report: "The 'San Francisco Chronicle,' San Francisco daily newspaper, and the 'Oakland Tribune,' Oakland daily newspaper, issues of July 10 and 9, 1958, respectively, carried an article which stated that JESSICA-FREEMAN-MITFORD TRUEHAFT, wife of Oakland attorney ROBERT TREUHAFT, had been disinherited by her father, Lord REDESDALE, and would not share in his estate. (U.S. Department of Justice, Federal Bureau of Investigation, Jessica Mitford File, FBI archives.)

220   "had never recovered": Lovell, *The Sisters*, 456.

220   "I knew I was cut out" Fursland, *Jessica Mitford*, 170.

220   "Bob came in in his undershorts": JM to Dinky, 21 November 1958, OSU.

221   "Off to meet with your fellow necrophilists?" Lovell, *The Sisters*, 478.

221   "a very *lively* group": JM to Muv, 24 October, 1958, OSU.

222   "In keeping with our high standard": JM, *PP*, 45.

222   "It should be borne in mind": JM, *PP*, 47.

222   "Have declared war on 'materialistic display'": JM, *PP*, 44.

222   "at the crack of Bob": JM to Dinky, 17 September 1958, OSU.

223   "I hope to be completely re-molded": JM to Dinky, 3 March 1959, in *Decca*, ed. Sussman, 187.

223   "How much more interesting could I": Ibid., 188.

223   "lift up": Mark Lapin, interview by author, March 2008.

225   "to gently fire Fles": JM to RT, 26 April, 1955, in *Decca*, ed. Sussman, 202.

225   "The book is sort of memoirs of my life": JM to Muv, 4 May 1959, OSU.

225   "that editors are a completely new": JM to RT, 11 August 1959 OSU.

225   "They just don't work that way in England": JM to RT and Dinky, 4 May 1959, in *Decca*, ed. Sussman, 208.

225   "there should be no bitterness in it": Muv, quoted by JM to Barbara Kahn, 11 May 1959, in *Decca*, ed. Sussman, 208.

226   "Oh Hen, I do hope": Debo, quoted in JM to Pele deLappe, 5 June 1959, in *Decca*, ed. Sussman, 217.

226   "Here is some exciting news": JM to Dinky, May 1959, in *Decca*, ed. Sussman, 210–211.

227   "to be prepared to deal": JM to Muv, 4 June 1958, in *Decca*, ed. Sussman, 175.

227   "Atom base I suppose—": NM to Muv, 30, May 1959, *Decca*, ed. Sussman, 216.

227   "Can you believe it? . . . cigarettes along with us": JM to Aranka, 1 June 1959 OSU.

228   "James MacGibbon was absolutely amazed": JM to Pele deLappe, 5 June 1959, OSU.

228   "cashing in on her stuff": JM to Pele deLappe, 5 June 1959, in *Decca*, ed. Sussman, 217.

228   "the knotty last chapter": Ibid.

228   "Set the record straight": Fursland, *Jessica Mitford*, 167.

229 "assiduously avoiding following Nancy's advice": JM to Marge Frantz, 26 June 1959, in *Decca*, ed. Sussman, 220.

229 "all mad about Benj": JM to Aranka Treuhaft, 10 July 1959, OSU.

230 "gloomy about it": JM to RT and Dinky, 9 July 1959, OSU.

230 "Life here is even-keelish": JM to Barbara and Ephraim Kahn, 3 July 1959, in *Decca*, ed. Sussman, 221.

230 "I get up pretty early (7:30)": 3 July 1959, OSU.

230 "THE BOOK IS FINISHED": JM to RT and Dinky, 10 July 1959, in *Decca*, ed. Sussman, 222.

CHAPTER 22

231 "Don't you think that is one hell of a nerve": JM to Dinky, 17 September 1959, OSU.

231 "hard work . . . in contrast for": JM to Dinky, 15 February 1960, in *Decca*, ed. Sussman, 232.

231 "Darling Dinkydonk, One is only really inwardly comfortable": JM to Dinky, 29 January 1960, in *Decca*, ed. Sussman 231.

232 "treading water—waiting for something": Dinky, interview by author, January 2007.

232 "in the good company": Daniels, "The Mad Mitfords and their Incredible Children," *Peoples Daily World*, January 11, 1960.

232 "I think it's *awfully* good": NM to JM, 11 March 1960, in *TM-LBSS*, ed. Mosley, 328.

233 "re written it or helped": NM to Heywood Hill, 9 March 1960, in *Love from Nancy*, ed. Mosley, 378.

233 "Clever of you to see the two voices": NM to Evelyn Waugh, 24 May 1960, in *Love from Nancy*, ed. Mosley, 382.

233 "theme song": Debo to NM, 28 March 1960, in *TM-LBSS*, ed. Mosley, 331.

233 "shameless but most diverting book": Earl of Birkenhead, review of *Hons and Rebels*, 25 March 1960, *London Daily Telegraph*, cited in *TM-LBSS*, ed. Mosley, 330n.

233 "much the best": JM to Muv, 2 April 1960, OSU.

234 "I soon discovered that as a published author": JM, *AFOC*, 295.

234 "all high-powered on the surface" JM to Pele deLappe, 13 June 1960, OSU.

235 "But my dear" JM to Dinky, 17 September 1960, in *Decca*, ed. Sussman, 238.

235 "wiggly nihilism": Lawrence Ferlinghetti, quoted in Adams, *San Francisco*, 137.

235 "beatnik raids": Tyler, "Why It Happened in San Francisco," *Frontier*, June 1960, 6.

235 "beards, sandals": Ibid.

236 "a meaningful alternative to the *status quo*": JM, "The Indignant Generation," part 1 of Rebels with a Cause Series, *The Nation* 192, 27 May 1961, 452 (italics in original).

237   "by no means uniform hostility": Ibid., 453.

238   "Let us in! Open the doors! Open the doors!" Marge Frantz, interview by author. July 2007.

238   "Let them in to see this travesty! What are you afraid of?" Archie Brown, quoted in Elmont Waite, "12 Thrown Out," *San Francisco Chronicle*, 13 June 1960.

238   "You gave all those people cards—why didn't you give me some for *my* friends?" Archie Brown, quoted in Tyler, "Why It Happened in San Francisco," 7.

239   "Jump!" Ibid., 5.

240   "Stop the Committee" . . . "so sue me!" Ibid., 5–7.

240   "The son of Aubrey can": Kathy Kahn, e-mail to author, 19 November 2008.

241   "What was new—wildly, unforeseeably": Tyler, "Why It Happened in San Francisco," 5.

                                      CHAPTER 23

243   "how the southern psyche": Notes for "You-All and Non-You-All: A Southern Potpourri," 1961, OSU.

243   "Stress the accent": Durr to JM, May 1960, in Durr and Sullivan, *Freedom Writer*, 206.

243   "funny, the moral to emerge by inference": JM to Dinky, 21 April 1960, in *Decca*, ed. Sussman, 236.

244   "The conversation turned, as they say": JM to RT, 13 May 1961, in *Decca*, ed. Sussman, 248–249.

245   "Go get the niggers!" Barnard, ed., *Outside the Magic Circle*, 297.

245   "One of the last riders": The description of Lucretia Collins is from Forman, *The Making of Black Revolutionaries*, 154.

246   "a hundred white men and women surged": McWhorter, *Carry Me Home*, 228. In Diane McWhorter's excellent book *Carry Me Home*, she describes the circumstances surrounding the officer's deliberate delay.

246   "cool as a cucumber": Zellner, with Curry, *The Wrong Side of Murder Creek*, 93.

247   "This is absurd—to be so scared": Barnard, ed., *Outside the Magic Circle*, 300.

247   "Southern costume—a lovely sort of fluffy green hat": Ibid.

249   "While the mob had been cleared": JM, quoting general of Alabama National Guard, in JM, "The Longest Meeting," 1961, OSU.

250   "All the funny ways she can write were muted": Barnard, *Outside the Magic Circle*, 301.

250   "Author JESSICA MITFORD TREUHAFT": U.S. Department of Justice, Federal Bureau of Investigation, Jessica Mitford File, FBI archives.

CHAPTER 24

251   "those who feel that burials": Roul Tunley, "Can You Afford to Die?" *Saturday Evening Post*, 17 June 1961, 24.

251   "the sharpest thorn in the morticians' sides": Ibid., 25.

251   "tireless recruiter": Ibid., 80.

251   "over the teacups": Ibid.

251   "widow's weeds": Ibid.

251   "more mail than they had ever received": RT and Larsen, *Robert E. Treuhaft*, 59.

252   "were forbidden to watch funerals": Devonshire, *Counting My Chickens*, 168.

252   "Children's Funerals": JM to Debo, 11 July 1962, OSU.

252   "New Bra-Form": JM to Kathleen Kahn, 2 February 1962, in *Decca*, ed. Sussman, 274.

252   "They only cost $11": Ibid.

252   "Thus making it worth one's while": JM to Muv, 20 February 1959, OSU.

253   "Funerals are becoming more and more": Sussman, *Decca*, 266.

253   "'It's a racket,' she exclaimed": JM, quoted in Tunley, "Can You Afford to Die?"

253   "to go for the jugular and expose": JM, *AFOC*, 302.

253   "I'm not concerned with what they do": Tunley, "Can You Afford to Die?" 82.

253   "69-year old woman, was 40 hours": JM to Kathleen Kahn, 2 February 1962, in *Decca*, ed. Sussman, 274.

254   "Bad and ghoulish . . . foolishness": JM to Dinky, 3 March 1960, OSU.

254   "I'm more and more beginning": JM to Candida Donadio, 2 March, 1962 in *Decca*, ed. Sussman, 276.

255   "like all the members": JM, *AFOC*, 301.

255   "police dogs to sic on any freedom riders": Branch, *Parting the Waters*, 571.

256   "She has all her": Robert Gottlieb, interview, *Portrait of a Muckraker: The Stories of Jessica Mitford*, produced by Stephen Evans, Ida Landauer, and James Morgan, KQED, 1990 (DVD and VHS).

257   "were now or once had been": Ibid.

257   "Essentially she did it": Ibid.

257   "make the comparison": Dinky, interview by author. January, 2007.

257   "besotted by money." Marge Frantz, interview by author, November, 2005.

258   "no real booze": JM to Barbara Kahn, 13 July 1939, in *Decca*, ed. Sussman, 290.

258   "I don't think so . . . good stiff drink in the p.m.": Ibid.

258   "Had tea with Hitler": JM, quoting Muv, to Barbara Kahn, 13 July 1939, in *Decca*, ed. Sussman, 289.

258   "Delicious cakes. Bobo [Unity] gets quite different when she's with him": JM, quoting Debo, to Barbara Kahn, 13 July 1939, in *Decca*, ed. Sussman, 289.

258   "Tea with the Führer. Muv kept talking about home-made": JM, quoting UM, to Barbara Kahn, 13 July 1939, in *Decca*, ed. Sussman, 289.

258   "freedom from fear of being boring": JM to Barbara Kahn et al., 15 July 1939, in *Decca*, ed. Sussman, 290.

258   "In fact, should I ever be faced with this exact problem": Ibid.

259   "Who is Constancia Romilly?" Dinky, interview by author, March, 2008.

260   "chucking her job and going to work": JM to Virginia Durr, 18 June 1963, OSU.

260   "feared the Klan would come around. He had nightmares about that": Dinky, interview by author. January, 2007.

                                CHAPTER 25

261   "How to get the book attacked as subversive": JM to RT, 26 April 1963, OSU.

261   "All these special letters and special approaches did so remind me of CRC": JM to RT, 26 April 1963, OSU.

262   "*marvelous* editor": Benedict, *Portraits in Print*, 110.

262   "Decca doesn't like research": Ibid., 107.

263   "to bury capitalist America's funeral customs": *Decca*, ed. Sussman, 267.

263   "the devil": Steve Coates, interview by author, February 2009.

264   "While hiding behind the commercial aspects of": James B. Utt, speech, 15 October 1963, *Congressional Record*, 15 October 1963, quoted in *Decca*, ed. Sussman, 267.

264   "Red herring": "Author Mitford Tagged Foe of Religion by Utt," *Washington Post*, 19 October 1963.

264   "lapsed into a steadfast condition of noncooperation": U.S. Department of Justice, Federal Bureau of Investigation, Jessica Mitford File, FBI archives.

264   "I think that only those who have been": JM, *PP*, 104.

264   "make thousands of jokes in succession": JM to Barbara Kahn, 13 November 1963, OSU.

264   "long-term viewing": Leroy F. Aarons, "It's Mitford vs. Undertakers," *Washington Post*, 6 November 1963.

264   "We shall bury you" . . . "muscling in on their territory": JM, *AFOC*, 311.

265   "I could put you away for $150" . . . "Sorry you're too late": JM, *AFOC*, 316.

265   "Unfortunately for the undertakers": JM, *AFOC*, 316.

265   "Benj is angling for a $2 weekly": JM to Aranka Treuhaft, 17 September 1963, in *Decca*, ed. Sussman, 306.

265   "I've already done a couple of daring things": Ibid.

265   "total fleabags"…"It was thrilling": Fursland, *Jessica Mitford*, 176.

265   "plainly stated attitude to death": JM to Debo, 7 October 1963, in *Decca*, ed. Sussman, xiii.

265   "Tell him of course I'm *against* it": Ibid.

266   "materialist denial of death": Guinness with Guinness, *The House of Mitford*, 569.

266   "spiritual aspects of death": JM, *PP*, 104.

266   "new-found respectability": JM, *PP*, 109.

266   "It is bad enough keeping up with the Joneses in life": Stephen H. Fritchman, "Expose of Funeral Industry Proves It's Cheaper to Live" *Peoples World*, September 7, 1963.

266   "the whole ghoulish paraphernalia": "Author Mitford Tagged Foe of Religion By Utt."

266   "crypt-o Communist": *Bulletin of the National Review*, December 1963, 466.

267   "synonymous with cheap funerals": JM, *PP*, 89.

267   "Mitford style" . . . "the plainest and least expensive": JM, *PP*, 89.

267   "masterpiece of black humor": Alvarez, "Memento Mori," *New York Review of Books*, 24 September 1998.

267   "made fun of the sacred cows of the time with equal glee": Ibid.

267   "death was on everybody's mind": Ibid.

267   Robert Kennedy had to choose: Schlesinger, *Robert Kennedy and His Times*, 610.

267   RFK had read *The American Way of Death*: JM to RT, 23 June 1964, OSU.

267   "a lot of sad things like Tom's first hair when it was cut, in a teeny envelope": JM to Barbara Kahn, 24 July 1964, OSU.

268   "Nancy was dressed by Chanel and I by J.C. Penney": Marge Frantz, interview by author, November 2005.

268   "loved Nancy's company": JM, *AFOC*, 250.

268   "Nancy treated Decca like shit": Marge Frantz, interview by author, November 2005.

268   "Oh dear, I regard her as Muv's greatest failure": NM to Debo, 31 August 1964, in *TM-LBSS*, ed. Mosley, 420.

269   "psycho-dramatist" . . . "meddle with these deep-seated desires": JM to Barbara Kahn, 6 March 1965, in *Decca*, ed. Sussman, 335.

270   "How do I go about getting accepted?" . . . "Oh come *on*": JM, *PP*, 288.

271   "linked together by mutual amorality": Earl of Birkenhead, *London Daily Telegraph*, 25 March 1960.

271   "Vietnam," she wrote, "nags unbearably": JM to Barbara Kahn, 5 March 1965, OSU.

271   "Jessica Mitford Treuhaft was the first speaker": U.S. Department of Justice, Federal Bureau of Investigation, Jessica Mitford File, FBI archives.

271   "a touch too sappy": JM to Durr, 27 January 1963, OSU.

271   "Hazel Grossman": JM to Barbara Kahn, 4 December 1967, OSU.

271   "I can't bear to join": JM to Debo, 11 September 1965, in *Decca*, ed. Sussman, 339.

272   "level of chaos . . . underdeveloped country": Hinckle, *If You Have a Lemon, Make Lemonade*, 192.

273   "The idea of actually owning": Ibid., 109.

273   "the ranking capitalists of the land, affording them the treat": Ibid.

273   "dithering manner": Toynbee, "Decca Mitford," 1, OSU.

273   "Darling, is the District Attorney the man who puts the rope": NM to JM, 4 May 1964, in *TM-LBSS*, ed. Mosley, 448.

274   "It was all worth it": JM to Leonard Boudin, 24 June 1966, OSU.

CHAPTER 26

275   "Decca loved parties": Marge Frantz, interview by author, November 2005.

276   "People who amused her . . . people in other contexts": Kathy Kahn, interview by author, December 2006.

276   "a lot of boring": JM to Maya Angelou, 7 May 1968, in *Decca*, ed. Sussman, 273.

277   "house on Regent Street": Herb Gold, interview by author, December 2007.

277   "makes one love everyone, they say": JM to NM, 4 May 1967, in *Decca*, ed. Sussman, 365.

277   "munching" . . . "There must be so many American children, surely some of them could be spared?" JM to Durr, 20 September 1967, OSU.

278   "quieter" . . . "the most bonded couple". . . "sense of intimacy": Herb Gold, interview by author, December 2007.

278   "enjoyed her fame" . . . "strong women": Mark Lapin, interview by author, March 2008.

279   "cold fish": Marge Frantz, interview by author, November 2005.

279   "about law cases" . . . "talked about writing, not literature" . . . "by an adoring husband": Herb Gold, interview by author, December 2007.

279   "The Arctic trails have their secret tales": Service, "The Cremation of Sam McGee," in *The Spell of the Yukon*, 50.

279   "The thing I'm most afraid of in": Mark Lapin, interview by author, March 2008.

280   "It really did take the edge off": JM to Durr, 20 September 1967, in *Decca*, ed. Sussman, 374.

280   "The inevitable has happened": Debo to NM, 13 March 1967, in *TM-LBSS*, ed. Mosley, 485.

280   "Is he *the* foreman?": NM to JM, 10 April 1967, in *TM-LBSS*, ed. Mosley, 488.

280   "Mrs. O slightly mis-reported me": JM to NM, 4 May 1967, in *TM-LBSS*, ed. Mosley, 491.

280   "I only said that now": JM to NM, 4 May 1967, in *TM-LBSS*, ed. Mosley, 491.

281   "a lot of anger": Herb Gold, interview by author, December 2007.

281   "they were impressed by him and liked what he was doing": Benjy, interview by author, January 2007.

281   "had a knock-down drag-out fight": Dinky, interview by author, May 2006.

281   "Caen mentioned subject after describing her": U.S. Department of Justice, Federal Bureau of Investigation, Jessica Mitford File, FBI archives.

281   "to disobey the draft law": JM to NM, 14 March 1968, OSU.

282   "Washington was rather extraorder": JM to Pele deLappe, 14 April 1968, in *Decca*, ed. Sussman, 377.

282   "The law of conspiracy is so irrational": JM, *The Trial of Dr. Spock*, 61.

282   "Spock and Coffin particularly were demanding". . . "a confrontation": JM to Marge Frantz, 17 June 1968, OSU.

283   "in violation of international conventions": JM, *The Trial of Dr. Spock*, 83.

283   "the people in power are nothing to fear": McCreery, "Queen of Muckrakers," 77.

283   "vaguely lavatorial": JM, *The Trial of Dr. Spock*, 89.

283   "Dan has a low threshold of boredom and mercifully enlivened": Ibid., 117.

283   "a very, very uphill job": JM to Durr, 17 April 1969, OSU.

283   "a workman like job": Ibid., 396.

CHAPTER 27

285   "great tradition of open, democratic meetings": Langer, "The Oakland Seven," *Atlantic Monthly*, October 1969, 77–81.

285   "opponents of the demo": Ibid.

285   "got to go": JM to Aranka Treuhaft, 28 March 1969, OSU.

285   "a kind of low-water mark for prosecutors": Packer, "The Conspiracy Weapon," *New York Review of Books*, 6 November 1969.

286   "slight tight-rope—between going up to her room": JM to Debo, 18 June 1969, OSU.

286   "another planet, another century": JM to Durr, 26 March 1969, OSU.

286   "rather lost interest in the book, in all the worry over Nancy": Ibid.

287   "swoop in" . . . "nothing but rapid-fire jokes": Ibid.

287   "To Virginia she said": Ibid.

287   Debo, "who was the go-between, the manager of it all": Fursland, *Jessica Mitford*, 181.

287   "Diana and I are getting on": JM to Marge Frantz, 22 May 1969, OSU.

287   "a really marvelous statue": Fursland, *Jessica Mitford*, 182.

288   "a sort of awful betrayal not to tell the truth" . . . "I do feel most": JM to Debo, 17 July 1969, OSU.

289   "Shall I give up writing & take Laurent's massage class, instead?" JM to Marge Frantz, 25 October 1969, OSU.

289   "state-of-mind trial" . . . "charged with carrying certain ideas across state lines": Abbey Hoffman, as depicted in the animated film *Chicago 10*, directed, produced, and written by Brett Morgan (Paramount, 26 August 2008; DVD); transcript of film.

292   "wouldn't it be equally unethical to publish a piece blasting them!!!": JM to Barbara Kahn, 2 December 1969, OSU.

292   "I am *furious*": Ibid.

292   "more pleasure from start to finish, than any other": JM, *PP*, 170.

293   "special stroke of genius": Alvarez, "Memento Mori," *New York Review of Books*, 24 September 1998.

293   "spontaneous and true": Patricia Holt, interview by author, March 2008.

293   "Of course, the whole thing is a terrific fraud": JM to Aranka Treuhaft, 3 January 1970, OSU.

293   "I'm an awful ham"... "a very hard sales pitch, an appeal to the gullible": JM, *PP*, 156.

293   "Would you prefer to paraphrase": JM, *PP*, 156.

294   "one of the clear-cut successes": JM, *PP*, 170.

294   "Wasn't it sad about Bennett Cerf croaking. I felt v. put out about that": JM to NM, 21 September 1971, in *Decca*, ed. Sussman, 434.

294   "I know in my heart of hearts": JM to Virginia, 5 March 1968, OSU.

295   "this cat": JM to Various Friends, 1 February 1993, in *Decca*, ed. Sussman,668.

295   "He slept in his clothes, seldom bathed, and lived on a diet of Gitane cigarettes and Nembutals": Ibid., 532.

295   "You're at Donald Sutherland's. I'll be right over": White, *Genet*, 530.

295   "wearing green socks": Ibid., 531.

295   "like a street fair": Herb Gold, interview by author, December 2007.

296   "Bay Area radicals, politicos": Herman, "Before I Forget," *Huffington Post*, 2 January 2008.

296   "to hear the latest news and to rally": Ibid.

296   his "fuse": Hilliard and Cole, *This Side of Glory*, 260.

297   "Isn't it nice": JM to Various Fiends, 1 February 1993, in *Decca*, ed. Sussman, 668.

297   "What do you think we should *do*?"... "*You* ask *me* how": JM to Various Friends, 1 February 1993, in *Decca*, ed. Sussman, 668.

297   "composed as a turtle": Herman, "Before I Forget."

297   "the sandbags and automatic weapons put them off": Albert, *Who the Hell Is Stew Albert?* 154.

298   "The old, balding": Ibid., 157.

298   "It's always the children who get hurt in wars": Decca was paraphrasing Michael McClure in a letter to various friends (JM to Various Friends, 1 February 1993, in *Decca*, ed. Sussman, 668.)

CHAPTER 28

303   "wit's end": Dinky, interview by author, February 2010.

303   "to protect the public."... "they never mention punishment": Don Wegars, "A Radical Switch," *San Francisco Chronicle*, 1973.

303   "... "hot stuff"... "nobody seems to know": JM to Robert Gottlieb, 5 September 1972, OSU.

304   "more proud of sticking pins": Leah Garchik, interview by author, March 2006.

304   "ruthless gutter fighter": Robert Gottlieb, interview, *Portrait of a Muckraker: The Stories of Jessica Mitford*, produced by Stephen Evans, Ida Landauer, and James Morgan, KQED, 1990 (DVD and VHS).

304   "I don't think of myself as a muckraker": "The Press; Queen of Muckrakers," *Time*, 20 July 1970.

304   "I really don't understand": JM, interview, *Portrait of a Muckraker: The Stories of Jessica Mitford*, produced by Stephen Evans, Ida Landauer, and James Morgan, KQED, 1990 (DVD and VHS).

304   "I'd got him": Ibid.

304   "This hard heart": JM, *PP*, 175.

305   "Miss Mitford is artful": Doug Smith, "James Dean Walker," quoted in, *Decca*, ed. Sussman, 538n196.

306   "gallant little" . . . "Her hair is thin": James Degnan, "Jessica Thumb Her Toes," *Change* (winter 1974–1975): 38–41.

307   "From a distinguished professor": Ibid.

307   "Every time she gets a chance she tries to stick": Ibid.

307   "Some day my prints will come": JM to Aranka Treuhaft, 17 January 1974, in *Decca*, ed. Sussman, 466.

307   "that the university's fingerprint requirement": JM, *PP*, 213.

308   "cremate them": JM, *PP*, 213.

308   "Pay the lady": JM, *PP*, 213.

308   "Jessica succeeds": Degnan, "Jessica Thumb Her Toes."

308   "Nancy's favorite symbol": JM, "The Saga of Swinbrook," *San Francisco Chronicle*, 24 March 1985.

309   "This he sold you . . . throw it at his head!" JM, *AFOC*, 145.

309   "Radical chic marches": Herb Caen, *San Francisco Chronicle*, 7 October 1975, quoted in U.S. Department of Justice, Federal Bureau of Investigation, Jessica Mitford File, FBI archives.

310   "grim feminist who talks sociologese": JM to Dinky, 9 November 1975, OSU.

310   "thoroughly muddled": Ibid.

310   "in adversary position against all comers": JM to Marge Frantz, 29 August 1974, OSU.

310   "I'm afraid I was a rather rotten mother": Decca to Tilla Durr, 6 March 1984, OSU.

311   "some of the *unutterably beastly*": JM to Katharine Graham, 9 April 1990, OSU.

311   "about the whole thing of Nicholas": JM to RT, 10 October 1990, OSU.

312   "really extreme prejudice . . . had to go to a psychiatrist": Dinky, interview by author, January 2007.

312   "I was militantly pro-mania": Benjy, interview by author, January 2007.

312   "the whole experience . . . farcical anecdote": Bernstein, *Loyalties*, 76.

312   "ex-menaces . . . had to be done": Marge Frantz, interview by author, November
       2005.

313   "incredibly upsetting . . . but then what else could it be?" JM to Sonia Orwell, 14
       October 1976, OSU.

313   "sibling rivalry—horrid phrase": JM, *AFOC*, 15.

313   "one experience but two outcomes, opposed in externals though in fact": JM,
       AFOC, 16.

313   "thousands simultaneously": JM, *AFOC*, 16.

314   "two sides of the same coin": JM, *Faces of Philip*, 101.

314   "Stalinism may well have been almost as horrible": Ibid.

CHAPTER 29

315   "I bloody well don't see why she is self-appointed arbiter": JM to Ann Farrer
       Horne, 23 February 1980, in *Decca*, ed. Sussman, 522.

315   "Victorian old ladies": Anthea Fursland, interview by author, 186.

316   "Obviously I applaud many of the changes you enumerate": JM to Hillary Rodham
       Clinton, 10 May 1980, in *Decca*, ed. Sussman, 527.

317   "When we hit Bilbao": Brahms, Sherrin, and Greenwell, *The Mitford Girls A
       Musical*, Warner/Chapel Music, 1998.

317   "the boy in the attic": Katie Edwards, interview by author, December 2006.

318   "it would be in no sense another spinoff": Patricia Holt, interview by author,
       March 2008.

318   "three packs a day . . . a Jack Daniels or two": Kevin Ingram, telephone interview
       by author, September 2006.

318   "I've never written a biography": JM to Kevin Ingram, 13 October 1981, in *Decca*,
       ed. Sussman, 550.

318   "rat-like cunning, a plausible": JM, *PP*, 1.

319   "If my parents believed in God": Dinky, interview by author, May 2009.

319   "I'm glad she's found": Ibid.

321   fretful "if Bob was out of her sight": Katie Edwards, interview by author, December
       2006.

321   "Oh he's perfectly splendid": Pele deLappe, interview by author, October 2006.

321   "My daughter tells me I'm an alcoholic": Dinky, interview by author, January
       2007.

322   "chuck in all sorts": JM to Kevin Ingram, 13 October 1981, in *Decca*, ed. Sussman,
       January 2007.

322   "narrative style is so peculiar": Raymond Mortimer, quoted in Hastings, *Nancy
       Mitford*, 219.

322   "Toynbee memoir proceeds": JM to William Abrahams, 20 July 1983, OSU.

322   "[Decca] has a strong element of genuine": Toynbee, "Decca Mitford," 1, OSU.

324	"riveted" . . . "I, of course": JM to Michael Straight, 25 February 1983, OSU.

324   "riveted" . . . "I, of course": JM to Michael Straight, 25 February 1983, OSU.

324   "caused temporary loss": Katie Edwards, interview by author, December 2006.

324   "indictment nor an expose": Patricia Holt, interview by author, March 2008.

325   "SURPRISINGLY good": JM to Edward Pattillo, 24 February 1985, OSU.

325   "happy that he'd finished it". . . "weighed in so": Kevin Ingram, telephone interview by author, September 2006 .

325   "SANE and AMUSING" . . . "You know how desperately worrying": JM to Robert Gottlieb, 26 May 1981, OSU .

325   "dreadful, and absurd": JM to Benjy, 24 January 1984, in *Decca*, ed. Sussman, 582.

325   "disgusting manic episodes": Ibid.

326   "snakepits," where "they shoot you full of thorazine": Benjy, interview by author, May 2006.

326   "you wouldn't be": JM to Benjy, 24 January 1984, in *Decca*, ed. Sussman, 582.

326   "Bob's affair was very very painful": Dinky, interview by author, March 2009.

326   "the Loved One" . . . "only interested in": JM to Sally Belfrage, 8 August 1985, OSU.

326   "SQUALOR of it all": *Decca*, ed. Sussman, 593.

326   "given persistence & good will": JM to Sally Belfrage, 22 August 1985, OSU.

327   "if it was easier & less painful for him to give up": JM to Sally Belfrage, 22 November 1985, OSU.

CHAPTER 30

329   "began in a cocaine": Benjy, interview with author, January 2007.

330   "And why not? Say I," JM, letter to the editor of *Harper's* magazine, November 1992.

330   "Hillary Clinton had interned": "Jessica Mitford's Diary," *The Times Magazine*, 9 October 1993.

330   "I think Decca probably": Diane Johnson, interview by author, May 2010.

330   "anything which sniffs of phoniness or misplaced earnestness": Toynbee, "Decca Mitford," OSU.

331   "There had, she said, been": Alexander Cockburn, "Farewell, Lady Decca," *Salon*, February 8, 2005.

331   "some v. catty items about me & Bob, many more": JM to Debo, 28 October 1994, OSU.

331   "to take out" Charlotte Mosley, letter to author, 19 October.

331   "before an interview a": Katie Edwards, interview by author, December 2006.

332   "Help I'm trapped at this ghastly dinner": Leah Garchik, interview by author, March 2006.

332   "Have I ever told you about my abortion?" . . . "grisly details" . . . "Of course we were going to America": Barbara Hall, telephone interview by author, February 2006.

332   "An obvious omission": JM, fax to Robert Boynton, August 1992, OSU.

332   "So get your safe, legal abortion": JM et al., "She's Come for an Abortion," *Harper's*, November 1992, 43–54.

333   "I don't think I'll get death threats": Robert Boynton. "Profile of Jessica Mitford" *Newsday*, 13 December 1992.

333   "were prob. due to being more than tiddly at the time": JM to Debo, 23 December 1994, in *Decca*, ed. Sussman, 689.

333   "grossly inflated with alcohol": Dinky, interview by author, March 2009.

333   "intellectual": Ibid.

333   "I've ruined your life": Dinky, interview by author, May 2006.

333   "eventually Decca thought that Dinky was the strongest person in the world": Kathy Kahn, interview by author, December 2006.

334   "I know I wouldn't be any good at it—all that appalling Frank Talk etc": JM to Debo, 23 December 1994, in *Decca*, ed. Sussman, 689.

334   "A time aeons ago Pele": JM to Dinky, 6 February 1995, OSU.

334   "I've gone on the wagon": JM to Debo, 23 December 1994, in *Decca*, ed. Sussman, 689.

335   "cut a Rock and Roll record": Karen Leonard, interview by author, October 2008.

335   "profound depths . . . which only bullfrogs could duplicate on a clear night": Cynthia Robbins, "The Gentle Art of Singing 'Bang! Bang!' Jessica Mitford Cuts a Record," *San Francisco Express*, 30 January 1995.

335   "doesn't have a lot": Patricia Holt, "Barroom Belter," *San Francisco Gate*, 28 July 1996.

336   "Can't you make her stop?": Katie Edwards, interview by author, December 2006.

336   "T'was on the ground of Swinbrook": Kathi Goldmark, interview by author, July 2009. Audrey deChadenedes and Tony Goldmark are also listed as lyricists.

337   "Needless to say I was absolutely astonished": JM to Fred Hill, 6 October 1995, OSU.

337   "cast SCI in a bad light clothed in wit and humor": JM, quoting Thomas McDade fax to JM, 27 January 1996, in *Decca*, ed. Sussman, 703n159.

337   "I'm extremely anxious to get the facts straight": JM to Thomas R. McDade, 27 January 1996, OSU.

338   "panic-stricken": Karen Leonard, interview by author, October 2008.

338   "Doesn't hurt at all". . . "Possibly late autumn or even Xmas": JM to Debo, [date unknown] July 1996, in *Decca*, ed. Sussman, 711.

338   "so much better than just being hit by a car or in plane wreck": JM to Debo, 11 July 1996, in *Decca*, ed. Sussman, 713.

339   "denounce wonderfully": Herb Gold, interview by author, December 2007.

339   "I know it must seem v. odd": JM and RT to Dinky and Benjy, March 1993, OSU.

340   "Bob—it's so ODD to be dying": JM to RT, 10 July 1996, in *Decca*, ed. Sussman, 711.

341   "Can you tell me who the President is?" to which she answered "That's not my fault!" Karen Leonard, interview by author, October 2008.

AFTERWORD

343   "most hated funeral director in California": Karen Leonard, interview by author, October 2008.

343   "goods and services": Karen Leonard to Robert Waltrip, 24 July 1996, in *Decca*, ed. Sussman, 717.

343   "$15.45 for the cremation container": Karen Leonard to Robert Waltrip, 24 July 1996, in *Decca*, ed. Sussman, 717.

SELECTED BIBLIOGRAPHY

Albert, Stew. *Who the Hell Is Stew Albert?* Los Angeles: Red Hen Press, 2004.

Aptheker, Bettina. *Intimate Politics: How I Grew Up Red, Fought for Free Speech, and Became a Feminist Rebel.* Seattle: Seal Press, 2006.

Barnard, Hollinger F., ed. *Outside the Magic Circle: The Autobiography of Virginia Foster Durr.* Tuscaloosa: University of Alabama Press, 1985.

Bechdel, Alison. *Fun Home: A Family Tragicomic.* Boston: Houghton Mifflin, 2006.

Belfrage, Cedric. *The American Inquisition, 1945–1960.* Indianapolis: Bobbs-Merrill, 1973.

Belfrage, Sally. *Freedom Summer.* Charlottesville: University Press of Virginia, 1990.

Bentley, Eric. *Are You Now or Have You Ever Been: The Investigation of Show-Business by the Un-American Activities Committee 1947–1958* in *Rallying Cries: Three Plays.* Evanston, Illinois: Northwestern University Press, 1987.

Bernstein, Carl. *Loyalties: A Son's Memoir.* New York: Macmillan, 1990.

Bernstein, Walter. *Inside Out: A Memoir of the Blacklist.* Cambridge, Massachusetts: Da Capo Press, 2000.

Branch, Taylor. *Parting the Waters: America in the King Years, 1954–63.* New York: Simon & Schuster, 1988.

DeLappe, Pele. *Pele: A Passionate Journey Through Art & the Red Press.* Petaluma, California: privately printed, 1999.

Dennis, Peggy. *The Autobiography of an American Communist: A Personal View of a Political Life, 1925–1975.* Westport, Connecticut: L. Hill, 1977.

Devonshire, Deborah Vivien Freeman-Mitford Cavendish. *Counting My Chickens and Other Home Thoughts.* New York: Farrar, Straus and Giroux, 2002.

Didion, Joan. *Slouching Towards Bethlehem.* New York: Farrar, Straus and Giroux, 1968.

Doctorow, E. L. *The Book of Daniel.* New York: Bantam Books, 1981.

Elliott, Jeff. "Decca." *Albion Monitor,* 9 October, 1995.

Evans, Steven, Ida Landauer, and James Morgan, producers. *Portrait of a Muckraker: The Stories of Jessica Mitford.* San Francisco: KQED/NABET, 1986.

Fariello, Griffin. *Red Scare: Memories of the American Inquisition*. New York: Norton, 1995.

Foner, Eric, and John A. Garraty, eds. *The Reader's Companion to American History*. Boston: Houghton Mifflin, 1991.

Forman, James. *The Making of Black Revolutionaries*. Seattle: Open Hand, 1985.

Frantz, Marge. Interview with Kelly Anderson, November 3–5, 2005. *Voices of Feminism Oral History Project*. Sophia Smith Collection. Northampton, Massachusetts: Smith College.

Freeman, Jo. *At Berkeley in the Sixties: The Education of an Activist, 1961–1965*. Bloomington: Indiana University Press, 2004.

Gerstein, Anna [Margaret Nelly "Nellie" Ogilvy Hozier Romilly]. *Misdeal*. London: Cassell and Co., 1932.

Ginsberg, Allen. *Howl and Other Poems*. San Francisco: City Lights Books, 1996.

Gornick, Vivian. *The Romance of American Communism*. New York: Basic Books, 1977.

Green, Martin Burgess. *Children of the Sun: A Narrative of "Decadence" in England After 1918*. London: Constable, 1977.

Healey, Dorothy, and Maurice Isserman. *Dorothy Healey Remembers: A Life in the Communist Party*. New York: Oxford University Press, 1990.

Hellman, Lillian. *Scoundrel Time*. New York: Bantam, 1976.

Hinckle, Warren. *If You Have a Lemon, Make Lemonade*. New York: Putnam, 1974.

Ingram, Kevin. *Rebel: The Short Life of Esmond Romilly*. New York: Dutton, 1986.

Jensen, Carl, ed. *Stories That Changed America: Muckrakers of the 20th Century*. New York: Seven Stories Press, 2000.

Kaplan, Judy, and Linn Shapiro, eds. *Red Diapers: Growing Up in the Communist Left*. Urbana: University of Illinois Press, 1998.

Kempton, Murray. *Part of Our Time: Some Ruins and Monuments of the Thirties*. New York: Dell, 1967.

Langer, Elinor. *Josephine Herbst*. New York: Little Brown, 1983.

Lapin, Adam [as Ben Adams]. *San Francisco: An Informal Guide*. New York: Hill and Wang, 1961.

Lapin, Mark. *Pledge of Allegiance*. New York: Dutton, 1991.

Lovell, Mary S. *The Sisters: The Saga of the Mitford Family*. New York: Norton, 2003.

Maas, Eva. *Looking Back on a Life in the Left: A Personal History*. San Francisco: WordRunner, 1998.

McWhorter, Diane. *Carry Me Home: Birmingham, Alabama: The Climactic Battle of the Civil Rights Revolution.* New York: Simon & Schuster, 2002.

Miller, Henry. *The Air-Conditioned Nightmare.* New York: New Directions Publishing, 1945.

Mitford, Jessica. *The American Way of Birth.* New York: Dutton, 1992.

—. *The American Way of Death.* New York: Simon & Schuster, 1963.

—. *The American Way of Death Revisited.* New York: Vintage Books, 1998.

—. *Faces of Philip: A Memoir of Philip Toynbee.* New York: Knopf, 1984.

—. *A Fine Old Conflict.* New York: Knopf, 1977. Appendix contains: *Lifeitselfmanship or, How to Become a Precisely-Because Man: An Investigation into Current L (or Left-Wing) Usage.* Oakland, California: originally privately printed, 1956.

—. *Grace Had an English Heart.* New York: Dutton, 1989.

—. *Hons and Rebels.* London: V. Gollancz, 1960 [published originally in the United States as *Daughters and Rebels: The Autobiography of Jessica Mitford.* Boston: Houghton Mifflin, 1960].

—. *Kind and Usual Punishment: The Prison Business.* New York: Knopf, 1973.

—. *Poison Penmanship: The Gentle Art of Muckraking.* New York: Knopf, 1979.

—. *The Trial of Dr. Spock: The Rev. William Sloane Coffin, Jr., Michael Ferber, Mitchell Goodman, and Marcus Raskin.* New York, Knopf, 1969.

Mitford, Nancy. *The Blessing.* London: Hamish Hamilton, 1951.

—. *Don't Tell Alfred.* London: Hamish Hamilton, 1960.

—. *Love in a Cold Climate.* New York: Random House, 1949.

—. *Madame De Pompadour.* Introduction by Amanda Foreman. New York: New York Review Books Classics, 2001.

—. *The Pursuit of Love.* New York: Random House, 1946.

—. *A Talent to Annoy: Essays, Articles and Reviews, 1929–1968.* Edited by Charlotte Mosley. London: Hamish Hamilton, 1986.

—. *Voltaire in Love.* New York: Harper, 1957.

—. *The Water Beetle.* New York: Harper & Row, 1962.

—. *Wigs on the Green.* London: T. Butterworth, 1935.

Mosley, Charlotte, ed. *Love from Nancy: The Letters of Nancy Mitford.* London: Hodder & Stoughton, 1993.

—. *The Mitfords: Letters Between Six Sisters*. New York: Harper, 2007.

Mosley, Nicholas. *Hopeful Monsters: A Novel*. London: Secker & Warburg, 1990.

Navasky, Victor S. *Naming Names*. New York: Viking, 1980.

Pomerantz, Charlotte, ed. *A Quarter-Century of Un-Americana, 1938–1963: A Tragico-Comical Memorabilia of HUAC, House Un-American Activities Committee*. New York: Marzani & Munsell, 1963.

Poniatowska, Elena. *Tinisima*. Translated by Katherine Silver. Albuquerque: University of New Mexico Press, 2006.

Pryce-Jones, David. *Unity Mitford: An Enquiry into Her Life and the Frivolity of Evil*. New York: Dial Press, 1977.

Rabinowitz, Victor. *Unrepentant Leftist: A Lawyer's Memoir*. Urbana: University of Illinois Press, 1996.

Richmond, Al. *A Long View from the Left: Memoirs of an American Revolutionary*. Boston: Houghton Mifflin, 1972.

Ritchie, Charles. *Undiplomatic Diaries: 1937–1971*. Toronto: Emblem Editions, 2008.

Romilly, Esmond Mark David. *Boadilla: A Personal Record of the English Group of the Thaelmann Battalion of the International Brigade in Spain*. London: Hamish Hamilton, 1937.

Romilly, Esmond, and Giles Romilly. *Out of Bounds: The Education of Giles Romilly and Esmond Romilly*. London: Hamish Hamilton, 1935.

Romilly, Giles, and Michael Alexander. *The Privileged Nightmare*. London: Pan Books Ltd., 1956.

Roraback, Eileen Mary. *The Defense of the Self: Autobiographical Responses of American Intellectuals to the McCarthy Era (Paul Robeson, W. E. B. Du Bois, Lillian Hellman, Jessica Mitford)*. Iowa City: University of Iowa, 1999.

Rosenstone, Robert A. *Crusade of the Left: The Lincoln Battalion in the Spanish Civil War*. New Brunswick, New Jersey: Transaction Publishers, 2009.

Rubin, Steve, and Karen Leonard. *The Jessica Mitford and Robert Treuhaft Memorial Site*. www.mitford.org.

Sayre, Nora. *Previous Convictions: A Journey Through the 1950s*. New Brunswick, New Jersey: Rutgers University Press, 1995.

Schiff, Karenna Gore. *Lighting the Way: Nine Women Who Changed Modern America*. New York: Miramax Books/Hyperion, 2006.

Schneider, Bart. *Secret Love*. New York: Viking, 2001.

Smith, John Saumarez, ed. *The Bookshop at 10 Curzon Street: Letters Between Nancy Mitford and Heywood Hill, 1952–73*. London: Frances Lincoln, 2004.

Starr, Kevin. *Embattled Dreams: California in War and Peace, 1940–1950*. New York: Oxford University Press, 2002.

Stone, I. F. [Isidor Feinstein]. *Business as Usual: The First Year of Defense*. New York: Modern Age Books, 1941.

Straight, Michael. *After Long Silence*. New York: Norton, 1983.

Sullivan, Patricia, ed. *Freedom Writer: Virginia Foster Durr, Letters from the Civil Rights Years*. New York: Routledge, 2003.

Sussman, Peter Y., ed. *Decca: The Letters of Jessica Mitford*. New York: Knopf, 2006.

Terkel, Studs. *Hard Times: An Oral History of the Great Depression*. New York: Pantheon, 1970.

Thompson, Laura. *Life in a Cold Climate*. London: Headline Book Publishing, 2003.

Toynbee, Philip. *Friends Apart: A Memoir of Esmond Romilly & Jasper Ridley in the Thirties*. London: MacGibbon & Kee, 1954.

Treuhaft, Robert E. Interview with Robert G. Larsen in 1988–9 in *Robert E. Treuhaft: Left-Wing Political Activist and Progressive Leader in the Berkeley Co-op: Oral History Project*. Berkeley: Berkeley Historical Society, 1989.

Trumbo, Dalton. *The Time of the Toad: A Study of Inquisition in America by One of the Hollywood Ten*. Hollywood: Hollywood Ten, 1950.

Vidal, Gore. *Washington, D.C.: A Novel*. New York: Pantheon Books, 1970.

Waugh, Evelyn. *The Loved One: An Anglo-American Tragedy*. Boston: Little Brown, 1948.

Wesker, Arnold. *Chicken Soup with Barley*. New York: Samuel French, 1961.

White, Edmund. *Genet: A Biography*. New York: Knopf, 1993.

Williams, Juan. *My Soul Looks Back in Wonder: Voices of the Civil Rights Experience*. New York: Sterling, 2005.

Woolf, Virginia. *Flush: A Biography*. New York: Harcourt Brace, 1933.

Worsley, Thomas Cuthbert. *Fellow Travellers: A Memoir of the Thirties*. London: London Magazine Editions, 1971.

Zellner, Bob, with Constance Curry. *The Wrong Side of Murder Creek: A White Southerner in the Freedom Movement*. Montgomery, Alabama: NewSouth Books, 2008.

Ziegler, Philip. *London at War: 1939–45*. New York: Knopf, 1995.

Zinn, Howard. *The Twentieth Century: A People's History*. New York: Perennial, 2003.

INDEX

Hastings, Selena, 315

Hawkins, Williametta, 170

Hayden, Tom, 289, 297

Hellman, Lillian, 164

Herman, Jan, 296, 297

Highlander Folk School in Tennessee, 92, 93, 137

Hill, Derek, 150

Hill, Frederick, 337

Hill, Heywood, 233

Hilliard, David, 294, 295, 296, 297

Hinckle III, Warren, 272

Hiss, Alger, 163

Hitler, Adolf: death of, 140; Decca on killing, 10; invades the Netherlands, 57; learns of Decca's elopement, 24; Mitford tea with, 258; Muv's sympathy for, 84; nonaggression pact with Stalin, 86–87; Unity's friendship with, 10, 55, 126; Unity's potential break with, 56; as witness to Diana's wedding, 23

Hoffman, Abbie, 284

Hollywood, 44

Hollywood Ten, 152

Holt, Patricia, 306

Hons and Rebels (Mitford): Nancy on, 232–233; publication of, 232; title debate, 228; writing of, 215–216, 225, 228–229

Hoover, J. Edgar, 163, 175

Hopson, Louise, 171

Horne, Ann Farrer, 191

Hôtel Paradis, 229

Houghton Mifflin, 225

House Committee on Un-American Activities: activism against, 236–241; the bar as terrorized by, 188–189; on civic activism as Communist, 164; Decca's first impression of, 122; jails writer Hammett, 175; Jerry Rubin at, 271; as making Decca American, 203; mandate of, 125; McCarthy era, 163, 179; Red Tide scare, 138; sentences Hollywood Ten, 152; subpoenas the Treuhafts, 176, 187–189

"Howl" (Ginsberg), 235

Hungary: Decca's misimpressions of, 212; Hungarians, 101; Soviets crush uprising in, 212; Treuhafts on socialism in, 204–205

Hurok, Sol, 104

I

immigrants, U.S.: Aranka as, 309; assimilation, 102; Bob as educated by, 101–102; Decca as, 309; NY Jewish, 101; Russian-Jewish, in Petaluma, 119

Inch Kenneth: Decca sells, 272–273; family reunion on, 200; Farve on, 85; last summer with Muv, 257; loneliness of, 267; memoir writing on, 225; Muv and Farve on, 140; as sisters' inheritance, 141; Treuhafts buy, 226–227; Unity and Muv on, 152

Independent Progressive Party, 180

Ingram, Kevin, 317–318, 323, 321, 324–326

Ingram, William, 307

inheritance: Decca as banned from Redesdale, 219–220; Inch Kenneth, 141, 142–144; from Nellie, 203, 212, 217

Internal Security Division, 290

International Brigades, 15, 37

Izzy Gomez's, 114, 118, 165

J

Jackson, Derek, 120, 233

Jackson, Mississippi, 169–170

Japanese internment, 114, 165

Jeanette Rankin Brigade, 271

Jeffers, Robinson, 114

Jew Süss, 9

jobs: Civil Rights Congress (CRC), 156–157; glamour of subversive, 146–147; ideology of employment, 207; jewelry sales in Miami, 53–54; lecture tour idea, 45–46; market researcher, 27, 39–40; Meyer commissions, 48–49, 52; OPA inspector, 105–107, 109, 115; performing career, 335–336; professorial, 305–308; and relational power balance, 46; secretary, 93–94, 106; *Washington Post* article/ad for, 70; Weinberger's dress shop, 73; *see also* activism; journalism

Printed in the United States
by Baker & Taylor Publisher Services